INSOLVENCY PRACTITIONERS

ELGAR CORPORATE AND INSOLVENCY LAW AND PRACTICE

Series Editors: Andrew Keay, *Professor of Corporate and Commercial Law, University of Leeds, UK* and *Chief Insolvency and Companies Court Judge* Nicholas Briggs

The Elgar Corporate and Insolvency Law and Practice series is a library of works by leading practitioners and scholars covering discrete areas of law in the field. Each title will be analytical in approach, highlighting and unpicking the legal issues that are most critical and relevant to practice. Designed to be detailed, focused reference works, the books in this series aim to offer an authoritative statement on the law and practice in key topics within the fields of company law, corporate governance, corporate insolvency and personal insolvency.

Presented in a format that allows for ease of navigation to a particular point of law, each title in the series is written by specialists in their respective fields, often with insight either from private practice or from an academic perspective.

Titles in the series include:

Creditor Treatment in Corporate Insolvency Law
Kayode Akintola

Insolvency Practitioners
Appointment, Duties, Powers and Liability
Hugh Sims QC, Rachel Lai, Neil Levy, Stefan Ramel, Holly Doyle, James Hannant and Samuel Parsons

INSOLVENCY PRACTITIONERS

Appointment, Duties, Powers and Liability

HUGH SIMS QC

Barrister, Guildhall Chambers, Bristol and London, UK

RACHEL LAI

Director, Menzies LLP, Cardiff, UK

NEIL LEVY

Barrister, Enterprise Chambers, Bristol and London, UK

STEFAN RAMEL

Barrister, Guildhall Chambers, Bristol and London, UK

HOLLY DOYLE

Barrister, Guildhall Chambers, Bristol and London, UK

JAMES HANNANT

Barrister, Guildhall Chambers, Bristol and London, UK

SAMUEL PARSONS

Barrister, Guildhall Chambers, Bristol and London, UK

ELGAR CORPORATE AND INSOLVENCY LAW AND PRACTICE

 Edward Elgar
PUBLISHING

Cheltenham, UK • Northampton, MA, USA

Published by
Edward Elgar Publishing Limited
The Lypiatts
15 Lansdown Road
Cheltenham
Glos GL50 2JA
UK

Edward Elgar Publishing, Inc.
William Pratt House
9 Dewey Court
Northampton
Massachusetts 01060
USA

A catalogue record for this book
is available from the British Library

Library of Congress Control Number: 2020950129

This book is available electronically in the **Elgar**online
Law subject collection
http://dx.doi.org/10.4337/9781788973984

MIX
Paper from
responsible sources
FSC
www.fsc.org FSC® C013604

ISBN 978 1 78897 397 7 (cased)
ISBN 978 1 78897 398 4 (eBook)

Typeset by Columns Design XML Ltd, Reading
Printed and bound by CPI Group (UK) Ltd, Croydon, CR0 4YY

CONTENTS

EXTENDED TABLE OF CONTENTS

PART III OFFICE-HOLDER LIABILITY

ABOUT THE AUTHORS

Hugh Sims QC (BSc (Hons)) is a barrister at Guildhall Chambers specialising in commercial and insolvency work. He has a particular interest in and has been involved in a number of cases concerning the professional liabilities of insolvency practitioners. He was appointed as Queen's Counsel in 2014 and a Deputy High Court Judge in 2019.

Rachel Lai (FCCA, MABRP, MIPA) is an insolvency practitioner at Menzies LLP, specialising in complex and investigatory cases. She has been involved in writing best practice guidance for the insolvency industry and currently writes questions for examinations relating to insolvency and receivership.

Neil Levy (LLB (Exon)) is a barrister at Enterprise Chambers. He specialises in banking and financial matters, having worked as part of Lloyds Bank's in-house legal team from 1987–92. He is editor of an online case database at *www.banknotesuk.com*.

Stefan Ramel (LLB, LLM (Cantab)) is an experienced commercial and insolvency barrister at Guildhall Chambers. He writes extensively on insolvency matters, including for Gore-Browne, Tolleys and LexisNexis.

Holly Doyle (BA (Hons)) is an experienced barrister at Guildhall Chambers and former guest lecturer at UWE. Her practice encompasses the broad span of insolvency and commercial work. She has a particular interest in professional negligence cases, including misfeasance claims against insolvency practitioners.

James Hannant (LLB, BCL) is a member of the insolvency and commercial teams at Guildhall Chambers. Before commencing practice, he was a judicial assistant to Lady Arden (then Lady Justice Arden). Before his career in law, James worked in the oil industry.

Samuel Parsons (BA, LLM (Harv)) is a specialist insolvency barrister, also practising at Guildhall Chambers. He regularly speaks and writes on insolvency matters alongside his practice. He was a senior associate teacher at the University of Bristol in 2018–19. In 2020, he was appointed to the Regional C Panel of Junior Counsel to the Crown.

FOREWORD

The authors of *Insolvency Practitioners* are to be congratulated for filling a real gap in the existing range of insolvency texts.

This new work looks at the subject from the perspective of the insolvency practitioners themselves, and is therefore of importance far beyond the legal profession. Its structure is simple and logical. It starts with 'Qualification and Appointment', moves through 'Duties and Powers in Office', and concludes with what the authors describe as the 'business end' of the book, namely 'Office-Holder Liability'.

The authors have adopted a relentlessly practical and up-to-date approach, discarding the format of the Insolvency Act 1986; instead, they have directly addressed the questions that arise every day in the working lives of all insolvency practitioners.

The book is made all the more useful by the invaluable contributions made by Rachel Lai, herself a leading insolvency practitioner. It is a successful team effort, plainly benefiting from the inspired helmsmanship of Hugh Sims QC.

I am particularly pleased to see that this new publication is also able to cover the important Corporate Insolvency and Governance Act 2020, to explain the new moratorium and restructuring process from a practitioner's standpoint. It remains to be seen whether these innovations will indeed combine with the UK's exit from the European Union to further a transatlantic drift towards the American approach to insolvency. As the authors say '[t]he UK's place in the world insolvency league table hangs in the balance in a post-Covid world'.

One thing is certain. This treatise will be of huge benefit to insolvency practitioners and lawyers operating before the Business and Property Courts. I am sure it will be often cited to the judges there.

I repeat my congratulations to each of the authors on an excellent piece of work.

The Rt. Hon. Sir Geoffrey Vos,
Chancellor of the High Court

PREFACE AND ACKNOWLEDGEMENTS

I always swore I would keep well away from doing anything close to what my Dad did. He was a frustrated accountant for much of his life. It is ironic therefore that I have ended up developing an interest in an area of law, insolvency, which involved more and more time spent with accountants. Unlike my Dad they seem to have enjoyed their work too, perhaps because insolvency practice has the relish of law, accountancy and litigation thrown in with equal measure.

About ten years ago I had a discussion with a colleague in Chambers about there being a gap in the market for a book on the professional liabilities of insolvency practitioners ('IPs'). We both agreed it was a worthwhile venture, there being no dedicated text on the subject, but busy practices and lives meant little progress was made beyond writing articles and giving seminar talks. The colleague was Nick Briggs, now the Chief Insolvency and Companies Court Judge and Deputy High Court Judge. After his elevation, Nick mentioned to me that Edward Elgar Publishing were looking for someone to write a book on the subject, and suggested I should take them up on it. By this time he was safely otherwise engaged. But we also had enjoyed an influx of new practitioners at Guildhall Chambers, who were enthusiastic about contributing, and who had experience of both insolvency and professional liability disputes, and so the writing commenced. Most notably we were joined by Sam Parsons, our most junior member, who has been the main cheerleader and organiser for this book. Thank you to the author team from Chambers for their hard work on the project and pooling their knowledge and efforts to make this project work. So, some years later, the first dedicated text on the liabilities of IPs is now to be published.

The authors, shape and contents are influenced by three main events.

First, shortly after signing up to the project, some of our members decided to move on to pastures new, to Enterprise Chambers. We were sad to see them go, but pleased that Neil Levy remained involved in the project, as a contributor, and we have enjoyed the benefit of his unparalleled expertise on receivers. And all of us who remain in the Insolvency Team in Guildhall Chambers remain indebted to those former members, including in particular Stephen Davies QC, who inspired our interest in insolvency disputes and helped to develop Chambers' expertise on the subject. We have drawn on many of the papers and talks Guildhall Chambers' Insolvency Team have produced over the years.

Secondly, we have enjoyed professional relationships and friendships with a number of IPs. We were delighted that Rachel Lai, of Menzies, agreed to join us as an author. She has contributed greatly, and her involvement has added a sense of perspective from the point of view of the IP. We hope that perspective has not been completely engulfed by the lawyers involved.

Thirdly, we have crossed the finishing line in the writing of this first edition just as Covid-19 has isolated us to our desks. Probably without that event we may have forever drifted towards an almost complete draft but never quite got there. We hope this is therefore a silver lining to that particularly nasty cloud. We touch on some of the new measures and insolvency procedures brought into force by the Corporate Insolvency and Governance Act 2020, as a result of Covid-19, including restructuring measures which were foreshadowed before the pandemic and will become permanent. Where appropriate, particularly in the introductory chapter of this book, we refer to potential comparisons which may be made between the new measures and existing procedures and appointments, and where there may be significant differences for the IP's role.

It is at this point the authors are normally supposed to thank their nearest and dearest for sacrifices made etc. However, given the team approach to this book that would not be appropriate. And I have in large part tried to work on my contributions to this book late at night, and amongst other commitments, without intruding too much into my other worlds. The only visible sacrifice, following a run of late-night editing before Christmas 2019, was an old car, written off due to a tired, and insufficiently careful, look on exiting the station car park. I hope the reader does not identify any particular drafting car crashes in the text. If they do then we accept liability for that too, though Simon Passfield, Head of Chambers' Insolvency Team, has kindly assisted us with a proof read, which will hopefully have averted any major ones.

Hugh Sims QC
June 2020

LIST OF ABBREVIATIONS

BA 1914	Bankruptcy Act 1914
CA 1948	Companies Act 1948
CA 1985	Companies Act 1985
CA 2006	Companies Act 2006
CDDA 1996	Company Directors Disqualification Act 1996
CFA	Conditional Fee Agreement
CIGA 2020	Corporate Insolvency and Governance Act 2020
CLCA 1978	Civil Liability (Contribution) Act 1978
CPR	Civil Procedure Rules 1998
DBA	Damages Based Agreement
DPA 2018	Data Protection Act 2018
EA 2002	Enterprise Act 2002
EIR	Regulation (EU) 2015/848 on Insolvency Proceedings
GDPR	General Data Protection Regulation (2016/679)
IA 1986	Insolvency Act 1986
IP	Insolvency Practitioner
IPO 1994	Insolvent Partnerships Order 1994
IPR 2005	Insolvency Practitioners Regulations 2005
IR 1986	Insolvency Rules 1986
IR 2016	Insolvency (England and Wales) Rules 2016
LASPO 2012	Legal Aid, Sentencing and Punishment of Offenders Act 2012
LPA 1925	Law of Property Act 1925
LRA 2002	Land Registration Act 2002
OR	Official Receiver
PDIP	Practice Direction (Insolvency Proceedings) (July 2018)
RPBs	Recognised Professional Bodies
SBEEA 2015	Small Business, Enterprise and Employment Act 2015
SIP	Statement of Insolvency Practice
TA 1925	Trustee Act 1925
TOLATA 1996	Trusts of Land and Appointment of Trustees Act 1996

TABLE OF CASES

ENGLAND AND WALES

OTHER JURISDICTIONS

Australia

Canada

Hong Kong

Ireland

New Zealand

Northern Ireland

Scotland

South Africa

INTERNATIONAL CASES

TABLE OF LEGISLATION

Statutory Instruments

Practice Directions

UNITED STATES OF AMERICA

EUROPEAN UNION

INTERNATIONAL CONVENTIONS

1

INTRODUCTION

A. OPENING REMARKS

This book is about insolvency practitioners ('IPs'), the roles that they play in the spectrum of **1.001**
insolvency procedures in England and Wales and the liabilities this exposes them to.[1] It seeks
to consider and analyse likely risk areas for IPs by reference to functions which are specific to
the different offices they may hold, but which also have common underlying themes having
regard to the three main overarching themes involved in the administration of any insolvent
estate: get in, realise and distribute.

Unlike other key texts routinely relied on by practitioners,[2] this book does not take the **1.002**
Insolvency Act 1986 ('IA 1986') as its starting point. Nor does it consider in detail the various
applications and claims that IPs may make in the course of their office. What distinguishes this
text from others is that it is the IP that is in the spotlight. The chapters move from the
qualification and appointment of the IP, to the duties that an IP is under and the powers that
they may exercise. It then considers aspects of an IP's liability in circumstances where those
duties are not complied with, or where the powers are exercised improperly, and under
headings where claims have been brought or may be brought against IPs in the future. The
final two chapters consider issues of causation, remedies, and defences that might be raised by
an IP to such claims.

---

1   References throughout this text to the law of England must be read as a reference to the law of England and Wales (being
    the same jurisdiction). There are no substantial variances in Welsh insolvency law from English insolvency law. The law
    is very different in Scotland, although Scottish authorities remain persuasive in English courts.
2   Such as *Sealy & Milman: Annotated Guide to the Insolvency Legislation 2020* (23rd edn, but updated annually).

Objectives of the text

1.003 This book aims to serve three purposes. The first is practical. It is hoped that this book will provide an overview of the IP's functions and liabilities that will be of assistance to IPs themselves, and insolvency lawyers. It is also hoped it will offer some more in-depth practical guidance to practitioners as to how claims might be framed, and defended, drawing on reported case law where available, and unreported cases known to the authors from their own practices. What this book does not seek to explain or give guidance on, are the many negotiating processes, deals, and workouts that IPs inevitably encounter in their work. However, it is hoped that the contents will nevertheless provide some clarity on the latitude that is given to IPs when they inevitably come to exercise their commercial judgment, as well as the chinks in the armour which may be probed successfully by the more seasoned operator.

1.004 The second purpose is to offer points of comparison and contrast between the various processes. The central theme of this book – and a subject that it explores – is the extent to which the role of an IP is constant, regardless of whatever statutory role the IP is playing at any given time. It is hoped that by compiling a book that encompasses the full range of roles that IPs play,[3] those similarities will be reinforced and, where there are differences, to explore the reasons and justifications for those differences. This may also offer some interest to academics, and postgraduate students, who are interested in the legal perspective on insolvency practice.

1.005 A common touchstone for comparison throughout the text is also the position of IPs vis-à-vis company directors. There is less reported case law on claims brought against IPs as compared with claims against directors.[4] In the authors' experience, however, there is no shortage of such claims,[5] and a growing trend for such claims to be brought by disgruntled stakeholders, especially where other recovery avenues (such as claims against directors) have been exhausted, or are not worth pursuing. In the circumstances, the next nearest touchstone for guidance on such claims are often claims against company directors who, like IPs, are fiduciaries, agents of the company, and stewards of the company's assets.[6] How this translates to the experience of trustees in bankruptcy also generates interesting questions, and in those circumstances the nearest equivalent in a solvent context would appear to be trustees appointed under private appointments.

1.006 The third purpose is to function as a springboard for further research. The relative breadth of this book means that, inevitably, the depth of discussions, at least outside the more detailed consideration of breaches of duties and powers, will be limited. It is hoped that the thorough referencing throughout will point the reader in the right direction and, because of the book's

---

3   In comparison with other key texts such as *Loose & Griffiths on Liquidators* (9th edn), *Lightman & Moss on the Law of Administrators and Receivers of Companies* (6th edn) and *Kerr & Hunter on Receivers and Administrators* (20th edn).

4   This may provide some comfort to IPs, though it is doubted it should offer too much. The professional training and licensing that IPs undergo, and are subject to, along with the general expectation that IPs will not take commercial risks in their work, may explain part of this difference. Another part of the difference may be due to the fact that IPs typically have professional indemnity insurance, and insurers tend to prefer to settle strong claims rather than fight them.

5   Many of which will settle before they go to trial, as noted in fn. 4 above.

6   It is a feature of English insolvency law that the directors no longer have any control over the company (whether directly or indirectly). This stands in stark contrast with the position in the USA, where directors who file for protection under Chapter 11 retain their power and control over the company.

exploration of commonalities as a starting point, possibly a different direction than other textbooks might encourage.

B. OVERVIEW OF INSOLVENCY REGIMES FOR IPs

The roles that IPs may be expected to play fall into or under five broad categories, each with their own sub-categories. **1.007**

1. Liquidators

A liquidator is the office-holder appointed in respect of a company in liquidation or winding up.[7] A liquidator may be appointed pursuant to a court order (a 'compulsory' liquidation), or pursuant to a resolution of the company (a 'voluntary' liquidation).[8] **1.008**

Within the voluntary mechanisms, two further sub-categories exist. A creditors' voluntary liquidation ('CVL') is generally a reference to an insolvent company, whereas a members' voluntary liquidation ('MVL') refers to a company that was solvent prior to its liquidation.[9] The labels are therefore something of a misnomer, but the reason for the nomenclature is that members (i.e., shareholders) will expect to receive a dividend in the liquidation, whereas in a CVL, it is assumed that the creditors will not be paid in full, and so the shareholders – who sit at the lowest level of priority in all insolvency processes – will not receive anything.[10] **1.009**

The role in compulsory liquidation is similar to that under a CVL,[11] and principles established in relation to companies in compulsory liquidations will, as a general rule, be applicable to companies in voluntary liquidations. There are, however, some crucial differences. One distinction that should be mentioned at this stage is that a CVL can still be wound up pursuant to a court order and, consequently, converted into a compulsory liquidation if cause is shown.[12] In that respect, compulsory liquidation is the 'backstop' insolvency process, and remains the 'centre of gravity' for the purpose of corporate English insolvency law.[13] Indeed, companies that enter some other form of insolvency process will often enter liquidation at some point prior to their dissolution. **1.010**

At the risk of oversimplification, the essential role of a liquidator is to get in, realise and distribute the assets of the company.[14] They replace the directors as the operating will and **1.011**

---

7   The terms are synonymous, although 'winding up' is more commonly used pre-order, and 'liquidation' is used during the currency of the insolvency process.
8   IA 1986 s73(2). More unusually, a company will be wound up if the purpose has been achieved, as defined in the company's articles: IA 1986 s84(1)(a).
9   IA 1986 s90.
10   See discussion of the statutory waterfall in *Re Nortel GmbH (in administration)* [2013] UKSC 52, [2014] AC 209, and discussed further in Chapter 4 at 4.004.
11   This essential role is unaffected by whether the liquidation is compulsory or voluntary.
12   *In re Crigglestone Coal Co Ltd* [1906] 2 Ch 327.
13   For example, companies often move from administration, CVL, or from a CVA into compulsory liquidation, before ultimately being dissolved. Companies moving in the opposite direction (i.e., out of liquidation) are seldom, if ever, encountered in practice.
14   IA 1986 s107.

mind of the company in question, and their duties will not usually be directed towards running the company for profit,[15] but rather ensuring that the company is wound up in an orderly fashion, with regard to the relative rights and priorities of the company's creditors and (in the uncommon event of there being a surplus) the shareholders. In England, liquidation has long been considered the centrepiece of the insolvency legislation, and for that reason the lion's share of authorities on IPs' duties and liabilities have been decided in the context of liquidation. This continues to be the case, notwithstanding the avowed commitment to creating a 'rescue culture', first promulgated by the Cork Report,[16] renewed in the Enterprise Act 2000 ('EA 2002'), and furthered by the Corporate Insolvency and Governance Act 2020 ('CIGA 2020'). Some recent cases however, do focus on claims against administrators, albeit in the context of claims being brought (not infrequently) by a liquidator.

1.012 Before turning to administrators, also falling within this first category are provisional liquidators ('PLs'), who normally play a limited role in the interim period between (i) presentation of a winding-up petition; and (ii) the making of a winding-up order. In those circumstances, it is common for the PL to become a liquidator in due course. A PL therefore gets a 'head start' in the liquidation. The appointment of a PL is usually reserved for cases where assets are at risk: likely to be distributed and later not be recovered for the benefit of creditors. The appointment has the effect of making the PL the agent of the company, removing control from the erstwhile directors and allowing the PL to begin the process of making investigations earlier than would otherwise be the case. Such appointments therefore undercut the principle of director control pre-order, and consequently are not commonly encountered.

2. Administrators

1.013 Compared with liquidators, administrators are a more recent legislative phenomenon, but as noted above their role has grown. Their status most recently underwent a transformation by virtue of the EA 2002. An administrator's role must be directed to one of three criteria set out in Schedule B1, para 3,[17] which includes at its apex rescuing the company as a going concern.[18] In practice, by far the most common purpose of administration is a more advantageous realisation of the company's assets than would be the case under a liquidation, which incorporates both 'Objective 2' and 'Objective 3' administrations.[19] In this way administrations

---

15 Although, as HHJ Purle QC noted in *Re Officeserve Technologies Ltd* [2017] EWHC 906 (Ch) at [14]: 'it is often overlooked that liquidators have power to carry on the business, and that they will in an appropriate case do so.' One such appropriate case was that of Carillion plc (and associated companies) which was described by the Official Receiver as the largest ever trading liquidation in the UK.

16 'Report of the Review Committee on Insolvency Law and Practice' (1982) Cmnd 8558, chaired by Sir Kenneth Cork.

17 Unless the administration is a special administration regime: see e.g., the Investment Bank (Amendment of Definition) and Special Administration (Amendment) Regulations 2017, Building Societies (Insolvency and Special Administration) Order 2009, Water Industry (Special Administration) Rules 2009, Building Society Special Administration (England and Wales) Rules 2010, Investment Bank Special Administration Regulations 2011. Consideration of these special types of proceeding fall outside the scope of this text. If there is no real prospect of one of the objectives in para 3 being met, then there can be no administration: see *Re Fortuna Fix Ltd* [2020] EWHC 2369 (Ch).

18 Often colloquially referred to as a 'light touch administration': see *Re Debenhams Retail Ltd* [2020] EWHC 921 (Ch) at [20] (Trower J).

19 See para 4.090.

now occupy ground which was previously the domain of the liquidator, and case law relating to liquidators may inform claims against administrators (and vice versa).

Where an administrator seeks to rescue the company, this may be achieved under a CVA **1.014** under Part I of the IA 1986,[20] or through a scheme of arrangement under Part 26 of the Companies Act 2006 ('CA 2006'). Both of these processes are considered below under the sub-section on 'Roles in Creditor Compacts'.

A further option open to administrators is to seek to sell the business and assets of the **1.015** company. This is commonly done by way of a 'pre-pack', which is the name given to situations where a sale will have been agreed in principle prior to the appointment of the administrators. The roles of an administrator as privately-appointed agent for sale and appointed office-holder therefore straddle the negotiation before and after completion of sale. These processes have given rise to particular controversy, not least because the sale will often be to a person or entity in some way connected with the previous business owner, and because the sale is negotiated without any creditor involvement.[21] Conversely, a 'pre-pack' allows for a swift sale of the business and assets of the company, with the potential for lower amounts of IP remuneration and other costs and expenses, and a reduction in the damage to any goodwill.

3. Trustees in bankruptcy

Trustees in bankruptcy are in many ways the equivalent of a liquidator in the personal **1.016** insolvency context. But there are crucial differences between the roles, and the courts have routinely cautioned over undue cross-pollination between authorities in both areas. One key difference is that the assets of a bankrupt will vest in the trustee in bankruptcy on the making of a bankruptcy order,[22] whereas in liquidation the assets remain the company's, and the liquidator will act, inter alia, as agent for the company.[23]

Another crucial difference is that the bankrupt is, of course, a natural person who will **1.017** invariably hope to be discharged so that they can return to a life of relative normality post-bankruptcy. Conversely, a company will usually be dissolved once an insolvency process has begun. Certain protections are therefore given to bankrupts that are not necessary in corporate insolvencies. An obvious example is that a bankrupt is permitted to retain certain property, such as their clothes, bedding and tools of their trade, and such property as is necessary to maintain the basic domestic needs of his or her family.[24] However, despite a flurry of interest in the impact of the Human Rights Act 1998 on bankruptcy legislation in the

---

20 Perhaps surprisingly, liquidators and administrators can also propose a CVA to creditors, providing a rare 'exit route' from insolvency: IA 1986 s1(3).
21 See paras 5.129 and 5.130.
22 IA 1986 s306.
23 Unless the jurisdiction under IA 1986 s145 is used to vest the company's property in the liquidation. In practice, s145 is seldom encountered.
24 IA 1986 s283(2). Before 6 April 2017, the OR became the receiver and manager of the bankrupt's estate on the making of the bankruptcy order. This change was brought about by the amendment to IA 1986 s287(1): SBEEA 2015 Sch 10, para 3.

early-to-mid-2000s (and in particular, the impact of Art 8),[25] the pre-existing statutory insolvency scheme has time and again been found to be compliant with human rights law.[26] More recently, issues relating to the General Data Protection Regulation ('GDPR') and the Data Protection Act 2018 ('DPA 2018') have given rise to renewed tensions, since Trustees in Bankruptcy are usually '*data controllers*' within the meaning of the GDPR and the DPA 2018.

4. The Official Receiver

1.018 The Official Receiver ('OR') is simultaneously an officer of the court, an officer of the Insolvency Service, and will be an officer of any company in respect of which he or she is appointed. Rather than being a separate type of IP, the OR will fulfil one of the other statutory roles, and will often act on an interim basis prior to the appointment of an IP. The office of official receiver was established by the Bankruptcy Act 1883. The role was originally confined to personal bankruptcy, but it was extended to companies in compulsory liquidation by the Companies (Winding Up) Act 1890.[27] By way of example, the OR will therefore be the first liquidator of a company in a compulsory liquidation,[28] and the first trustee in bankruptcy on the making of a bankruptcy order.[29] The OR will however, never fulfil the role of administrator, and very rarely as supervisor.[30] This in itself shows that the statutory system historically tends towards liquidation and bankruptcy as a default, which stands in contrast to the avowed commitment to a 'rescue culture'. It is also a reflection of the fact that the demands of heavy and substantial administrations are better suited to private appointments.

5. Roles in creditor compacts

1.019 Closely related to the above processes are what can broadly be described as 'creditor compacts', which can be seen as relations of the above insolvency processes, although often the purpose of

---

25 See e.g., Trower, 'Bringing human rights home to the insolvency practitioner' Part 1 (2000) 13(6) *Insolv Int* 41–3, and Part 2 in 13(7), 52–3.

26 See, e.g., *Ford v Alexander* [2012] EWHC 266 (Ch), [2012] BPIR 528 and case comment from Holly Doyle and Simon Passfield: https://www.guildhallchambers.co.uk/files/Personal_and_corporate_update_Holly_Doyle_and_Simon _Passfield_May2012.pdf (accessed 3 April 2020). Art 6 of the European Convention on Human Rights may also be engaged in applications to remove IPs, since their appointment is personal and such applications may be dealt with without an oral hearing: IR 2016 r12.28; *Werner v Poland* (26760/95) (2003) 36 EHRR 28.

27 *Re Pantmaenog Timber Co Ltd* [2003] UKHL 49 at [43] (Lord Millet):

> It is a statutory office held by persons appointed by the Secretary of State from among the civil servants employed within the Department of Trade and Industry. They are members of the Insolvency Service, which is an executive agency of the Department with overall responsibility for the administration of insolvency in England and Wales, and acts under the ultimate direction and control of the Secretary of State. The Insolvency Service is headed by the Secretary of State but her involvement in day to day matters is normally exercised on her behalf by officials. She must make arrangements to ensure that there is at least one official receiver attached to each court having bankruptcy jurisdiction. The official receiver is an officer of the court to which he is attached and is answerable to the court for the carrying out of its orders and for the discharge of his statutory functions. As the holder of a statutory office, he has standing to bring proceedings and has a right of audience before the court to which he or she is attached. He sues and is sued not in his personal name but as 'the official receiver'. The definite article is appropriate because in the case of each company there is only one official receiver.

28 IA 1986 s136(2).

29 Ibid s291A(1).

30 The OR did act as supervisor in fast-track voluntary arrangements under EA 2002, Sch 22. They were abolished by SBEEA 2015 s135(3)(b).

such a compact will be precisely to avoid those processes from becoming engaged. They are creatures of the IA 1986, and as such go beyond contractual agreements that may be entered into on a bilateral or multilateral basis as between creditor(s) and debtor. They can also be used in conjunction with one another. For example, an administrator (or even a liquidator) may put in place a scheme of arrangement or achieve a CVA. In practice, however, they seldom do so.

During the currency of a CVA or IVA, the role of the IP will generally be that of a supervisor. **1.020** Prior to the approval of the proposal and the coming into being of the CVA/IVA, IPs act as nominees, and will offer advice to directors or individuals who wish to put a CVA or IVA proposal to creditors. It is also not unusual for a supervisor to intercede on behalf of the debtor in communications with creditors, in an attempt to continue the arrangement, in circumstances where the terms of the CVA/IVA are not met by the debtor.

A CVA allows a company, whether solvent or insolvent, to reach a binding agreement with its **1.021** creditors to repay all, or part, of its debts over an agreed period of time. There is no need for there to be any judicial involvement in the process.[31] It may also result in a quicker return to creditors.

The essential characteristic of a CVA or IVA, therefore, is that it contains an offer and **1.022** acceptance.[32] The offer is a proposal, formally offered by the director or individual, but which will normally be produced by an IP. The IP will habitually include an 'Estimated Outcome Statement', showing that the creditors will receive a greater return than they would in the relevant insolvency process (i.e., liquidation or bankruptcy).

Where CVAs and IVAs differ from a conventional contract or settlement to pay a particular **1.023** creditor is that the proposal is offered to the creditors as a whole. If the requisite majority of creditors agree to the proposal, then they will bind or 'cram down' the dissenting minority. In this sense, although CVAs and IVAs are not insolvency processes, they are similar to those processes in that the outcome represents the interests of the creditors as a whole, determined by a democratic process, and by reference to each class of creditor in accordance with their respective voting rights.

If the majority of creditors agree to the arrangement, the IP who drafted the proposal will **1.024** routinely be appointed as a supervisor. As the name suggests, IPs supervise debtors, and ensure that they comply with the agreement arrived at under the arrangement. If the debtor defaults, the IP will commonly (subject to the views of creditors) present a petition and commence the liquidation or bankruptcy process. The IP will then usually transition into one of the roles set out above.[33]

---

31 Although a report and result of the meeting must be filed with the court: IA 1986 s2(2) 4(6), 4(6A). The arrangement may however be challenged by a creditor: IA 1986 s6.

32 Despite this similarity with the law on the formation of contracts, CVAs are unlikely to be contracts for the purposes of the Contracts (Rights of Third Parties) Act 1999: *Rhino Enterprises Properties Ltd* [2020] EWHC 2370 (Ch) (an application for permission under Sch B1 para 75(6)).

33 Provision is given in IA 1986 s140(2) for a supervisor to continue directly as liquidator of a company in CVA, thereby displacing the presumption that the OR will be the first liquidator: IA 1986 s140(3). Similarly, provision is given in IA 1986 s291A(2) for a supervisor of an IVA to be appointed as the debtor's trustee in bankruptcy.

1.025 Schemes of arrangement under Part 26 of the CA 2006 are also a form of collective compact, which require a majority in number representing at least 75 per cent in value of each class of creditors to agree to the scheme. The decision of the 75 per cent is therefore capable of binding the minority, so long as the court approves the scheme. Schemes of arrangement are not governed by the IA 1986, and can be agreed to, whether or not a company is insolvent.[34] It also follows that initiating a scheme of arrangement will not provide a moratorium or stay against creditor claims. The moratorium included in IA 1986 ssA1–A33 by virtue of the amendments brought about by CIGA 2020 ss1–6 may be used in conjunction with a scheme under Part 26 (or as standalone process in relatively straightforward cases of turnaround), but the intention appears for them to be used in conjunction with so-called 'super schemes' under Part 26A.[35] The relevance of schemes to an IP's practice is therefore limited to situations where IPs act in their capacity as agent for the company, i.e., as liquidator or administrator. Where the company is solvent, there is no need for an IP to be engaged. The prospect of insolvent 'super schemes' would however seem to bring the IP into the picture, at least as a monitor, for as long as the moratorium continues to operate in the background.

1.026 Outside their official roles as IPs within one of the above recognised insolvency processes, an IP may also act by giving advice to a company during a restructuring, which takes place wholly outside any court-based process. In situations where solvency is in issue, these are commonly referred to as 'workouts'. Where a company or corporate group seeks to settle the debts owed to one or several lenders by way of new financing, the process is referred to as a 'refinance'. IPs are not required to be involved in such processes, although concerns about transactions where a party to the transaction is of dubious solvency may justify the advice of an IP as to how best to structure the transaction.

Special managers

1.027 There has been a trend in some recent liquidations carrying media or political interest for there to be no licensed IP prepared to take on the role of liquidator. The solution arrived at by some courts has been for the OR to be appointed as liquidator, and for the OR to delegate much of the day-to-day management of the liquidation to special managers. Those special managers have, in those cases at least, been licensed IPs.[36] The advantage from the IP's perspective is that they are not official office-holders, and so are not subject to the same statutory duties (and potential for liability). While this may be understandable in cases such as *British Steel*[37] and *Thomas Cook*,[38] there is possibly a risk that it creates a slippery slope for IPs who will continue

---

34 For a similar reason, they are not included in Annex A to the EU Insolvency Regulation (Regulation (EU) 2015/848 of the European Parliament and of the Council of 20 May 2015 on insolvency proceedings).

35 Schemes under Part 26 were described by Tribe in 2009 as being the lost cousin of insolvency practice: (2009) 7 *JIBFL* 386. Since their conception, they have been available to companies in financial difficulty: see e.g., *Re NEF Telecom Co BV* [2012] EWHC 2944 (Ch).

36 Although need not necessarily be so: IA 1986 s177(1).

37 [2019] EWHC 1304 (Ch). A trading liquidation coupled with the appointment of special managers means the process starts to take on similar characteristics to a trading administration: see Keay and Walton, 'British steel: is it a wind up?' (2019) 4 *CRI* 125.

38 [2019] EWHC 2626 (Ch).

to be remunerated for carrying out the *de facto* role of liquidator,[39] but without the *quid pro quo* of being subject to the same duties and regulatory strictures.

Sui generis insolvency processes

There are also special administration regimes for water and sewerage undertakings, protected railway companies, air traffic service companies, public-private partnership companies and building societies. These regimes are not encountered sufficiently often to justify their inclusion in this text.   **1.028**

6. New roles

Other roles, apparently taking inspiration from the other side of the Atlantic, have been raised and considered in government consultations for the last decade. Plans for a restructuring model and moratorium, similar to those found in US Chapter 11, were suddenly brought onto the Parliamentary agenda in May 2020 by the Covid-19 pandemic.[40] The resulting legislation, CIGA 2020, and the creation of the *sui generis* role of the IP as a 'monitor' of the statutory moratorium, is discussed in more detail in Section H below and also in Chapter 3, Section F. Of particular note however, for IPs' liabilities, is the carve-out in CIGA 2020 for monitors, which provides that compensation claims cannot be brought against them in relation to their conduct in that role.[41]   **1.029**

C. HISTORICAL CONTEXT

English insolvency law has a long history, with provisions dating from as long ago as 1542 and 1571 still being observable in the modern statutory framework.[42] As the idea of separate corporate personality gained traction in the early nineteenth century and led to the Joint Stock Companies Act 1844 for the incorporation of private companies,[43] the Joint Stock Companies Winding-Up Act 1844 provided for their liquidation. Around the time of the 1844 Acts, there   **1.030**

---

39   They may have such powers as are entrusted to them by the court, and may extend to any of the powers of a liquidator: IA 1986 ss177(3), (4).

40   Administrators also made applications to determine whether they could benefit from the Coronavirus Job Retention Scheme: *Re Debenhams Retail Ltd* [2020] EWCA Civ 600.

41   See Chapter 3 below at para 3.126.

42   The Statute of Bankrupts of 1542 34 & 35 Henry VIII, c. 4 was described as 'an act against such persons as do make bankrupts'. It introduced the concept of rateable distribution. The Preamble memorably underscores the then-prevailing immorality of being insolvent:

> Whereas divers and sundry persons, craftily obtaining into their hands great substance of other men's goods do suddenly flee to parts unknown, or keep their houses, not minding to pay or restore to any of their creditors their debts and duties, but at their own will and pleasures consume the substance obtained by credit of other men, for their own pleasure and delicate living, against all reason, equity and good conscience.

This same statutory purpose served by the provisions designed to counter post-petition dispositions, transactions at undervalue, preferences, and transactions defrauding creditors in IA 1986 ss127/284, 238/239, 339/340 and 423 can be traced to the Statute of Elizabeth 1571.

43   Corporate bodies established before 1844 required their own Act of Parliament or Royal Charter. Their purposes often extended far beyond the functions of what would commonly be expected of a limited company, such as the railway and canal companies, many older universities, and the infamous example of the East India Company, established in 1600 by Elizabeth I.

were concerns that, while there were obvious commercial and entrepreneurial advantages of limited companies, so was the potential for abuse. Incorporators could simply establish a limited company, rack up enormous debts at the risk to creditors, and then dissolve the company before moving on. Records of debates in Hansard shows how real these concerns of abuse of limited liability were.[44] One of the purposes of the company entering a period of winding up prior to dissolution, therefore, was that someone else would take over the company, get in and realise the company's assets, and (as part of that exercise) bring claims against potential defendants. Those core features remain central to the modern insolvency regime.[45] It might be said the potential for abuse still remains, and failure by IPs to provide an effective role in making recoveries to creditors may be said to provide fuel to the concerns of creditors and, in doing so, continue the upward risk trend for IPs.

1.031   However, returning to the historical perspective, one of the problems with this process was that there were few limitations on who could act as a liquidator. Concerns and suspicions about 'friendly' or partisan IPs being appointed still crop up today, particularly where allegations are made that, but for the acts of the IP, a surplus would have flowed to the shareholder or bankrupt who stands at the bottom of the insolvency waterfall.

1.032   In response to those concerns, IPs must nowadays be licensed professionals. Perhaps remarkably, it was not until the Cork Report that the requirement for IPs to be registered professionals was introduced.[46] Before then, the role of liquidator could be undertaken by anyone, although even by the time of the Cork Report, the role was increasingly being filled by accountants.

1.033   In more recent times, English insolvency law has moved further away from the European tradition of considering bankruptcy to be a sinful[47] or even criminal[48] act. Through a series of modernising reforms (the most recent of which are discussed below), it has moved closer to the predominantly American view that there is a substantial economic benefit to society in rehabilitating bankrupts quickly, dealing with the insolvency process itself as efficiently as possible,[49] and ultimately attempting to rescue any part of a business that remains economically viable. The role of the IP over time can therefore be interpreted as a tectonic shift from being non-existent, towards a predominantly quasi-judicial role as an officer of the court, and more recently away from that quasi-judicial role towards a greater emphasis on the managerial role of the IP, and in particular in the growing requirement of IPs to strike deals with stakeholders within the insolvency process. It is nevertheless a curious feature of the IP's role that they continue to straddle roles that are both quasi-judicial and quasi-directorial, and tensions between those roles are inevitable.

---

44   HC Deb 29 June 1855 vol 139 cc310–58.
45   Conversely, applying to strike off a company (and thereby attempting to bring about its dissolution without an intervening liquidation) without giving notice to creditors is a criminal offence: CA 2006 s1006(4).
46   Discussed in Chapter 2.
47   The German word for 'debt' (*Schuld*) is also the same as 'guilt'.
48   The debtors' prisons, memorably described in Charles Dickens' *Little Dorrit* (1857), were abolished by the Debtors Act 1869 s4, which provided that (absent some exceptions), no person would be arrested or imprisoned for making default in payment of a sum of money.
49   For example, in the deemed consent procedure: IA 1986 s246ZF.

Notwithstanding the slow but increasing trend in the UK towards greater speed and **1.034** out-of-court arrangements,[50] the starting point remains that creditors rank *pari passu*,[51] that payments made before the onset of insolvency are recouped as far as possible,[52] and that the deleterious effects of misfeasance (including breaches of director duties), fraudulent behaviour, and wrongful trading are ameliorated as far as possible.[53] Indeed, in some circumstances, the most valuable asset a company will have will be a chose in action against another company or its former director(s). Without IPs to bring those claims, there would be far fewer recoveries for the estates over which they preside. More cynically, there would also be a much smaller body of decided law on the subject. It is also the case that a failure to provide for an expected recovery may provide a liability risk for the IP.

Recent government statements that the 'financial rehabilitation of a company in distress is key **1.035** to a modern economy'[54] and a sustained commitment to re-invigorating the UK's rescue culture all indicate that the legislative intention will continue to tend towards deals and workouts between creditors and debtors, with judicial supervision where appropriate and the backstop of liquidation as an 'exit route' should a deal not be forthcoming. In that context, the prediction must be that more and more of the getting in, realising and restructuring work may be done pre-appointment, with less and less work of such nature after appointment. And the IP's role, as office-holder, may steadily move away from getting in and realising the assets of a company, and more towards the role of part-director and part-mediator. Indeed, it is entirely possible to imagine that the role of the professional IP could in future take the form of a totally supervisory role, looking over the shoulders of the directors who remain at the helm of the company.[55]

D. OVERVIEW OF LEGISLATIVE FRAMEWORK

The insolvency processes discussed in this book are largely found in the IA 1986. Predecessor **1.036** provisions from the Companies Act 1948 and the Bankruptcy Act 1914 (and their predecessors) can often be traced into the provisions of the IA 1986, to the extent that those provisions were not impacted upon by the review. For the purposes of this volume, the IA 1986 is by far the most important piece of legislation.

The IA 1986 has itself been the subject of a number of reforms, namely the Insolvency Act **1.037** 1994, the Insolvency (No. 2) Act 1994, the Insolvency Act 2000, the EA 2002, and the Small Business, Enterprise and Employment Act 2015 ('SBEEA 2015'). The Insolvency Act 2000 introduced provisions relating to voluntary arrangements and moratoriums,[56] which were designed to increase the efficacy of such arrangements.

---

50 Such as CVAs, IVAs, and other compacts with creditors.
51 Cf. Mokal, 'Priority as pathology: the pari passu myth' (2001) 60(3) *CLJ* 581–621.
52 Visible in IA 1986 ss127, 238, 239, 339, 423.
53 IA 1986 ss212–214.
54 Government response to the Corporate Governance Reform (26 August 2018), 8.
55 As happens occasionally with US Trustees under the US Chapter 11 procedure.
56 In practice the moratoriums have been seldom used. It is suggested this is because of both the strict criteria for eligibility for the moratoriums, and the relatively rare use of CVAs at all. See Marks, 'Insolvency Act 2000: the practitioner's

1. The Enterprise Act 2002

1.038 The most significant reform to date has been the EA 2002, which introduced the current administration regime into the IA 1986, and which is largely self-contained in Schedule B1 to the IA 1986.[57] The EA 2002 also largely abolished the institution of administrative receivership, and the jurisdiction to make an administration order was correspondingly expanded so as to occupy many situations which would previously have been governed by administrative receivership. From the perspective of an IP, one of the biggest changes ushered in by the EA 2002 was the realignment of the IP's duty towards all of the company's creditors, even though, in the context of an 'Objective 3' administration, the duty is simply not to cause unnecessary harm to the unsecured creditors.

2. Small Business, Enterprise and Employment Act 2015

1.039 The second significant reform came with the SBEEA 2015. Unlike the EA 2002, its reforms are better characterised as being more a case of evolution than revolution. Nevertheless, many of the changes it brought about are of particular relevance to how IPs perform their roles, particularly in the amendments made to the Company Directors Disqualification Act 1986 ('CDDA 1986'),[58] opening the gate for administrators to bring actions for fraudulent or wrongful trading,[59] removal of the general requirement to seek sanction from creditors or the Secretary of State before commencing certain claims,[60] some revisions to the administration procedure,[61] and the automatic appointment of the OR as trustee in bankruptcy on the making of a bankruptcy order.[62] The SBEEA 2015 also revises the regulation of IPs, and gives the power to establish a single regulator of IPs.[63]

3. Insolvency Rules 2016

1.040 The Insolvency (England and Wales) Rules 2016 ('IR 2016') are the current insolvency rules, applicable to all types of insolvency process. They replaced the Insolvency Rules 1986 which had themselves been subject to a substantial number of amendments. The replacement and codification has, however, not led to a significant re-drafting or amendment to the substance of the provisions, and cases considering the 1986 Rules will still generally be applied to the equivalent rule under the IR 2016. The starting point is that the equivalent rule is likely to be interpreted in the same way.[64]

---

exposure to the cold winds of the moratorium' (2003) 16(8) *Insolv Int* 57–9. It is anticipated that these criteria will in any event be subsumed by the amendments brought about by the Corporate Insolvency and Governance Act 2020.

57 For a discussion of the changes brought about by the EA 2002 at the time of enactment, written by members of Guildhall Chambers' Insolvency Team and edited by Stephen Davies QC, see *Insolvency and the Enterprise Act 2002* (1st edn, 2003).
58 SBEEA 2015 ss104–111 and Sch 7.
59 Ibid ss117–119.
60 Ibid ss120, 121.
61 Ibid ss127–130.
62 Ibid s133 and Sch 10.
63 Ibid ss137–146 and Sch 11.
64 Chapter 2 IR 2016 contains some specific rules and definitions to aid interpretation.

The IA 1986 was drafted primarily with limited liability companies and individuals in mind. The IA 1986 does, however, also apply to partnerships by virtue of the Insolvent Partnerships Order 1994 (SI 1994/2421) (as amended by the Insolvency Partnerships (Amendment) Order 2005 (SI 2005/1516) and the Insolvency (Miscellaneous Amendments) Regulations 2017 (SI 2017/1119)). One of the principal distinctions is, of course, that a partnership is not an entity in itself. It does not have any limited liability, and so the individuals in a partnership may also be subject to personal insolvency proceedings in tandem with any proceedings in which the partnership is involved. The same IP will usually be appointed as the partners' trustee in bankruptcy and liquidator of the partnership. **1.041**

The Limited Liability Partnerships Regulations 2001 (SI 2001/1090) extend the application of the IA 1986 to LLPs,[65] by broadly amending the wording of the IA 1986 into terms that more readily apply to such entities. From an IP's perspective, therefore, it will not usually matter whether the entity is a limited liability company or a limited liability partnership. LLPs have their own legal personality and, as such, a partner in an LLP will more accurately reflect the position of a shareholder in a company than will a partner in a partnership. **1.042**

Reference should also be made, where appropriate, to the Insolvency Practice Direction of 2018 ('PDIP'),[66] although it is not of special relevance to the issues raised in this volume, because the PDIP is principally concerned with questions of procedure. One key exception, however, are the principles applicable in cases of challenge to an IP's remuneration, which are described in some detail in part six of the PDIP. **1.043**

4. Corporate Insolvency and Governance Act 2020

For at least ten years prior to its introduction, there had long been a dissatisfaction among practitioners and directors at the lack of a standalone, renewable moratorium process. UK law did not provide for an automatic stay of the type that is available to debtors in, for example, the USA.[67] Despite consultations up to and including in 2018, the matter was never given any significant Parliamentary time, not least because of the effect of Brexit on the legislature's diary. That all changed with the Covid-19 pandemic in March 2020, which promised the worst economic downturn since at least the 2007–08 financial crisis, and possibly since the end of the Second World War. This prompted the Corporate Insolvency and Governance Bill to be fast-tracked through Parliament. It was presented on 20 May 2020. It passed all stages in the House of Commons on 3 June 2020. Royal Assent was granted on 25 June 2020. **1.044**

Notwithstanding the impetus of the Covid-19 pandemic, the Act brings about temporary and permanent amendments to the legislative scheme in the IA 1986. For the purposes of this text, the most important changes are the creation of the role of 'monitor', where the freestanding moratorium is engaged. The long-term role of the monitor is overtly limited to certifying that the company is likely to be rescued as a going concern and bringing about the end of the moratorium where it is not able to be so rescued. It is anticipated that their role will also overlap with that of an IP advising on restructuring plans under CA 2006 Part 26A. **1.045**

---

65   As amended by the Limited Liability Partnerships (Amendment) Regulations 2005 (2005/1989).
66   [2018] *Bus LR* 2358. Introduced, for the second time, in July 2018.
67   See US Bankruptcy Code: 11 USC §362.

E. SOURCES OF IP DUTIES

1.046   IPs are subject to a range of duties, stemming from a variety of sources. These sometimes overlap, are sometimes consecutive, and can occasionally lead to contradiction. However, the starting point for most considerations of duty will be statute, and that will almost always mean the IA 1986.

1.047   Those statutory obligations must be understood in light of the authorities that have elaborated on and explained the provisions of the IA 1986. So, for example, a liquidator's core duty to get in and realise assets will include ensuring that property is sold in such a way that will swell the general pool of realised assets for the benefit of the company's creditors.[68] In other words, the general starting point is that the liquidator will perform his or her duties for the benefit of creditors, and that remains the touchstone of the liquidator's office. That same principle applies generally to all types of liquidator, administrator, and trustee in bankruptcy (and, by extension to supervisors, where maintaining the arrangement is a manifestation of the intention to get a better return for creditors).

1.048   The language of trusts has always pervaded discussions of insolvency law in England. Despite their description as a *trustee* in bankruptcy, however, the role of this particular type of office-holder is very different from that of a conventional trustee in, for example, a bare express trust. Nevertheless, it is clear that a liquidator will owe fiduciary duties directly to the company and – as a result of those fiduciary obligations – indirectly to the company's creditors (though which is ordinarily not actionable other than via the company vehicle). Conversely, a trustee in bankruptcy probably owes no such fiduciary duties to the bankrupt,[69] but the bankrupt's assets are still understood to be impressed with a statutory trust, and the trustee has a continuing obligation to recognise the fundamental rights of the bankrupt.

1.049   In practice, IPs may find the IR 2016 to be more directly relevant to their day-to-day job than the IA 1986. The rules themselves vary from delving into considerable depth on particular aspects of their role in some areas, while still leaving a great deal to be worked out by the courts in others, and often cannot be properly understood without also considering the relevant interlinking (or oversailing) provision in the IA 1986.

1.050   Finally, when acting as an officer of the court, the IP will also be subject to a general obligation to act fairly, equitably and even-handedly, even if the office-holder does nevertheless have a strict right that can prima facie be exercised. This is discussed in more detail in Chapter 4 below, at paragraphs 4.041–4.045, in relation to the rule in *Ex parte James*.[70]

---

68   See paras 4.004 ff.

69   *Oraki v Bramston* [2017] EWCA Civ 403; [2018] Ch 469.

70   The proper definition of the principle in *Ex parte James* continues to trouble the courts. It has been applied recently by the Court of Appeal in *Lehman Brothers Australia Ltd (in liquidation) v Macnamara and others (Joint Administrators of Lehman Brothers International (Europe) (in administration))* [2020] EWCA Civ 321, when David Richards LJ gave further guidance confirming that 'unconscionability' (applied by Hildyard J at first instance) is not the touchstone. Instead it is said the principle rests on 'unfairness', judged objectively and by reference to how the court itself would act – no lesser standard being acceptable from an officer of the court. The concept of 'fairness' is sometimes said to be an 'unruly horse', without further guidance as to the underlying factors. Whether this case goes further, to the Supreme Court, and how

F. EXPLANATION OF BOOK STRUCTURE

The remainder of this book is broadly divided into three parts. The first (Chapters 2 and 3) **1.051** deal with issues of qualification, regulation and appointment. Part II (Chapters 4 and 5) considers the duties and powers of office-holders, including the power of office-holders generally to bring claims and applications (whether as agent or in their own right). Part III may be said to be the 'business end' of the book: it considers, in Chapter 6, the claims that may be brought against office-holders for breach of their duties or obligations, and in Chapter 7, the remedies that may be available should a claim be successful and causation be established. Chapter 8 closes matters off, by considering the defences that may be raised by an IP in response to a claim.

The object of the book is, where possible, to begin in each section by observing what is **1.052** common between each type of office-holder, before moving onto specifics that relate to a smaller category or sub-category of office-holders. The reason for this is twofold. First, there are many principles that apply to IPs broadly. Second, by starting from that common position, it is hoped that the description will throw into relief the differences between the principles as they apply to IPs, enabling those differences between them and the reasons and justifications for them to be explored.

G. RECEIVERS

Two roles that IPs may occasionally play are those of receiver and administrative receiver, and **1.053** are discussed in Chapter 3 of this volume at paragraphs 3.130–3.148. They have not been included in the foregoing discussion of types of office-holder and types of insolvency process, because their roles are peripheral to those played by IPs. This book simply touches on them lightly, and reference should be made to specialised texts for more detailed consideration of their duties.[71]

Receivers need not be qualified IPs in the same way as the other insolvency office-holders must **1.054** be. They are routinely appointed by mortgagees via the out-of-court mechanism created by the Law of Property Act 1925, ss101 and 109. Their task is essentially to realise one property over which they have been appointed receiver, for the benefit of that secured creditor. As a result, the authorities considering that duty including, in particular, the obligation to obtain the best price reasonably obtainable, is still of some import in respect of the obligation to get in and realise the assets of an insolvent person or company.

Administrative receivers have become something of an endangered breed in the wake of the **1.055** EA 2002. Aside from some rare exceptions, their role has largely been subsumed by that of the administrator, particularly where the purpose of the administration is to realise property for the benefit of a secured creditor.[72]

---

reliable or effective this test is in practice, remains to be seen. The principle has, however, been given a new lease of life by the decision of the Court of Appeal, and circumstances in which this principle will now be applied will be fact sensitive.

71 See *Kerr & Hunter* (above, fn 3).
72 Sch B1, para 3(1)(c).

H. FUTURE DEVELOPMENTS

1.056   As already noted above, litigation involving and against IPs is unlikely to abate, even though much of it does not end up in a reported case. We live in an increasingly litigious culture ('where there's blame there's a claim') and IPs are certainly not immune from that. Disgruntled creditors, and others involved in the insolvency process, are more aware of their rights as information is much more easily available than it has been in the past. However, wider access to information does not necessarily mean a wider access to legal understanding, and so as there has been a growth in potential litigation, practitioners will also be familiar with the growth of creditor frustration arising from a misunderstanding of the insolvency scheme. The various issues we have seen in the banking sector (e.g., IRHP mis-selling, PPI claims) make people more likely to complain about institutions, and their treatment by regulated bodies or persons, in the hope of receiving compensation.

1.057   At the same time, there are more options available for people looking to bring claims. The litigation funding market is developing all the time, and there are specialist funders and brokers who market to IPs, to bring claims against other IPs as well as against other parties.

1.058   There is increased scrutiny of pre-packaged administrations in particular, and IPs' regulators review each and every SIP 16 disclosure.[73] However, there are still allegations of transactions at undervalue involving IPs. IPs are regularly contacted by disgruntled creditors, wanting to replace a liquidator or other office-holder, and reverse an asset sale, including but not limited to pre-pack sales. We suggest this is likely to happen more and more.[74]

1.059   The trend of recent case law also tends to invite further scrutiny on the conduct of IPs.[75] Such case law also tends to encourage focus on the particular facts of each case and make the outcome of any challenge less easy to predict, though arguably resulting in a more just outcome.[76]

1.060   In terms of general challenges, or changes ahead, these are likely to include the following: a new Code of Ethics is effective from 1 May 2020, which is moderately expansive in effect;[77] draft regulations were published on 8 October 2020 for reforms to connected party sales in pre-packaged administrations which would remove the need for the Pre-pack Pool;[78] changes to corporate governance and increased liability of directors are expected, which could have an impact on the duties and actions of IPs as much as directors;[79] a new moratorium and restructuring process has been created by CIGA 2020 that possibly furthers the 'transatlantic

---

73   Statement of Insolvency Practice 16, introduced on 1 November 2015, detailing how the decision to opt for a pre-packaged administration has been arrived at.

74   Spurred on by decisions such as that of Chief ICC Judge Briggs in *Brewer v Iqbal* [2019] EWHC 182 (Ch).

75   Illustrated by *Brewer v Iqbal* above.

76   See, e.g., the decision of the Court of Appeal in *Lehman Brothers Australia* [2020] EWCA Civ 321.

77   This is discussed further in Chapters 5 and 6 below.

78   The Pre-pack Pool was set up following the 2015 Graham Review, conducted by Teresa Graham, and enables a person who proposes to enter into a pre-pack to refer the case to the Pool for guidance as to whether it is not unreasonable to proceed, though it is a voluntary process. Some commentators support the expansion of the Pool: see Vaccari, 'English pre-packaged corporate rescue procedures: is there a case for propping industry self-regulation and industry-led measures such as the pre-pack pool?' (2000) 31(3) *ICCLR* 170–97.

79   This has been ongoing since March 2018.

drift' currently experienced in the UK, as the legislation moves towards the American Chapter 11 model,[80] and – depending on where Brexit negotiations end up – possibly away from the European model and automatic recognition given by the EU Regulation on Insolvency Proceedings ('EIR').[81] The UK's place in the world insolvency league table hangs in the balance in a post-Covid world, and how the UK responds to that test could have serious implications for IPs in terms of the types and amount of work they do, and the ability of the economy to rescue viable businesses (if not viable companies). The re-introduction of the Crown preference will further have an impact on lending.[82] None of these potential changes or challenges suggest a lessening of the burdens or duties on IPs.

Overall, therefore, the risks for IPs are unlikely to decrease and most likely to increase. Perhaps somewhat unfairly for the IP, this is likely to come with greater challenges to the reward and remuneration to be gained from that work, which likely involves increased risk exposure. **1.061**

---

80   Many of the measures in the Bill have been described as heading in the direction of Chapter 11 as exists in the US. They do not go quite that far, but they have been described as being important steps in the right direction: see Hansard (2 June 2020), Vol. 676, Cll 924–925.

81   Regulation (EU) 2015/848 of the European Parliament and of the Council of 20 May 2015 on insolvency proceedings. See Hertz, MacLennan, Bennett, 'Back to the Future' (2016) 8 *JIBFL* 476.

82   The Chancellor announced in the March 2020 budget that this would be implemented, but delayed until December 2020.

PART I

QUALIFICATION AND APPOINTMENT

2

QUALIFICATION AND AUTHORISATION OF INSOLVENCY PRACTITIONERS

A. AUTHORISATION OF INSOLVENCY PRACTITIONERS UNDER THE INSOLVENCY ACT 1986

1. History and background

2.001 Prior to 1986 there were no specific requirements for authorisation or regulation of insolvency practitioners ('IPs'). Insolvency procedures were often administered by accountants and other professionals and, in some cases, those with no practical experience or relevant qualifications.

2.002 This problem was particularly acute in relation to voluntary liquidations. Although there always remained the option of seeking a compulsory winding up, on cause being shown,[1] that remedy could itself be worthless if the assets had already been dissipated. Past abuses were associated particularly with those who had no practical experience or relevant qualifications, and occasionally had some connection with the erstwhile directors of the company whose conduct had resulted in the liquidation. At the time of *The Insolvency Law and Practice Report of the Review Committee* (1982) ('The Cork Report'), those concerns still remained live.

2.003 The Cork Report recommended that, to ensure a high standard of competence and integrity, a private IP should 'be a member of a professional body approved by the Department of Trade, and to have been in general practice for five years prior to acting as an insolvency practitioner', and that all practitioners should be subject to compulsory bonding to ensure they performed their duties correctly.[2] The requirement of regulatory oversight and accountability tied in with the recommendations made in the Cork Report to the effect that: 'The insolvency practitioner

---

1 See the well-known decision of the Court of Appeal in *Re Crigglestone Coal Co Ltd* [1906] 2 Ch 327.
2 *The Cork Report* paras 758 and 763.

will be a professional man charged with the responsibility of managing and realising property belonging to others' who 'must act honestly, reasonably and prudently, and display proper professional skill and competence'.[3]

2.004 As a result, the IA 1986 made specific provisions for the authorisation of private IPs when acting in a formal capacity as office-holders of insolvent estates. As well as introducing the meaning of 'act as an insolvency practitioner', the definition of an 'office-holder' was created by IA 1986.[4] It also introduced a criminal liability for acting in such a capacity without meeting the requirements.

2.005 Seven recognised professional bodies (RPBs) were designated by the Insolvency Practitioners (Recognised Professional Bodies) Order 1986 to authorise and regulate IPs.[5] In addition, the Department of Trade and Industry authorised some IPs directly; however, it ceased to carry out this role in line with the introduction of the regulatory objectives (which are discussed later in this chapter) and with the Insolvency Service taking more of an oversight role rather than directly monitoring practitioners.

2.006 The RPBs have authority to issue licences to individuals to act as IPs and are responsible for ensuring that standards are maintained, by monitoring work and investigating complaints. They are professional membership bodies and also have a role in supporting their members, such as through issuing guidance, running training courses and webinars, and providing a helpline or e-mail address to assist with queries. The RPBs may additionally authorise and regulate professionals who do not work in the insolvency arena. Like other areas of professional liability, when assessing whether negligence is established, it is to be expected that the court will have regard to the standards expected and guidelines laid down by the RPBs.[6]

2.007 The Joint Insolvency Committee ('JIC') is made up of representatives from the RPBs, along with lay members which have an interest in insolvency, such as HM Revenue and Customs, and representatives from the Insolvency Service and the Insolvency Service, Northern Ireland. The JIC provides an opportunity for its members to work together to discuss issues affecting the profession and to develop and maintain standards and to promote consistency across the RPBs and the practitioners they authorise. As an example, Statements of Insolvency Practice ('SIPs') are developed by the JIC via working groups.

---

3 Para 781. Of course, 'man' should today be read as 'person'. IP accountability is essential to public confidence in insolvencies. See also Finch, 'Insolvency practitioners: the avenues of accountability' (2012) 8 *JBL* 645–67, which starts from the premise that it is possible to analyse IP accountability with reference to different activities.

4 This was introduced through an unusual route, under IA 1986 s233(1) dealing with the supplies of gas, water, electricity etc. This defines 'the office-holder' by reference to the same categories as those defined as acting as insolvency practitioners; see IA 1986 s388 discussed further below.

5 (SI 1986/1764).

6 See, e.g., *Mortgage Express Ltd v Bowerman & Partners* [1996] 2 All ER 836 at 842a–d, in *Shore v Sedgwick Financial Services Ltd* [2007] EWHC 2059 (QB) (Beatson J) and *O'Hare v Coutts* [2016] EWHC 2224 (QB) (Kerr J) at [207].

In 2010 a market study undertaken by the Office of Fair Trading ('OFT')[7] commented that the interests of unsecured creditors were harmed in some corporate insolvency appointments and that the system of regulation did not stop this harm. The study proposed three remedies: **2.008**

A. establishing an independent complaints body to increase the efficacy and consistency of after-the-event complaint and review, restore creditor trust in the regulatory regime, and allow a cost-effective route of fee assessment

B. setting clear objectives for the regulatory regime, and changing some of the regulatory processes and responsibilities, to increase its ability to meet those objectives, and

C. amending some of the detailed regulations to better align the interests of the IP with the interests of the wider creditor group.

A Memorandum of Understanding (MoU) was entered into in 2011 between the Insolvency Service and the RPBs 'for the purposes of achieving consistency in the authorisation and regulation of insolvency practitioners'.[8] It sets out agreed principles and more detailed guidance to be followed. **2.009**

A report was produced for the Insolvency Service by Professor Elaine Kempson in 2013 which focused on the fees charged by IPs.[9] This report made a number of recommendations including 'enhanced monitoring by regulator(s)' and raised the possibility of a single regulator.[10] **2.010**

In response to the reports by the OFT and Professor Kempson, the government introduced new legislation to deal with some of the shortcomings identified. The Small Business, Enterprise and Employment Act 2015 ('SBEEA 2015') changed the regulatory framework in that statutory objectives were introduced of which the RPBs were required to take account. There is some overlap between the SBEEA 2015 and the MoU, although the MoU terms are more detailed than the legislation. The MoU may therefore be removed in the future, leaving the RPBs with some more flexibility when deciding how to regulate IPs. **2.011**

Where the Official Receiver is acting as an office-holder, there is no requirement for the Official Receiver to be authorised by an RPB. Under IA 1986 s399(2) the Secretary of State may appoint persons to the office of Official Receiver. The role is carried out by civil servants working for the Insolvency Service and subject to the Insolvency Service's internal requirements in terms of experience and qualification. As explained in the introduction, this book focuses on private IPs rather than the Official Receiver as office-holder. **2.012**

---

7   The market for corporate insolvency practitioners, A market study, June 2010 https://webarchive.nationalarchives. gov.uk/20140402172033/http://oft.gov.uk/shared_oft/reports/Insolvency/oft1245 (accessed on 11 April 2020).

8   Memorandum of Understanding between the Secretary of State for Business, Innovation and Skills and the Recognised Professional Bodies (October 2011), Foreword (https://www.gov.uk/government/uploads/system/uploads/attachment_data/file/301579/MoU_between_RPBs_and_SoS_October_2011.doc) (accessed on 11 April 2020).

9   Elaine Kempson, *Review of Insolvency Practitioner Fees Report to the Insolvency Service* (July 2013) https://www.gov.uk/government/publications/insolvency-practitioner-fees-a-review (accessed on 11 April 2020)

10   See Wood, 'One ring to rule them all: has the call for a single regulator been answered?' (2020) 33(2) *Insolv Int* 55–62.

2. Statutory requirements to be qualified as an Insolvency Practitioner

(a) Roles which may be carried out only by an insolvency practitioner

2.013 Where an office-holder is appointed, they must be appropriately qualified to act as such. Acting as an office-holder while not appropriately authorised is a criminal offence: 'A person who acts as an insolvency practitioner in relation to a company or an individual at a time when he is not qualified to do so is liable to imprisonment or a fine or both.'[11] This does not apply to the Official Receiver, who does not need to be qualified to act in the same way as private IPs.[12] The offence applies to all of the common insolvency procedures and some of the less common ones. However, even if an IP commits an offence, their acts carried out as an IP will remain valid notwithstanding a defect in appointment or qualification.[13] This may be compared with situations where the appointment is defective, rather than where it is a complete nullity.[14]

2.014 In relation to a company, acting as 'insolvency practitioner' includes acting as its liquidator, provisional liquidator, administrator, administrative receiver, monitor, or as nominee or supervisor of a voluntary arrangement.[15] It should be noted that this definition does not require the company to be insolvent, and includes a liquidator appointed by a company in members' voluntary winding up where there may be no insolvency issues.

2.015 In relation to an individual, it includes acting as trustee in bankruptcy, interim receiver of the individual's property, trustee of a deed of arrangement, nominee or supervisor of a voluntary arrangement, or administrator of a deceased insolvent estate which is subject to an order under IA 1986 s421.[16]

2.016 In relation to insolvent partnerships, this includes acting as liquidator, provisional liquidator, administrator, trustee under Article 11 of the Insolvent Partnerships Order 1994 ('IPO 1994'),[17] or nominee or supervisor of a voluntary arrangement.

2.017 Note that the requirements to be qualified only apply in respect of certain types of receivers. For example, a receiver appointed under the Law of Property Act 1925 ('LPA 1925') or a receiver appointed by powers under a charge (who is not an administrative receiver) is not required to be qualified under IA 1986. Indeed, such roles are often carried out by other professionals such as chartered surveyors. The only restrictions under IA 1986 are that 'a body corporate is not qualified for appointment as receiver of the property of a company'[18] and that an individual may not act:

---

11 IA 1986 s389(1).
12 Ibid s389(2).
13 Ibid s232 and Sch B1 para 104.
14 *Portman Building Society v Gallwey* [1955] 1 WLR 96; *Re Frontsouth (Witham) Ltd* [2011] BCC 635.
15 IA 1986 s388(1).
16 Ibid s388(2).
17 Art 11 applies where a petition is presented to court for the bankruptcy of the individual members of an insolvent partnership and for the winding up of the partnership business and administration of its property without the partnership being wound up as an unregistered company under IA 1986 (otherwise known as a consolidation order if granted).
18 IA 1986 s30.

as receiver or manager of the property of a company on behalf of debenture holders while:

(a) he is an undischarged bankrupt,

(aa) a moratorium period under a debt relief order applies in relation to him, or

(b) a bankruptcy restrictions order or a debt relief restrictions order is in force in respect of him.[19]

Similarly, in keeping with the general notion that schemes of arrangement are not strictly insolvency processes, there is no such requirement in relation to those who advise or assist with schemes of arrangement, even though they will frequently be IPs licensed by an RPB. **2.018**

(b) Requisites in order to act as an insolvency practitioner

Appointment as an insolvency office-holder is personal to the IP, and therefore only individuals may be qualified to act as IPs.[20] There are three main requisites in order for an individual to act as a practitioner in accordance with IA 1986. **2.019**

First, the individual must be a member of an RPB and permitted to act as an IP by or under the rules of the RPB.[21] Each of the RPBs has its own specific requirements and procedure for authorisation; however, the requisites are largely similar and partially set out in statute. See paras 2.024–2.025 below on RPBs for further details. **2.020**

Secondly, there must be security which meets the prescribed requirements.[22] This is frequently known as a 'bond' which effectively insures the IP against their own fraud in relation to the estates over which they are appointed. This is discussed in more detail in paras 2.046–2.058 below. **2.021**

Thirdly, the individual must not be subject to formal insolvency proceedings (as an undischarged bankrupt or subject to a moratorium period under a debt relief order), subject to a disqualification order or disqualification undertaking under the Company Directors Disqualification Act 1986 ('CDDA 1986'), lack capacity within the meaning of the Mental Capacity Act 2005[23] or be subject to a bankruptcy restrictions order or a debt relief restrictions order.[24] **2.022**

If an individual has ever been subject to any of the above, the RPB may consider that person not to be 'fit and proper' and may decline a request for authorisation as an IP. See paras 2.029–2.032 below for further discussion on the meaning of 'fit and proper'. **2.023**

---

19 Ibid s31(1). Note that this does not apply if the court makes the appointment: s31(3).

20 Ibid s390(1). Ordinarily this means that an IP should be sued in their sole name. For an interesting discussion as to whether there might be vicarious liability on the part of a firm for the actions of a member as receiver, by reason of s6(4) of the Limited Liability Partnership Act 2000, see *Christakis Kashourides v Allsop LLP* [2017] EWHC 2958 (Comm) (Sir Jeremy Cooke), who refused to strike out a claim brought against a firm, where reliance was placed on the earlier Inner House, Scottish decision, of *Kirkintilloch Equitable Cooperative Society Ltd v Livingstone* [1972] SC 111.

21 IA 1986 ss390(2) and 390A(2). Whilst this also refers to the Department for Enterprise Trade and Investment in Northern Ireland (now the Department for the Economy) as authorising IPs, this ability was removed via the Insolvency (Amendment) Act (Northern Ireland) 2016 (subject to transitional provisions).

22 Ibid s390(3) and the Insolvency Practitioners Regulations 2005 (SI 2005/524) Sch 2.

23 Ibid s390(4). Equivalent restrictions arising from Northern Irish and Scottish law apply.

24 Ibid s390(5).

3. Recognised professional bodies (RPBs)

(a) Overview of RPBs and the granting of insolvency licences

2.024 The identity of the RPBs is determined by an order of the Secretary of State.[25] A body may be recognised if it regulates the practice of a profession and it maintains and enforces rules to ensure that IPs (a) are fit and proper persons so to act, and (b) meet acceptable requirements as to education and practical training and experience.[26]

2.025 Currently there are five RPBs as follows:

- Association of Chartered Certified Accountants (ACCA)
- Institute of Chartered Accountants in England and Wales (ICAEW)
- Institute of Chartered Accountants in Ireland, now known as Chartered Accountants Ireland (CAI)
- Institute of Chartered Accountants of Scotland (ICAS)
- Insolvency Practitioners Association (IPA).[27]

2.026 The Deregulation Act 2015 removed the ability for a competent authority to grant, refuse and withdraw authorisation to act as an IP. The only competent authority was the Secretary of State and, as a result of the reform brought in by the Deregulation Act 2015, the Secretary of State no longer authorises IPs directly (subject to transitional provisions). The purpose of the reform was to 'reduce inconsistency of regulation by ensuring that all insolvency practitioners are authorised by one of the recognised professional bodies' and to remove 'a perceived conflict of interest with the Secretary of State's role as an oversight regulator of the professional bodies'.[28] The role of the Secretary of State in regulation is discussed further below.

2.027 Each RPB has its own procedure for issuing authorisation to IPs in the form of an insolvency licence. The procedure will involve the individual completing an application form, which will be considered by staff or a committee of the RPB. The reader should refer to the websites of the RPBs for details of their current processes.[29]

2.028 Licences may be appointment taking (allowing the individual to act as an IP in accordance with the IA 1986) or non-appointment taking. As the name suggests, a non-appointment

---

25 Ibid s391(1).

26 Ibid s391(4).

27 The Insolvency Practitioners (Recognised Professional Bodies) Order 1986 (SI 1986/1764), which has since been modified to remove The Law Society and The Law Society of Scotland as RPBs following requests from those bodies. On 31 December 2019 ACCA ceased authorising and regulating IPs and will be removed as an RPB when parliamentary time allows: see Annual Review of Insolvency Practitioner Regulation 2019 (26 August 2020) https://www.gov. uk/government/publications/insolvency-practitioner-regulation-process-review-2019/annual-review-of-insolvency-practitioner-regulation-2019 (accessed 24 October 2020).

28 Explanatory notes to the Deregulation Act 2015 para 594.

29 For ICAEW: https://www.icaew.com/technical/insolvency/become-an-insolvency-practitioner-with-icaew/becoming-an-icaew-insolvency-licensed-practitioner; for CAI: https://www.charteredaccountants.ie/Professional-Standards/Authorisations/Insolvency/Application-renewal-of-insolvency-certificate-licence; for ICAS: https://www.icas.com/regulation/how-to-become-an-icas-insolvency-practitioner; for IPA: https://www.insolvency-practitioners.org.uk/insolvency-practitioner/becoming-an-ip (all accessed on 11 April 2020). Note that in accordance with a collaboration agreement between ACCA and IPA, IPA carried out licensing, monitoring and complaints handling for ACCA from 2017.

taking licence does not permit the holder to act as office-holder in insolvency cases. However, it will give confidence to the outside world that the individual is suitably qualified and experienced in insolvency matters such that one of the RPBs thought fit to issue a licence to that person. As an example, non-appointment taking licences are common amongst solicitor IPs who wish to advise appointment-taking IPs rather than compete with them for insolvency appointments.

(b) Fit and proper

An individual will need to demonstrate to the RPB that they are fit and proper. The MoU **2.029** states that RPBs will have regard to regulation 6 of the Insolvency Practitioners Regulations 2005 in this respect. Regulation 6 refers to matters to be taken into account by competent authorities and includes matters surrounding offences committed, evidence of dishonesty, systems of control within the individual's practice and whether the individual acts in an ethical manner.

The RPB is also likely to wish to be satisfied that the individual has not been: **2.030**

- subject to any form of insolvency proceedings personally;
- a director of a company which has been involved in insolvency proceedings;
- the subject of a disqualification order;
- the subject of an adverse finding against him or her by a professional body;
- removed as an insolvency office-holder for misconduct;
- found guilty or pleaded guilty to a criminal offence; or
- the subject of a negligence claim.[30]

If one or more of the above circumstances does apply, further information is likely to be **2.031** required to be supplied to the RPB, which will decide whether or not the individual is deemed to be fit and proper. Given that an individual authorised as an IP will invariably act in the position of a trustee or fiduciary, it is important that high standards are upheld.

In addition, the individual will need to confirm that they will abide by the Insolvency Code of **2.032** Ethics.[31]

(c) Education and experience

The RPB will need to be satisfied that an applicant for an insolvency licence is appropriately **2.033** qualified and has a sufficient level of education.

The qualification requirement can be met by way of passing the Joint Insolvency Examination **2.034** Board (JIEB) examination. There are two papers: a corporate paper and a personal paper, and an individual must pass both papers in order to obtain a full licence. The examinations are set once a year, and individuals may choose to sit one paper at a time or both together. The papers examine insolvency legislation and practice and are considered to be a rigorous test. There are

---

30 As an example of matters which the RPB will take into account, see https://www.insolvency-practitioners.org.uk/insolvency-practitioner/authorisation-criteria (accessed on 11 April 2020).

31 See https://www.gov.uk/government/publications/insolvency-practitioner-code-of-ethics. Note that Code of Ethics was revised with effect from 1 May 2020 (accessed on 13 April 2020).

no education pre-requisites in order to sit the examinations, but it is usually recommended that applicants have several years' insolvency experience before attempting them. Frequently, applicants already hold a professional qualification, such as an accountancy or legal qualification or the Certificate of Proficiency in Insolvency.[32] Candidates do not need to be a member of an RPB in order to sit JIEB examinations, but the application must be made via one of the RPBs.[33]

2.035 In order to obtain a partial licence, only one of the two JIEB papers needs to be passed. See paras 2.062–2.067 below in respect of partial licences.

2.036 Alternatively, where an individual has obtained a professional or vocational qualification overseas which is equivalent to the JIEB examination in terms of its knowledge and competency requirements, the RPB may accept the overseas qualification instead. Under the European Union (Recognition of Professional Qualifications) Regulations 2015, where an applicant possesses an attestation of competence or evidence of formal qualifications required by another relevant European State, and where appropriate subject to an adaptation period or aptitude test, access to the profession must be allowed.[34]

2.037 Where the individual is or has been authorised by the Secretary of State or by an RPB, the authorisation may be transferred to another RPB (whether or not a suitable qualification has been obtained). Many individuals who acted in the capacity of IPs prior to the introduction of IA 1986 were 'grandfathered in' to the post 1986 regime under transitional provisions and were not required to pass examinations.

2.038 Practical training and experience are normally demonstrated by a particular number of hours of insolvency experience over a number of years prior to the application for a first insolvency licence. Each RPB has its own requirements in this regard. Details of the insolvency experience may need to be evidenced by way of timesheets or a list of examples of matters on which the applicant has worked. In addition, RPBs may have requirements relating to types of work carried out or the level of responsibility held by the applicant.

2.039 Details of the continuing professional development carried out by the individual prior to the licence application may be required by the RPB, to demonstrate that the individual is keeping their knowledge and skills up to date. There may be a minimum number of hours to be undertaken in the period prior to the licence application.

---

32 The Certificate of Proficiency in Insolvency is an examination set by the Insolvency Practitioners Association which tests knowledge of insolvency law and practice at a lower level than that of the JIEB qualification. There are also personal and corporate versions of the examination for those wishing to specialise.

33 See the Insolvency Practitioners Association's website http://www.insolvency-practitioners.org.uk/examinations/jie and JIEB website http://jieb.co.uk/the-exams/ (both accessed on 11 April 2020).

34 See European Union (Recognition of Professional Qualifications) Regulations 2015 (SI 2015/2059), Reg 29. In the context of these Regulations, a 'relevant European State' means an EEA State (Reg 2). At the time of writing, the terms of the UK's exit from the EU remain uncertain. It is therefore not clear whether these Regulations will continue to apply to individuals wishing to practice insolvency in the UK.

(d) Additional requirements

The RPB will require the IP or their firm to hold professional indemnity insurance, which will **2.040** be available to cover loss caused by any negligence of IPs or those working for them.[35]

The RPB will also require arrangements to be in place to deal with succession planning issues, **2.041** to ensure that the estates over which the IP is appointed can be maintained and transferred to an alternative IP in the event of the death or incapacity or other inability to act of the original IP.[36]

In addition, where the IP is a member of an accountancy body, that body may require the **2.042** individual to hold a practising certificate, regardless of whether that body is an RPB or is the RPB which regulates the IP.

Fees will have to be paid to the RPB to meet the costs of the obligations on the RPBs to **2.043** administer the licence and regulate the IP, and also for the onward payment of levies to the Insolvency Service, Department for the Economy in Northern Ireland and Complaints Gateway service.

(e) Ongoing requirements

Insolvency licences are usually issued for up to one year and renewed on an annual basis. **2.044** Renewal of a licence is likely to require completion of a form (or verification of the content of a pre-completed form) and RPBs may request information relating to:

- confirmation of continuing to be a fit and proper person; and
- continuing professional development, which may include confirmation that a minimum number of hours of education and training has been carried out, or that in the view of the IP sufficient professional development has been undertaken.

Annual fees will be payable to maintain an IP's licence, including levies to government services **2.045** as above. The RPB's fees may be charged at a fixed level or staged according to the fee income of the IP in the preceding year.

4. Security requirements

(a) The bonding system

In order to take appointments as an IP, it is necessary to hold a specific bond for each estate **2.046** and a general bond which comes into effect if the relevant specific bond is insufficient for any reason. The bond provides protection for creditors and other stakeholders by insuring the estate against fraud committed by the IP. It does not cover non-fraudulent misconduct or negligence, which would normally be covered by a professional indemnity policy.

---

35 Chapter 7 discusses the professional indemnity insurance requirements of the RPBs.
36 See insolvency guidance paper on succession planning, available at https://www.insolvency-practitioners.org.uk/regulation-and-guidance/insolvency-guidance-papers (accessed 13 April 2020).

2.047 Prior to 1986 security had to be held by trustees in bankruptcy and liquidators in compulsory liquidations, as well as receivers appointed by the court, but not by office-holders in other types of appointment. The Cork Report recommended 'that the distinction should be abolished and that the appointment of all insolvency practitioners should require to be covered by insurance and bonding against all types of fraud, dishonesty and professional negligence'.[37]

2.048 The recommendation was accepted and the requirements for security in all insolvency appointments were first introduced by the Insolvency Practitioners Regulations 1986 alongside the IA 1986. They are now set out in the Insolvency Practitioners Regulations 2005 ('IPR 2005'). The bond must cover:

> losses in relation to the insolvent caused by (i) the fraud or dishonesty of the insolvency practitioner whether acting alone or in collusion with one or more persons; or (ii) the fraud or dishonesty of any person committed with the connivance of the insolvency practitioner.[38]

Cover in respect of professional negligence without fraud or dishonesty is not a statutory requirement, but all of the RPBs nevertheless require IPs to hold such insurance.[39]

2.049 The bond must provide for a 'specific penalty sum' which is the maximum sum payable in each estate in respect of the IP's liability for losses.[40] The sum is calculated as

> at least the value of the insolvent's assets as estimated by the insolvency practitioner at the date of his appointment but ignoring the value of any assets –
>
> (a) charged to a third party to the extent of any amount which would be payable to that third party; or
> (b) held on trust by the insolvent to the extent that any beneficial interest in those assets does not belong to the insolvent

subject to a minimum of £5,000 and a maximum of £5,000,000.[41]

2.050 Similarly, in voluntary arrangements, the specific penalty sum is 'at least the value of those assets subject to the terms of the arrangement'.[42]

2.051 Effectively, this means that the specific penalty sum must cover the assets available to preferential and non-preferential unsecured creditors, including any surplus once those claims have been met. Note that no provision for costs or expenses may be deducted when calculating the specific penalty sum.

2.052 If the IP becomes aware that the specific penalty sum is less than the value of assets in the estate as calculated above, the value of the specific penalty sum must be increased.[43] Such a

---

37 *The Cork Report* para 763.
38 IPR 2005 (SI 2005/524) Sch 2 para 3(1)(a).
39 See Chapter 7 for further details of professional indemnity insurance requirements.
40 IPR 2005 Sch 2 para 3(2)(a).
41 Ibid paras 4, 6 and 7. Note that the role of monitor as created by CIGA 2020 carries with it the requirement for the IP to obtain a bond. The specific penalty sum is calculated as the value of the company's assets in the same way as other corporate insolvency appointments despite the moratorium being a debtor in possession procedure.
42 Ibid para 5.
43 Ibid para 3(2)(d).

situation may arise if an asset is discovered after the original calculation is carried out, or if an asset such as a property increases in value over time.

Schedules (also called bordereaux) must be submitted to the surety and the IP's RPB on a monthly basis detailing the relevant estates and levels of the specific penalty sums.[44] **2.053**

In addition, the bond must provide for a 'general penalty sum' of £250,000 in the event that a specific penalty sum is insufficient to meet claims arising out of an estate.[45] **2.054**

IPs must retain records relating to their bonds, which must be available for inspection where requested by a person with authority to make that request. Such persons include the Secretary of State, the IP's RPB and creditors and other stakeholders of an estate over which the IP is or was appointed.[46] **2.055**

There are a number of sureties who offer security to IPs on a commercial basis. Each general bond and specific bond carries with it a premium, which will be set by the surety based on the level of cover and commercial factors such as the perceived level of risk attaching to the cover. For this reason, larger firms of IPs dealing with greater numbers of estates holding greater value may be offered cheaper premia than smaller firms and sole practitioners with smaller portfolios. **2.056**

The cost of the specific bond premium may be charged to the estate to which it relates. However, the premium must always be paid regardless of the sufficiency of funds in the relevant estate, leaving the IP or their firm to pick up the cost where estate funds cannot bear it. **2.057**

Where a potential claim on the bond within an estate is identified, a successor IP is often appointed to investigate and make a claim if appropriate. If the surety agrees to meet the claim, the proceeds are paid into the estate as an asset and will be subject to the usual rules on priority of payments from the estate. **2.058**

(b) The future of bonding

The bonding system has been reviewed by the Insolvency Service and was the subject of a *Call for Evidence* in September 2016.[47] This paper identifies a number of perceived weaknesses in the current system, such as the levels of maximum cover being too low, the regime having not been changed since 1986, and concerns around the costs associated with investigating a bond claim meaning there may be no overall benefit to creditors. **2.059**

A number of suggestions were put forward in that paper including voluntary and regulatory changes through to abolition of the system altogether. A claims management protocol was also **2.060**

---

44 Ibid paras 3(2)(c) and 13.
45 Ibid para 3(2)(b).
46 Ibid paras 9–11.
47 *Bonding arrangements for insolvency practitioners: Call for Evidence* (15 September 2016) https://www.gov.uk/government/consultations/bonding-arrangements-for-insolvency-practitioners-call-for-evidence (accessed 13 April 2020).

suggested which would regulate the relationship between RPBs, bond providers and successor IPs.[48]

2.061   A summary of responses was published in September 2017. The majority of responses were in favour of legislative change. The paper states: 'We will consider the costs and benefits of legislative change in this area, which in the event of Ministerial agreement can be achieved through secondary legislation and so will require less parliamentary time.'[49] At the time of writing, there is no indication as to whether there will be any amendments to the existing legislation.

5.   Partial authorisation

2.062   Historically, where an individual was authorised to act as an IP, they were able to act over any estate, whether personal, corporate or a partnership.

2.063   The Deregulation Act 2015 introduced the ability for RPBs to issue partial licences to IPs. A partial licence permits insolvency appointments over individuals only or corporate entities only. This regime was 'intended to remove barriers to entry to the insolvency practitioner profession and improve competition. It will also reduce the cost of training for applicants who wish to specialise'.[50]

2.064   The requirements on IPs with partial licences are the same as on those with full licences, except that a pass in only the personal or the corporate paper of the JIEB examination (or other equivalent qualification) is required to satisfy the relevant education requirement of the RPB. The RPB may expect to see experience substantially in respect of the type of work in which the applicant intends to specialise.

2.065   Partially authorised IPs are not permitted to act in relation to partnerships. This is because knowledge of both individual and corporate insolvency is required in order to carry out the role of office-holder of a partnership.

2.066   There is a further restriction on holders of partial licences where the individual or company which is the subject of the appointment is a member of a partnership. An IP who is authorised to act only in relation to companies or to individuals is not permitted to take an appointment if the IP is aware that the subject of the appointment is a member of a partnership (other than a Scottish partnership if the subject is an individual) and there are outstanding liabilities in relation to the partnership.[51]

2.067   If a partially authorised IP becomes aware of this situation only after their appointment, then they are not permitted to continue to act unless permission is granted by the court.[52] The court

---

48   As above.

49   *Summary of Responses: Bonding arrangements for insolvency practitioners* (1 September 2017). See web page as above.

50   Explanatory notes to the Deregulation Act 2015, para 86.

51   IA 1986 s390B(1) & (2).

52   Ibid s390B(3) & (4).

may give such permission if it satisfied that the IP is competent to act in the matter.[53] The IP has a grace period of seven business days to make an application to court either for permission to continue to act or for the appointment of a replacement office-holder. Provided the application is made within this time frame, the IP will not commit an offence under s389 IA 1986.[54]

B. COMPLAINTS AND SANCTIONS

1. The regulatory framework

The insolvency industry is self-regulating with each RPB responsible for monitoring the IPs it authorises and for dealing with work falling below the required standard. Sub-standard work may be identified by the RPB or via a complaint made by a third party. IPs may also be required to self-report failings to their RPB.   **2.068**

RPBs are expected to carry out visits to the IPs they regulate on a periodic basis, to carry out reviews of their systems and of a selection of their cases. Where deficiencies are found, an RPB may offer assistance and guidance to the IP as to how they can improve their practices and overall quality of work. Serious or recurring issues may lead to a sanction against the IP.   **2.069**

The overall aim is to provide confidence to the public that the profession is giving a competent service. The Secretary of State has a reserve power to establish a single regulator in place of the RPBs should it be deemed necessary or desirable.[55]   **2.070**

The court has the power to issue sanctions directly against an IP where they have failed to comply with a requirement or professional standard of their RPB.   **2.071**

Liquidators, receivers, and administrative receivers may also be disqualified for up to 15 years under CDDA 1986 s4 if they are found to have breached their duties. The extent of such misconduct will typically be severe for disqualification to follow.[56] A disqualification will mean that the IP no longer meets the requisites for acting as an IP under IA 1986.[57]   **2.072**

2. Complaints against insolvency practitioners

Complaints may be made directly to an IP's firm and may be resolved without the need to involve any external body. However, any complaints which cannot be resolved this way should be referred to the Insolvency Service's Complaints Gateway. The Complaints Gateway was introduced in June 2013, upon a recommendation in the report of the OFT. It acts as a triage system to review complaints and decide whether or not they should be passed on to the IP's RPB for investigation. In addition, statistics are collected on the categories of complaints,   **2.073**

---

53   Ibid s390B(5).
54   Ibid s390B(9).
55   SBEEA 2015 s144(1) and see para 2.098.
56   *Re Asegaai Consultants Ltd* [2012] EWHC 1899 (Ch).
57   IA 1986 s390(4)(b).

whether they are referred to an RPB and the eventual outcomes. These statistics are published periodically by the Insolvency Service.[58]

2.074 Each RPB has its own system for dealing with complaints. This is likely to involve review by an investigating officer, correspondence with the complainant and an opportunity for the IP to provide comments and evidence on the issues raised. The complaint may be referred to a disciplinary committee or tribunal which will decide whether there is a case made out or no case for the IP to answer. There may also be an ability to appeal against the decision made.

3. Sanctions against insolvency practitioners issued by RPBs

2.075 Where there is a finding against an IP arising from a complaint, or conduct falling below the required standard identified through the RPB's monitoring processes, the RPB may issue a sanction. To improve consistency amongst the RPBs, common sanctions were introduced in 2013. Sanctions may be financial or non-financial and, in addition, the RPBs and the Insolvency Service publish all such sanctions unless there is an order by the RPB's committee or tribunal for no publicity or publicity on an anonymous basis.[59]

2.076 Non-financial sanctions range from a reprimand or severe reprimand through to restrictions on an IP's licence, exclusion from the RPB and removal of the licence altogether. The latter sanctions can seriously impact on the IP's livelihood and should only be used in the most extreme of cases.

2.077 A financial sanction is a fine at a fixed level or it may be linked to the profit made by the IP from the misconduct. In addition, the costs of the RPB in investigating the conduct may be payable by the IP.

2.078 In deciding on a suitable sanction, the disciplinary committee or tribunal may consider the common sanctions guidance and also whether any aggravating or mitigating factors are present.

2.079 The common sanctions guidance recommends that the following factors should be considered when deciding whether to issue a sanction and, if so, what sanction:

- protecting and promoting the public interest;
- maintaining the reputation of the profession;
- upholding the proper standards of conduct in the profession;
- correcting and deterring breaches of those standards.[60]

2.080 Aggravating factors (which may contribute to a heavier sanction being imposed) include matters such as concealment of the misconduct, repeated breaches and financial loss to one or

---

58 See Wood, 'Review of the regulatory system: how effective has the Complaints Gateway been?' (2017) 30(7) *Insolv Int* 106–13 at 112: '*the true level of justifiable complaints is unknown*'. The latest report of the Insolvency Service is available at https://www.gov.uk/government/publications/insolvency-practitioner-regulation-process-review-2019/annual-review-of-insolvency-practitioner-regulation-2019 (accessed 24 October 2020).

59 See www.gov.uk/government/publications/disciplinary-sanctions-against-insolvency-practitioners/common-sanctions-guidance ('Common Sanctions Guidance') (accessed 13 April 2020).

60 Ibid.

more estates over which the IP has control. Mitigating factors include personal factors such as illness, self-reporting and minimal risk of re-occurrence.

Most sanctions are split into three categories depending on the seriousness of the IP's misconduct: **2.081**

(a)   very serious – generally deliberate and/or dishonest conduct
(b)   serious – generally reckless conduct
(c)   less serious – usually an inadvertent breach.

As an example, where an IP is found to have failed to have taken adequate steps to realise assets, the indicative sanctions guidance is as follows: **2.082**

(a)   very serious – severe reprimand and fine of £7,500
(b)   serious – reprimand and fine of £2,000
(c)   less serious – reprimand and fine of £1,500.[61]

As its name suggests, the indicative sanctions guidance is meant as a guide to the RPBs when deciding on an appropriate level of sanction rather than as a fixed penalty. The RPBs should take into account all of the circumstances in each case, including whether any aggravating and/or mitigating factors are present. However, by setting out indicative levels, consistency across the RPBs is more likely to be maintained, leading to a fairer, more level playing field for IPs. One RPB should not be seen as being 'softer' than another. **2.083**

Where the RPB believes that misconduct has taken place, the IP may be given an opportunity to agree to a disciplinary consent order rather than the RPB imposing an order without consent. The advantage of agreeing to a consent order is that it reduces committee time and associated costs in hearing any further arguments and in having to decide on an appropriate sanction. Such costs would normally be passed on to the IP where a finding is made against them by the committee. **2.084**

A finding and/or a sanction against an IP may be appealed against according to the rules and procedures of the RPB. The court may become involved to settle matters which cannot be resolved between the IP and RPB. This was the case in *Mond v The Association of Chartered Certified Accountants*,[62] where Collins J quashed the orders made by ACCA's Disciplinary Committee and Appeals Committee against the IP, Mr Mond. The process which had been followed was found to be contrary to ACCA's regulations and unfair to Mr Mond.[63] **2.085**

---

61   https://assets.publishing.service.gov.uk/government/uploads/system/uploads/attachment_data/file/564872/Common_Sanctions_Guidance_2016_table.pdf (accessed 24 October 2020).
62   [2005] EWHC 1414 (Admin).
63   See also *Hollis, R (on the application of) v The Association of Chartered Certified Accountants* [2014] EWHC 2572 (Admin), an application for judicial review of a decision of the Disciplinary Committee of ACCA.

4. Direct sanctions by the Secretary of State and the court

2.086   The SBEEA 2015 introduced changes to the IA 1986 which allow the Secretary of State to agree a sanction with an IP, or to make an application to court for a sanction against an IP, where it is in the public interest to do so. It is normally expected that the RPB has the primary responsibility for issuing sanctions against IPs in line with the RPB's procedures as referred to above. However, where the Secretary of State is not satisfied with the actions (or inactions) of the RPB, they may now take matters into their own hands.

2.087   A 'direct sanctions direction' is given by the Secretary of State to the RPB of an IP, but the IP must give their consent.[64] Alternatively, the Secretary of State may make an application to court for a 'direct sanctions order' against an IP.[65]

2.088   In either case there are five conditions to be considered. The Secretary of State (in the case of a direct sanctions direction) or the court (in the case of a direct sanctions order) must be satisfied that condition 1 has been met and at least one of conditions 2, 3, 4 and 5 has been met in relation to the IP.[66]

2.089   Condition 1 is that the person has failed to comply with a requirement imposed by the RPB or any standards or code of ethics for the profession adopted by the RPB.[67] This underlines the importance for IPs of complying with professional standards. Note, however, that the Statements of Insolvency Practice and Code of Ethics are increasingly intended to be principles-based rather than rules-based approaches, creating a degree of subjectivity in ascertaining whether or not a particular element of them has been followed. The court, in particular, may find it difficult to make a determination and perhaps would need to rely on expert evidence as to how the standards and codes are used in practice.

2.090   Condition 2 is that the person is not a fit and proper person to act as an IP, either at all or in relation to companies or to individuals.[68] There are no defined criteria to determine whether a person is 'fit and proper' and, again, this carries a substantial amount of subjectivity.

2.091   Condition 3 is that it is appropriate for the person's authorisation to act as an IP to be suspended for a period of time or until one or more requirements are complied with.[69]

2.092   Condition 4 is that it is appropriate to impose other restrictions on the person.[70]

2.093   Condition 5 is that loss has been suffered by one or more creditors of an estate over which the person was acting, as a result of a failure to comply with a requirement imposed by the RPB or

---

64   IA 1986 s391R(1) & (2).
65   Ibid s391P(1).
66   Ibid ss391R(1) and 391P(3).
67   Ibid s391Q(1).
68   Ibid s391Q(2).
69   Ibid s391Q(3).
70   Ibid s391Q(4).

with professional standards.[71] Note that it is only a loss suffered by creditors which may be considered. In a case where the loss is suffered by the debtor, the members of a company or partners of a partnership, such loss would not be a matter for consideration under this condition.

The court must take into account the action taken by the IP's RPB when deciding whether or not to make a direct sanctions order, and whether or not that action is insufficient to address the failure on the part of the IP.[72] **2.094**

A direct sanctions order or direction includes one or more of the following, as a declaration or requirement of the court (in the case of an order) or a requirement of the RPB to take all necessary steps to secure (in the case of a direction): **2.095**

(a)   That the person is no longer authorised to act as an IP
(b)   That the person is no longer fully authorised but remains partially authorised
(c)   That the person's authorisation is suspended for a period of time or until such time as specified requirements are complied with
(d)   That the person must comply with specified requirements whilst acting as an IP
(e)   That the person makes a specified contribution to one or more creditors of an estate over which the person is acting or has acted.[73] However, the maximum contribution is the amount of remuneration that the person has received or will receive for acting as an IP in the case.[74]

5.   Oversight of RPBs by the Secretary of State

The SBEEA 2015 introduced the Secretary of State (acting through the Insolvency Service) as the 'regulator of regulators', or oversight regulator, giving him or her the ability to issue a range of sanctions on an RPB. Prior to this, the only sanction available was the revocation of an RPB's recognition as an RPB. **2.096**

Regulatory objectives were enshrined in law through the SBEEA 2015. The RPBs must have regard to these objectives when regulating IPs. **2.097**

Finally, the Insolvency Service has a reserve power to establish a single regulator of IPs.[75] This power must be exercised within seven years of its coming into force, this is, within seven years of 1 October 2015.[76] There is no clue as to the identity of the single regulator. It may be a new body established for the purpose, or a body already in existence, either private or public.[77] **2.098**

---

71   Ibid s391Q(5).
72   Ibid s391P(5).
73   Ibid ss391O(1) and 391R(3).
74   Ibid ss391O(4) and 391R(5).
75   SBEEA 2015 s144(1).
76   Ibid s146(1) and (2).
77   Ibid s144(2).

2.099 The RPBs must (so far as is reasonably practicable) act in a way which is compatible with the regulatory objectives, whilst the Secretary of State must have regard to them. The regulatory objectives cover the following areas:

(a) Having a system of regulation for IPs which secures fair treatment for those affected by their acts and omissions

(b) Encouraging an independent and competitive profession

(c) Promoting maximisation of returns to creditors

(d) Protecting and promoting the public interest.[78]

2.100 The Secretary of State may issue a direction to an RPB where an act or omission of the RPB has had or is likely to have an adverse impact on the achievement of one or more of the regulatory objectives. The direction may include requiring the RPB to take steps within its powers or to amend its arrangements for authorisation and regulation of IPs, or to institute regulatory proceedings.[79]

2.101 At least 28 days' notice must be given to the RPB prior to the Secretary of State issuing the direction and an explanation as to how the Secretary of State reached the conclusion must be provided. The notice period gives the RPB an opportunity to make representation to the Secretary of State, following which the Secretary of State will decide whether or not to issue the direction.[80]

2.102 Where an RPB fails to comply with such a direction or with a provision of the IA 1986 (or subordinate legislation), the Secretary of State may issue a financial penalty on the RPB at a level which the Secretary of State thinks appropriate.[81] A 28-day notice period applies to allow the RPB to make representations, after which the proposed penalty may be imposed or reconsidered by the Secretary of State.[82] If a penalty is imposed, the RPB has the right to appeal to the court to quash the penalty, to reduce the amount or to change the time period in which it must be paid.[83]

2.103 The Secretary of State also has the power to reprimand RPBs by publishing a statement setting out the acts and omissions of the RPB to which attention should be drawn,[84] and retains the power to revoke recognition of a body as an RPB.[85]

6. The future of insolvency practitioner regulation

2.104 As mentioned above, the Insolvency Service has a reserve power to establish a single regulator of IPs, which must be exercised by 1 October 2022. In order to assist the government in

---

78 IA 1986 s391C(3).
79 Ibid s391D.
80 Ibid s391E.
81 Ibid s391F.
82 Ibid s391G.
83 Ibid s391H.
84 Ibid ss391J and 391K.
85 Ibid s391L.

making a decision as to whether to appoint a single regulator, a *Call for Evidence*[86] was issued in July 2019. This paper sought responses from interested parties such as IPs, RPBs and creditors on a number of questions surrounding the current regulatory framework and regulatory objectives including whether or not they are working as intended.

One of the areas for consideration raised by the paper was whether there has been increased confidence in the regulatory regime since October 2015, in line with the regulatory objectives. It asked whether complaints are investigated fairly and RPBs issue appropriate sanctions. **2.105**

A number of options were put forward which would involve changes to the current system but would not go so far as to introduce a single regulator. These were mostly centred around complaints and misconduct and included the introduction of a single body to progress complaints against IPs[87] or a tribunal system to consider misconduct. The identity of the single regulator, were one to be established, was also raised for comment. The existing legislation does not permit the Insolvency Service to be the single regulator, but the *Call for Evidence* asked whether the government should play a role in the regulatory framework and hinted at possible further legislative change. **2.106**

As discussed earlier in this chapter, IPs are authorised and regulated as individuals, in line with the personal nature of the appointment of an office-holder over an insolvent estate. However, the *Call for Evidence* asks respondents to consider whether firms should be authorised instead of, or alongside, individual IPs. This suggestion appears to have been driven by the high volume market for individual voluntary arrangements (and protected trust deeds in Scotland), where, according to the *Call for Evidence*, 'the IP is often an employee, supervising several thousand cases, with little control or say over the actions and policies of the firm'. Authorisation at firm level would shift the weight of responsibility, either such that it would be shared between firm and IP, or solely to the firm.[88] **2.107**

Finally, the funding of regulation is raised. The current model is self-funding, with the IPs funding both the RPBs and the Complaints Gateway. If IP regulation were to be become a function of a government body, this would no doubt result in a huge set-up expense and ongoing costs to run the system. However, the Insolvency Service is keen to point out that no decision has been made as of July 2019 as to the future of IP regulation and any proposed changes would require further consultation. **2.108**

---

86 *Regulation of insolvency practitioners Review of current regulatory landscape: Call for evidence* https://www.gov.uk/government/consultations/call-for-evidence-regulation-of-insolvency-practitioners-review-of-current-regulatory-landscape (accessed 13 April 2020).

87 Whilst the Complaints Gateway receives complaints about IPs, as noted above, it acts as a triage system only, referring the complaint on to the RPB or reverting to the complainant due to insufficient information or due to the complaint not being a matter appropriate for consideration by the RPB.

88 Although note the decision in *Christakis Kashourides v Allsop LLP* [2017] EWHC 2958 (Comm) and para 2.019 above, which might suggest, in the case of LLPs, the argument might already be made that such liability is shared with the LLP.

3

APPOINTMENT, TERMINATION AND REMOVAL

A. INTRODUCTION

1. Overview

3.001 Before turning, in Chapter 4 onwards, to set out in more detail the duties and powers of an insolvency practitioner ('IP') and going on to look at their liabilities, it is important to have an understanding of the manner in which office-holders are appointed, and of the circumstances in which they can be removed or otherwise cease to act. This is because the statutory underpinning for, and methodology of, office-holder's appointment and/or removal, is of obvious relevance to that office-holder's prospective liabilities.

3.002 In an ordinary civil claim against a professional for negligence, it is likely that the starting point of any analysis will involve identifying the basis upon which the professional was appointed and remunerated. To take an obvious example, a lawyer retained by a client will invariably be retained upon the basis of a formal written retainer, which will contain the terms and conditions upon which the lawyer agrees to act. The retainer will also delineate the duties and standards which the lawyer agrees to abide by. The retainer's impact on the lawyer's potential liabilities is immediately obvious.

IPs are, however, professionals that are in a slightly different category. Unlike accountants, **3.003** architects, financial advisers, lawyers, doctors and surveyors, who are retained (for the entirety of the professional relationship) to act for a specific client or group of clients, an IP, upon appointment, exercises a more wide-ranging statutory function as set out in the IA 1986, having to balance the interests of several stakeholders (e.g., and most obviously, the debtor on the one hand and the debtor's creditors on the other). Therefore, once appointed, an IP is not, in the sense that other professionals are, retained by a single client or homogenous group of clients.

That is not to say that there are never bilateral relationships (professional/client) in an **3.004** insolvency context. Prior to their appointment it is possible, and indeed common, for the relevant practitioner to have had an advisory relationship with one of the stakeholders in the insolvency process, frequently the debtor or a particular creditor or class of creditors. Indeed, it is also possible that the office-holder will be appointed at the behest of a specific stakeholder. It is a relatively common feature of out of court administration appointments by a qualifying floating charge holder that the office-holder will have had a prior professional relationship with the company's banker or first-tier lender, who will be the holder of the relevant charge.

The extent to which particular stakeholders are able to play a role in the appointment of an IP **3.005** is plainly potentially relevant in considering the subsequent actions of the individual once appointed, particularly in the event of an assertion that the individual preferred one set of stakeholders' interests over others.

Against that backdrop, it is helpful therefore to have some understanding of how IPs come to **3.006** be appointed (and subsequently removed) as trustees in bankruptcy, liquidators, or any other type of office-holder. This chapter sets out to achieve that aim, with the caveat that this work focuses on the liabilities of IPs, and not their appointment. Accordingly the treatment of IPs' appointment, remuneration and removal is, of necessity, intended to provide a full overview, rather than a detailed analysis. Reference can however be made to existing texts which consider specific categories of insolvency office-holders.[1] A similar caveat is appropriate in relation to Schemes of Arrangement under Part 26 of the Companies Act 2006 ('CA 2006'), which although frequently used as a restructuring tool in situations when a corporate entity is insolvent, are not, strictly, an insolvency process; reference should therefore be made to specialist texts on the topic.[2]

---

1   See e.g., Robinson and Walton (eds), *Kerr & Hunter on Receivership and Administration* (21st edn, 2020), *Lightman & Moss on the Law of Administrators and Receivers of Companies* (2017, 6th edn), Briggs and Tribe (eds), *Muir Hunter on Personal Insolvency* (loose-leaf), *Loose and Griffiths on Liquidators* (9th edn, 2019).
2   See e.g., O'Dea, Long and Smyth, *Schemes of Arrangement: Law and Practice* (2012); Pilkington, *Schemes of Arrangement in Corporate Restructuring* (2nd edn, 2017).

2. Appointment

3.007 Office-holders may be appointed by a variety of different methods, depending upon the type of insolvency. This chapter focuses on the appointment process for one IP but it should be noted that joint appointments are common and this has potential significance in the context of liability. Joint appointments are considered further in paras 3.029–3.033 below. In general, the person or group of persons which has the major financial interest in the insolvent person or entity has the ability to choose the identity of the office-holder appointed to manage their interests, with the court as a backstop in most cases if that fails. However, there are many exceptions to this general rule. For example, in an administration, the directors may be able to appoint an administrator, even though they may have no financial interest in the outcome of the procedure.[3] In bankruptcies and compulsory liquidations, the Secretary of State has the power to appoint a trustee or a liquidator. Whilst in some circumstances, the Secretary of State may refer to the major creditors when identifying an IP to act, at other times, such as when there is an urgent need for an office-holder other than the official receiver, an IP may simply be appointed without reference to any of the stakeholders.[4]

3.008 In the case of Secretary of State appointments, the Insolvency Service Technical Manual contains, at part 5 of Chapter 17, detailed provisions which explain the approach taken by the Secretary of State to the appointment of liquidators and trustees.

3.009 Any person appointed as an Official Receiver ('OR') should normally seek a Secretary of State appointment either where the skills of an IP are desirable, or the majority of creditors request the appointment. Where such an appointment is sought, the OR should normally seek to appoint the next IP on the 'Insolvency Practitioner Rota' maintained by the Insolvency Service. A copy of the rota can be viewed online.[5]

3.010 However, that is not, it seems, intended to be an absolute rule. For example, in the case of a connected insolvency (e.g., a liquidator of a connected company or the trustee in bankruptcy for a spouse/partner or a business partner) the OR should seek the appointment of the same IP. There is therefore a tension between the complete independence of an IP (which might be preserved if the rota were to be adhered to strictly) and where the rota will be departed from in cases where it is efficient to do so.[6] It will also be relevant whether or not a proposed IP has a conflict of interest, and/or special skills which make them more suitable for the particular insolvency (e.g., where there are assets abroad).

3.011 Further, in the event that there is a clear majority creditor, the Technical Manual directs that that creditor should be contacted, and that their preferred IP should be appointed, rather than

---

3 See paras 3.073–3.074 below.

4 For example, under IA 1986 s124A.

5 https://www.gov.uk/government/publications/insolvency-practitioner-rota (accessed on 19 April 2020). The appointment of an insolvency practitioner from the Official Receiver's rota would only be made out of turn in very exceptional circumstances and this would only be if there were clearly recognisable reasons for doing so: see 'Guidance to Official Receivers on appointing liquidators and trustees' (2017) 30(4) *Insolv Int* 63.

6 But see the comments made in *Re Barings Plc* [2001] 2 BCLC 159 at [51] for concerns over when cross-over appointments become too numerous.

the next practitioner on the rota. If creditors representing over 50 per cent of creditors by value seek the appointment of a specific IP, the OR should normally accede to such a request.

In those cases where Her Majesty's Revenue and Customs ('HMRC') are the petitioning **3.012** creditor, the Technical Manual records HMRC's preference for an appointment to be made from the rota, although it is open to HMRC to specify that a non-rota appointment will be sought and that HMRC will seek the appointment of a specific practitioner.

Before an IP decides whether to accept an appointment, they will receive from the OR a **3.013** 'teaser' form which will contain basic details in relation to the debtor's assets and liabilities. The tasks to be undertaken and any matters which may specifically arise will be drawn to the attention of the relevant practitioner.

3. Removal

As a general rule, the stakeholder(s) entitled to appoint an office-holder also have the power to **3.014** remove him or her from office.

In an insolvent liquidation and a bankruptcy, creditors may remove the office-holder via a **3.015** decision procedure instigated specifically for that purpose.[7] Members have this power in a members' voluntary liquidation via a general meeting of the company (or written resolutions) in accordance with the company's articles of association.

The court also has the power to remove an administrative receiver, a liquidator, a provisional **3.016** liquidator, a trustee in bankruptcy, administrator, or monitor.[8]

If the liquidator or trustee was appointed by the Secretary of State, he or she may also be **3.017** removed by the Secretary of State.[9]

In an administration, the appointor of the administrator may replace the administrator, **3.018** although consent of the qualifying floating chargeholder or the permission of the court may be required depending on the circumstances.[10]

There are no provisions in legislation relating to the removal of a supervisor of a voluntary **3.019** arrangement. The proposal may contain such provisions.

4. Resignation

The circumstances in which office-holders may resign office are limited. For a liquidator or a **3.020** trustee, it must be for one of the following reasons:

---

7 In a CVL: IA 1986 s171(2)(b); in a compulsory liquidation: IA 1986 s172(2); in a bankruptcy: IA 1986 s298(1).
8 In administrative receivership: IA 1986 s45(1) (note only the court has the power to remove an administrative receiver); in CVL and MVL: IA 1986 s108(2); in a compulsory or provisional liquidation: s172(2); in a bankruptcy: IA 1986 s298(1); in an administration: IA 1986 Sch B1 para 88; in a moratorium: IA 1986 sA39.
9 IA 1986 ss172(4) and 298(5).
10 IA 1986 Sch B1 paras 92–94.

(a)   On grounds of ill health;

(b)   Because of the intention to cease to practice as an insolvency practitioner;

(c)   Because further discharge of duties is prevented or made impractical by a conflict of interest or a change in personal circumstances;

(d)   Where there are two or more office-holders and it is no longer expedient for there to be that many.[11]

Other than if the reason for resignation is (d) above, then the office-holder should seek appointment of a replacement,[12] as it not desirable for there to be no office-holder in office during an insolvency procedure.

3.021 An administrator may resign for one of reasons (a), (b) or (c) above, or, with the permission of the court, on other grounds.[13]

3.022 There are no restrictions as to when an administrative receiver may resign.[14] Five business days' notice must be given of the intention to resign.[15]

5.   Fixing remuneration on appointment

3.023 Office-holders have a general entitlement to remuneration: 'an administrator, liquidator or trustee in bankruptcy is entitled to receive remuneration for services as office-holder.'[16] The Insolvency (England and Wales) Rules 2016 ('IR 2016') specify the different bases, of which there are three, by reference to which the remuneration of an administrator, a liquidator or a trustee in bankruptcy must be fixed at the commencement of the office-holder's appointment.[17] The first basis is, in the case of an administrator, as a percentage of the value of the property with which the administrator has to deal.[18] In the case of a liquidator or a trustee in bankruptcy, it is as a percentage of the value of the assets which are realised, distributed, or both realised and distributed.[19] The second basis is by reference to the time properly given by the IP and the IP's staff in attending to the matters in the insolvency.[20] This second basis is, by far, the most commonly encountered basis of remuneration in insolvency cases, and is usually the basis favoured by IPs. The final basis is as a set amount.[21] The possibility of adopting different bases for different tasks undertaken by the IP is expressly provided for in the IR 2016.[22]

---

11 In an MVL: IR 2016 r5.6(1); in a CVL: IR 2016 r6.25(1); in a compulsory liquidation: IR 2016 r7.61(1); in a bankruptcy: IR 2016 r10.77(1).

12 In an MVL: IR 2016 r5.6(2); in a CVL: IR 2016 r6.25(2); in a compulsory liquidation: IR 2016 r7.61(2); in a bankruptcy: IR 2016 r10.77(2).

13 IR 2016 r3.62.

14 IA 1986 s45(1).

15 IR 2016 r4.18.

16 Ibid r18.16(1).

17 Further details on the general right to charge for work done, the method for fixing in each process, the right of recoupment, and the priority rule, are covered in paras 5.192–5.213 below.

18 IR 2016 r18.16(2)(a)(i).

19 Ibid r18.16(2)(a)(ii).

20 Ibid r18.16(2)(b).

21 Ibid r18.16(2)(c).

22 Ibid r18.16(3).

In general, the stakeholders with a financial interest in the outcome of the procedure are **3.024** responsible for agreeing the basis of remuneration of the office-holder. Ordinarily, if there is a creditors' committee or a liquidation committee, it will decide the basis of remuneration. Where there is no committee, the decision generally falls to the general body of creditors. In an administration the secured and/or preferential creditors may be responsible where there will not be a distribution to the unsecured creditors (other than through the prescribed part).[23] In a members' voluntary liquidation, the members have the primary interest in the outcome and therefore the company decides on remuneration via a general meeting.[24] The Rules impose a requirement on the IP (other than in an MVL) to supply relevant information to the stakeholders responsible for deciding on remuneration in advance of a decision being made.[25] The information includes details of the work which the IP proposes to undertake and details of the expenses which the IP will incur, or which are likely to be incurred. In reaching a decision on the basis of remuneration, the stakeholders must take into account the complexity of the case, whether the case imposes any exceptional responsibility on the IP, the effectiveness with which the IP has or appears to have carried out his or her duties, and finally, the value and nature of the property with which the IP has to deal.[26] Except in the case of a members' voluntary liquidation, if an IP wishes to take his or her remuneration on the basis of the time properly given, it is necessary, before the basis of remuneration is fixed, for the IP to deliver a fee estimate to the relevant stakeholders.[27]

In bankruptcy and compulsory liquidation, if the basis of remuneration has not been fixed **3.025** upon request, or if 18 months have passed and the basis of remuneration has not been fixed, then the scale rate applies, calculated as a percentage of realisations and distributions in the estate.[28]

The court is always a backstop if either the office-holder's basis of remuneration is not fixed or **3.026** the office-holder considers the amount or rate to be insufficient or the basis to be inappropriate. However, if the basis of remuneration has not been fixed at all, an administrator and a voluntary liquidator may only apply to court within 18 months of appointment[29] and the office-holder must attempt to agree remuneration via creditors or the committee first.[30] There is no such deadline in a bankruptcy or compulsory liquidation as, if there has been no decision with 18 months of appointment, the office-holder's remuneration is automatically fixed at the scale rate. In any situation in which the court is called upon to determine the remuneration of an IP, reference must be made to Part 6 of the Insolvency Practice Direction ('IPD').[31] The

---

23 Ibid r18.18(4).
24 Ibid r18.19.
25 Ibid r18.16(6)(7).
26 Ibid r18.16(9).
27 Ibid r18.16(4).
28 Ibid r18.22. The scale is set out in Sch 11 to the IR 2016. Note that if no assets have been realised and no distributions made, the application of the scale rate will mean the IP is not entitled to any remuneration at all. This may be retrospectively altered by the court under its general power to do so in IA 1986 s363: see *Re Colgate* [1986] Ch 439. However, there also appears to be scope for the alternative view, which is that the power in IA 1986 s363 must be exercised in accordance with and subject to IR 2016, chapter 4, and after 18 months have elapsed the scale rate must apply.
29 Ibid r18.23(3).
30 Ibid r18.23(2).
31 'Applications Relating to the Remuneration of Office-Holders'.

objective set out therein is to 'ensure that the amount and/or basis of any remuneration fixed by the Court is fair, reasonable and commensurate with the nature and extent of the work properly undertaken ...'. There are nine guiding principles to which the court must have regard in determining the remuneration of the IP.[32] The Practice Direction also prescribes, in some detail, the information which an IP must supply in advance of any hearing at which the court determines the remuneration.[33] The practice direction received judicial endorsement by the Court of Appeal in *Brook v Reed*.[34]

3.027 There are no specific provisions in respect of the remuneration of administrative receivers. Such remuneration should be agreed between the office-holder and the chargeholder. There may be provisions in the charge documentation which deal with this issue. Remuneration of receivers is also a private matter to be agreed between appointor and receiver.

3.028 Similarly in a voluntary arrangement, the remuneration of the supervisor should be covered in the terms of the proposal which is approved by creditors. Where they are not sanctioned by the terms of the arrangement, fees may be incurred where they correspond to those which would be payable in an administration or winding up (CVA) or in a bankruptcy (IVA).[35] In addition, the fees of nominees are ordinarily agreed before appointment; a nominee does not have a statutory entitlement to remuneration. A similar approach will be taken in respect of monitors, whose remuneration will be a matter for agreement between the IP and the debtor company.

6. Joint appointments

3.029 Trustees in bankruptcy, liquidators and administrators will often be appointed in pairs, and described as, for example, 'the Joint Administrators of' the relevant company or 'the Joint Trustees in Bankruptcy of' the relevant debtor.[36]

3.030 This is done for predominantly practical reasons, so that if one office-holder should be incapacitated or unavailable, the process can continue with minimal difficulties. Typically, the terms of the insolvency practitioner's appointment will mean that when one acts in respect of the company or debtor, those acts will be on behalf of, and indeed bind, both office-holders. This is consistent with the general theory that the *office* of the insolvency practitioner is juridically distinct from the individual who steps into the shoes of that office-holder.[37]

3.031 In some instances, a second office-holder might be appointed as a 'conflict office-holder'. An example of such an appointment occurring is *Re Angel Group*.[38] In that case, the former director of the company had concerns over the impartiality of the administrators who had been

---

32 IPD para 21.2.
33 Ibid para 21.4.
34 [2011] EWCA Civ 331, [2012] 1 BCLC 379 at [48].
35 IR 2016 rr2.43 and 8.30.
36 Court documents are conventionally headed in this way, with both office-holders being named as the First and Second Applicants (or Respondents as appropriate) and subtitled 'in their capacity as Joint [Administrators/Trustees] of [the company/debtor]'.
37 So, e.g., the acts of one office-holder will bind all future IPs in that role. Obviously, any personal liability will remain with the outgoing IP.
38 [2015] EWHC 3624 (Ch). See also *Re Zinc Hotels (Holdings) Ltd* [2018] EWHC 1936 (Ch).

appointed by a bank, who was by far the largest creditor and holder of a qualifying floating charge. The former director sought the appointment of the additional liquidators for the primary purpose of investigating and potentially bringing a claim against the bank. The day-to-day working of the liquidation in that case was governed by a Memorandum of Understanding ('MoU'), which Rose J confirmed was a sensible and pragmatic solution to the problem raised in that case, and it is suggested that it will often be sensible and pragmatic for joint officeholders to enter into a similar protocol or MoU.

A further reason for joint appointments occurs where two or more creditors (or groups of **3.032** creditors) wish for the appointment of different IPs as office-holders. Rather than proceeding with a potentially adversarial race to the highest value of creditor votes, a practical solution to satisfy both sides may be for two office-holders to be appointed jointly. Or the point may be that there is simply a need for extra resources and it is considered a second IP will result in greater efficiency. Original administrators may make an application, for example, to appoint a second set of administrators to act concurrently.[39]

How the functions within the administration will be divided between joint and concurrent **3.033** administrators is set out in Sch B1, paras 100–103, which require it to be stated which functions are to be exercised by the person acting jointly and which functions are to be exercised by any or all of the persons appointed. This also specifies, under para 101(4), joint liability on the part of joint office-holders in the event of offences of omission. Disputes over the division of remuneration between joint administrators, liquidators and trustees are covered by the Rules, with such matters capable of referral to the committee, the creditors (by decision procedure), the company (in a members' voluntary liquidation) or in any case to the court.[40]

B. LIQUIDATORS

1. Liquidators – compulsory liquidations

(a) Appointment

The appointment of a liquidator in a winding up by the court (i.e., compulsory liquidation) is **3.034** provided for in IA 1986 ss135–140. The IA 1986 draws a distinction between those instances in which the company has been in administration or in a CVA under the IA 1986 before the winding-up order is made, and those where it has not.

By IA 1986 s140, if the company was in administration or in a CVA prior to the court making **3.035** a winding-up order, the court has a discretion to appoint the former administrator or supervisor as liquidator of the company. It is a discretionary power which has been described as enabling the court to bypass the normal appointment provisions contained in IA 1986 ss135–139.[41] It is thought to be justified by the fact that the IP who has already acted as administrator or supervisor in relation to the company will generally be aware of the company's background and will have an understanding of the issues that arise and need addressing in the

---

39   As happened in *Re BHS Ltd* [2016] EWHC 1965 (Ch), [2016] BCC 609.
40   IR 2016 r18.17.
41   *Re Exchange Travel (Holdings) Ltd* [1992] BCC 954 (Edward Evans-Lombe QC).

company's insolvency. It is clear however from the express wording of the statute that the power given to the court by s140 does not extend to appointing as liquidator of a company which immediately before the winding-up order was in administration or a CVA a person other than the administrator or supervisor (indeed that was the view taken by the court in *Re Exchange Travel*).

3.036 Before the court can make an appointment under s140 (and a similar requirement is replicated as regards the other methods of appointment), it is necessary for the relevant individual seeking appointment to file with the court a statement to the effect that the individual is an IP, and is duly qualified under IA 1986 to become a liquidator.[42] A liquidator's appointment pursuant to s140 takes effect from the date of the court's order, or on such other date as the court orders.[43] Prior to making a statement of consent to act, however, this situation is specifically mentioned in the Insolvency Code of Ethics (the 'Code') as one where the individual must consider whether there are any circumstances that give rise to an unacceptable threat to ethical principles. The appointment of a liquidator as a subsequent office-holder provides an opportunity for that individual to review and scrutinise the actions of the former office-holder. Such a review cannot be objective if both office-holders are the same person. That said, successive appointments of the same office-holder are not uncommon, and it would occur where a particular, unmanageable threat exists in the circumstances of the case that an individual may be expected to decline to act as subsequent office-holder.

3.037 In any other case, by IA 1986 s136(2), the OR becomes liquidator of a company on a winding-up order being made against the company. This means that if, prior to the winding-up order being made, the company was in a CVL or an MVL, the liquidator in those proceedings will cease to be in office.[44]

3.038 At any time when the OR is a liquidator of a company, he or she will be able to exercise a power under s136(4) to invite nominations from the company's creditors and contributories for the appointment of an insolvency practitioner as liquidator. Moreover, within 12 weeks beginning with the day on which the winding-up order was made, the OR must decide whether to exercise the power to seek nominations for a liquidator.[45] If the OR does not exercise that power within 12 weeks, it is open to the creditors of the company (provided that they represent at least one-quarter in value of the company's creditors) to request, at any time, the OR to exercise the power.

3.039 The IR 2016 contain detailed provisions which specify the process which must be followed when the OR invites nominations under s136(4). Creditors have five business days from receipt of a notice under s136(4) to make a proposal to the OR.[46] If any proposals are received, the OR must seek a decision on the nomination of a liquidator from the creditors or contributories as appropriate, such decision to be taken by a decision procedure or a deemed

---

42 IR 2016 r7.56(2).
43 Ibid r7.56(7).
44 See IR 2016 r6.31, which deals with the consequences that follow from a liquidator vacating office on the making of a winding-up order.
45 IA 1986 s136(5)(a).
46 IR 2016 r7.52.

consent procedure. The rules contain provisions to determine the decision on nomination.[47] It is in effect a majority decision. It is open to contributories or creditors, in some circumstances, to apply to court under IA 1986 s139(4) (within seven days of an appointment being made) for an order appointing some other person as the liquidator.

In addition to the procedure set out in s136, IA 1986 also contains, in s137, provisions for the appointment of a liquidator by the Secretary of State. By s137(1), at any time when the OR is liquidator, he can apply to the Secretary of State for the appointment of a person as liquidator. Further, by s137(2), if nominations for a liquidator are sought under s136(5)(a), but no liquidator is appointed as a result, the OR has a duty to consider whether to refer the need for an appointment to the Secretary of State. It is open to the Secretary of State, to either make an appointment, or decline to make one.[48] In the case of a Secretary of State appointment, the relevant certificate must specify the date from which the liquidator's appointment is effective.[49] **3.040**

If there is ever a vacancy in the office of liquidator whilst a company is being wound up by the court, the OR automatically becomes liquidator of the company.[50] **3.041**

(b) Resignation

As explained above, by IR 2016 r7.61(1), a liquidator can resign on the grounds (a) of ill health, (b) because of an intention to cease to practice as an insolvency practitioner, (c) because the liquidator is unable to continue to discharge their duties because of a conflict of interest or a change in personal circumstances or (d) because, in the case of a joint appointment, all joint appointees agree that it is no longer expedient for there to be that number of liquidators. **3.042**

(c) Removal

Further, a liquidator in a winding up by the court can be removed, pursuant to IA 1986 s172, either by the court or by a decision of the creditors, or by the Secretary of State. Further, by s172(5), a liquidator must vacate office if they cease to be a person who is qualified to act as an IP. It is important to note that, by IA 1986 s172(3), in respect of certain liquidators (e.g., a liquidator appointed by the Secretary of State), a qualifying decision procedure to remove that liquidator can only be instigated if the liquidator thinks fit, the court so orders, or one-quarter in value of the creditors make a request to that effect. **3.043**

The court will order a decision procedure to be instigated if the applicant can show that in all the circumstances, it will be in the best interests of the liquidation for the order to be made.[51] It is, however, open to the court to decline to order a decision procedure to be instigated if the court considers that instigating a decision procedure would not be conducive to the proper process of liquidation, for example, where claims had been made against some of the creditors who were seeking to remove the liquidator.[52] However, in keeping with the general conduct of the insolvency process in line with the wishes of the majority of creditors, where that majority **3.044**

---

47   Ibid r7.54.
48   IA 1986 s137(3).
49   IR 2016 r7.57(3).
50   IA 1986 s136(3).
51   *Managa Properties Ltd v Brittain* [2009] EWHC 157 (Ch), [2009] 1 BCLC 689.
52   *Re a company CR-2017-000393* (unreported, 20 March 2017).

requests a decision procedure to be instigated, the court will usually order one.[53] The authorities described below in connection with the removal of voluntary liquidators are also likely to be relevant to a compulsory liquidator (see paras 3.060 and 3.061).

(d)   Other termination of appointment

3.045   A final circumstance in which an IP may leave office as liquidator is where the winding up of the company is complete. In that instance, it is necessary for the liquidator to send a final account to the company's creditors, the court and the registrar of companies.[54]

(e)   Release

3.046   Finally, upon ceasing to be a liquidator (for whatever reason, and by whatever method), the relevant IP will always seek their 'release'. The same is determined by reference to IA 1986 s174. The effect of an IP receiving their release is that, with effect from the time specified in the Act, the individual is discharged from all liability both in respect of acts or omissions of theirs in the winding up and otherwise in relation to their conduct as liquidator. However, the Act also makes clear that release has no impact on the exercise, in relation to a now former liquidator, of the court's powers under IA 1986 s212.[55] This may, however, have an impact on potential bond claims. This is considered further in Chapter 7 below.[56]

3.047   In relation to liquidators in a compulsory liquidation, there are four different possible times at which a release takes effect. First, if the person has been removed from office by a decision of the company's creditors (and those creditors have not decided against the release) or the person has died, the time of release is the time at which notice is given to the court in accordance with the rules.[57] Secondly, if the person has been removed as liquidator by the company's creditors (and those creditors have decided against the release), or the person has been removed by the court or the Secretary of State or the person has ceased to be qualified as an IP, the time is such time as the Secretary of State determines upon an application by the individual.[58] Thirdly, in the event of a liquidator that resigns, the time is the time which is prescribed by the Rules; that is to say 21 days after the date on which the notice of resignation is filed with the court.[59] Finally, in the case of a liquidator who ceases to be a liquidator because they have filed a final account with the court, they are released either, if a creditor objected to release, at such time as the Secretary of State may determine, or, if no creditors objected to the release, the time at which the liquidator vacated office.[60]

---

53   *Autobrokers Ltd v Dymond* [2015] EWHC 2691 (Admin).
54   IA 1986 s146.
55   IA 1986 s174(6).
56   See paras 7.089–7.093 below.
57   IA 1986 s174(4)(a).
58   Ibid s174(4)(b).
59   Ibid s174(4)(c) and IR 2016 r7.61(7).
60   Ibid s174(4)(d).

2. Liquidators – voluntary liquidations

(a) MVL / CVL

In the ordinary course, the voluntary winding up of a company commences with the passing **3.048**
(by the company) of a special resolution that it be wound up voluntarily.[61] It is also possible for
a company to move from administration into a creditors' voluntary liquidation. There are two
different types of voluntary winding up. First, a members' voluntary liquidation (an MVL)
which, as its name suggests is a process instigated solely by the company with no creditor
involvement, and which requires the directors of the company to make a statutory declaration
of solvency. Because of the company's solvency, there will almost always be a surplus available
to the company's members; it is for that reason that it is said to be a *members'* voluntary
liquidation. The second category is a creditors' voluntary liquidation (a CVL), which by
contrast with an MVL does entail creditor involvement. The two different types of voluntary
liquidation are defined in IA 1986 s90. Each will be considered in turn below.

(b) Appointment (MVL)

In an MVL, a liquidator is appointed by the company in a general meeting.[62] The relevant **3.049**
formalities are described in IR 2016 r5.2. In the event that a vacancy occurs as a result of the
death, resignation or otherwise in the office of liquidator, it falls to the company, in general
meeting, to fill the vacancy.[63] The power of the company is said to be subject to any
arrangement with the company's creditors, although the scope of that phrase has not yet been
explored in reported cases.

(c) Resignation and termination (MVL)

By IR 2016 r5.6, the liquidator may resign on the grounds (a) of ill health, (b) because of an **3.050**
intention to cease to practise as an IP, (c) because the liquidator is unable to continue to
discharge their duties because of a conflict of interest or a change in personal circumstances or
(d) because, in the case of a joint appointment, all joint appointees agree that it is no longer
expedient for there to be that number of liquidators.

Once the company's affairs have been fully wound up in the MVL, the liquidator is obliged to **3.051**
send a final account of the winding up to the company's members and the registrar of
companies.[64]

(d) Appointment (CVL)

In a normal CVL, the company's creditors play a much more significant role in the process. **3.052**
Indeed, within seven days of the company passing a special resolution for winding up, the
company's directors must send a statement of affairs to the company's creditors.[65] By IA 1986
s100(1B), the directors of the company must seek a nomination from the creditors of a person

---

61 Ibid ss84 and 86.
62 Ibid s91.
63 Ibid s92.
64 Ibid s94.
65 Ibid s99.

to act as liquidator of the company.[66] It is also open to the company to nominate its own chosen liquidator,[67] however, by s100(2), the creditor's choice of liquidator (if there is one) always trumps the company's choice.

3.053   The rules which govern the process by which a liquidator is nominated in a CVL are contained in IR 2016 r6.14 ff. In summary, the directors of a company must deliver to the creditors a notice requiring their decision on the appointment of a liquidator either by the deemed consent procedure, or by a virtual meeting. The decision date for the purposes of this decision procedure must be not earlier than three days from the aforesaid notice, but not later than 14 days from the date of the winding-up resolution. It is possible for creditors to request that a physical meeting be held. Whichever decision procedure applies, as a result of r6.18, the decision to nominate a liquidator is determined by reference to which nominee obtains the most support, and if there are more than three nominees, if one nominee has a clear majority, that one is appointed (and voting continues until that point is reached, with one nominee being eliminated at each round). By IR 2016 r6.20, the appointment of the liquidator takes effect from the date of the passing of the resolution of the company, or, if the creditors did not appoint the company's choice of liquidator, the date of the creditors' meeting. *Cash Generator Ltd v Fortune* was an early case to consider the interrelationship between mandatory provisions such as IA 1986 s100 and the deemed consent provisions in the IR 2016.[68]

3.054   The CVL process described in the preceding paragraphs applies in the event that the company enters a CVL without first having been in an MVL. It is possible, despite the directors' declaration of solvency, that it will become clear during the course of an MVL that the liquidator will not be able to pay all of the company's debts (and interest thereon) within the time specified in the declaration of solvency (a maximum of 12 months). If that situation occurs, the liquidator has a duty to prepare a statement of the company's affairs and to send it to the company's creditors within seven days of the date on which the liquidator formed the view that the company's debts and interest thereon would not be paid within the specified period.[69] In this scenario, a liquidator is obliged to seek a nomination to the office of liquidator from the company's creditors,[70] and indeed, the creditors can nominate a liquidator (who may of course be different from the MVL liquidator). The MVL converts to a CVL on the day on which the creditors decide to (or decline to) appoint a liquidator. If the creditors fail to appoint a different liquidator, the MVL liquidator becomes the CVL liquidator.[71]

3.055   The Rules contain the detailed provisions which govern the process which must be followed as regards the nomination of a liquidator in the case of an MVL converting to a CVL. A decision on a new liquidator must be taken within 28 days of the date on which the liquidator decided that the company's debts could not be paid within the relevant period, but not earlier than 14

---

66   This may be achieved via the deemed consent procedure in IA 1986 s246ZF. Should the creditor(s) object, they can do so under s246ZF(3).

67   IA 1986 s100(1).

68   [2018] EWHC 674 (Ch). See Rogers (2018) 11(3) *CRI* 107. IR 2016 r15.15 establishes a presumption that the deemed consent procedure was duly initiated and conducted, even if not everyone to whom the notice is to be delivered has received it.

69   IA 1986 s95(1A).

70   Ibid s95(4C).

71   Ibid s96(3).

days after the notice to creditors.[72] As regards the decision whether to nominate the MVL liquidator, or another liquidator, it is taken in the same way as in a normal CVL case.[73]

A further method of appointment of a CVL liquidator is when a company which has been in **3.056** administration under Schedule B1 moves from administration into a CVL under Schedule B1 para 83. The trigger for a move from administration into CVL is that the administrator has formed the view that each secured creditor has received (or the same has been set aside for the secured creditor's benefit) the total amount which each such creditor was likely to receive and that there will be a distribution to unsecured creditors other than pursuant to the prescribed part.[74] Upon registration of the notice that the administrator is required to send to Companies House, the company is treated as moving from administration to CVL.[75]

As regards the identity of the liquidator in such a scenario, Schedule B1 para 83(7) provides **3.057** that it will be either the person nominated by the creditors or, if there is no such person, the former administrator.

As regards nomination by the creditors, IR 2016 r3.60(6) provides that the nomination takes **3.058** the form of the creditors' approval of administrator's proposals or revised proposals or their nomination of a different person, through a decision procedure, but before their approval of the proposals.

IA 1986 s104 deals with the position where there is a vacancy in the office of liquidator in a **3.059** CVL. If such a vacancy occurs whether as a result of death, resignation or otherwise, then, except in the case of a liquidator appointed by the court, the creditors may fill the vacancy. IR 2016 r6.21 provides that in order to select a new liquidator, the creditors (or, if there is more than one liquidator, the continuing liquidator) may initiate a decision-making procedure to fill the vacancy.

(e)   Removal (MVL and CVL)

The removal of a liquidator in an MVL or a CVL is, somewhat oddly, dealt with in two **3.060** different sections of the IA 1986. By s108(1), if from any cause whatever there is no liquidator acting, the court can appoint a liquidator. More significantly, by s108(2), the court has a discretion, on cause being shown, to remove a liquidator and appoint another. Section 171 also deals with the removal of a liquidator in a voluntary winding up. By s171(2), a liquidator can only be removed by the court or, in the case of an MVL by a general meeting of the company summoned for that purpose and in the case of a CVL by a decision of the creditors instigated for that purpose. The apparently wide power conferred by s171(2) is, however, restricted by the next two subsections, insofar as the liquidator sought to be removed was appointed under s108. The restrictions relate to the circumstances in which a meeting can be held or decision procedure can be instigated: only if the liquidator thinks fit, the court so directs or one half of the members (MVL) or one half of the creditors (CVL) so request. The relevant procedural rules are at IR 2016 r6.27.

---

72   IR 2016 r6.11(5), (6).
73   Ibid r6.18.
74   Sch B1 para 83(1).
75   Ibid para 83(6).

3.061   The modern jurisprudence on the extent of IA 1986 s108(2) starts with a decision of Millet J in *Re Keypak Homecare Ltd*[76] where he emphasised that the burden lies on the applicant to show cause (which, he observed, is different to the court thinking it fit to remove the liquidator). According to *Keypak*, it is not necessary to show any personal unfitness or misconduct by the sitting liquidator, rather, the court will act and remove a liquidator if it is to the advantage of those interested in the assets of the company. The liquidator in that case, although a professional, independent and experienced liquidator, had conducted the liquidation un-impressively, and had been complacent and relaxed in his attitude to the liquidation. Neuberger J, in *AMP Music Box Enterprises Ltd v Hoffman* later warned, however, that it should not be seen as easy to remove a liquidator, and a court should think carefully before removing a liquidator.[77] Liquidators may be removed using this power on account of conflicts of interest.[78] Such a potential conflict might be cured by appointing a conflict liquidator.[79] Other bases for removal include disregarding creditors' interests,[80] for defaulting in the performance of their duties,[81] or as a result of their connection with the directors or promoters of the company.[82]

(f)   Resignation and termination (CVL)

3.062   In a CVL, resignation is dealt with in IR 2016 r6.25, by which the liquidator may resign on the grounds (a) of ill health, (b) because of an intention to cease to practise as an insolvency practitioner, (c) because the liquidator is unable to continue to discharge their duties because of a conflict of interest or a change in personal circumstances or (d) because, in the case of a joint appointment, all joint appointees agree that it is no longer expedient for there to be that number of liquidators.

3.063   Once a liquidation has run its course, and the liquidator has produced a final account according to IA 1986 s94 (MVL) or IA 1986 s106 (CVL) and sent a copy of the final account to the registrar of companies, the liquidator vacates office.[83]

(g)   Release

3.064   Finally, upon ceasing to be a liquidator (for whatever reason, and by whatever method), the relevant IP will always seek their 'release'. In the context of voluntary liquidators, release is determined by reference to IA 1986 s173. As explained above in the context of compulsory liquidators, the effect of an IP receiving their release is that, with effect from the time specified in the Act, the individual is discharged from all liability both in respect of acts or omissions of theirs in the liquidation and otherwise in relation to their conduct as liquidator. However, the

---

76   (1987) 3 BCC 558.
77   [2002] BCC 996 at 1001H.
78   *Sisu Capital Fund Ltd v Tucker* [2005] EWHC 2170 (Ch), [2006] BCC 463 and *Beattie v Smailes* [2011] EWHC 1563 (Ch), [2012] BCC 205.
79   *Re York Gas Ltd* [2010] EWHC 2275 (Ch), [2011] BCC 447.
80   *Re Rubber & Produce Investment Trust* [1915] 1 Ch 328.
81   *Re Ryder Installations* [1966] 1 WLR 524.
82   *Re Charterland Goldfields* (1909) 26 TLR 132.
83   IA 1986 s171(6), (7).

Act also makes clear that release has no impact on the exercise, in relation to a now former liquidator, of the court's powers under IA 1986 s212.[84]

In the case of a voluntary liquidator, the time of release is determined by IA 1986 s173(2). The **3.065** Act allows for five different possibilities. First, if a liquidator has been removed from office by a general meeting of the company, or by a decision of the creditors (and the creditors have not decided against the release) or has died, the time of release is when notice is given to the registrar of companies that the person has ceased to hold office.[85] Secondly, if the liquidator has been removed from office by the creditors (and the creditors have decided against the release), or the liquidator has been removed by the court or has vacated office as a result of ceasing to be qualified as an insolvency practitioner, the time of release is such time as determined by the Secretary of State on the application of the outgoing liquidator.[86] The third situation is when the liquidator resigns;[87] in that case, the date of release is 21 days after the date of delivery of the notice of resignation to the registrar of companies.[88] The fourth and fifth situations deal with vacation of office after the liquidator in the MVL or CVL has sent a final account to creditors. The release occurs at the time that the insolvency practitioner vacates office, or, in the case of a CVL where the creditors (on receipt of the final account) object to the release, the outgoing liquidator is released at such time as the Secretary of State may specify.[89]

3. Provisional liquidators

(a) Appointment

By IA 1986 s135(1), the court has power to appoint a provisional liquidator to a company. The **3.066** power can only be exercised after a winding-up petition has been presented, and so is not available in a voluntary liquidation. In England and Wales, the appointment of a provisional liquidator cannot be made after the making of the winding-up order.[90] According to the same subsection, the provisional liquidator can be either the OR, or any other fit person. It is more usual for a private sector IP to be appointed as a provisional liquidator. In any event, the reference to 'any other fit person' is taken to be a reference to the person being a licensed IP who is qualified to act in relation to the company.[91]

The circumstances in which, and the court's approach to its discretion, to appoint a provisional **3.067** liquidator are the subject of extensive authority. The modern recent authorities commence with the decisions in *Re Union Accident Insurance Co Ltd*[92] and *Re Highfield Commodities Ltd*,[93] both of which emphasised that the then-applicable statutory power was wide and seemingly unfettered.

---

84   Ibid s173(4).
85   Ibid s173(2)(a).
86   Ibid s173(2)(b).
87   Ibid s173(2)(c).
88   IR 2016 rr5.6(6) and 6.25(7).
89   IA 1986 s 173(3)(d), (e).
90   Ibid s135(2).
91   Ibid ss388(1)(a) and 389(1).
92   [1972] 1 All ER 1105.
93   [1985] 1 WLR 149.

3.068 The court's approach has most recently been summarised and digested at Court of Appeal level in *Revenue and Customs Commissioners v Rochdale Drinks Distributors Ltd.*[94] In *Rochdale*, Rimer LJ emphasised that, in the case of a trading company, the court should give anxious consideration to the appointment of a provisional liquidator to a company, in view of the serious consequences that the appointment would have on the company's trading life. Rimer LJ drew attention to two matters which the court must have regard to in order to appoint a provisional liquidator. They were, first, whether the applicant is likely to obtain a winding-up order in relation to the company, and secondly, whether, in all the circumstances of the case, it was right that a provisional liquidator should be appointed.

3.069 By IA 1986 ss135(4) and (5), the order appointing the provisional liquidator must specify the functions and powers of the provisional liquidator.

(b) Termination of appointment

3.070 Chapter 5 of Part 7 of the IR 2016 deals with the position of provisional liquidators. In particular, r7.39 deals with the termination of a provisional liquidator's appointment. It provides that the appointment of a provisional liquidator can be terminated by the court, either on the provisional liquidator's application, or on the application of a person entitled (in the first place) to appoint a provisional liquidator (as to which, see IR 2016 r7.33(1)). Further, there seems to be little doubt that, if the winding-up petition is, for whatever reason dismissed, then the appointment of the provisional liquidator ceases. In addition, the Rules envisage that, on the making of a winding-up order, the provisional liquidator's appointment will terminate: r7.39(3) assumes that the making of a winding-up order terminates (presumably automatically) the provisional liquidator's appointment. That is consistent with the decision of Harman J in *Re WF Fearman Ltd*[95] in which he declined to order that provisional liquidators should be appointed as liquidators on the making of a winding-up order since he took the view that the same would interfere with the creditors' right, at the first meeting, to express a view on the appointment of a liquidator.

C. ADMINISTRATORS

1. Introduction

3.071 Since the coming into force of the Enterprise Act 2002 ('EA 2002'), the statutory law relating to administrators can be found in Schedule B1 IA 1986. Further rules relating to the administration regime can be found in Part 3 of the IR 2016. Schedule B1 paragraph 3(1) fixes three alternative purposes of administration, being (1) the rescue of the entity as a going concern, (2) achieving a better result for the company's creditors as a whole than would be likely if the company were wound up without first being in administration, and finally (3) realising property to make a distribution to one or more secured creditors.

---

94 [2011] EWCA Civ 1116, [2012] 1 BCLC 748.
95 [1988] 4 BCC 141.

It has become accepted since the enactment of the EA 2002, as regards the appointment of an **3.072** administrator, that there is a distinction between administrators who are appointed by court order, and administrators who are appointed 'out of court'. It is worth noting that, save in relation to the route by which they come to be appointed, a court-appointed administrator and an 'out of court' appointed administrator have the same role, functions, duties and powers. For the avoidance of doubt, this includes the duty of the administrators to the creditors as a whole, notwithstanding that the administrators may have been appointed by a director or by a qualifying floating charge holder (a 'QFC' holder).[96]

2. Appointment (court)

By paragraph 11 of Schedule B1, a court can make an administration order on an adminis- **3.073** tration application made to it by the company, the directors of the company or a creditor of the company. The list of eligible applicants also includes the designated officer for a magistrates' court, the holder of a QFC[97] and the liquidator of the company.[98] Additionally, certain regulators have the right to make an application for the making of an administration order against an entity which they regulate; for example, the Financial Conduct Authority and the Prudential Regulation Authority have that power under section 359 of the Financial Services and Markets Act 2000 ('FSMA 2000'). Before the court makes an order, it must be satisfied that the company is unable to pay its debts, and that one of the purposes of administration is reasonably likely to be achieved. The court ultimately retains a discretion whether or not to make an administration order.[99] By paragraph 36 of Schedule B1, it is open to a QFC holder who is not the applicant on an administration application to intervene in the application and ensure that their preferred administrator is appointed.

3. Appointment (out of court)

So far as out of court appointments are concerned, they can be made at the behest of the holder **3.074** of a QFC,[100] or the company[101] or the directors of the company.[102] Out of court adminis- tration appointments by QFC holders are now often the route used by secured creditors where an administrative receivership appointment would previously have been made. Unsecured creditors of the company cannot make an out of court appointment of an administrator. By contrast with the court route, an out of court appointment is designed to be quick and easy, and in some circumstances will also be available outside court opening hours if an electronic method is used.[103]

---

96 Although under an 'Objective 3' administration, the duty towards unsecured creditors is limited to ensuring that their interests are not harmed.
97 Sch B1 para 35.
98 Ibid para 38.
99 Ibid para 13. Appeals against the exercise of discretion will therefore be rare. However in *Rowntree Ventures Ltd v Oak Property Partners Ltd* [2017] EWCA Civ 1944, the Court of Appeal allowed the appeal on the basis that it was illogical for the judge to: (i) find that the company was insolvent; but (ii) the main reason not to exercise his discretion to make the order was because of the possibility of turnaround: see [28].
100 Sch B1 para 14.
101 Ibid para 22(1).
102 Ibid para 22(2).
103 See para 3.076 below.

3.075   However, out of court administration filings are not without their complexities, and indeed, there is a growing body of case law which deals with the formal validity of such appointments. A detailed consideration of those complexities is beyond the scope of this chapter; reference can of course be made to the standard texts on insolvency law. By way of example, in *Re BXL Services*,[104] it was held that a failure to give a required notice to a company did not invalidate the appointment. More recently, in *Re Spaces London Bridge Ltd*,[105] the court held that the failure to specify a separate date and time of appointment in a notice of appointment did not invalidate the appointment.

3.076   Further complexities have arisen with regard to 'out of hours' appointments, which are defined as situations where the appointment has taken place and the notice of appointment is filed with the court when the relevant court office is shut. Notwithstanding the breadth of paragraph 8.1 of the IPD and the Electronic Working Pilot,[106] which seemed to create a presumption in favour of the use of CE-filing to commence all insolvency proceedings, ICC Judge Burton held in *Re SJ Henderson & Co Ltd*[107] that the exceptional case of out of hours appointments is only open to QFC holders, the route having been created as a *quid pro quo* for the loss of administrative receivership. QFC holders must, in turn, rely on the procedure in IR 2016 rr.3.20–3.22 for out of hours appointments, which requires the use of e-mail or fax to give notice of appointment. Use of CE-filing and PD51O by QFC holders is likely to constitute a remediable defect,[108] but will still mean that the appointment takes effect at the time the notice is filed. For director and company appointments made 'out of hours', the pragmatic solution arrived at by ICC Judge Burton in *Re SJ Henderson* was that such appointments would take effect when the court office next opened. This practical workaround stands in contrast with the relatively strict approach adopted in cases such as *Re NJM Clothing*,[109] which highlighted the need for a notice of appointment to state the correct time and date of the appointment – neither of which would be correct if the appointment is deemed to take place when the court office next opens.

3.077   The current state of what was described by Barling J as a 'byzantine' legal framework in *HMV Ecommerce Ltd*[110] has led to much confusion. Indeed, the generally permissive approach of Barling J in *HMV Ecommerce* with regard to out of hours director appointments appeared unstable in light of *Re SJ Henderson*, although it is suggested the further decisions in *Re Keyworker Homes (North West) Ltd*[111] and *Re All Star Leisure (Group) Ltd*[112] have pointed the practice again towards a more permissive approach. In the former, HHJ Hodge QC held that the company or its directors may e-file an NOA at any time, irrespective of whether or not the court is closed. While that contradicts the position in *Re SJ Henderson*, the later judgment must be considered to be correct unless and until the matter is decided by the Court of Appeal.

---

104   [2002] EWHC 1877 (Ch), [2012] BCC 657.
105   [2018] EWHC 3099 (Ch).
106   CPR PD51O, para 2.2.
107   [2019] EWHC 2742 (Ch).
108   *Re Skeggs Beef Ltd* [2019] EWHC 2607 (Ch).
109   [2018] EWHC 2388 (Ch).
110   [2019] EWHC 903 (Ch).
111   [2019] EWHC 3499 (Ch).
112   [2019] EWHC 3231 (Ch).

Contrary to the statutory intention of giving a fast and effective way of appointing administrators without the involvement of the court, many unchallenged applications have been made for declarations that administrators were validly appointed. This is an unfortunate result, which has been compounded by the flurry of contradictory decisions. The practical response of the Chancellor was to issue guidance on 30 January 2020 to the effect that all 'out of hours' appointments will now be reviewed on the papers by a High Court Judge.[113] Three further cases then followed under the paper review procedure: *Carter Moore Solicitors Ltd*,[114] *Symm & Company Ltd*,[115] and *Statebourne (Cryogenic) Ltd*.[116] In *Carter Moore*, the court held that a CE-filing made when the court was open but then rejected was curable. In *Symm & Co*, Zacaroli J agreed with the approach in *Re SJ Henderson* and *Skeggs Beef* that the company and its directors may not appoint out of hours. The purported appointment was capable of cure under r12.64, but on the basis that the filing would be effective from the time the court next opened for business. In *Statebourne (Cryogenic)*, the court held that the ten-day period under paragraph 28(2) commences on the day the NOIA is filed. That is a departure from the calculation in *Keyworker Homes*. This position has continued under the Temporary Insolvency Practice Direction ('TIPD').[117] The TIPD therefore continues, at paragraphs 3.3–3.6, the distinction for appointments by QFC holders.

4. Resignation

The circumstances in which an administrator can resign from office are dealt with in Schedule B1 paragraph 87 and IR 2016 r3.62 onwards. In short, an administrator can resign on grounds of ill health, because of an intention to cease to practise as an IP, or because the further discharge of functions as administrator is made impossible by a conflict of interest or a change of personal circumstances. Interestingly, it is also possible for an administrator to resign, with the permission of the court, on other grounds.[118] The exact scope of the phrase 'other grounds' is yet to be determined in case law. The Rules also contain the procedural rules which govern the resignation of an administrator; they include, for example, an obligation on a resigning administrator to serve notice of intention to resign,[119] before serving a notice of resignation.[120] In *Ve Vegas Investors IV LLC v Shinners*,[121] Registrar Jones considered various procedural issues arising in the context of a claim by creditors for the removal of administrators during the hearing of which the administrators decided to resign, including the decision of the court to give reasons (with the attendant professional ramifications for doing so) notwithstanding the administrators' decision to step down at the hearing.

3.078

---

113 https://www.judiciary.uk/wp-content/uploads/2020/01/Administration-Notices-For-release-FINAL.docx (accessed 21 April 2020).
114 [2020] EWHC 186 (Ch) (Snowden J).
115 [2020] EWHC 317 (Ch) (Zacaroli J).
116 [2020] EWHC 231 (Ch) (Zacaroli J).
117 Issued in response to the COVID-19 pandemic (7 April 2020). The TIPD was drafted by Zacaroli J.
118 IR 2016 r3.62(2).
119 Ibid r3.63.
120 Ibid r3.64.
121 *Re Ve Interactive* [2018] EWHC 186 (Ch).

3.079   Of course, an administrator who ceases to be qualified to act as an IP in relation to a company must vacate office as administrator.[122] Such an individual is required to give notice to various parties depending on the route of their appointment, for example, in the case of an administrator appointed by the court, notice must be given to the court.[123]

5. Removal

3.080   By Schedule B1 paragraph 88, a court can remove an administrator from office. The relevant procedural rules can be found in IR r3.65. Those rules deal principally with issues of service. Neither paragraph 88, nor r3.65 identify the persons that can make an application for an order under paragraph 88. It is likely, however, that the court would expect the applicant for an order under paragraph 88 to be able to demonstrate some financial interest in the administration.[124] An administrator that has been removed is vulnerable to a costs order in relation to the removal application.[125]

3.081   In *Sisu Capital Fund Ltd v Tucker*,[126] Warren J had to consider an application under paragraph 88 to remove administrators. Although he accepted that the words of paragraph 88 were wide, and the discretion of the court was apparently unfettered, he concluded nonetheless that cause had to be shown for the removal, and that in the case before him, cause had not been shown.

3.082   In *Clydesdale Financial Services Ltd v Smailes*,[127] David Richards J (as he then was) made clear that, although there had to be a good ground for ordering the removal of an administrator, that need not involve misconduct or personal unfitness by the individual. He held that the views of the majority creditors were an important factor which had to be taken into account in the balancing exercise. In the case before him, he decided to remove the administrator because he took the view that a transaction undertaken by the administrator was susceptible to further investigation, and that the administrator could not be expected to conduct an independent review. In *Smailes*, the applicants had also sought an order under Schedule B1 paragraph 74(4)(d) for the appointment of the administrator to cease to have effect. In the course of his judgment, David Richards J observed that reliance on that provision added little to the court's powers under paragraph 88, and indeed, the circumstances in which paragraph 74 could be relied upon were seemingly narrower.

3.083   In *Finnerty v Clark*,[128] the Court of Appeal had to deal with a case in which the largest group of unsecured creditors of a company had sought to remove the company's administrators because those administrators had declined to bring legal proceedings. Mummery LJ endorsed the Chancellor's decision in the same case that there must be a good ground for making the order, and what will be a good ground will depend on the purposes of the office, and the facts of the case. In *Finnerty*, Mummery LJ endorsed the approach taken in *Sisu* and *Smailes*. Given that the administrators in *Finnerty* had been acquitted of bias and had taken independent legal

---

122   Sch B1 para 89(1).
123   Ibid para 89(2).
124   Cf. *Deloitte v Johnson* [1999] 1 WLR 1065 (PC).
125   *Coyne v DRC Distribution Ltd* [2008] EWCA Civ 488, [2008] BCC 612.
126   [2005] EWHC 2170 (Ch), [2006] BCC 463.
127   [2009] EWHC 1745 (Ch), [2009] EWHC 3190 (Ch), [2011] 2 BCLC 405.
128   [2011] EWCA Civ 858, [2012] 1 BCLC 286.

advice on whether to bring proceedings, and at each instance it was accepted that they had taken a decision which was properly open to them, there were no grounds for their removal.

6. Replacement

In the event that an administrator resigns, ceases to be qualified, or is removed by the court, **3.084** Schedule B1 paragraphs 91–95 contain the relevant rules which enable a replacement administrator to be appointed. If the administrator was appointed by the court, then by Schedule B1 paragraph 91, it is the court that will make an order replacing the administrator. If the administrator was appointed by a QFC holder, then it is that creditor that can appoint a replacement (Sch B1 para 92). In the case of a company or director appointment, then by Schedule B1 paragraphs 93 and 94, it is the company or the directors who, subject to certain conditions (including the consent of any QFC holder) can appoint a replacement administrator.

Finally on the question of removal, it is necessary to make a brief reference to Schedule B1 **3.085** paragraphs 96 and 97 which do not require a vacancy in the office of administrator. The former is engaged when an administrator has been appointed by a QFC holder. In such a case, it is open to a prior floating charge holder to apply to the court to replace the administrator. The provision is seemingly open-ended, and there do not yet appear to be any reported decisions which have explored the breadth of the court's powers under paragraph 96.

By contrast, pursuant to Schedule B1 paragraph 97, where an administrator has been **3.086** appointed by the company or the directors of the company, and there is no holder of a QFC, it is open to the creditors to replace the administrator by a qualifying decision procedure.

7. Ending administration

In addition to the circumstances described above in which an administrator can resign or be **3.087** removed, it is also necessary to deal with the circumstances in which an administrator ceases to be in office because the administration of the company comes to an end. There are a number of ways in which an administration can come to an end.

By Schedule B1 paragraph 76(1), the appointment of an administrator ceases to have effect at **3.088** the end of the period of one year beginning with the date on which it takes effect. In the event that paragraph 76(1) is engaged, plainly an administrator will no longer be in office. Although it is an aspiration of Schedule B1 that administrations are concluded within one year, extensions of the administration (whether by court order or with the consent of relevant creditors) are common. Extensions of an administration can give rise to difficult issues in relation to whether the office-holder has remained in office. For example, Schedule B1 paragraph 77(1)(b) provides that an extension by court order cannot be made after the expiry of the administrator's term of office, although in such circumstances, it would be open to the court to make a fresh administration order, albeit with retrospective effect.[129]

---

129   *Re Frontsouth (Witham) Ltd* [2011] EWHC 1668 (Ch), [2011] BCC 635.

3.089 Pursuant to Schedule B1 paragraph 79, it is open to the court, in specified circumstances, and on the application of the administrator, to provide for the appointment of the administrator to cease to have effect. The circumstances include a situation where the purpose of the administration cannot be achieved[130] or conversely where the purpose has been sufficiently achieved (in the case of the latter, only where the company entered administration as a result of a court order). The circumstances also include a situation in which the company's creditors compel the administrator to make an application under paragraph 79.

3.090 A creditor can also apply, under paragraph 81 of Schedule B1, albeit in much more limited circumstances (the appointor must have had an improper motive), for the appointment of an administrator of a company to cease to have effect. In *Thomas v Frogmore Real Estate Partners GP1 Ltd*[131] the court was confronted with an application by a creditor under paragraph 81. The judge found that the allegation of improper motive was not made out, but in any event, simply demonstrating an improper motive of the appointor was not, by itself, enough to mean that the court must make an order under paragraph 81.

3.091 In the event of an out of court appointment, and if the administrator thinks that the purpose of the administration has been sufficiently achieved in relation to the company, then by notice given to the court and to the registrar of companies, the administrator can procure for his appointment to cease to have effect.[132]

3.092 By Schedule B1 paragraph 83, if an administrator thinks that the total amount which each secured creditor is likely to receive has been paid to them or set aside, and there will be a distribution to the unsecured creditors of the company (other than from the prescribed part), then on the registration of the relevant notice, the company moves from administration to CVL, and the administrator ceases to be the company's administrator. It is usual, and indeed provided for in paragraph 83(7), for the creditors to nominate the person that will become the liquidator. Frequently, and absent a creditor wishing to take action against the soon to be former administrator, the administrator becomes the liquidator in the CVL.

3.093 Finally, by Schedule B1 paragraph 84, if the administrator thinks that the company has no property which might permit a distribution to its creditors, it is possible for the company to move straight from administration to dissolution on the filing of the relevant notice taking effect.

8. Release

3.094 In the same way that there is a statutory provision for other office-holders to be discharged from liability, Schedule B1 paragraph 98 addresses the position of administrators who cease to be (for whatever reason) administrators. Paragraph 98(2) specifies the various times at which the discharge from liability takes effect. Save in the case of paragraph 98 applying because of

---

130 The court will similarly not direct a qualifying decision procedure where there is insufficient evidence to indicate that alternative administrators will be able to meet the statutory objective under Sch B1 para 3: *Re Fortuna Fix Ltd* [2020] EWHC 2369 (Ch). In such a case where the administrators' proposals have already been rejected by the creditors, the response of the court may well be to make a winding-up order.

131 [2017] EWHC 25 (Ch), [2017] 2 BCLC 101.

132 Sch B1 para 80.

the death of the administrator, in other cases, the time of discharge is the time fixed by the creditors or by the court. Again, this may have implications so far as bond claims are concerned, as considered further in Chapter 7 below.

9. The paragraph 99 charge

Lastly, it is important to mention paragraph 99. That paragraph applies in any case in which a **3.095** person ceases to be the administrator of a company. By paragraph 99(3), the former administrator's remuneration and expenses are a charge on and payable out of property of which the administrator had custody or control immediately before the cessation of the administration appointment. This plainly has implications for successor office-holders, whether new administrators, or liquidators if the company goes into compulsory liquidation or into a CVL.

D. BANKRUTPCY

1. Trustees in bankruptcy

The rules which govern the appointment and removal of trustees in bankruptcy are contained **3.096** in IA 1986 ss291A to 300.

(a) OR automatically trustee in bankruptcy

In a change introduced by the Small Business, Enterprise and Employment Act 2015 **3.097** ('SBEEA 2015'), on the making of a bankruptcy order, and subject to one exception, the OR automatically becomes trustee in bankruptcy.[133] Prior to this amendment, the IA 1986 did not provide for the automatic appointment of a trustee in bankruptcy on the making of the bankruptcy order, and indeed, the OR did not become a trustee in bankruptcy until (within a period of 12 weeks from the bankruptcy order) he or she had decided whether or not to summon a meeting of creditors to appoint a trustee, and if not, notice had been given to prescribed persons. It was only upon the giving of that notice that the OR became trustee, having previously been a receiver and manager, as it stood prior to the changes implemented by the SBEEA 2015.[134] As a result, under the old rules, there was a gap between the making of the bankruptcy order, and the vesting of the bankruptcy estate in a trustee in bankruptcy under IA 1986 s306. There will now be no such gap following the amendments made by the SBEEA 2015, which brings the law on personal insolvencies into line with the position in compulsory liquidations.[135]

The exception mentioned above is to cater for the position where the bankruptcy petition is **3.098** presented, and the order made at a time when the debtor was subject to an individual voluntary arrangement and a supervisor was in place. In that instance, the court has a discretion to appoint the supervisor of the IVA as the trustee in bankruptcy of the bankrupt.

---

133 IA 1986 s291A.
134 Ibid s293.
135 Of course, title to the company's property remains with the company, and does not automatically vest in the office-holder.

(b) Appointment of an IP other than the OR

3.099 By IA 1986 s296, the OR, at any time when acting as trustee in bankruptcy of a bankrupt, can apply to the Secretary of State for the appointment of a person as trustee instead of the OR. It is open to the Secretary of State to either make an appointment, or to decline to make an appointment.[136]

3.100 It is important to note that the provision pursuant to which creditors could request the OR to summon a meeting of creditors for the purposes of appointing a trustee in bankruptcy[137] has been omitted by the changes made by the SBEEA 2015. It seems therefore that, at least so far as the IA 1986 is concerned, the time at which the creditors' power to influence the appointment of a trustee arises is pursuant to s298, which deals with the removal of a trustee, or the trustee's vacation of office.

3.101 Before turning to that, it is necessary to make clear that, by s300, in the event of a vacancy in the office of trustee in bankruptcy (including if, for whatever reason, an appointment fails to take effect), the OR will be trustee until the vacancy is filled.[138] It is open to the OR to ask the bankrupt's creditors to appoint a trustee in bankruptcy, and the OR must ask the bankrupt's creditors if requested by not less than one-tenth in value of the bankrupt's creditors.[139] If, by the end of the period of 28 days beginning with the date upon which the fact of a vacancy first came to the OR's attention, he has not asked and is not proposing to ask the creditors to fill the vacancy, the OR must refer the need for an appointment to the Secretary of State.

(c) Removal of a trustee in bankruptcy

3.102 Section 298(1) identifies two principal means by which a trustee in bankruptcy can be removed. First, a trustee in bankruptcy can be removed from office by an order of the court. Secondly, a trustee in bankruptcy can be removed pursuant to a creditors' decision procedure instigated for that purpose. There are restrictions, imposed by IA 1986 s298(4), which affect the creditors' ability to remove a trustee: indeed, where the OR is trustee pursuant to s291A(1), or the trustee has been appointed by the Secretary of State or by the court (other than under s291A(2)), a decision procedure can only be instigated if the trustee thinks fit, the court directs, or one of the bankrupt's creditors so requests, but with the concurrence of not less than one-quarter, in value, of the creditors.

3.103 In the event that the creditors decide to remove a trustee in bankruptcy, they may, in accordance with the IR 2016 r10.67 appoint another person as trustee in place of the outgoing trustee,[140] and indeed, a decision by the creditors to remove a trustee in bankruptcy under s298(4) does not take effect until a new trustee in bankruptcy is appointed.[141]

3.104 There is limited jurisprudence on the circumstances in which a trustee in bankruptcy can be removed under section 298 of the Act, by either the court or the creditors. Occasionally, a

---

136 IA 1986 s296(2).
137 Ibid s294.
138 Ibid s300(2).
139 Ibid s300(3).
140 Ibid s298(4A).
141 Ibid s298(4B).

bankrupt will make an application to remove his trustee. In *Smedley v Brittain*,[142] Registrar Nicholls refused to remove a trustee in bankruptcy on the application of the bankrupt. The Registrar commented that, if it could be shown that the trustee's conduct had been honest, reasonable and without misconduct or maladministration, then it would be necessary for the court to think carefully before removing the trustee in bankruptcy. In cases where the applicant was the bankrupt, the Registrar commented that the 'test was a particularly high one and he must show a very real and substantial cause' for the removal of the trustee. The Registrar drew support from the decisions in liquidator removal cases of *Keypak* and *AMP Music Box*, which are mentioned above (see para 3.061).

3.105 Proudman J also had to consider an application to remove a trustee in bankruptcy, against a backdrop of conflict of interest allegations, in *Doffmann v Wood*.[143] She declined to order the removal of the trustees. She considered that it would be appropriate to have regard to the authorities which apply in the case of removal of a liquidator under IA 1986 ss108 and 172, including *Keypak* and *AMP Music Box*. Her view was that cause had to be shown before a trustee in bankruptcy could be removed. The question whether to remove an office-holder, including a trustee in bankruptcy, had to be measured by reference to 'the real substantial, honest interests' of the process.' In a case where no surplus to the bankrupt was expected, that interest was the interests of the creditors, and not the bankrupt.[144]

3.106 In *Re Birdi (In Bankruptcy); Miles v Price*,[145] the court had to determine whether to remove a trustee in bankruptcy or to direct the calling of a creditors' meeting to consider such a removal. The court declined the application. In so doing, it was held that the question of whether to remove an insolvency practitioner of any kind had to be measured by reference to the real substantial, honest interests of the process, and to the purpose for which the office-holder was appointed. The trustee in bankruptcy's conduct was of course material, as were the wishes of the creditors. The court expected any office-holder to be efficient, vigorous and unbiased in his conduct of the insolvency process, and it should have no hesitation in removing an office-holder if satisfied that he had failed to live up to those standards at least unless it could be reasonably confident that he would live up to those requirements in future. The judge found that in *Birdi*, none of the applicants' complaints (e.g., incurring unnecessary costs) were made out. The court also declined to order the convening of a creditors' decision-making procedure.

3.107 By IA 1986 s298(5), there is a third means by which a trustee in bankruptcy can be removed, which is that if the trustee was appointed by the Secretary of State, the trustee can be removed by the Secretary of State.

(d) Ending of bankruptcy

3.108 As regards a trustee in bankruptcy vacating office, the IA 1986 envisages at least three different scenarios. First, by s298(6), the trustee can vacate office if he ceases to be qualified to act as an IP. Secondly, by s298(8), the trustee will vacate office after he has given notice to the court that

---

142 [2008] BPIR 219.
143 [2011] EWHC 4008 (Ch), [2012] BPIR 972.
144 See also, on the issue of sufficient interest in the absence of a surplus: *Deloitte & Touche AG v Johnson* [1999] 1 WLR 1605 (PC) (Lord Millett).
145 [2019] EWHC 291 (Ch), [2019] BPIR 498 (Adam Johnson QC, sitting as a Deputy High Court Judge).

he has complied with the provisions of s331, which deal with the final report to creditors upon the administration of the bankrupt's estate being completed. Finally, if the bankruptcy order made against the bankrupt is annulled pursuant to s282 of the Act, the trustee in bankruptcy will also vacate office,[146] and the trustee's release will be at such time as the court may determine.[147] The trustee must still deliver up a final report to the Secretary of State.[148]

(e) Resignation

3.109 As with other office-holders, a trustee in bankruptcy can resign from office.[149] By IR 2016 r10.77, a trustee in bankruptcy can resign on the grounds (a) of ill health, (b) because of an intention to cease to practise as an IP, (c) because the trustee in bankruptcy is unable to continue to discharge their duties because of a conflict of interest or a change in personal circumstances or (d) because, in the case of a joint appointment, all joint appointees agree that it is no longer expedient for there to be that number of trustees in bankruptcy. Before resigning, a trustee in bankruptcy must invite the creditors to consider appointing an alternative trustee, either by a decision-making procedure or by a deemed consent procedure.[150]

(f) Release

3.110 The time at which a trustee in bankruptcy has their release is determined by reference to IA 1986 s299. Subsections (1) and (2) deal with the position of the OR. If the OR is replaced as trustee in bankruptcy by the creditors or the Secretary of State, the OR will have his release at the time that he gives notice to the prescribed person. If the OR is replaced as a result of a court order, then the time of the OR's release is at such time as the court may determine. Lastly, if the OR, as trustee in bankruptcy, concludes the administration of the bankruptcy estate, then the OR has their release with effect from such time as the Secretary of State may determine, following the OR having given notice to the Secretary of State.

3.111 The IA 1986 envisages four different scenarios for release where the trustee in bankruptcy is not the OR.[151] First, if either the trustee in bankruptcy has died, or the bankrupt's creditors have resolved to remove the trustee from office (and the creditors have not decided against release), then the trustee's release will be when notice is given to the persons prescribed by the Rules.[152] Secondly, in the event that a trustee in bankruptcy has been removed by a decision of the creditors, and the creditors voted against release, or if the trustee has been removed by the Secretary of State, or has vacated office as a result of ceasing to be qualified, then the trustee in bankruptcy will have their release at such time as the Secretary of State may decide on an application by the outgoing trustee.[153] Thirdly, and if the trustee in bankruptcy resigns, the outgoing trustee has their release 21 days after the date on which notice of resignation was filed with the court (in a bankruptcy which was flowed from a petition) or delivered to the Official

---

146 IA 1986 s298(9).
147 Ibid s299(4).
148 IR 2016 r10.141.
149 IA 1986 s298(7).
150 IR 2016 r10.77(2).
151 IA 1986 s299(3).
152 IR 2016 rr10.83 and 10.84; IA 1986 s299(3)(a).
153 IA 1986 s299(3)(b).

Receiver (in a bankruptcy which was made on a debtor's application).[154] Finally, if the trustee vacates office because the administration of the bankruptcy estate is complete, release occurs either at the time that the Secretary of State determines (if any of the bankrupt's creditors objected to release) or otherwise the time at which the person vacated office.[155]

Finally, the IA 1986 makes clear that release has no impact on the exercise, in relation to a now **3.112** former trustee in bankruptcy, of the court's powers under IA 1986 s304.[156] In *Borodzicz v Horton*,[157] the Chief Bankruptcy Registrar, having referred to the decision of Walton J in *In Re Munro ex parte Singer v Trustee in Bankruptcy*,[158] endorsed this proposition of Walton J's that the effect of release is to 'wipe the slate completely clean so far as the trustee is concerned, so that he may thereafter pay no thought to the previous course of his actions as the trustee in bankruptcy'.

E. SUPERVISORS AND NOMINEES

1. Introduction

IA 1986 envisages two possible types of voluntary arrangements. In relation to companies, Part **3.113** I IA 1986 contains provisions which enable the company to propose a company voluntary arrangement ('CVA') to its creditors, and for the creditors to vote to approve (or reject) the arrangement. Similarly, Part VIII contains rules which enable individual debtors to propose a voluntary arrangement ('IVA') to their creditors, which their creditors can then vote on and either approve, modify or reject.

Whilst IVAs have proved popular with debtors,[159] CVAs have not proved popular as a means **3.114** of rescuing companies. Insolvency Service statistics suggest that there have never been more than 1,000 CVAs per year, and in the last few years the number has been far lower, below 500. In 2019, there were just 351.[160]

2. Contractual basis of voluntary arrangements

Voluntary arrangements are different to other insolvency processes inasmuch as they are based, **3.115** in large part, on the contract between the relevant debtor and the debtor's creditors which is contained in the proposals put forward by the debtor. These will incorporate any standard terms and conditions which accompany those proposals or are otherwise incorporated into

---

154 IR 2016 r10.77(8); IA 1986 s299(3)(c).
155 IA 1986 s299(3)(d).
156 Ibid s299(5).
157 [2016] BPIR 24.
158 [1981] 1 WLR 1358.
159 In 2019, there were 77,982 IVAs (the highest number ever recorded), as compared with 16,702 bankruptcies (a slight increase on the previous year). Statistics available at https://www.gov.uk/government/collections/insolvency-service-official-statistics (accessed 21 April 2020).
160 https://assets.publishing.service.gov.uk/government/uploads/system/uploads/attachment_data/file/861187/Commentary_-_Company_Insolvency_Statistics_Q4_2019.pdf (accessed 21 April 2020).

them.[161] The 'contract', once agreed, is given statutory force by IA 1986 ss5(2) (CVAs) and 260(2) (IVAs). The contractual underpinning of a voluntary arrangement is readily apparent from the court's approach to the interpretation of voluntary arrangements, which involves adopting the general law principles of contractual interpretation as in *Welsby v Brelec Installations Ltd*,[162] and its statutory underpinning is equally evident from the court's reluctance to imply terms into an arrangement, as in *Johnson v Davies*.[163]

3. Appointment

3.116   All of the above means that there are remarkably few provisions in either the IA 1986 or the IR 2016 which directly concern the appointment of an IP to be, first, the nominee in relation to the proposal for the voluntary arrangement, and then, if the arrangement is approved, the supervisor of the arrangement. In the case of both CVAs and IVAs, the nominee must be qualified to act as an IP.[164] Invariably, the nominee is selected, in the first instance at least, by the debtor.

3.117   It is open to creditors, at the time that they are able to vote on the proposals, to propose a modification to the proposals which will have the effect of replacing the proposed supervisor chosen by the debtor with their own choice of insolvency practitioner.[165] It is important to note that a modification proposed in relation to an IVA cannot be approved by the creditors unless the debtor consents.[166]

3.118   In the case of both CVAs and IVAs, the decision whether to approve the proposal (including any appropriate modifications and of course the identity of the future supervisor) is taken in accordance with the rules for decision-making contained in IR 2016 Part 15. The rules pertaining to CVAs and IVAs are contained in IR r15.34. As regards CVAs, there is a two-stage process. First, three-quarters or more (in value) of those voting must vote in favour of the relevant resolution. Secondly, a decision will not be considered to have been made by the creditors if more than half of the total value of unconnected creditors voted against the proposal.[167] The position in relation to voting for IVA proposals is similar: first, a proposal or a modification is passed if more than three-quarters in value vote in favour of it, provided, secondly, that a decision will not have been made if more than half of the total value of creditors who are not associates of the debtor voted against it.

---

161   See, e.g., the R3 IVA Standard Conditions: https://www.r3.org.uk/technical-library/england-wales/technical-guidance/standard-conditions/ (accessed 21 April 2020).
162   [2000] 2 BCLC 756.
163   [1999] Ch 117. But notwithstanding the contractual underpinnings of such arrangements, they do not appear to be able to affect property-based rights, such as the right to forfeiture: *Discovery (Northampton) Ltd v Debenhams Retail Ltd* [2019] EWHC 2441 (Ch) (Norris J).
164   IA 1986 ss1(2) and 253(2).
165   Ibid s4(2) (CVAs). Note that no consent is required of the company or the company's directors for the modification to be adopted. IA 1986 s258(3) applies in relation to IVAs.
166   Ibid s258(2).
167   IR 2016 rr15.34(3), (4).

4. Termination of appointment

As regards the termination of a supervisor's appointment, plainly, if an arrangement is **3.119** successfully challenged by a creditor, for example on the grounds of unfair prejudice or material irregularity,[168] or subsequently fails (e.g., because a debtor breaches the arrangement leading the supervisor to petition for bankruptcy), the supervisor's appointment will cease.[169] Outside those instances, there is little regulation in the IA 1986 or IR 2016 which caters for a scenario whereby the office-holder is replaced, but the arrangement remains ongoing.

5. Replacement of supervisor

IA 1986 ss7(5) (CVAs) and 263(5) (IVAs), which are similarly drafted, give the court power to **3.120** appoint a person who is qualified to act as an IP or otherwise authorised to act as a supervisor either in substitution for an existing supervisor, or to fill a vacancy. The power is exercisable when it is expedient to appoint a person as supervisor and it is inexpedient, difficult, or impracticable for an appointment to be made without the assistance of the court. There is remarkably little authority on the sections, at least as regards applications by dissatisfied creditors. It is likely that the reason for that lies in the fact that the terms of the arrangement will contain provisions dealing with the removal or replacement of the supervisor.

For example, the insolvency trade body R3 has prepared a set of Standard Conditions for **3.121** Individual Voluntary Arrangements.[170] Clause 19 of the current version contains provisions which enable a supervisor of the IVA to be replaced by a decision of the creditors requested specifically for that purpose. According to the clause, the relevant creditor must specify the grounds of the proposed removal. By clause 21 of the R3 Standard Conditions, the creditors (or the court, presumably under IA 1986 s263(5)) have the power to fill a vacancy in the office of supervisor. Clause 66 of the R3 Standard Conditions specify the relevant voting majorities. It is very likely that the terms of a CVA proposal will contain like provisions for the removal and/or replacement of a supervisor.

F. MONITORS

1. Introduction

With the coming into force of the Corporate Insolvency and Governance Act 2020, a new Part **3.122** A1 has been introduced to the IA 1986. It enables the directors of an eligible company to apply for a temporary moratorium. This is designed to create a 'breathing space' to enable the directors to attempt to rescue the company as a going concern.

---

168   IA 1986 ss6 (CVAs) and 262 (IVAs).

169   A chair or convener of a creditors' meeting will usually only be personally liable for the costs of an appeal against a decision to admit or reject a proof of debt in special circumstances, such as where the decision is self-interested, irrational or unreasonable, or where there is some other good reason to impose personal liability: *Re Rochay Productions Ltd* [2020] EWHC 1737 (Ch).

170   The latest version (v4) is dated 4 January 2018. See https://www.thedebtadvisor.co.uk/wp-content/uploads/2015/11/IVA-Standard-Terms-Version-4-Jan-2018.pdf (accessed 20 November 2019).

3.123 In order to apply for a moratorium, the directors need to obtain statements from an IP ('the proposed monitor') that: (i) the proposed monitor is a qualified person and consents to act as the monitor in relation to the proposed moratorium; (ii) the company is an eligible company; and (iii) in the proposed monitor's view, it is likely that a moratorium for the company would result in the rescue of the company as a going concern.[171]

2. Appointment of the monitor

3.124 On the coming into force of a moratorium, the proposed monitor becomes the monitor in relation to the moratorium.[172]

3. Function and status of the monitor

3.125 The monitor is an officer of the court.[173] During a moratorium, the monitor must keep updated with the company's affairs for the purpose of forming a view as to whether it remains likely that the moratorium will result in the rescue of the company as a going concern.[174] However, monitors are generally entitled to rely on the information provided to them.[175] If the monitor's view as to the company being rescued as a going concern changes (i.e., if the monitor is no longer able to support the statement that a going concern is likely), the monitor must bring the moratorium to an end by filing a notice with the court.[176]

4. Replacing the monitor

3.126 The new sA39 of the IA will empower the court to remove a monitor, replace them with another IP or appoint another IP as an additional monitor. The Act is silent as to the grounds on which the court will make such orders. Challenges to the monitor's actions can also be brought under IA sA42(1). It is presumed that the court will have regard to the case law considered above in relation to liquidation and administrations. However, it does not seem possible that a monitor can be liable to pay compensation in the way that liquidators and administrators can be.[177] Given the monitor's involvement in potential dispositions of the company[178] and their licensed status, this appears to give IPs an unjustifiably high level of protection.

G. BLOCK TRANSFERS

3.127 The vast majority of IPs are members of a firm or, at least, some form of corporate entity. Nevertheless, an appointment as an office-holder in an insolvency is personal to the relevant practitioner, even if, in practice, the practitioner inevitably draws on the resources of their firm

---

171 IA 1986 sA6.
172 Ibid sA7(2).
173 Ibid sA34(1).
174 Ibid sA35(1).
175 Ibid ssA28(4), A35(2).
176 Ibid sA38(1).
177 Ibid sA42(4)(c).
178 Ibid sA28(1)(a).

for the purposes of managing the relevant estate.[179] In modern times, it is far more frequent than previously that IPs move between firms. This gave rise to a situation where the new practitioner found themselves in a different firm with different support staff and managers, who did not necessarily have the same detailed knowledge of the relevant insolvency estates. For a time, the common law filled a gap in the Act and the Rules to enable the court to order that, in such cases, a replacement IP from the departing IP's firm would be appointed to act in respect of the relevant insolvency estates: that way, there was a simple change in the named office-holder, and the disruption was minimal and the transition was seamless. Often, those rules were to the benefit of majority creditors, such as HMRC, who had a particular view as to how such transfers should be handled.

Those common law rules have now been placed on a statutory footing. Sub-division B in **3.128** Chapter 6 of Part 12 of the Insolvency Rules deals with block transfer orders. When an office-holder dies, retires from practice or is otherwise unable or unwilling to continue in office, it is open to that office-holder (or to others, who are specified in r12.37(4) IR 2016) to make an application for a block transfer order. In the event that the court forms the view that it is expedient to do so, then pursuant to IR 2016 r12.36(2), the court is able to appoint a replacement office-holder as liquidator in any winding up, as an administrator in an administration, as trustee in a bankruptcy, or as a supervisor in a CVA or an IVA. By IR 2016 r12.36(3), the proposed replacement office-holder must of course be qualified to act in relation to the relevant insolvency.

The evidence which supports the application must set out the circumstances as a result of **3.129** which it is expedient to appoint a replacement office-holder.[180] IR 2016 r12.38 contains important provisions dealing with when the costs of an application for a block transfer order can be treated as an expense of the relevant insolvency proceeding.

H. RECEIVERS

1. Introduction

In a book concerning office-holders' liabilities, discussion of the position of receivers may be **3.130** thought to be misplaced to the extent that receivers are not within the classes of office-holders mentioned within the IA 1986 who are required by statute to be qualified insolvency practitioners.[181] Nevertheless receivers are office-holders in a wider sense[182] and appointment of receivers remains a powerful process for the protection and realisation of assets. Receivers are either appointed by the court, or out of court pursuant to contract or statute.[183]

---

179 The nature of liability being personal rather than corporate is subject to review.
180 IR 2016 r12.37(9).
181 IA 1986, ss1(2), 2(4), 4(2) and 7(5) require nominees and supervisors of voluntary arrangements to be qualified IPs; s230 requires provisional liquidators, liquidators and administrative receivers to be qualified IPs; Sch B1 para 6 makes equivalent provision for administrators.
182 *Mirror Group Newspapers plc v Maxwell* [1998] 1 BCLC 638 at 647 (Ferris J).
183 See, e.g., the analogous context in criminal law in the Proceeds of Crime Act 2002 ss48–51.

2. Court-appointed receivers

3.131 The court has power to appoint a receiver in all cases in which it appears to be just and convenient to do so.[184] Court appointments are generally made either to preserve property during the course of litigation or by way of so-called equitable execution which is a remedy for the realisation of property to satisfy a judgment or order.[185] The power extends to enforcement of foreign debts.[186] The relevant court procedure is set out in Part 69 of the Civil Procedure Rules ('CPR'),[187] which provides that a receiver may be appointed before[188] or during proceedings and on or after judgment.[189] The receiver must be an individual[190] but there is no other restriction in the rules as to who may be appointed. The court will usually try to avoid appointing a person with any conflict of interest,[191] unless there is good reason to do so.[192] A court-appointed receiver is an officer of the court, not the agent or trustee of any party,[193] and has a duty to act fairly in the interests of all parties, adopting high standards of honesty and straightforward dealing.[194] Subject to those considerations, a court-appointed receiver is in a similar fiduciary position to a receiver appointed out of court and will have similar duties to those discussed below in the context of out of court appointments.[195] The receiver's powers should be set out in the order appointing him. In dealing with third parties the receiver acts as principal with personal liability.[196] Possession of property by the receiver is possession by the court and can only be disturbed by the court.[197] The court may at any time terminate the appointment and appoint a replacement receiver.[198] Court rules cover the application process, provision of security by the receiver,[199] applications for directions by the receiver, fixing the receiver's remuneration,[200] preparation and service of receivership accounts, remedies for non-compliance by the receiver and applications for the appointment to be discharged or terminated.[201]

---

184 Senior Courts Act 1981 s37(1), applied in the county court by County Courts Act 1984 s38.

185 The principles applicable to the appointment of receivers by way of equitable execution were reviewed in *JSC v VTB Bank v Skurikhin* [2015] EWHC 2131 (Comm).

186 *Masri v Consolidated Contractors International (UK) Ltd (No. 2)* [2008] EWCA Civ 303, [2009] QB 450.

187 See also Practice Direction 69 – Court's power to appoint a receiver.

188 The court may, e.g., order the appointment of a receiver in support of a pre-action freezing order.

189 CPR r69.2(1).

190 CPR r69.2(2).

191 *Re Lloyd* (1879) 12 Ch D 447.

192 *Re Prythgerch* (1889) 42 Ch D 590 (mortgagee appointed as receiver); *Pawley v Pawley* [1905] 1 Ch 593 (judgment creditor appointed as receiver by way of equitable execution).

193 *Burt, Boulton & Hayward v Bull* [1895] 1 QB 276 at 279 (CA); *In re Flowers & Co* [1897] 1 QB 14 at 16 (CA); *Parsons v Sovereign Bank of Canada* [1913] AC 160 at 167 (PC).

194 *Re Condon, ex p James* (1874) 9 Ch App 609.

195 In the context of court appointed receivers, see, e.g., *Procopi v Maschakis* (1969) 211 Estates Gazette 31 (Megarry J) (duty to realise property for the best price reasonably obtainable), and *Mirror Group Newspapers plc v Maxwell* [1998] 1 BCLC 638 at 648–9 (duty to account and maintain proper records).

196 *Burt, Boulton & Hayward v Bull* at 279, 284.

197 *Russell v The East Anglian Railway Company* (1850) 42 ER 201 at 206.

198 CPR r69.2(3).

199 If the receiver is a licensed IP, a bond provided as security under the Insolvency Practitioners Regulations 2005 (SI 2005/524) may be sufficient.

200 As to which see generally *Mirror Group Newspapers plc v Maxwell* [1998] 1 BCLC 638.

201 CPR rr69.3–69.11.

Given the out of court procedure discussed below, there is generally little need for receivers to **3.132** be appointed by the court in relation to security, unless the security is in jeopardy[202] at a time when the right to appoint out of court has not arisen or is disputed, or the security is in a form which does not confer the right to appoint out of court or does not confer adequate powers on the receiver.[203]

3. Receivers appointed out of court by mortgagees

(a) Introduction

The most common out of court appointments are by a mortgagee under an express power **3.133** contained in a mortgage or charge or under the statutory power conferred on mortgagees by the Law of Property Act 1925 ('LPA 1925').[204] The purpose of such an appointment is to place the management of the security in the hands of the receiver whose primary duty in exercising his powers of management is to try to bring about a situation in which the secured debt is repaid.[205] It is important to appreciate that the appointment derives its authority from the mortgage or charge and is one of a number of proprietary remedies available to mortgagees.[206] This puts the receiver in a different position to that of most office-holders. The receiver is not an officer of the court and owes no duties to unsecured creditors. Although the receiver owes duties in equity to the mortgagor, the mortgagee and others with an interest in the equity of redemption, the receiver manages the property for the benefit of the mortgagee, not for the benefit of the mortgagor.[207] The appointment process can be quick, inexpensive and is entirely in the control of the mortgagee. The appointment shields the mortgagee from the liabilities which would otherwise attach to him if he were a mortgagee in possession, so long as the mortgagee does not intermeddle in the conduct of the receivership in such a way as to assume responsibility for the receiver's acts and defaults.

(b) The mortgagee's power to appoint a receiver

The statutory power to appoint a receiver is conferred in every case where the mortgage or **3.134** charge is made by deed and the mortgage money has become due.[208] The power is not limited to mortgages of land and applies equally to mortgages or charges of personal property and things in action.[209] The statutory power is confined to appointing a receiver only when the power of sale has become exercisable and is then only to receive the income,[210] but it can be

---

202 *Cryne v Barclays Bank plc* [1987] BCLC 548 at 554.

203 For example, if the security, not made by deed, comprises only an equitable charge: *Swiss Bank Corpn v Lloyds Bank Ltd* [1982] AC 584 at 594–5 (CA).

204 See ss101(1)(i) and 109.

205 *Silven Properties Ltd v Royal Bank of Scotland plc* [2004] 1 WLR 997 (CA) at [27].

206 Other proprietary remedies available to the mortgagee will usually include the right to possession, to sell or (though little used) to foreclose.

207 *Silven* at [27].

208 LPA 1925 s101(1)(iii). Mortgage is defined to include any charge or lien on any property for securing money or money's worth: s205(1)(xvi). The power is therefore available to the holder of an equitable mortgage or charge made by deed. For discussion as to realisation of property under an equitable mortgage see *Swift 1st Ltd v Colin* [2011] EWHC 2410 (Ch).

209 See the definition of property: LPA 1925 s205(1)(xx).

210 LPA 1925 s109(1) and (3). Unless the mortgage deed provides otherwise, a receiver can be appointed by a mortgagee who is already in possession: *Refuge Assurance Co Ltd v Pearlberg* [1938] Ch 687 (CA).

extended by the terms of the mortgage deed.[211] Well-drawn mortgage deeds usually extend the power so as to allow the receiver to be appointed at any time after the mortgagee has demanded payment and confer on the receiver wide powers to sell and do anything else which can be done by the mortgagor.[212] The timing of the appointment is entirely a matter for the mortgagee who owes no duty to the mortgagor in this respect.[213] The mortgage will usually specify any formalities for the appointment and removal of the receiver. The only statutory formality is for the appointment to be made in writing by the mortgagee.[214] Unless the mortgage provides otherwise, more than one individual can be appointed.[215] The appointment takes effect from the time it is accepted by the receiver.[216]

3.135   Receivers do not need to be qualified IPs, although they often will be.[217] Only an individual can be a receiver of company property[218] and such a receiver must not be a bankrupt or subject to a moratorium or bankruptcy restriction under a debt relief order.[219] If the mortgage or charge is invalid, an appointment under it will also be invalid, exposing the appointee to possible liabilities such as for trespass or conversion.[220] In the case of an invalid appointment over company property, the appointor may be ordered to indemnify the appointee against any such liability.[221]

(c)   The receiver's agency

3.136   Modern forms of mortgage or charge usually provide for the receiver to act as agent for the mortgagor. The statutory position is the same.[222] This means that the mortgagor, not the mortgagee, is liable for the receiver's acts or default. But the position can be reversed if on its proper interpretation the mortgage contains an express power which does not provide for the

---

211   LPA 1925 s101(3) and (4).

212   An appointment made on an incorrect ground may be valid if another ground existed at the time: *Byblos Bank SAL v Al-Khudhairy* [1987] BCLC 232; or if the borrower is estopped from disputing the validity of the appointment: *Bank of Baroda v Panessar* [1987] Ch 335.

213   *Silven* at [13]; assuming the mortgagee is not acting in bad faith or for an improper purpose.

214   LPA 1925 s109(1) and (5).

215   For consideration of joint and multiple appointments see *Gwembe Valley Development Co Ltd v Koshy (No 2)* [2000] 2 BCLC 705.

216   *Windsor Refrigerator Co Ltd v Branch Nominees Ltd* [1961] Ch 375 (CA); acceptance may be tacit: *Cripps (Pharmaceuticals) Ltd v Wickenden* [1973] 1 WLR 944, 954 (Goff J). For the time from which the appointment of a receiver of a company takes effect, see IA 1986 s33.

217   For consideration of whether a claim against a receiver requires expert evidence see the discussion in *Devon Commercial Property Ltd v Barnett* [2019] EWHC 700 (Ch), [112] – [140] (HH Judge Paul Matthews). This might be contrasted with the approaches taken in *McDonagh v Bank of Scotland Plc* [2018] EWHC 3262 (Ch) (Morgan J) and *Centenary Homes v Gershinson* (unreported, LTL 15/12/2017).

218   IA 1986 s30.

219   IA 1986 s31.

220   *Ford & Carter Ltd v Midland Bank Ltd* (1979) 10 LDAB 182, 129 NLJ 543 (HL). An application for an injunction to restrain receivers from acting under a charge alleged to be defective is likely to be approached applying *American Cyanamid* principles, as in *Rushingdale v Byblos Bank SAL* (1986) 2 BCC 99 (CA); *BCPMS (Europe) Ltd v GMAC Commercial Financial plc* [2006] EWHC 3744 (Ch) at [51] (Lewison J).

221   IA 1986 s34.

222   LPA 1925 s109(2); for the history of this provision see the dissenting judgment of Rigby LJ in *Gaskell v Gosling* [1896] 1 QB 669 (CA), affirmed on appeal [1897] AC 575 (HL).

receiver to be the agent of the mortgagor.[223] The receiver may also become the agent of the mortgagee if the mortgagee intermeddles in the receivership by giving directions or instructions for the conduct of the receivership which the receiver accepts.[224] In the case of an appointment over company property, the agency ceases if the company goes into liquidation.[225] In that event the receiver continues to act as principal in his own right, unless the mortgagee, by words or deeds, makes the receiver its own agent and the receiver, by words or deeds, accepts that new status.[226] Whilst acting as principal, the receiver continues to have power to hold and dispose of the mortgaged property.[227]

By virtue of the receiver's agency for the mortgagor, the receiver is not personally liable on contracts he makes, so long as the contract makes this clear, and the receiver is entitled to an indemnity out of the assets.[228] Whilst in occupation as agent for the mortgagor, the receiver incurs no personal liability for business rates.[229] Nevertheless, the receiver's agency is not an ordinary species of agency because it is primarily a device to protect the mortgagee, and the receiver's primary duty is to bring about a situation in which the secured debt is repaid. The mortgagor has no say in the appointment, has no unrestricted right to receivership documents, cannot give instructions to the receiver or dismiss him[230] and may be restrained by injunction from interfering in the receivership.[231] In addition, the receiver is not obliged to accept proposals made by the mortgagor to repay the secured debt to put an end to the receivership,[232] and it has been held that a power conferred on a receiver by the mortgage contract to take possession of the mortgaged property can be asserted against the mortgagor notwithstanding the agency.[233]

3.137

---

223 *Re Vimbos Ltd* [1900] 1 Ch 470; *Deyes v Wood* [1911] 1 KB 806 (CA); it may be that the receiver will be regarded as the agent of the mortgagee if the mortgagee takes possession after the receiver's appointment, see *North American Trust Co v Consumer Gas Co* (1997) 147 DLR (4th) 645 (Court of Appeal for Ontario).

224 *Standard Chartered Bank v Walker* [1982] 1 WLR 1410 (CA) at 1415–6; *American Express International Banking Corp v Hurley* [1985] 3 All ER 564 (Mann J); *Morgan v Lloyds Bank plc* [1998] Lloyds Rep Bank 73 (CA) at 82; *National Bank of Greece SA v Pinios Shipping Co (No 1)* [1990] 1 AC 637, 647; *Bicester Properties Ltd v West Bromwich Commercial Ltd* (Unrep) 10 September 2012 (Ch D); *Davey v Money* [2018] EWHC 766 (Ch), [2018] Bus LR 1903 at [697]–[700] (Snowden J).

225 *Gough's Garages Ltd v Pugsley* [1930] 1 KB 615 (CA); *Re Beck Foods Ltd* re [2001] EWCA Civ 1934, [2002] 1 WLR 1304 (CA), [76]. It is thought the same may apply if the company goes into administration.

226 *Royal Bank of Scotland plc v O'Shea* (Unrep), 3 February 1998 (CA).

227 *Sowman v David Samuel Trust Ltd* [1978] 1 WLR 22, 30A. There is some doubt whether, after liquidation, a receiver can convey property in the name of the company. For support for the view that this can be done, see *Barrows v Chief Land Registrar*, Times 20 October 1977 and Land Registry Practice Guide 36 on Administration & Receivership, para 7.

228 IA 1986 s37(1)(a) and (b).

229 *Ratford v Northavon District Council* [1987] QB 357; *Brown v City of London Corporation* [1996] 1 WLR 1070. Even following termination of the agency on liquidation or bankruptcy of the mortgagor, the fact that the receiver's occupation derives from the charge enables him to avoid incurring personal liability to rates: *Re Beck Foods Ltd*.

230 *Gomba Holdings UK Ltd v Minories Finance Ltd* [1988] 1 WLR 1231 at 1233; *Silven* at [27].

231 See, e.g., *Bower Terrace Student Accommodation Ltd v Space Student Living Ltd* [2012] EWHC 2206 (Ch).

232 *Lloyds Bank plc v Cassidy* [2003] BPIR 424 (CA).

233 *Menon v Pask* [2019] EWHC 2611 (Ch), (Mann J) at [27]; it was also held that the mortgagor is entitled to rely on the court's powers to postpone possession under s36 of the Administration of Justice Act 1970 because the receiver derives title from the mortgagee within the meaning of s39 of that Act: [42].

(d) The receiver's duties

3.138 As an agent with control of the mortgaged property, the receiver owes fiduciary duties to the mortgagor, the mortgagee and anyone interested in the equity of redemption.[234] In the conduct of the receivership, the receiver is obliged to act in good faith and for proper purposes, meaning obtaining repayment of the debt owed to the mortgagee.[235] Similarly, in discharging his duties to manage the property, the receiver has a duty to deal fairly and equitably with the mortgagor and others interested in the equity of redemption, and to take account of their interests.[236] Breach of the duty of good faith does not necessarily involve dishonesty because bad faith is capable of embracing a failure to act in a commercially acceptable way and sharp practice of a kind falling short of outright dishonesty.[237] Given these duties, the receiver cannot purchase the property himself without permission of the court.[238] As in the case of a mortgagee, it has traditionally been thought that if the receiver sells to a connected party, the burden of proof is on the receiver to prove that the price paid was the best price reasonably obtainable.[239] This proposition was not accepted, however, in a recent case concerning a sale by a receiver to a person connected to the mortgagee, on the basis that there was no 'self-dealing' or conflict of interest on the part of the receiver.[240] The commercial circumstances of the appointment may suggest, however, that there is the potential for such a conflict, and there are other first instance decisions which go the other way.[241] It has been held at first instance that the duty to act for proper purposes is not breached if the receiver is, at least in part, acting for a proper purpose.[242] In the case of a sale to a connected party, however, it is for the receiver to show that the desire to obtain the best price was given absolute preference over any desire that the associate should obtain a good bargain.[243]

3.139 In managing the property, a receiver cannot remain entirely passive if this would be damaging to the mortgagor or mortgagee. The receiver must act to protect and preserve the charged

---

234 The duty extends to guarantors of the secured indebtedness: *Standard Chartered Bank v Walker* [1982] 1 WLR 1410; *American Express International Banking Corp v Hurley* [1985] 3 All ER 564. It does not extend to directors, shareholders, employees or unsecured creditors of the mortgagor: *Standard Chartered v Walker* above at 1415–6; *Lathia v Dronsfield Bros Ltd* [1987] BCLC 321 at 324; *Burgess v Auger* [1998] 2 BCLC 478.

235 *Quennell v Maltby* [1979] 1 WLR 318 (CA), *Downsview Nominees Ltd v First City Corporation Ltd* [1993] AC 295 (PC) at 312; *Medforth v Blake* [2000] Ch 86 at 98, 102. In *O'Kane v Rooney* [2013] NIQB 114 discouraging purchasers in a sales process, providing inaccurate information to them, and suggesting a preferred bidder lower his bid was held sufficient evidence of an arguable case of bad faith to grant an injunction.

236 *Palk v Mortgage Services Funding plc* [1993] Ch 330 at 337–8; *Medforth v Blake* at 101.

237 *Medforth v Blake* above, as explained in *Horn v Commercial Acceptances Ltd* [2011] EWHC 1757 (Ch), [77], upheld on appeal without this point being specifically discussed (see [2012] EWCA Civ 958). See also *Niru Battery Manufacturing Co v Milestone Trading Ltd* [2004] QB 985 (CA) at 999-1000; *Fattal v Walbrook Trustees (Jersey) Ltd* [2010] EWHC 2767 (Ch), [181]; *Armstrong DLW GmbH v Winnington Networks Ltd* [2012] EWHC 10 (Ch), [2013] Ch 156 at [108].

238 *Nugent v Nugent* [1908] 1 Ch 546.

239 *Tse Kwong Lam v Wong Chit Sen* [1983] 1 WLR 1349 (PC); *PK Airfinance SARL v Alpstream AG* [2015] EWCA Civ 1318, [245] (CA), and Lightman and Moss, *The Law of Administrators and Receivers of Companies* (6th edn, 2017), at 13-047.

240 *Devon Commercial Property Ltd v Barnett* [2019] EWHC 700 (Ch) at [28] (HHJ Paul Matthews).

241 In addition to the authorities and commentary referred to above, see *Watts v Midland Bank plc* [1986] BCLC 15 at 23 (Peter Gibson J).

242 *Meretz Investments NV v ACP Ltd* [2007] Ch 197, [134] (reversed in part on other grounds, see [2008] Ch 244).

243 *Australia and New Zealand Banking v Bangadilly* (1978) 139 CLR 195; *Alpstream* at [221].

property.[244] So a receiver may be in breach of duty by failing to let a vacant property[245] or, if property is let, by failing to inspect the lease and to ensure that an upwards rent review is triggered in time.[246] The receiver is not obliged to carry on a business formerly carried on by the mortgagor, but if he has power and decides to do so, he must take reasonable steps to trade profitably.[247]

The equitable or fiduciary duties of care owed by mortgagees and receivers in respect of the exercise of a power of sale conferred on the receiver by the mortgage are the same. This means that, like mortgagees, receivers owe a duty to the mortgagor, the mortgagee and others interested in the equity of redemption, to take reasonable steps to obtain the best price reasonably obtainable. Like mortgagees, receivers are not obliged before sale to spend money on repairs, to make the property more attractive before marketing it, to refurbish, to investigate and proceed with applications for planning permission, or to continue any existing planning application.[248] But the duty to obtain a proper price requires the receiver to ensure that the property is adequately advertised and marketed for sale.[249] It will also require a receiver who wishes to sell the property within a portfolio with other properties, to consider whether this is in the best interests of the mortgagor and to form the view that this is likely to produce a better result than a more conventional stand-alone sale.[250] A receiver realising assets is liable for the acts, defaults and advice of his agents and cannot avoid liability by saying that he retained a competent professional.[251] In deciding whether a receiver has acted in breach of duty, the facts must be looked at broadly and he will not be adjudged to be in default unless he is plainly on the wrong side of the line.[252] **3.140**

The receiver also has an agent's duty to account[253] and, in the case of a receiver of company property, a duty to file accounts with the registrar of companies.[254] In the absence of any other provision in the mortgage deed, statute obliges the receiver to apply money he receives in the following order, namely to pay (i) rents, taxes, rates and outgoings affecting the mortgaged property, (ii) any sums payable in priority to the mortgage under which he is appointed, (iii) his commission, insurance premiums, and the cost of repairs, (iv) mortgage interest, (v) mortgage principal, and any residue to the person entitled but for the receivership.[255] **3.141**

(e) The receiver's powers and remuneration

The receiver's powers and remuneration are usually governed by express terms in the mortgage deed and the terms of appointment. Otherwise the receiver's powers are limited to the **3.142**

---

244 *Silven* at [23].
245 *Nautch Ltd v Mortgage Express* [2012] EWHC 4136 (Ch) at [82]–[88].
246 *Knight v Lawrence* [1993] BCLC 215; *Silven* at [23].
247 *Medforth v Blake* above.
248 *Silven* at [27]–[29].
249 *Standard Chartered Bank v Walker* above; *American Express International Banking Corp v Hurley; Glatt v Sinclair* [2011] EWCA Civ 1317, [2012] BPIR 306.
250 *McDonagh v Bank of Scotland plc* [2018] EWHC 3262 (Ch); [2019] 4 WLR 12, [144]–[149] (Morgan J).
251 *Raja v Austin Gray* [2003] BPIR 725 (CA) at [30]–[36].
252 *Centenary Homes Ltd v Liddell* [2020] EWHC 1080 (QB) at [72].
253 *Silven* at [28].
254 IA 1986 s38.
255 LPA 1925 s109(8).

statutory powers to recover the income from the mortgaged property, to exercise any other powers delegated to the receiver by the mortgagee,[256] to use receipts to pay costs, charges and expenses incurred in the receivership and his commission,[257] and to insure (if directed to do so by the mortgagee).[258] A receiver of company property also has a statutory right to apply to the court for directions in relation to any matter arising in connection with the performance of his functions.[259]

3.143   Statutory remuneration is limited to commission of up to 5 per cent of the receiver's gross receipts, as specified in his appointment. If the appointment is silent on this, commission of 5 per cent is allowed, or else the receiver can apply to the court to fix such rate as it thinks fit.[260] In a receivership of the property of a company in liquidation, the liquidator can apply to the court to fix the receiver's remuneration.[261]

(f)   Ending the receivership

3.144   The receivership ends if the mortgagee removes the receiver,[262] the receiver dies, the receiver is required to vacate by the administrator of a company in administration,[263] a receiver is appointed under a higher ranking security, or if the receiver terminates the appointment on completion of the receivership after having repaid the secured indebtedness and accounted for any surplus to those entitled to it.[264]

I. ADMINISTRATIVE RECEIVERS

1.   Introduction

3.145   Administrative receivers are true office-holders, in the sense that they are within the classes mentioned within the IA 1986 and are required to be qualified insolvency practitioners.[265] They are, however, a dying breed as a result of the restrictions on new appointments introduced by the EA 2002.[266] What follows is therefore only a brief review.

3.146   Although part of the same family as other receivers, administrative receivers fall within a class defined by and subjected to a specific statutory regime established by the IA 1986. They are receivers or managers:

---

256   Ibid s109(3).
257   Ibid s109(6).
258   Ibid s109(7).
259   IA 1986 s35(1).
260   LPA 1925 s109(6).
261   IA 1986 s36(2).
262   LPA 1925 s109(5).
263   IA 1986 Sch B1 para 41.
264   *Rottenberg v Monjack* [1992] BCC 688.
265   IA 1986 s230. See further Chapter 2.
266   There was only one in 2019: see The Insolvency Service Company Insolvency Statistics (30 January 2020), 8: https://www.gov.uk/government/collections/insolvency-service-official-statistics (accessed 21 April 2020).

of the whole (or substantially the whole) of a company's property appointed by or on behalf of the holders of any debentures of the company secured by a charge which, as created, was a floating charge, or by such a charge and one or more other securities.[267]

There is some room for doubt whether there can be more than one administrative receiver in office in respect of company property at the same time,[268] whether a receiver of the assets of a foreign company is included,[269] and whether a court-appointed receiver can be an administrative receiver.[270]

2. Overview of administrative receivership

(a) The power to appoint an administrative receiver

An instrument which purports to empower the holder of a floating charge to appoint an administrative receiver falls within the definition of a QFC in the IA 1986.[271] With limited exceptions, the holder of a QFC created on or after 15 September 2003 may not appoint an administrative receiver.[272] The limited exceptions[273] cover special cases of appointments in respect of certain capital market arrangements, public-private partnerships which include step-in rights, utilities, urban regeneration projects, project finance which includes step-in rights, financial market charges, registered social landlord companies and protected railway companies.[274] It follows that outside those special cases, corporate receivership under a post-15 September 2003 security is generally limited to cases where the receiver is appointed under a fixed charge on specific assets, although this may be supplemented by a floating charge which is limited in scope so as not to catch substantially all of the company's property. Where administrative receivership remains available, the appointment formalities do not differ from those detailed above for appointments by mortgagees.

3.147

(b) The administrative receiver's agency

The IA 1986 deems an administrative receiver to be the company's agent, unless and until the company goes into liquidation.[275] It imposes personal liability on the administrative receiver on any contract he makes (except insofar as the contract otherwise provides) and any employment contracts which he adopts (for wages and pension contributions for services provided after

3.148

---

267   IA 1986 ss29(2)(a) and 251(a); see to the same effect CA 2006 s1170A.
268   This seems unlikely; the receiver appointed under the higher ranking security is likely to displace any other appointment.
269   This was held possible in *Re International Bulk Commodities Ltd* [1993] Ch 77 but the definition of company is limited to companies registered under the CA 2006: IA 1986 s28.
270   This also seems unlikely given that such a receiver is appointed by the court and not as agent for any other party. See *Re A & C Supplies Ltd* [1998] BCC 708.
271   Sch B1 para 14(2)(c).
272   IA 1986 s72A(1) and (4), and the Insolvency Act (Administrative Receivership and Urban Regeneration etc) Order 2003, SI 2003/1832.
273   Which can be extended or restricted by order: IA 1986 s72H.
274   For details see IA 1986 ss72B–72GA.
275   IA 1986 s44(1)(a).

adoption).[276] It also confers on the receiver a right to be indemnified out of the assets of the company.[277] Subject to those express provisions, the same principles apply as described above in respect of the agency of receivers appointed by mortgagees.

(c)   The administrative receiver's duties

3.149   As office-holders, administrative receivers have a number of statutory duties in addition to the general duties of receivers appointed by mortgagees described above. On appointment, an administrative receiver is required forthwith to send to the company and publish in the prescribed manner a notice of his appointment, and to send notice to creditors for whom he has an address within 28 days.[278] He is also required forthwith on appointment to call for a statement of affairs in prescribed form from officers of the company and/or certain persons involved in the company's affairs.[279] Within three months (or longer if the court allows), he must send a report to the registrar of companies, certain creditors and (within a further seven days) any liquidator, covering events leading to his appointment, actual or proposed disposals and the carrying on of any business, sums due to the debenture-holder and preferential creditors, amounts likely to be available for payment of other creditors, and a summary statement of affairs.[280] The company's unsecured creditors can then establish a creditors' committee which may require the administrative receiver to provide information relating to the receivership.[281] Unlike an administrator, an administrative receiver does not have a duty to consider a rescue of the company, nor is he under a duty to trade on or to conclude that trading on is not realistic before seeking to sell assets.[282]

(d)   The administrative receiver's powers and remuneration

3.150   The IA 1986 confers on administrative receivers a wide range of powers, except insofar as they are inconsistent with the provisions of the debenture under which they are appointed.[283] They include power to take possession of and sell property, borrow money, give security, appoint lawyers and other agents, engage in legal proceedings and arbitration, insure, execute deeds, carry on the company's business, grant and surrender leases, make compromises, prove for debts in insolvency processes, and present or defend winding-up petitions. Third parties dealing with the administrative receiver in good faith and for value are not concerned to inquire whether he is acting within his powers.[284]

3.151   The court may also authorise an administrative receiver to dispose of property which is subject to security which has priority to the debenture under which he is appointed, if this would be

---

276   Ibid s44(1)(b) and see s44(2)–(3). This liability is confined, in general, to new contracts made by the administrative receiver. He is not personally liable under existing contracts: *Re Atlantic Computer Systems plc* [1992] Ch 505, 524–5 (CA).

277   IA 1986 s44(1)(c).

278   Ibid s46.

279   Ibid s47.

280   Ibid s48.

281   Ibid s49.

282   *Ahmad v Bank of Scotland plc* [2016] EWCA Civ 602 at [38].

283   IA 1986 s42(1) and Sch 1.

284   Ibid s42(3).

likely[285] to promote a more advantageous realisation of the company's assets than would otherwise be effected.[286] Such orders are conditional on the net sale proceeds and any sum required to make up the open market sale value (as determined by the court), being applied in discharging the sums secured by the prior security or securities.[287]

The remuneration of an administrative receiver is governed by the same principles as have been **3.152** set out above in relation to receivers appointed out of court by mortgagees. In essence their remuneration is usually governed by the debenture and terms of appointment.

(e) Ending administrative receivership

Administrative receivers may only be removed from office by court order or may resign by **3.153** giving notice as prescribed.[288] They must vacate office if they cease to be a qualified IP.[289] If they vacate office their remuneration and expenses, and any indemnity to which they are entitled from the assets, are charged to be paid out of the assets within their control at that time in priority to the security under which they were appointed.[290] If they vacate office otherwise than by death, they must give notice to the registrar of companies within 14 days.[291]

---

285   This probably requires there to be a reasonable prospect: compare *Re Harris Simons Construction Ltd* [1989] 1 WLR 368 at 371.
286   IA 1986 s43(1)–(2). A copy of the order must be filed with the registrar of companies: s43(5). For the equivalent power of an administrator, see s15.
287   Ibid s43(3)–(4).
288   Ibid s45(1). The court has no power to appoint a replacement: *Re A & C Supplies Ltd* [1988] BCC 708.
289   Ibid s45(2).
290   Ibid s45(3).
291   Ibid s45(4).

PART II

DUTIES AND POWERS IN OFFICE

4

THE DUTIES OF OFFICE-HOLDERS

A. INTRODUCTION

As outlined above at paragraphs 1.046–1.050, the duties that IPs must comply with stem from **4.001** a number of sources, and in turn depend on whether the IP is acting as a contracted professional, an appointed agent of the company and/or as an officer of the court. As a matter of law, those sources are: (i) statute; (ii) equity (i.e., fiduciary duties); (iii) contract; and (iv) tort. The remainder of this chapter sets out how those sources interact, overlap,[1] and the potential for conflict between them. It then considers some examples of how the standard of skill and care applies in practice, and how those standards vary depending on which role the IP plays.[2]

1. Statutory duties

The appointments and offices that IPs fill are generally created by statute, and in particular the **4.002** Insolvency Act 1986 ('IA 1986'). It follows that the primary obligations of an IP are governed

---

1 See *Bristol & West v Mothew* [1998] Ch 1; Taylor (2019) 82(1) *MLR* 17–45.
2 For example, an IP may first be instructed by a director on a private basis to provide advice on insolvency matters. If the administrator is subsequently appointed as the administrator of the company, the administrator's statutory obligations will supplant the previous contractual duty owed to the director.

by primary and secondary legislation, principally found in the Insolvency (England and Wales) Rules 2016 ('IR 2016'), and must be fulfilled by IPs in the exercise of their powers.[3]

4.003 Further, it is a result of the office-holder's statutory duties that they are properly described as officers of the court,[4] and as such will act subject to its control,[5] although this will apply to the extent that the appointment of the IP is statutory.[6] One important exception to this principle is the position of a liquidator in a voluntary winding up, whereby a liquidator is (anomalously) not an officer of the court.[7]

4.004 The core role of the IP in the context of an insolvency process is normally to get in, realise,[8] and distribute the assets of the company in accordance with the stakeholders' rights relative to one another, and in accordance with the *pari passu* principle.[9] The general starting point for the order of priority, set out by Lord Neuberger PSC in *Re Nortel* is as follows:[10]

(1) Fixed charge creditors;
(2) Expenses of the insolvency proceedings;
(3) Preferential creditors;
(4) Floating charge creditors;
(5) Unsecured provable debts;
(6) Statutory interest;
(7) Non-provable liabilities; and
(8) Shareholders.

This hierarchy has come to be known as the 'waterfall' of statutory priorities, and is now referred to as such.[11] The reason for its description as a waterfall is that each rank of creditor must be paid off in full before the next creditor can receive any dividend in the insolvency. So, for example, only when the expenses of the insolvency proceedings (rank (2)) have been paid in

---

3   For example, IA 1986 Schs 4 (liquidators) and 5 (trustees in bankruptcy). See Annexes I and II at pp 297 and 302 for a comparison of the powers granted to each type of office-holder.
4   IA 1986 s160 explicitly delegates these duties to the liquidator of a compulsory winding up 'as an officer of the court', and as such will be subject to the court's control. Section 165 applies in voluntary liquidations, and does not include a similar proviso.
5   Section 167(3), applicable to voluntary liquidations by virtue of s112.
6   Sch B1 para 5; *Re Atlantic Computer Systems plc* [1992] Ch 505 (CA) at 529. Therefore, where advice is sought from an IP on a purely contractual basis, it is doubtful whether they could be described as acting as an officer of the court. However, their position as a licensed practitioner (obviously) does not change, and so this will inform the standard of skill and care to be expected from an IP, even when acting pursuant to a contract.
7   *Re TH Knitwear (Wholesale) Ltd* [1988] Ch 275 (CA).
8   Sch 4 para 6 gives a 'power to sell any of the company's property *by public auction or private contract with power to transfer the whole of it to any person or to sell the same in parcels*'. This includes choses in action: *Seear v Lawson* (1880) 15 Ch D 426; *Re Oasis Merchandising Services Ltd* [1998] Ch 170, [1997] BCC 282. Other actions contained in IA 1986 Sch 4 para 3A, such as preference claims, can also now be assigned in light of the amendments brought about by SBEEA 2015 s118 (reflected in IA 1986 s246ZD).
9   IA 1986 s143; IR 2016 r14.12(2). The *pari passu* principle is itself subject to a number of qualifications. The usefulness of the *pari passu* principle has been the subject of academic criticism: see Rizwaan Mokal, 'Priority as pathology: the pari passu myth' (2001) *CLJ* 581.
10 *In re Nortel GmbH (in administration)* [2013] UKSC 52 at [39].
11 For example, *In re Lehman Brothers International (Europe) (in administration)* [2015] EWCA Civ 485, [2016] Ch 50 at [198] (Briggs LJ).

full will the preferential creditors (rank (3)) be entitled to receive a distribution.[12] This description is a generalised summary of the distribution priorities in an insolvency. As Lord Neuberger himself made clear, it was not intended to be treated as some sort of quasi-statutory statement of immutable legal principle.[13] It has however been consistently affirmed, and cannot be re-ordered by the court on grounds of discretion or equitable principles, no matter how outwardly deserving.[14] See paragraph 4.088 for the effect of the changes brought about by CIGA 2020 and the status of moratorium debts within the waterfall.

This essential duty[15] can be viewed as the primary purpose from which all other statutory **4.005** duties flow. Therefore, where an IP investigates the affairs of a company or individual, adjudicates on creditor proofs,[16] makes a distribution or dividend,[17] or sells property belonging to a company, it follows that this will be performed with a view to maximising returns to the creditors in accordance with their respective rights.[18]

Where share capital is not fully paid-up, the IP is also under a duty to make calls on **4.006** contributories,[19] which effectively triggers the repayment due from the contributory to the company.[20] This provision is less commonly used in modern times, because generally shares are paid for in full on transfer.[21] The contributory rule applies only in liquidation, and not generally in administration.[22] There is no provision for calls on contributories to be made by administrators of the sort provided for in s74(1).

Unlike the position in bankruptcy, whereby the assets of the bankrupt (as defined in s283) will **4.007** vest automatically in the trustee[23] on the making of the bankruptcy order, the position in corporate insolvencies is generally that the company's property will remain vested in the company. The liquidator may apply to the court to have the assets vested in them, usually after

---

12   The distinction between what is an expense and what is an unsecured provable debt can sometimes be a fine one, as is illustrated by *Re Nortel* itself, which turned on where certain pension liabilities fell within the waterfall. Note also that a proportion of the funds (known as the 'prescribed part') which would otherwise be available for a floating charge creditor must be set aside for the unsecured creditors where the floating charge was created on or after 15 September 2003: IA 1986 s176A and The Insolvency Act 1986 (Prescribed Part) Order 2003 SI 2003/2097, as amended by The Insolvency Act 1986 (Prescribed Part) Order 2020 SI 2020/211.

13   *In re Lehman Brothers International (Europe) (in administration) (No 4)* [2017] UKSC 38 at [17].

14   *Re Nortel* at [116]; *Re London Bridge Entertainment Partners LLP* [2019] EWHC 2932 (Ch) at [25], [50]. As Lord Briggs JSC described it in *Re Stanford International Bank Ltd* [2019] UKPC 45 at [40]:

    [t]he applicable insolvency scheme may be good, bad or indifferent, but the liquidator takes it as he finds it, and his statutory duty is to apply it, both for the purpose of getting in the company's assets, and for the purpose of deciding how they should be allocated among those, including creditors, with a claim in the liquidation.

15   Enforceable by those who have an interest in the insolvency: IA 1986 ss212, 303/304, Sch B1 para 75.

16   IR 2016 Part 14 Ch 1.

17   Ibid Ch 3.

18   The IP is nevertheless given a great deal of discretion in deciding how to achieve this objective.

19   IA 1986 s74(1) (in voluntary winding up), subject to the exceptions in s74(2). See also ss149 and 150 (compulsory liquidation). The same principles apply in respect of unregistered companies: IA 1986 s226.

20   Ibid s80.

21   Ibid s74(2)(d). Unlimited companies, which are even less frequent features of modern-day corporate life, are a different matter: see *Re Lehman Brothers International (Europe) (in administration) (No 4)* [2017] UKSC 38 at [35].

22   *Re Lehman Bros (No 4)* at [165]. There may be an exception for distributing administrations.

23   IA 1986 s306.

giving an indemnity.[24] However, this is an exceptional course, and is not often encountered in practice, since the liquidator will, by default, act as agent of the company, and as such will usually be able to administer the estate without the need for the assets to vest in him personally.

4.008   Once the company's affairs are fully wound up, the IP must provide an account of the insolvency process, showing how it has been conducted and how the property has been disposed of.[25] This is emblematic of a number of more compliance-oriented aspects of the IP's role within insolvency processes which, while they will not necessarily result in any particular financial advantage accruing to creditors, their purpose is obviously to enable creditors to assess the conduct of the IP (often on an ongoing basis), and sufficiently inform them so as to be in a position to challenge that conduct, if necessary. There is also the not-insignificant consideration that the efficacy of English insolvency law as a whole, and its attraction as a jurisdiction in which to commence proceedings, depends on its transparency.[26]

4.009   Once the requirement for a final account has been complied with, the office-holder will usually vacate office,[27] and where the company is being wound up it will be dissolved three months later.[28] From the point when a liquidator obtains his release, he will no longer be liable in respect of acts or omissions in the winding up.[29] A bankruptcy continues until the bankrupt obtains their discharge,[30] which is (by default) a period of one year from the date of the bankruptcy order.[31] The trustee will however remain that individual's trustee in bankruptcy until he obtains his release under IA 1986 s299, and is therefore independent from whether or not the bankrupt has obtained his discharge. A claim may therefore be brought against a trustee in bankruptcy under IA 1986 s304 at any time, but the leave of the court must first be obtained if the claim is brought after the trustee obtains his release.

4.010   Within this basic structure, there are an infinite combination of things that may happen, such as claims being brought by the IP,[32] applications for information,[33] applications for directions from the court,[34] applications for recognition in other jurisdictions (where such recognition is

---

24   IA 1986 ss112 and 145.

25   IA 1986 ss38 (receivership accounts); 94 (compulsory liquidations); 106 (voluntary liquidations).

26   See, e.g., McCormack, 'Jurisdictional competition and forum shopping in insolvency proceedings' (2009) *CLJ* 169, 197.

27   See paras 3.046 and 3.047 above on release; IA 1986 ss171(6), (7); 172(8).

28   IA 1986 ss201 and 205.

29   IA 1986 ss173(4) (voluntary liquidation); 174(6) (compulsory liquidation).

30   IA 1986 s278.

31   IA 1986 s279. The trustee in bankruptcy can apply to suspend discharge for a certain period under IA 1986 s279(3), usually in response to non-compliance by the bankrupt with his obligation to cooperate with the trustee's investigations. See *Muir Hunter on Personal Insolvency* (Release 80, June 2019) at 3–521ff.

32   Either by causing the company to bring a claim, or in his own right, pursuant to IA 1986 Sch 4 para 3A (which applies to proceedings under IA 1986, ss212–214, 238–239, 242–243, and 423). See *Kirkpatrick v Snoozebox Ltd* [2014] BCC 477. Sanction is no longer required for such claims: SBEEA 2015 s120, which amended IA 1986 ss165, 167, 169 and Sch 4 paras 3 and 6A.

33   Such as through examination of individuals (IA 1986 ss133, 236, 289), or by application for delivery up of the books and records of the company (IA 1986 s234). Applications under IA 1986 s236 probably do not have extraterritorial effect: *Re Akkurate* [2020] EWHC 1433 (Ch); *Re MF Global UK Ltd* [2015] EWHC 2319 (Ch). Recognition in another jurisdiction will however be likely to enable the same power to be exercised extra-judicially.

34   IA 1986 ss35 (receivers and managers); 168 (compulsory liquidation); 112 (voluntary liquidations); 303(2) (bankruptcy); Sch B1 para 63 (administration).

not automatic),[35] disclaimers of onerous property,[36] and conversions from one type of insolvency process to another[37] (or even the concurrent use of multiple types of procedure[38]). Again, the touchstone throughout these applications are that they are intended to be made for the benefit of creditors and for the furthering of their interests. Although IPs are remunerated for their work, they must not lose sight of this fundamental point, and must remain vigilant of conflicts of interest, so that creditors will have no sense of grievance that the process is not being conducted in their interest.[39]

The above outline is not generally applicable in cases where there is a voluntary agreement (i.e., in the context of CVAs, IVAs, insolvent schemes of arrangement, or contractual compacts with creditors). In those circumstances, the role of the IP is dramatically different, and reference should be made to paragraphs 4.096–4.098 below as to how those procedures are conducted. Indeed, schemes of arrangement are not generally considered to be 'insolvency processes', even if the company in question is insolvent.[40]   **4.011**

2. Fiduciary duties

An office-holder becomes a fiduciary on appointment, because their task is to take into their custody or control 'all the property and things in action to which the company is or appears to be entitled.'[41] In doing so, the directors in a corporate insolvency will be supplanted, and their functions are taken over by the IP, who will act as agent for the company. The duty is one of 'single-minded' loyalty and, just as a director must act in respect of a particular company,[42] so an IP must similarly only take into account the effects on group companies to the extent that they do not interfere with his fiduciary duty in respect of a single company or individual.[43] It is difficult to see how such a person could not owe fiduciary duties, given that the IP's task is to   **4.012**

---

35 IA 1986 s426; European Insolvency Regulation 2015/848, Arts 19–21; The Cross-Border Insolvency Regulations 2006, Art 15 (incorporating the UNCITRAL Model Law on cross-border insolvency). See further Segal, Harris, Morrison, 'Assistance to foreign insolvency office-holders in the conflict of laws: is the common law fit for purpose?' (2017) 30(8) *Insolv Int* 117–27. Applications for recognition are subject to a duty of full and frank disclosure: *In re Dalnyaya Step llc (in liquidation) (No 2)* [2017] EWHC 3153 (Ch) (failure to notify court of Home Office refusal to give recognition to Russian criminal proceedings).

36 IA 1986 ss178 (liquidation) and 315 (bankruptcy).

37 Such as moving from administration to liquidation under Sch B1 para 82.

38 Such as the implementation of a voluntary arrangement within an insolvent administration or liquidation under IA 1986 s1(3).

39 *Re Zirceram Ltd (in liquidation)* [2000] 1 BCLC 751; *Re Barings plc* [2001] 2 BCLC 159 at [51]; *Sisu Capital Fund v Tucker* [2006] BCC 463 at [94]–[97].

40 By way of illustration, schemes of arrangement are notably absent from Annex A to the EU Regulation on Insolvency Proceedings (recast), and are therefore not classified as 'insolvency processes' for the purpose of Art 6 of the Regulation. See *Tolley's Insolvency Law Service* at [E10002] for further discussion.

41 IA 1986 s144(1). This analysis is bolstered by the power to collect in such property, books and records under s234. In Scotland, all the property of the company is deemed to be in the custody of the court: s144(2).

42 *Re Charterbridge* [1970] Ch 62 (Pennycuick J). Although a case on directors, there would appear to be no justifiable distinction between directors and office-holders on this point.

43 The common practice of IPs taking on multiple appointments within corporate groups and/or being appointed as trustees in bankruptcy of directors or other stakeholders has the potential to place the IP in a position of potential or actual conflict: see *Re D C L Hire Ltd* [2018] EWHC 3457 (Ch) at [11]–[13]. Possible solutions include the appointment of the Official Receiver: see *Re Barings plc*, or the appointment of a so-called 'conflict liquidator': see *Re Arrows Group* [1992] BCC 121 (Hoffmann J).

gather in the money and property of a company or another individual and to distribute it to others. Such a person is:

> obviously required to act in good faith, prohibited from making a secret profit out of dealings with the company's property and money, not at liberty to act out of self interest in the performance of his/her duties, and not entitled to unapproved reward.[44]

It is therefore suggested that fiduciary duties flow in the same way as they will in a director-company relationship.[45] As an agent of the company, an IP's duties will also incorporate a tortious duty of care at common law to act with reasonable care and skill.[46]

4.013 However, IPs are categorically distinct from trustees. The language of trusts has also pervaded insolvency law for some time, which gives rise to some difficult issues with regard to how the IP must act. The view of the author is that this may have been because in the early days of joint stock companies[47] it provided a convenient and pre-existing framework to explain a new phenomenon, that is, a situation where property was held by one party (like a trustee) while another party had a right to demand the transfer of that property (like a beneficiary). The trust-oriented perspective still appears to have remained as an undercurrent in insolvency jurisprudence. For example, the reasoning in *Ayerst v C & K (Constructions) Ltd*[48] was premised on the assumption that the company was divested of beneficial interest in its property, while legal title remained in the company. This view was endorsed in *Cambridge Gas Transport Corporation v Official Committee of Unsecured Creditors of Navigator Holdings plc*,[49] but has not found favour in Australia.[50] Although it is accepted that the language of trusts has some utility, its limits become apparent when one discusses remedies. For example, where a claim succeeds under the transaction avoidance provisions,[51] it appears that there is no one answer as to whether the claim itself will be based on the law of constructive trusts, unjust enrichment, or even the tort of conversion. Instead, it will depend on the characteristic of the particular claim.[52] The better view now appears to be that the substantive rights of creditors remain untouched by the overlay of the statutory insolvency scheme. Although creditors are confined to a collective enforcement procedure that results in *pari passu* distribution of the company's assets, the insolvency process neither creates new substantive rights nor destroys the old ones.[53]

4.014 The conclusion, therefore, is that IPs will often act as fiduciaries, but not over trust property in the sense as conventionally understood in the law of trusts, and they are not trustees in the

---

44 *Re Mama Milla Ltd* [2014] EWHC 2753 (Ch) at [40].
45 See paras 4.046–4.050 below for discussion of this comparison.
46 *Bristol & West v Mothew* [1998] Ch 1 (CA), 16–18; *Kyrris v Oldham* [2003] 2 BCLC 305.
47 Placed on a statutory footing by the Joint Stock Companies Act 1847. Their winding up was governed by the Joint Stock Companies Winding-up Act 1848.
48 [1976] AC 167 (HL). *Re General Rolling Stock Ltd* (1871–72) LR 7 Ch App 646 may also have been decided on that same basis: see *Re Cases of Taff's Well Ltd* [1991] BCC 582, 586.
49 [2006] UKPC 26, [2007] 1 AC 508.
50 *Commissioner of Taxation v Linter Australia Ltd (in liquidation)* [2005] HCA 20.
51 Broadly, IA 1986 ss127, 238/239, 423.
52 See the discussion in relation to *Officeserve Technologies Ltd v Annabel's (Berkeley Square) Ltd* [2018] EWHC 2168 (Ch) (HHJ Paul Matthews).
53 *Wight v Eckhardt Marine GmbH* [2003] UKPC 37 at [26]–[27].

strict sense either. For that reason, the better view is that the closer analogy of an office-holder is a company director, who is subject to strict fiduciary duties.

3. Contractual duties

The courts have, on numerous occasions, made it clear that it is not possible for parties to contract out of the statutory scheme set out in the IA 1986.[54] For similar reasons, it is also not possible to contract out of insolvency set-off.[55] Such contracts will generally be contrary to public policy.[56] This applies with equal force to IPs themselves, whose statutory duty is delegated to them alone, and the statutory responsibility cannot be further delegated by way of contract.[57] It is for this reason that, although an IP's firm will often be referred to as a shorthand for 'the office-holder', it must constantly be borne in mind that the IP remains personally responsible.[58] However, this does not preclude the IP from contracting out his duties to agents or to others within his or her firm, and this routinely happens as a matter of practice. **4.015**

A distinction must be made, however, where an IP is engaged to provide insolvency advice prior to entry into a formal insolvency procedure. An IP's duty will be primarily governed by contract prior to appointment, for example, where advice is given directly to a director of a company facing financial difficulties. This gives rise to a potential for problems where the company in question later enters a formal insolvency process. That problem is most acute if the practical object of an administration is to effect a pre-pack sale, on which, see paragraphs 6.178–6.181 below.[59] **4.016**

Once the formal insolvency process is underway, however, it would be inadvisable and potentially contrary to public policy for an IP to enter into a contract with the company of which he is agent and/or with the company's directors. It would similarly be highly irregular for a trustee to enter into a contractual relationship with a bankrupt, not least because such contractual obligations could well conflict with the trustee's overriding statutory obligations.[60] Trustees may however occasionally choose to authorise the bankrupt to have conduct of a sale of a particular asset in the bankruptcy estate. This may apply where, for example, the asset is unique or specialist or of uncertain value (such as, e.g., technical intellectual property rights) and the bankrupt is well-placed to negotiate the sale. The trustee must however act reasonably in making such authorisation. It is suggested that prior compliance from the bankrupt will be required as a minimum, and the bankrupt will normally have an interest in any surplus from **4.017**

---

54 *British Eagle International Airlines Ltd v Compagnie Nationale Air France* [1975] 1 WLR 758, [1975] 2 All ER 390 (HL) 780–81 and *Belmont Park Investments Pty Ltd v BNY Corporate Trustee Services Ltd* [2011] UKSC 38 at [6]–[15].
55 See *National Westminster Bank Ltd v Halesowen Presswork and Assemblies Ltd* [1972] AC 785, [1972] 2 WLR 455, [1972] 1 All ER 641 (HL), 805.
56 Although if a party agrees to take a lower ranking position in the 'waterfall', such agreement will probably be given effect to by the courts: *Re SSSL Realisations Ltd* [2004] EWHC 1760 (Ch).
57 *Bakal v Petursson* [1953] 4 DLR 449; *London Joint City & Midland Bank v Herbert Dickinson & Co* [1922] WN 13. This is an illustration of the maxim *delegata potestas non potest delegari*: see *Denis v More* 123 ER 953.
58 Unless the contractual liability is instead formed with the company alone, which will be a matter of construction of the relevant contract: *Wright Hassall LLP v Morris* [2012] EWCA Civ 1472.
59 Section 6.F.3.
60 *Kyrris v Oldham* [2003] EWCA Civ 1506; *Reynard v Fox* [2018] EWHC 2141 (Ch). This is perhaps subject to the rare exception where a trustee may engage the bankrupt to perform a pre-existing contract.

the bankruptcy estate before it will be appropriate to adopt such a course. It follows that the same principle must also apply as between liquidators or administrators in relation to the company of which they are an agent, once the company in question is in liquidation or administration.

4.018 It is possible for an IP to enter into a contract with third parties, such as creditors.[61] One obvious example is where a claim is brought by the IP against, for example, a recipient of company property and the claim is settled,[62] in which case the contract will often be between the IP and the defendant/respondent, although it is a matter of construction of the particular contract. It is also possible for IPs to cause the company to enter into contracts with creditors, particularly where such contracts will support the efficient resolution of the insolvency process.[63] Such contracts will be governed by the normal principles of contractual formation and interpretation,[64] and will bind the parties accordingly.[65]

4.019 Although IPs will often engage third parties to assist with the insolvency process, such as valuers and solicitors, they generally do so in such a way that limits their contractual liability. This is usually achieved by contracting as an agent for the company,[66] and those expenses will usually be treated as an expense of the insolvency process. However, this starting point is subject to the clear wording of any contract of engagement (which may include a conditional contract of engagement), which may fix the IP with personal liability.[67] Should the company fail to pay in accordance with the applicable priority of expenses, the third party should prove in the insolvency in the same way as any other creditor.[68]

4.020 Where the IP contracts with a third party directly, however, any fees arising will normally be '*payable, not provable*'.[69] Although, as is explained above, the office of an IP is a personal one, IPs will usually be able to take advantage of an indemnity from the corporation where they practice, where fees are incurred in this indirect way. Such an indemnity will usually be sweeping in its terms and application. It is unlikely that IPs will ever pay for services out of

---

61 There is no longer a requirement for an IP to obtain sanction in respect of any compromise decision, although he may choose to do so, particularly if the decision is a momentous one: see *Re Nortel Networks UK Ltd* [2016] EWHC 2769 (Ch) at [46].

62 The power is given in IA 1986 Sch 4 para 2 (compulsory liquidations), applied in voluntary liquidations by s165(2); IA 1986 Sch 1 para 18 (administrators).

63 See, e.g., the use of so-called claims determination deeds in *Lehman Brothers Australia Ltd (in liquidation) v Lomas* [2018] EWHC 2783 (Ch). The practice greatly reduced the amount of work to be conducted in the insolvencies resulting from the collapse of Lehman Brothers.

64 Cf. *Hamid v Francis Bradshaw Partnership* [2013] EWCA Civ 470.

65 It is therefore unlikely that the principle in *ex parte James* (see paras 4.041–4.045 below) will have any application where a contract is entered into between company and creditor, although at the time of going to press an appeal in *Lehman Brothers Australia* appears likely.

66 *Wright Hassall v Morris* [2012] EWCA Civ 1472.

67 See *Stevensdrake v Hunt* [2015] EWHC 1527 (Ch).

68 Goode, *Principles of Corporate Insolvency Law* (4th edn, 2011) at para 11–99.

69 IA 1986 s115. Professor Goode explains this on the basis that it is a new liability that occurs after the commencement of the insolvency process. However, the author's view is that it is best explained as a matter of contractual interpretation according to the usual applicable principles. It does not necessarily follow that just because a liability arises post-liquidation, it will necessarily create a personal liability on the part of the company's agents, i.e., the IP. It is suggested that Professor Goode's statement can be understood as reflecting the relative priority of expenses of the insolvency process as compared with provable unsecured debts: see para 4.004 above.

their own pockets, although there are limits to that principle, in which case the IP may (or may not) be able to rely on professional indemnity insurance.[70]

B. STANDARD OF SKILL AND CARE

For practical purposes, neither IPs nor the courts will generally engage heavily in parsing out which source is of primary importance when measuring the conduct of the IP. Indeed, whether the source of the duty is statutory, based on common law or equitable principles, or regulatory guidance, they will generally inform each other. It is suggested that by interpreting that framework together as an iterative process, it enables the court to locate and set the requisite benchmark and determine whether the IP's conduct meets (or has met) the requisite standard. The standard is that of a reasonable IP.[71] **4.021**

1. Challenges to approach and strategy

There are two standards that apply in relation to IPs, which must be considered in turn as part of a two-step process. There is a critical difference between, first, challenges to the strategy or decisions adopted by the IP and, second, the way in which that strategy has been implemented. It is generally understood that, although every form of insolvency process is generally under the supervision of the court,[72] the court will not generally interfere with an IP's exercise of their discretion in the conduct of their office,[73] which is explicitly delegated.[74] This is a result of both the protection afforded to stakeholders in insolvency processes by IPs necessarily being licensed professionals,[75] and the general reluctance of the courts to intrude into what are essentially decisions made by commercial actors.[76] The exercise of the IP's powers will therefore almost always be by reference to what the IP – and not the court – considers to be in the best interests of the liquidation.[77] The stance routinely taken by the courts in such matters is therefore one of deference in the context of an office that is both personal and delegated,[78] unless he or she is acting unreasonably,[79] or the conduct of the IP is absurd.[80] That principle is extended further still in situations where an IP enlists the assistance of other professionals, such **4.022**

---

70 Itself another form of contract, albeit one that may have been entered into between the IP's firm and the insurer.
71 It is an objective standard, and no allowance is made for more junior IPs. Cf. the general principle in *Nettleship v Weston* [1971] 2 QB 691.
72 For example, IA 1986 ss112 and 363.
73 *Re a Debtor, ex parte the Debtor v Dodwell* [1949] Ch 236 (a bankruptcy case).
74 In the case of compulsory liquidations: IA 1986 s168(4) and in bankruptcy: s305(2).
75 See IA 1986 Pt XIII and Chapter 2 (above).
76 *Re Longmeade Ltd* [2016] EWHC 356 (Ch); *Re Lehman Brothers International (Europe) Ltd* [2009] BCC 632, [45]. A parallel can be seen, for instance, in the general unwillingness of courts to re-write contracts for parties (or to be seen to be doing as such): *Braganza v BP Shipping Ltd* [2015] UKSC 17 at [18] (Lady Hale).
77 *Re International Contract Co* [1872] WN 63; *Re East of England Banking Co* (1872) 7 Ch App 309.
78 *Davey v Money* at [590]. It follows that the court will also be reluctant to give directions on commercial decisions: *Re T&N Ltd* [2005] 2 BCLC 488; *MTI Trading Systems Ltd v Winter* [1998] BCC 591. This stands somewhat in contrast with other aspects of the insolvency framework, and indeed commercial law more generally: Wood, 'Insolvency office holder discretion and judicial intervention in commercial decisions' (2020) 6 *JBL* 451–71. See also Mace, 'Challenging administrators: can they ever do any wrong?' (2010) 4 *Corporate Rescue and Recovery* 141.
79 *Pitman v Top Business Systems Ltd* [1984] BCLC 593.
80 *Leon v York-O-Matic Ltd* [1966] 1 WLR 1450.

as valuers or solicitors. However, an IP's conduct, particularly with regard to pursuing applications promptly, may be relevant to the issue of costs.[81]

4.023 The test to be applied in reviewing an IP's decision or strategy (or what an administrator 'thinks') is similar to that which the court applies when reviewing decisions taken by company directors in the exercise of their powers.[82] It would appear, then, in the context of administration that the administrator's decision to pursue the second objective will only be open to challenge if it was made in bad faith or was clearly perverse in the sense that no reasonable IP could possibly have thought about the matter and come to that conclusion. In the bankruptcy context, as Registrar Baister put it in *Osborn v Cole*,[83] the test is that the trustee has acted in bad faith or so perversely that no trustee properly advised or properly instructing himself could so have acted, alternatively if he had acted fraudulently or in a manner so unreasonable and absurd that no reasonable person would have acted in that way.

4.024 The standard is therefore akin to the *Wednesbury* standard, which sets a high, familiar, and yet not totally certain standard for the review of the IP's conduct.[84] In the administration context, this is in keeping with the intention behind the legislative history, which expressly sought to make such decisions subject to a 'rationality' test.[85] It is therefore notoriously difficult to challenge the strategy or views of an IP, for the reason that the conduct of the insolvency is a matter for the IP, and not for the court. In the context of administrations, therefore, a wide degree of latitude is given to administrators over whatever method of sale he or she thinks appropriate,[86] the extent and breadth of advertising, and the basic requirement is only to take reasonable care to obtain the true value of the property at the moment he or she chooses to sell it.[87]

4.025 One particular area, however, where the courts have demonstrated a more interventionist approach in terms of challenges to IP strategy is in the context of pre-pack sales, especially

---

81 For example, where an extension of an administration is sought within six weeks of the administration expiry date: PDIP para 8.3; *Re Japan Leasing (Europe) Plc* [1999] BPIR 911; *Re Sabre International Products Ltd* [1991] BCC 694.

82 *Re Smith & Fawcett Ltd* [1942] Ch 304 (CA); *Charterbridge Corp Ltd v Lloyds Bank* [1970] Ch 62; *Regentcrest plc v Cohen* [2001] BCC 494; *Extrasure Travel Insurances Ltd v Scattergood* [2003] 1 BCLC 598; *Colin Gwyer & Associates Ltd v London Wharf (Limehouse) Ltd* [2002] EWHC 2748 (Ch), [2003] BCC 885; *Ultraframe (UK) Ltd v Fielding* [2006] FSR 17, [1292]–[1295], [1300]–[1302].

83 [1999] BPIR 251.

84 *Re Hans Place Ltd* [1992] BCC 737. But see *Bramston v Haut* [2012] EWHC 1279 (Ch), [2012] BPIR 672, where Arnold J suggested that the growing flexibility inherent in the *Wednesbury* test could also lead to greater flexibility with regard to applications brought under s303. See also Milman, 'Governance, stewardship and the insolvency practitioner' (2012) 321 *Co LN* 1–4.

85 See Hansard, H.L. Deb. 29 July 2002, col.768:

> The present wording would mean that if the administrator's view were then to be tested, it would be subject to a 'rationality' test – that is, his decisions would be subject to successful challenge if it could be shown that no reasonable administrator would have acted in such a way in the particular circumstances of a case. As I said, we do not think that the courts should or will second-guess the administrator's professional or commercial judgment in exercising his or her duties. The administrator is best placed to determine what is appropriate … without prejudice to the rights under para.74 of creditors or members to challenge the administrator's decision where that decision has unfairly prejudiced his or her interests.

86 *Davey v Money* [2018] EWHC 766 (Ch) at [255].

87 *Cuckmere Brick Co Ltd v Mutual Finance Ltd* [1971] Ch 949.

where a sale is arranged back to management. These particular issues are considered in more detail at paras 6.178–6.181 below.

2. Reasonable standard of skill and care

Notwithstanding that the decisions of *how* to carry out their tasks is unlikely to be interfered **4.026** with by the court, it is now well-settled that IPs owe a duty of care, enforceable through the relevant statutory processes[88] in the performance of their duties and in the exercise of their powers. This is more likely to apply in relation to the tasks which IPs *must* carry out, that is, matters in respect of which IPs do not enjoy any discretion. The requisite standard of care in relation to administrators was described by Millett J in *Re Charnley Davies Ltd (No 2)*:[89]

> An administrator must be a professional insolvency practitioner. A complaint that he has failed to take reasonable care in the sale of the company's assets is, therefore, a complaint of professional negligence and in my judgment the established principles applicable to cases of professional negligence are equally applicable in such a case. It follows that the administrator is to be judged, not by the standards of the most meticulous and conscientious member of his profession, but by those of an ordinary, skilled practitioner. In order to succeed the claimant must establish that the administrator has made an error which a reasonably skilled and careful insolvency practitioner would not have made.

The duty of care owed by a liquidator is the same as that owed by an administrator,[90] and it **4.027** seems that the same standard applies to trustees in bankruptcy.[91] Indeed, there would seem to be no justifiable basis for differentiating between the standard required of an IP in the corporate and personal contexts.

3. Misapplications and breaches of fiduciary duty

It is doubtful whether the test of reasonable care and skill applies in the context of **4.028** misapplications of company property and/or breaches of fiduciary duty. The question of whether there has been such a breach is whether the IP honestly (even if mistakenly) believed that the payment was in accordance with their fiduciary duty;[92] this will usually resolve into a question of whether the payment was in accordance with the respective rights of creditors in accordance with the statutory waterfall. A failure to exercise independent judgment, or acting for an improper purpose,[93] will constitute a breach of fiduciary duty.

4. The *Bolam* test

The measure of the standard of reasonableness in relation to a professional who exercises a **4.029** special skill means that the standard of skill and care to be expected of an IP will be raised over

---

88 Provided by IA 1986 ss212 (in liquidation in relation to a prior office-holder); 304 (in bankruptcy); Sch B1 paras 74–75 (in administration); s263(3) (in an IVA context).

89 [1990] BCLC 760, [1990] BCC 605, ChD at 618D–E.

90 *Re Mama Milla* [2014] EWHC 2753 (Ch) at [28].

91 The language of IA 1986 s304 mirrors that of s212.

92 Cf. *Progress Property Co Ltd v Moore* [2010] UKSC 55 at [32].

93 Cf. *Madoff Securities International Ltd v Raven* [2013] EWHC 3147 (Comm) at [200] ff.

that of the 'man on the Clapham omnibus'.[94] That will be, by its very nature, a relatively high standard of skill and care. But at the same time, a degree of protection is probably afforded to the IP by means of the well-known principle in *Bolam v Friern Hospital Management Committee*.[95] The test was formulated in that case as being that a doctor 'is not guilty of negligence if he has acted in accordance with a practice accepted as proper by a responsible body of medical men skilled in that particular art'.[96] The same test applies, *mutatis mutandis*, in the insolvency context as it does in the medical context.

4.030   If a claim is brought against an IP, therefore, and she can point to a reasonable body of opinion that would have acted (or refrained from acting) in the same way, then it follows that the IP will have discharged her duty, and there will have been no breach. However, the standard is that which, in the opinion of the court, members of the profession ought to achieve and not that which members of the particular profession do in fact achieve ordinarily. Thus, evidence as to general and approved practice, although of very considerable importance, is not automatically conclusive in every case.[97] In particular, the courts will take heed of the many codes of practice and other guidelines specifying what professionals should do in particular situations.[98] There is a wealth of such guidance for IPs, which will include the Code of Conduct, and 'Dear IP' updates.

4.031   Further, following the prevailing position in medical negligence law in *Montgomery v Lanarkshire Health Board*,[99] the *Bolam* test may not apply in circumstances where there is a duty to advise. This principle is more likely to come to the fore where the IP plays a pre-appointment, advisory role, and so will normally depend on the proper construction of the retainer or engagement letter.[100] This has been applied outside of the medical context in a conveyancing negligence case in Northern Ireland,[101] and in the context of risk warnings in the context of the provision of financial services in *O'Hare v Coutts & Co*.[102] In that case, Kerr J cited the decisions in *Montgomery* and *Baird*, and noted that, in the context of investment advice too, there must be proper dialogue and communication between adviser and client. He concluded at [204] that: 'I do not think the required extent of communication between financial adviser and client to ensure the client understands the advice and the risks attendant on a recommended investment, is governed by the *Bolam* test.' This might be relevant to the standard of care to be expected by the IP acting in an advisory capacity pre-appointment, but the underlying reasoning by Kerr J in *O'Hare v Coutts & Co* goes beyond that.

4.032   In drawing his conclusion, Kerr J pointed out that the relevant regulatory regime (there the Conduct of Business Rules Sourcebook ('COBS')) was strong evidence of what the common

---

94   See, e.g., *Hall v Brooklands Auto Racing Club* [1933] 1 KB 205.
95   [1957] 1 WLR 582.
96   *Bolam* at 587. The thrust of the test is that if the professional can demonstrate there was a responsible body of opinion in the same field that would have acted in the same way, no liability will attach for the purposes of the law of negligence.
97   *Jackson & Powell on Professional Liability* (8th edn) at 2-131 and 2-132. See also *Brewer v Iqbal* [2019] EWHC 182 (Ch) at [82] for an example of the unchallenged expert evidence of an IP, which appears to have been determinative of the issue of reasonable skill and care.
98   See paras 4.034 and 4.035 below.
99   [2015] UKSC 11.
100   *Minkin v Landsberg* [2015] EWCA Civ 1152 at [38]; *Lyons v Fox Williams LLP* [2018] EWCA Civ 2347.
101   *Baird v Hastings* [2015] NICA 22.
102   [2016] EWHC 2224 (QB).

law requires,[103] and a duty to explain in terms not dissimilar to the *Montgomery* formulation is found in the COBS rules.[104] He considered the content of those rules would be very difficult to square with the application of a conventional *Bolam* approach, as they do not include reference to a responsible body of opinion within the profession.[105] He was not swayed by the defendant's submission that there were differences between the medical and financial contexts – how much to say to a client was not a question to be decided according to whether the adviser acted in accordance with a practice accepted as proper by a responsible body of persons skilled in the giving of financial advice, because expert evidence tended to indicate that there is little consensus in the financial services industry about how the treatment of risk appetite should be managed by an adviser, and, as in the medical context, the extent of required communication with the client should not depend on the attitude of the individual adviser.[106]

Whether, and to what extent, these same principles could be transplanted into the duties of an **4.033** IP have not yet been the subject of detailed analysis by the courts post-*Montgomery*. However, it is the view of the authors that there may be a distinction between IPs who act as office-holders (and who are answerable primarily to the court) and a surgeon or financial adviser (who is answerable primarily to their patient or client). The duty to advise and keep creditors updated by way of reports, for example, is less likely to have any causative impact on the direction of the insolvency, although it is conceivable that a mis-advised creditor may be persuaded not to act in light of (for example) a negligent report, where it might otherwise have challenged the IP's decision by way of a decision procedure. When acting privately under a contract, however, that distinction would appear to be nugatory.

5. Professional guidance

IPs must comply with a substantial number of professional, regulatory, and ethical guidelines. **4.034** Clearly, such guidelines can be used to assist with interpreting the standard that should be achieved by IPs themselves, and will inform what the position ought to be under the common law.

Of particular relevance are the Statements of Insolvency Practice ('SIPs'). Of these, SIPs 13 **4.035** ('Disposal of assets to connected parties in an insolvency process') and 16 ('Pre-packaged sales in administrations') are the most commonly encountered. Failure to appreciate the applicability or to have regard to either SIP will be strong indicators of a failure to act with due care and skill in respect of the IP's dealings as the IP in relation to the Company.[107] One point that is made clear in both SIPs 13 and 16 is the need for IPs to keep track of their changing role in pre- and post-appointment scenarios. The overriding obligation can be interpreted as one of transparency, and the need to disclose how the IP has acted with due regard to creditors' interests, by providing them with a proportionate and sufficiently detailed justification of why the sale was undertaken, and the alternatives that were not taken.[108] Additional colour may be added to

---

103 Citing *Loosemore v Financial Concepts (a firm)* [2001] Lloyds Rep PN 235, 241 (HHJ Jack QC); *Green v Royal Bank of Scotland (FCA intervening)* [2013] EWCA Civ 1197, [2014] Bus LR 168 (Tomlinson LJ) at [18].
104 In particular rr2.2.1(1) and 2.2.2(1)(b); r4.2.1(1); rr9.2.1, 9.2.2, 9.2.3 and 9.2.6.
105 [208]–[209].
106 [204]–[205].
107 *Brewer v Iqbal* [2019] EWHC 182 (Ch) at [80].
108 SIP 13 paras 5 and 9; SIP 16 paras 2, 5, 10, 16–17.

the IP's role through the 'Dear IP' newsletter circulated by the Insolvency Service, and may be referred to in court as evidence of common or competent practice.[109]

6. Reliance on advice

4.036   The duty of an IP to act in accordance with the above standard of skill and care must also be interpreted in light of the availability of advice. Often an IP will not need to rely on the *Bolam* test, or even the protection generally afforded to him as a commercial actor, as he will often be able to rely on the advice of experts, including solicitors and/or counsel. As Maugham J observed in *Re Home & Colonial Insurance Co Ltd*:[110]

> ... a high standard of care and diligence is required from a liquidator in a voluntary winding up. He is of course paid for his services; he is able to obtain whenever it is expedient the assistance of solicitors and counsel; and, which is a most important consideration, he is entitled, in every case of serious doubt or difficulty in relation to the performance of his statutory duties, to submit the matter to the Court, and to obtain guidance.

4.037   It also relevant that an IP will not normally have to pay out of his own pocket for such advice, as such advice will usually rank as an expense of the insolvency process and be payable from the estate. IPs (and most commonly trustees) will routinely rely on the services of estate agents and surveyors when realising real property for the benefit of the estate.[111] A failure properly to ascertain the value of a company's assets by failing to obtain a proper valuation will likely constitute a failure to exercise reasonable care and skill.[112]

4.038   A recent illustration of this principle is *Brewer v Iqbal*.[113] Chief ICC Judge Briggs held that the administrator had placed too much reliance on the directors of the company to provide a value for certain Guides (known as 'EPGs'), approval for marketing on a website, and the timing of the sale of the EPGs. Therefore, while ascertaining the views of stakeholders will not necessarily go against the grain of the IP's duty,[114] if there is undue reliance on those views, then the IP will expose himself to liability. This principle may be more likely to apply where there is something unusual about the asset. The EPGs in *Brewer v Iqbal* were a specific category of intangible asset with a *'restrictive but competitive'* market. There were specialist EPG acquisition and sales agents, and it appears that knowledge of this fact should have been acted on by the IP for him to have discharged his duty to the company. This was the type of case where a competent administrator would probably have taken independent advice as to the marketing and selling from more than one agent, as the asset class was unusual and unfamiliar.[115] By not taking such advice, the IP ran the risk that the sale would be for an undervalue.

---

109   As in *Safier v Wardell* [2017] EWHC 20 (Ch) at [22]. The Dear IP guidance was used as evidence of common practice and, in turn, whether the Secretary of State fee was to apply to sums paid into the Insolvency Services Account.

110   [1930] 1 Ch 102.

111   The most common being sale of the family home under IA 1986 s 283A.

112   See *American Express International Banking Corp v Hurley* [1985] 3 All ER 564, (1986) 2 BCC 98993, a case concerning a receiver.

113   [2019] EWHC 182 (Ch).

114   See *Davey v Money* at [592].

115   *Brewer v Iqbal* at [88].

A liquidator who exercises powers in good faith after taking proper advice is not generally open to challenge.[116] This also extends to the situation where an IP who relies upon apparently competent advice should not be liable if that advice turns out to be wrong, unless the decision which he takes is outside the scope of his powers or contrary to the law. IPs will therefore generally be likely to obtain appropriate advice (and especially legal advice) prior to commencing litigation or entering into compromises and, to an extent, this will be expected by the court.[117] The costs of obtaining such advice will almost always rank as an expense of the insolvency process,[118] and will usually be paid out of the assets of the company. There is therefore every reason for an IP to seek such advice. **4.039**

The obvious caveat to the proposition that reasonable advice will offer a degree of protection to the IP is that instructions must have been correctly given in the first place.[119] Where advice has been sought on the basis of erroneous or incomplete instructions, therefore, the potential for protection falls away. It is imperative that the IP still investigates the affairs of the company accurately and gives the correct impression to those from whom advice is sought. **4.040**

7. The rule in *ex parte James*

The duties of an IP are also subject to a requirement that, in rare instances, IPs should not rely on their strict legal rights. The statutory or common law duties to pay or discharge only liabilities which are legally enforceable is tempered by the rule in *ex parte James*,[120] which has been stated in various terms by the courts. The statement of the principle given by Salter J in *In re Wigzell* is the most often cited:[121] **4.041**

> The legal right is clear. The money claimed by the trustee is vested in him and divisible among the creditors by the express terms of the Act. The Court of Appeal, however, have repeatedly decided that where a bankrupt's estate is being administered by the trustee under the supervision of a court that court has a discretionary jurisdiction to disregard legal right, and that such jurisdiction should be exercised wherever the enforcement of legal right would, in the opinion of the court, be contrary to natural justice.

The purpose of the rule stems from the expectation that, in the administration of assets on an insolvency, the court will expect its own officer to behave as honestly as other people.[122] It will accordingly direct him to act 'in an honourable and high-minded way',[123] even if this means **4.042**

---

116 *Davey v Money, Re Burnells Pty Ltd (in liq) ex p Brown and Burns* (1979) 4 ACLR 213; *Re Charnley Davies Ltd (No 2)*; *Re Home & Colonial Insurance Co Ltd* and *Pitt v Holt* [2013] UKSC 26, [2013] 2 AC 108.

117 *State Bank of NSW v Turner Corp Ltd* (1994) 14 ACSR 480, 483.

118 IR 2016 rr7.108(4)(a)(ii) (compulsory liquidation); 6.42(4)(a) (creditors' voluntary liquidation); 10.149(a)(i) (bankruptcy). However, in a liquidation, litigation expenses of more than £5,000 may not be paid from floating charge assets unless the necessary approval or authorisation has been provided: IA 1986 s176ZA(3) and IR 2016 rr7.111–116 (compulsory liquidation) and 6.44–48 (creditors' voluntary liquidation).

119 *Re Mama Milla* [2014] EWHC 2753 (Ch) at [170].

120 LR 9 Ch.App. 609.

121 *Ex parte Hart* [1921] 2 KB 835, 845. This statement was affirmed by the Court of Appeal.

122 *Ex parte James* at 614 (James LJ).

123 *Ex parte Simmonds* (1885) 16 QBD 308 (Lord Esher MR).

'overriding rights which persons interested might otherwise be entitled to claim on a strict application of the rules of law and of equity, in the technical sense'.[124]

4.043 The rule in *ex parte James* is of some antiquity and, as a result, now seems somewhat entrenched, notwithstanding that it has been described as inherently vague,[125] anomalous,[126] difficult to apply,[127] and the facts of the case itself that established the principle (where a liquidator retained money paid under a mistake of law), would in any event lead to the case being decided differently today.[128] It is submitted that the rule is also outdated, because of its reliance on morality, conscience, and general fairness as the touchstone of its application. That is inherently difficult to square with the wholly different way in which insolvency processes are conducted in the modern day, by licensed IPs in line with the wishes of creditors, who are often themselves commercial actors. The anomalies of *ex p James* are also exacerbated by the lack of clarity as to which office-holders will be bound its application. For example, in *Re TH Knitwear*, it was held that the rule did not apply in cases of voluntary liquidation, although the opposite conclusion was reached in *Re Temple Fire & Accident Assurance Co*[129] on the basis that the alternative conclusion would give rise to an unjustifiable distinction between voluntary and compulsory liquidations.[130]

4.044 In sum although the rule is widely known and is still good law, the view of the author is that it has now become superfluous to requirements. It is unlikely that Parliamentary time in the modern era would be given over to debate of the rule, and so the general restriction of the rule by the courts is to be welcomed. In the view of the author, it is submitted that the rule has outlived its purpose, and it would be better if the rule were to be abolished.

4.045 The rule has, however, been revitalised in *Lehman Brothers Australia Ltd v MacNamara*.[131] The circumstances of that case involved the so-called 'claims determination deeds' used in the administration of Lehman Brothers International (Europe). The deeds were intended to fix (on an agreed basis) the creditors' claims in the administration. One creditor assented to a deed on a figure which, it later transpired, was significantly lower than the creditor had been entitled to. After consideration of the authorities, the Court of Appeal allowed the creditor's appeal and permitted the creditor to submit a proof in excess of the deed, holding that 'no right-thinking person would think it fair for the administrators to stand on their strict contractual rights and refuse to correct a shared mistake for which they were responsible'.[132] The case may turn on the particular fact that the fault for the currency conversion error was shared between creditor and office-holder, but in the view of the author it is nevertheless disconcerting that the effect of the decision will have undermined the finality and utility of the claims determination deeds, which were entered into by sophisticated commercial parties.

---

124 *Re TH Knitwear* [1988] Ch 275, 288C.
125 *Re Wigzell* [1921] 2 KB 835, 858 (Scrutton LJ).
126 *Lomas v Burlington Loan Management Ltd* [2015] EWHC 2270 (Ch) (David Richards J).
127 See Dawson, 'Corporate rescue by the upright rescuer – a trap for the unwary' (2016) 29(6) *Insolv Int* 81–6.
128 The crucial distinction between mistakes of fact and law having been removed by the House of Lords in *Kleinwort Benson Ltd v Lincoln CC* [1999] 2 AC 349.
129 (1910) 129 LTJo 115.
130 Milman argues that the justification for the distinction between office-holders and officers of the court has largely disappeared: 'Insolvency office-holders: recent developments and future possibilities' (2018) 412 *Co LN* 1–5.
131 [2020] EWCA Civ 321.
132 *Lehman Brothers Australia* at [103].

8. Comparison with directors

Passing references have been made above to some of the similarities that exist between the roles **4.046** played by directors and IPs when they take office. As has been noted above, the appointment of a liquidator or administrator will effectively replace the directors on the making of the winding-up order, the resolution to wind up, or the company being placed into administration.[133] With the exception of a company that exits administration and returns to solvency (such as a comparatively rare 'Objective 1' administration), or where the IP acts as supervisor, the IP will be the agent for the company until the administration or liquidation comes to an end and the IP vacates office.

As such, the IP generally has all the powers of a director, including to continue trading.[134] **4.047** However, the first key difference is that IPs must exercise those powers with a view to achieving their fundamental purpose, which will usually be to realise the company's assets for the benefit of creditors. IPs will therefore be unlikely in practice to take the kind of commercial risks that directors may be more accustomed to taking, although as long as they undertake those strategies in a way that is rational and in good faith, it is submitted that those decisions would be unlikely to be challenged successfully.[135]

The emphasis on realising, selling, and distributing as a 'default position' as a matter of practice **4.048** and of law therefore stands in contrast to the so-called 'rescue culture' that was one of the original guiding principles behind the Cork Report,[136] and continued to underpin the reforms in the Enterprise Act 2002 ('EA 2002') and Small Business Enterprise and Employment Act 2015 ('SBEEA 2015').[137] The duty of augmenting the assets of the company[138] and achieving the best result for creditors is therefore a moderate one; notwithstanding the power of IPs to continue to trade,[139] there is no obligation to achieve the very best result for creditors, and there is correspondingly no need for IPs to take on commercial risk with a view to achieving better results.

One obvious exception to the above principle is where an IP acts as an administrator of a **4.049** company, and where he thinks that the company may be rescued as a going concern. In such cases, the IP may be more accustomed to taking commercial risks with a view to achieving that goal. In doing so, the IP typically plays a role closer to that of a turnaround manager.

Like directors, the duties of IPs are enforceable by the provisions of the IA 1986. In particular, **4.050** the same mechanism that is used to provide a summary remedy against delinquent directors in IA 1986 s212 may also be used to bring a claim of the company against a liquidator, and so opens the way for claims in respect of 'any misfeasance or breach of any fiduciary or other duty'

---

133 Unless the exceptional step is taken by a liquidation committee or the company's creditors sanctioning their continuance in office: IA 1986 s103. Note however in s103 that whilst the powers of the directors cease, the duties do not.

134 Sch 1 para 14 (administrators and administrative receivers); Sch 4 para 5 (liquidators); Sch 5 para 1 (trustees in bankruptcy); Sch B1 para 59(1).

135 For the reasons stated above at 4.022–4.025.

136 See the Cork Report at paras 218, 496, 732, 1500–1502, 1511, 1800.

137 Productivity and Enterprise: Insolvency—A Second Chance (DTI, TSO, 2002).

138 *Re Tavistock Ironworks Co* (1871) 24 L.T. 605.

139 For example, IA 1986 Sch 4 para 5 (in the case of liquidators).

in connection with carrying out the functions of his office.[140] IA 1986 s212 is however not available to administrators, and so as a matter of procedure the company must be a claimant to any such claim in administration.[141] Claims brought against administrators may be brought under paragraphs 74 and/or 75 of Schedule B1 to the IA 1986. Both creditors and the current IP have standing to bring proceedings, but the court can only make an order in favour of the company, because it is the claim of the company that is being brought.

C. GENERAL DUTIES

4.051 In fulfilling their statutory and fiduciary duties, and in acting with reasonable care and skill, the following general duties apply generally to IPs, whichever type of role they fulfil.

1. Duty to act within powers

4.052 As a fiduciary, an IP must act within his powers. Unlike a director, whose powers are established by the company's constitution, an IP's powers will primarily be found in the IA 1986 and the IR 2016. In particular, the powers of the IP are set out in the Schedules to the IA 1986. For the purposes of this volume, the key Schedules are in relation to: administrators/administrative receivers (Sch 1), liquidators (Sch 4), and trustees in bankruptcy (Sch 5). If an IP doubts whether he has power to take a particular course of action, the IP may be able to seek the consent of creditors (by analogy with the director-shareholder protection afforded by the *Duomatic* principle),[142] or make an application to the court for directions.

4.053 However, any act done by the IP will not be void solely because the IP was not appointed in accordance with the correct procedure.[143] This is to be contrasted with where the appointment is a complete nullity from the outset.[144] Therefore, while an IP may not have any *de jure* power at all to perform the act in question, it appears that such acts will be voidable, rather than void. Further or alternatively, they will also be capable of ratification under IR 2016 r12.64, which has come to provide a safety valve in respect of invalid or questionably valid appointments.[145]

---

140 IA 1986 s212(2).

141 The company must be joined as a co-claimant in cases where the administrators seek to bring other claims that are those of the office-holder (and not of the company).

142 There was previously a requirement for IPs to seek the creditors' sanction before commencing some forms of litigation: see IA 1986 Sch 4 para 3A. Although the requirement for sanction has been abolished by SBEEA 2015 s120, it may still be prudent for IPs to seek the views of creditors, particularly where the claim is to be brought against a defendant/respondent whose asset position is unknown.

143 IA 1986 s232; *Cash Generator Ltd v Fortune* [2018] EWHC 674 (Ch) (non-compliance with the notice provision in IA 1986 s100 did not result in an invalid appointment). See also *SJ Henderson & Co* [2019] EWHC 2742 (Ch).

144 *Re Kaupthing Capital Partners II Master LP Inc* [2010] EWHC 836 (Ch).

145 See, e.g., the discussion on out-of-court appointments at paras 3.074–3.077.

2. Duty to act independently

As a fiduciary, an IP must exercise independent judgment. He must not simply allow another **4.054** person to dictate to him how he should exercise his powers as administrator. Nor should he unquestioningly act in accordance with the wishes of another. That proposition has been described as:

> an obvious consequence of the fact that the office of administrator is a personal office under the Insolvency Act 1986 and the relevant authority and statutory powers are given to the administrator and not anyone else. They are also consistent with the general principles that govern the exercise of discretionary powers by fiduciaries.[146]

However, this does not mean that IPs cannot take into account the wishes of the relevant **4.055** creditor(s) whose interests are likely to be affected by the decisions he takes. IPs are at liberty to consult with those creditors to ascertain their views, and in many cases it will be entirely sensible that they do so. They are not, however, bound to follow their wishes.[147] Where IPs are considering whether to bring, settle, or assign a claim, it may also be prudent for them to seek the views of creditors before taking that course, so as to ensure that the interests of creditors are being served. As a matter of practice, seeking informed consent from creditors before taking any step in litigation will make it difficult for those creditors later to challenge the conduct of the IP.

3. Duty to investigate affairs

As intimated above, the purpose of IPs investigating the affairs of an insolvent company or **4.056** bankrupt is directed towards the fuller ascertainment and realisation of the relevant assets, including any choses in action, so that a distribution can be properly effected in accordance with the statutory scheme. Under this rubric falls the investigation of any books and records,[148] interviews and examinations of relevant persons involved with the insolvent person or entity.

The starting point for any investigation will be the statement of affairs, which must be signed **4.057** by the bankrupt or a director. The director or bankrupt has a statutory duty to comply with the requests of the IP,[149] although in practice cooperation may not be forthcoming (particularly in bankruptcy cases). Cooperation can be enforced by way of an application to court, for example, under IA 1986 s236 for inspection of the books and records of the company,[150] or by an application to suspend a bankrupt's discharge,[151] which is intentionally penal in nature.[152]

The IP may also seek an examination of an officer of the company, or parties who may have **4.058** relevant property or information in their possession, which would enable them better to understand the company's position. Where an examination is conducted by the OR, it will be

---

146 *Davey v Money* at [590]. See also *Pitt v Holt* [2013] 2 AC 108 at [66] and [81] in relation to trustees.
147 *Davey v Money* at [592].
148 IA 1986 s234.
149 Ibid s235(3); *Smedley v Brittain* [2008] BPIR 219 at [71].
150 Section 236 also carries extraterritorial effect: see *Re Carna Meats (UK) Ltd* [2019] EWHC 2503 (Ch).
151 Under IA 1986 s279(3).
152 *Shierson v Rastogi* [2007] EWHC 1266 (Ch) at [65].

in public,[153] although both private IPs and the OR may seek an interview, which is inevitably more informal, and takes place outside of the statutory regime. Evidence given in the interview will, however, be admissible in court. There is no general requirement for a bankrupt to be 'cautioned' or warned about the import of giving evidence in interview, although as a matter of practice and transparency, that may be desirable.

4.059 There is also a general duty to carry out duties with appropriate vigour, speedily and responsibly.[154] Therefore, even where a trustee in bankruptcy may be considered to have been over-zealous in the conduct of his office, it is unlikely that that will by itself expose him or her to liability.[155] However, notwithstanding this provision, applications to court to extend the period of an administration are still likely to be granted, so long as one of the objectives sought to be achieved by the administration may still be possible.[156] There is therefore a tension between the requirement to act with appropriate speed and the relatively 'light touch' that courts apply when it comes to extensions of the administration, provided that the application is made at least a month before the end of the period of administration.[157]

D. ACCOUNTING AND DISCLOSURE REQUIREMENTS

4.060 The first duty of an IP will usually be to inform others that the insolvency process has begun. Therefore, the first task of a voluntary liquidator will be to publish a notice in the London Gazette and to file a copy with the registrar of companies.[158] Where a compulsory winding up or bankruptcy order is made, the OR must as soon as reasonably practicable cause the notice to be advertised, stating the date of the order. Administrators must similarly send a notice of their appointment to the company, advertise the making of the order and lodge a notice with the registrar of companies.[159]

1. Progress reports

4.061 In all insolvency procedures, progress reports must be produced in order to provide an update to creditors, members in MVLs, and to the public via Companies House in corporate cases. These are usually at annual intervals, apart from in administrations where they are at six-monthly intervals.[160] In an administration and a receivership which either is an administrative receivership, or where the receiver is otherwise dealing with property which falls under a qualifying floating charge, a proposal or report is required close to the outset in order to inform stakeholders of what has been done to date and what the office-holder proposes to do. The purpose of the reporting is to keep stakeholders appraised of developments in the case and to give confidence as regards the work being undertaken by the IP.

---

153   IA 1986 s133.
154   *Re Keypak Homecare Ltd* (1987) 3 BCC 558; Sch B1 para 4.
155   *Smedley v Brittain* at [24], [73].
156   IA 1986 Sch B1 paras 76(2), 77(1).
157   Practice Direction on Insolvency Proceedings para 8.3.
158   IA 1986 s109; IR 2016 r6.23.
159   Ibid Sch B1 para 46.
160   The reason being that the 'default' duration of an administration is one year: Sch B1 para 76.

The Legislative Reform (Insolvency) (Miscellaneous Provisions) Order 2010 removed the **4.062** requirement to hold annual meetings of members and (in CVLs) creditors for voluntary liquidation cases commenced from 6 April 2010, and at the same time the Insolvency (Amendment) Rules 2010 brought in a requirement for a progress report instead for these types of cases and also for bankruptcies and compulsory liquidations which previously had no annual reporting requirements. This created a consistency in reporting across all types of liquidation and bankruptcy.

SIP 7 sets out principles relating to disclosure of information which apply in all cases. In **4.063** particular:

> Information provided by an office holder, including information about receipts and payments, should be presented in a manner which is transparent, consistent and useful to creditors and other interested parties, whilst being proportionate to the circumstances of the case.[161]

Failure to comply with the requirement to deliver or make any return, account, or document, **4.064** or failure to give any notice may lead to an application by a creditor or contributory or by the registrar of companies (where appropriate) ordering the liquidator to make good the default within a specific time.[162] IPs also have obligations to report criminal offences in certain circumstances.[163]

2. Accounting for funds held

SIP 11 sets out general principles and standards around the handling of funds by IPs. It is **4.065** important that office-holders can clearly identify at any time the funds belonging to each estate over which they are appointed, and therefore that creditors and other stakeholders have confidence that their interests are protected. The key compliance standard relating to record keeping is: 'Office holders should ensure that records are maintained to identify estate money (including interest earned thereon) for each case for which they are office holder and document transactions involving such funds.'[164]

In the case of compulsory liquidations and bankruptcies, office-holders are required to bank all **4.066** funds received into the Insolvency Services Account.[165] There is an exception where the office-holder intends to carry on the business of the company or the bankrupt, in which case the office-holder may obtain permission from the Secretary of State to open a local bank account for ease of use.[166] However, it is rare for a liquidator or trustee to trade the business of the company or debtor, and therefore the provision is seldom used.[167]

---

161 SIP 7 para 3.
162 IA 1986 s170.
163 Ibid ss7A, 218(3), (4), 262B. Where an offence of false representation under IA 1986 ss6A or 262A is made with respect to a proposal for the purpose of obtaining a voluntary arrangement, the Insolvency Service will pass potential offences on to the BEIS Criminal Enforcement for consideration where appropriate. See further, 'Potential criminal offences and how to report' (2013) 26(3) *Insolv Int* 33–7.
164 SIP 11 (England and Wales) para 5.
165 The Insolvency Regulations 1994 regs 5(1) and 20(1).
166 Ibid regs 6(2) and 21(1).
167 See comment at para 4.048 above.

4.067 In all other types of case, office-holders are free to open an account with any bank of their choosing, provided that the requirements of SIP 11 are met. A variety of high street and online banks are used for this purpose.

3. Progress reports in administration, winding up and bankruptcy

4.068 The basic contents of progress reports are the same across administration, all types of winding up, and bankruptcy. As well as standard details about the case, office-holders are required to provide details of the progress made in the period including a summary of receipts and payments, information about remuneration, expenses and distributions, and what remains to be done.[168]

4.069 In administrations, a progress report is required every six months starting from the date the company entered administration. It must be delivered to the creditors and to the registrar of companies within one month of the period covered by the progress report.[169]

4.070 In liquidations and bankruptcies, a progress report must be prepared every 12 months starting on the date of appointment of the first liquidator or trustee (other than the OR).[170] The office-holder has two months from the end of the period covered by the report to deliver it to the creditors and, in corporate cases, to the members of the company and to the registrar. However, there is no requirement to deliver a progress report to creditors in an MVL as all creditors should have been paid by this point in accordance with the declaration of solvency.[171]

4. Progress reports in voluntary arrangements

4.071 In a CVA and an IVA, the supervisor must produce reports 'on the progress and prospects for the full implementation' of the arrangement.[172] Where the supervisor is handling funds belonging to the estate, the report should also include a summary of receipts of payments.[173] There are no detailed requirements as to the contents of the reports, although the proposals could prescribe matters for disclosure. Reports must be prepared every 12 months starting on the date of approval of the voluntary arrangement[174] and delivered within two months of each anniversary.[175] The report must be delivered to the creditors bound by the arrangement, and in an IVA, to the debtor, whilst in a CVA the report must also be delivered to the registrar, the company, the members[176] and the auditors (if any and if the company is not in liquidation).[177]

---

168 IR 2016 r18.3(1).
169 IR 2016 r18.6.
170 IR 2016 rr18.7(1) and 18.8(1).
171 IR 2016 rr18.7(6), 18.8(5) and 18.8(6). This is subject to the conversion of an MVL into CVL should it transpire that, notwithstanding the declaration of solvency, the creditors are not able to be paid in full.
172 IR 2016 rr2.41(4) and 8.28(4).
173 IR 2016 rr2.41(9) and 8.28(8).
174 IR 2016 rr2.41(6) and 8.28(5).
175 IR 2016 rr2.41(7) and 8.28(6).
176 Although the court may dispense with or alter the requirement to deliver the report to members, perhaps if the company is public and there is a large number of shareholders.
177 IR 2016 rr2.41(4) and 8.28(4).

5. Final reports and accounts

At the conclusion of an insolvency procedure, office-holders are required to produce a final **4.072** account or report to the stakeholders. The contents are similar to those required for progress reports,[178] although the detailed provisions vary by case type. The requirement to provide a final account also exists where a bankruptcy is annulled,[179] notwithstanding that the effect of the bankruptcy is generally that the bankruptcy is deemed not to have existed. It is suggested that this step is something of a formality where an application for annulment has been made soon after the bankruptcy order, but nevertheless must be complied with.

6. Disclosure relating to office-holder's remuneration

There is a particular sensitivity surrounding office-holders' remuneration. Office-holders are **4.073** often in the unusual position of, on one hand via their firm issuing a request for payment of fees to the estate and, at the same time, deciding on behalf of the estate whether certain fees should be paid, including their own fees. Criticisms of IP fees are often made by bankrupts, ex-directors, and even judges (especially in county courts), even though it is axiomatic that the process exists for the benefit of creditors, who routinely affirm the proposed bases and rates of remuneration proposed by IPs themselves.[180] In light of this responsibility and the sensitivities involved, a high degree of transparency and accountability is expected of office-holders.

Information about the remuneration and expenses of the office-holder is required in progress **4.074** reports in administration, winding up and bankruptcy, including the basis fixed for remuneration, the amounts charged in the period of the report, whether any fees estimate or estimate of expenses is likely to be exceeded and a statement of the rights of creditors and members to request further information and to challenge the office-holder's remuneration and expenses.[181] A challenge can also be brought by a bankrupt in bankruptcy cases where a surplus accrues to the bankrupt, or in conjunction with an application for annulment on the basis that all the debts and expenses of the bankruptcy have been paid.[182]

SIPs 7 and 9 set out disclosure requirements in addition to those in statute surrounding **4.075** payments to office-holders and their associates. As well as such payments, an office-holder should disclose:

> any business or personal relationships with parties responsible for approving his or her remuneration or who provide services to the office holder in respect of the insolvency appointment where the relationship could give rise to a conflict of interest.[183]

---

178 Ibid r18.14.
179 Ibid r10.141.
180 Although in the majority of insolvencies, many creditors often choose not to play any active role in the insolvency process.
181 IR 2016 r18.4.
182 That is, under IA 1986 s282(1)(b); IR 2016 r10.134.
183 SIP 9 para 6.

7. Requests for further information in administration, winding up and bankruptcy

4.076   Creditors and members (with security, 5 per cent voting value or the permission of the court) may request further information about the remuneration or expenses of the office-holder in an administration, winding up or bankruptcy.[184] The request (or application to court for permission) must be made within 21 days of receipt of a progress report or a final report.[185] This provides a window of opportunity for more details to be obtained, and may be a precursor to a challenge to the office-holder's remuneration.[186]

4.077   Where the office-holder receives such a request for information, he or she has 14 days within which either to provide some or all of the information requested or to decline all or part of the request,[187] in which case an explanation must be given of the reasons for refusal.[188] The allowable reasons for refusal are set out in the Rules.[189]

4.078   If any creditor or member is dissatisfied with the reason for refusal (or if the office-holder has not responded within the 14-day time frame), the creditor or member may make an application to court,[190] and the court may make such order as it thinks just.[191]

8. Requests for further information in voluntary arrangements

4.079   Where a nominee or supervisor of a voluntary arrangement is remunerated on the basis of time costs, details of the time spent must be provided on request.[192] In a CVA the request may be made by a director of the company and, where the proposal has been approved, any creditor or member.[193] In an IVA the debtor and, where the proposal has been approved, a creditor bound by the IVA may make the request.[194] The information provided must cover a period from appointment to the end of the most recent six month anniversary of appointment or, if the office-holder has ceased to act, for the whole of the period during which he or she was appointed.[195] The content is somewhat limited: the total hours spent, average hourly rate per grade of staff engaged on the matter and the number of hours spent by each grade of staff must be provided.[196]

---

184   IR 2016 r18.9(1).
185   IR 2016 r18.9(2).
186   On which, see paras 6.240–6.248 below on challenges to office-holder remuneration.
187   IR 2016 r18.9(3).
188   IR 2016 r18.9(5).
189   See IR 2016 r18.9(4).
190   IR 2016 r18.9(6).
191   IR 2016 r18.9(7).
192   IR 2016 rr2.45(1) and (2), 8.38(1) and (2).
193   IR 2016 r2.45(3).
194   IR 2016 r8.38(3).
195   IR 2016 rr2.45(4), 8.38(4).
196   IR 2016 rr2.45(5), 8.38(5).

E. VALUATION OF CREDITOR CLAIMS

In broad terms, insolvencies are conducted democratically, by reference to the voting power of **4.080** creditors.[197] The votes of creditors are to be determined by reference to the relative weight of their financial interest in the estate and – it should follow – the outcome of the process. In general, the views of the majority in value will dictate how the process is conducted, within the scope of the IP's statutory and fiduciary obligations.[198] In turn, this requires that the liquidator ascertains the debt outstanding to each creditor, by reference to their proof of debt.[199]

These issues are particularly acute in the context of CVAs, IVAs, and the appointment of IPs, **4.081** where votes cast will have the greatest impact on: (i) the outcome of the procedure or (ii) who will take office as an IP. Reference should be made in particular to IR 2016 Part 15, and the revised SIP 6. The key starting point is IR 2016 r15.31, which provides that votes are to be calculated according to the amount of each creditor's claim. Once the correct date has been identified and the currency exchange rate (if there is one) has been settled, ascertained or certain claims, principally liquidated debts, will usually give rise to little difficulty.

Issues arise where a creditor's claim is yet to be ascertained. IR 2016 r15.31(2) gives the **4.082** creditor a right to vote in respect of a debt of an unliquidated or unascertained amount 'if the convenor or chair decides to put upon it an estimated minimum value for the purpose of entitlement to vote and admits the claim for that purpose'. This is qualified slightly in the cases of CVAs and IVAs, where an unliquidated or unascertained debt is to be valued at £1 for the purposes of voting unless the convenor or chair or an appointed person decides to put a higher value on it.[200]

The IP's decision is subject to appeal to the court by a creditor, contributory, bankrupt, or **4.083** debtor.[201] In practice, this will bring about the determination of the claim by the court; the review is *de novo*, and is not limited to a review of whether the IP adopted the appropriate process.[202] It is therefore different from other types of challenge to the IP's decision, which are subject to a *Wednesbury*-type standard of review.[203] It must be sought within 21 days of the date of the decision under review.[204] If the decision is reversed or varied, the court may order another decision procedure to be initiated, or make such order as it thinks just,[205] but, in the CVA/IVA situation, the court may only make an order if it considers that the circumstances gave rise to unfair prejudice or material irregularity.[206]

---

197 Significant inroads have been made into the concept of creditors' meetings, however, through the introduction of virtual meetings and the 'deemed consent procedure' in IA 1986 ss246ZF and 379ZB, inserted by SBEEA 2015 ss122, 123.
198 IR 2016 r15.34.
199 If a creditor has not proved, they will not be entitled to vote: IR 2016 r15.28.
200 IR 2016 r15.31(3).
201 Ibid r15.35(1). And also by a member in the case of a CVA: r15.35(2).
202 *Revenue and Customs Commissioners v Maxwell* [2010] EWCA Civ 1379. The IP will only in a rare case be liable for the costs of the appeal: *Nimat Halal Food Ltd* [2020] EWHC 734 (Ch).
203 See Trower, 'Challenging officeholder decisions' (2020) 33(1) *Insolv Int* 23–6, referring to *Re Nortel Group* [2016] EWHC 2769 (Ch).
204 IR 2016 r15.35(4).
205 Ibid r15.35(3).
206 That is, the two bases on which a CVA or IVA can be challenged by a creditor.

F. DUTIES PARTICULAR TO DIFFERENT TYPES OF IP

4.084 The core duties of an IP will remain constant, regardless of the office that they hold. Whether the assets of a bankrupt vest in a trustee in bankruptcy, or whether the liquidator remains in charge of those assets (which remain vested in the insolvent company), will not normally have any bearing on how the IP goes about their job. It is suggested that the ordering of the powers in Schedules 1, 4, and 5 (relating to administrators, liquidators, and trustees in bankruptcy, respectively) reflect the nuances in their respective offices.[207]

4.085 Comparing the various powers of administrators, liquidators, and trustees in bankruptcy shows that there are many similarities between their roles. Some of the differences are apparently the result of the paragraphs being worded differently; there is no distinction of substance between the roles. However, there are some key differences, which are discussed below. Tables AI.1 and AII.1 in Annexes I and II attempt to compare and contrast the relevant paragraphs, although some comparisons are more exact than others.

4.086 Schedule 1 paragraph 1 gives administrators the power to '*take possession of, collect and get in the property of the company*'. The secondary part of that power, that is, '*to take such proceedings as may seem to him expedient*' arguably encompasses all of the other powers of the administrator.[208] This is a noticeable omission from Schedules 4 and 5, but is readily explicable on the basis that the liquidator's core duty[209] requires them to do what paragraph 1 permits administrators to do. Similarly, trustees in bankruptcy do not require the power to get in the assets of the bankrupt, because the assets will have vested on the making of the bankruptcy order.[210]

1. Duties of liquidators in CVLs and MVLs

4.087 The duties of liquidators in CVLs and MVLs are essentially the same as the duties of liquidators in compulsory liquidations. The core duty remains a requirement to get in and realise the assets of the estate for the benefit of creditors, and then to distribute the assets in accordance with the interests of those interested in the process in accordance with the statutory 'waterfall'.

4.088 The assets of the company must be distributed in accordance with the following scheme. Only where the liabilities of the higher level have been fully paid will assets be available for the next level of creditor (hence the 'waterfall' description):[211]

    (1) fixed charged creditors (which fall outside of the liquidation);
    (2) Official Receiver fees and expenses;[212]

---

207   See Annexes I and II at pp 297, 302.
208   See also Sch B1 para 59(1).
209   IA 1986 s107. See para 4.004 above.
210   IA 1986 ss283 and 306.
211   See para 4.004 above.
212   IA 1986 s174A(2)(a).

(3)   moratorium debts;[213]

(4)   the expenses of the winding up, including the liquidator's remuneration;[214]

(5)   the preferential debts;[215]

(6)   any preferential charge on goods distrained that arises under IA 1986 s176(3);

(7)   floating charge creditors;

(8)   the company's general unsecured creditors;

(9)   statutory interest;

(10) non-provable liabilities;

(11) any debts or other sums due from the company to its members qua members.[216]

Therefore, while CVLs strictly take place outside the court's processes, and liquidators in CVLs are not officers of the court,[217] a liquidator of a CVL has all of the powers of a liquidator in a compulsory liquidation. The *quid pro quo* is that they can be made subject to the oversight of the court in a similar way.[218]

The key difference with MVLs is that, unlike in most insolvency processes, there will often be **4.089** a surplus for the benefit of shareholders. The statutory waterfall remains the same, but the company will usually be solvent, meaning that the assets will make it to the plunge basin at the bottom of the waterfall. The IP's duties will therefore extend to shareholders. However, IPs must bear in mind that their duties are still governed by their above sources of duty, including the central requirement that IPs must rely on their own judgement, and not merely defer to the opinion of their appointees (the shareholder(s)). In particular, if it transpires that the company is in fact insolvent, then the liquidator must report that fact, and the MVL can be transferred into CVL.[219] The option remains for the creditors to seek to place the company into compulsory liquidation instead, should they wish to do so.

2. Administrators

The particular duties of administrators are determined by, and directed to fulfilling, the **4.090** purpose of the administration. This will in turn be determined by reference to the terms of the administrator's appointment, namely whether it is:[220]

---

213   Where a winding up commences within 12 weeks of the day after the end of any moratorium: IA 1986 ss174A(1), 175(1). 'Moratorium debt' is defined in IA 1986 sA51. Also within this category are certain pre-moratorium debts, defined in IA 1986 s174A(2)(b) (as defined in sA18).

214   IA 1986 ss115 and 175(1)(b).

215   Ibid ss386, 387 and Sch 6 (IA 1986 s175). At the time of writing, a return of the preferential status of HMRC debts is anticipated, although only in relation to a limited number of categories and with secondary preferential status. It is suggested that, where relevant, the reader consults the Finance Act 2020. Relatedly, the 'maximum prescribed part' of floating charge realisations which are set aside and paid to unsecured creditors in an insolvency increased from £600,000 to £800,000 under the Insolvency Act 1986 (Prescribed Part) (Amendment) Order 2020 art 2(2).

216   IA 1986 s74(2)(f).

217   *Re TH Knitwear (Wholesale) Ltd* [1988] Ch 275.

218   IA 1986 s156.

219   Ibid s95.

220   Ibid Sch B1 para 3(1).

(a)   rescuing the company as a going concern ('*Objective 1*'), or

(b)   achieving a better result for the company's creditors as a whole than would be likely if the company were wound up (without first being in administration) ('*Objective 2*'), or

(c)   realising property in order to make a distribution to one or more secured or preferential creditors ('*Objective 3*').

4.091   Schedule B1 creates a hierarchy of objectives. Objective 1 is clearly the most desirable from the perspective of the 'rescue culture', but is unlikely in practice to be achieved often. The use of the administration process gives some 'breathing space' to the company, and allows for new management to take over the reins of the company. In this respect, it is suggested that the administrator's role will be similar to that of a turnaround practitioner (albeit that the company is an insolvency process).

4.092   Objective 3, at the other end of the spectrum, has subsumed the role of administrative receivers into Schedule B1. Administrators appointed under Objective 3 will usually be so-called 'hostile appointments' made by qualifying floating charge holders ('QFC' holders). Objective 3 appointments will therefore be directed towards selling property (often real property) for the benefit of one or more secured creditors, usually on the basis that the security will only be sufficient to meet the security of those creditors (if that). However, unlike receivers appointed under the Law of Property Act 1925 ('LPA 1925') s101, 'Objective 3' administrators also have a duty to unsecured creditors, and should not detrimentally impact the rights of such creditors.[221] Cases where that distinction is thrown into relief will by their very nature be rare, since the administrator's core task is to obtain the best price reasonably achievable for the property on the day – in that sense, it is consistent with the same obligation that arises in respect of liquidators and, indeed, in respect of receivers. However, if the IP is presented with an option that provides the secured creditor with a better deal, but to the detriment of the general body of unsecured creditors, then it appears that the administrator will be constrained not to accept it, in a way that receivers are not. Once the property has been sold, it is common for the company to transfer into liquidation, or else to be dissolved without the interim stage of being in liquidation.[222]

4.093   Objective 2 administrations lie between these two extremes. It is suggested that the comparison with liquidations is a starting point, albeit that there must be an expectation on the part of the administrators that creditors will get a better return than in liquidation. It generally used to be considered that administration would almost always offer a better return to unsecured creditors because of the applicable fee structure. However, this is not always correct.[223] Aside from that distinction, the general statutory purpose of 'Objective 2' administrations is that it enables a greater level of flexibility than liquidations. For example, an administrator need not make a distribution (although he may), and the administrator may decide to continue trading some parts of the company, sell off others, and realise assets separately.

---

221   Ibid Sch B1 para 3(4)(b) and see generally Chapter 3, Section G.

222   Ibid Sch B1 para 84.

223   *Baltic House Developments Ltd v Wing Keung Cheung* [2018] EWHC 1525 (Ch), where the court lacked jurisdiction to make an administration order.

However, the assumption is that the company will eventually enter liquidation (and ultimately, **4.094** dissolution), and given the breadth of the powers given to liquidators, the question remains whether 'Objective 2' administrators will in truth be undertaking a substantially different task from that of a liquidator. The recent trend for orders appointing the OR as liquidator with the assistance of special managers in respect of industrially and/or politically sensitive companies throws this issue in relief further, as the lines between liquidation and administration appear to be blurring.[224]

The better answer may be that it is one of presentation and emphasis; some companies may **4.095** obviously be so sick that liquidation is the only realistic solution. For companies where a greater return to creditors may be obtained by greater flexibility, Objective 2 administrations may be more appropriate. It is suggested that while this has little impact on the *duties* of IPs per se, it does inform the way that administrators will often go about their role. It may also inform the appetite for risk that the administrators have in their commercial dealings. IPs must also keep under review during an Objective 2 administration whether an Objective 1 administration can instead be achieved, thereby hauling the company out of the administration process altogether. Such a route is generally precluded by liquidation, where the possibility of rescue can be achieved via a CVA[225] (but which course is seldom encountered), and the assumption in liquidation is that it will end in the dissolution of the company.

3. Nominees and supervisors

A nominee is (as the name suggests) an individual who is nominated to act as a supervisor of a **4.096** CVA or IVA. Although the proposal is, as a matter of law, proposed by the director[226] or individual[227] who wishes to take advantage of the statutory process, this is something of a legal fiction. In practice, the proposal will usually be drawn up by the same IP who will then act as the supervisor in the event that the requisite majority of the creditors agree to the proposal.

The duty of the nominee is, in essence, to ensure that the creditors have the necessary and **4.097** accurate information before them in order to form a view and vote on the proposal. If a proposal is later found to contain a material irregularity, that irregularity can give rise to a basis for challenge by a creditor, thereby unravelling the voluntary arrangement altogether.[228]

This places the nominee in a potentially difficult position, since they are usually unable fully to **4.098** investigate the affairs of the insolvent individual or company. However, they cannot simply defer to the information given to them by the insolvent person and assume that that information is correct or complete. If there are aspects of the information that appear to require

---

224 *Re Sovereign Hospitals Services Ltd* [2018] EWHC 815 (Ch); *Re British Steel Ltd* [2019] EWHC 1304 (Ch); *Re Thomas Cook Group plc* [2019] EWHC 2626 (Ch). The advantage of being appointed as a special manager from the perspective of an IP is that they will not be liable *qua* liquidator. Such appointments are made under IA 1986 s177(1) and IR 2016 r7.93. Special managers must provide security to the OR to the value of the business or property in relation to which they are appointed: IR 2016 r7.94.

225 IA 1986 s1(3).

226 Ibid s1(1).

227 Ibid s256A(1). The nominee must produce a report: s256A(3).

228 Ibid ss 6(1)(b), 262(1)(b).

an explanation, then it is the IP's duty to ask further questions.[229] It is suggested that the guiding principle is that

> Where such doubts have reasonably arisen it cannot be right for the nominee unquestioningly to accept whatever is put in front of him on the supposed basis that it is not for him but for the creditors to accept or reject the proposal; it is fundamental to the intended operation of IVAs that what the creditors vote upon is not the debtor's raw material but a proposal that, at least to the qualified extent I have described, has survived scrutiny and which, to at least that extent, has commended itself to an independent professional insolvency practitioner as proper to be put to, and capable of being not unfairly voted upon by the creditors. Although it may be said, in the broadest terms, that the plan of the 1986 Act in relation to IVAs is 'Leave it to the creditors', it is not, in other words, anything that is so to be left; the formalities apart, the 'it' to be left to them by the nominee has (at least in the cases of doubt which I have described and with which I am, for the moment, concerned) to have met the three minima I have mentioned.[230]

4.099 Further guidance can be taken from SIPs 3, 3.1, and 3.2. The core principle in those SIPs is that the IP should differentiate clearly between the stages and roles that are associated with the IVA/CVA, namely the provision of initial advice, assisting in the preparation of the proposal (for it is the debtor's proposal), acting as the nominee, and acting as supervisor.[231] This type of distinction is also similar to the distinction between the pre- and post-appointment roles often played by IPs when they advise a director before being appointed as an administrator.

4. Monitors

4.100 The role of a monitor is somewhat similar to that of a nominee, in that their duty is essentially to ensure that the statutory moratorium under CIGA 2020 is not abused. We have already noted in paragraph 4.098 above the difficult role that nominees may be in. This is also likely to apply to monitors but, unlike nominees,[232] the monitor has the benefit of a specific carve out in relation to compensation claims. Under CIGA 2020 compensation claims cannot be brought against a monitor.[233]

---

229   *Greystoke v Hamilton-Smith* [1997] BPIR 24 (Lindsay J).
230   Ibid at 29.
231   SIP 3.1 para 2; SIP 3.2 para 3.
232   IA 1986 Sch A1 paras 26 and 27: cf. paras 27(1), (3)(c) and 27(4).
233   Ibid sA42(4)(c).

5

POWERS OF OFFICE-HOLDERS

A. INTRODUCTION

To fulfil their statutory functions, office-holders are given a selection of express powers by the Insolvency Act 1986 ('IA 1986'), which are found in Schedule 1 (for administrators[1]), Schedule 4 (for liquidators[2]) and Schedule 5 (for trustees in bankruptcy[3]). Many of these powers are broadly similar as between office-holders, despite the differing emphasis between the functions of the various roles.[4] **5.001**

In bankruptcy and liquidation, the office-holders' powers are largely directed towards achieving their functions of getting in, realising and distributing the bankrupt's estate[5] or the assets of the company[6] respectively. This reflects the fact that liquidation and bankruptcy are both, in a sense, 'terminal' processes. In liquidation, the company is wound up and ultimately dissolved, whereas bankruptcy spells the end not for the individual but for their insolvency; divested of their estate and discharged from their debts, the bankrupt can move on from both as the phoenix, leaving them to the trustee to administer and close. **5.002**

---

1 See also Sch B1 para 60.
2 See IA 1986 s165(2) in respect of companies being voluntarily wound up (but cf. s166 with regard to CVLs) and s167(1) for companies being wound up by the court.
3 IA 1986 s314.
4 See Annexes I and II for a tabular comparison of Schedules 1, 4 and 5.
5 IA 1986 s305.
6 Ibid s143.

5.003 By contrast, administration does not always spell the end for a company – it may involve the company continuing to trade, at least for a period, even if sale as an ongoing concern is not possible. For that purpose, the administrator has broad powers to do anything necessary or expedient to manage the affairs, business and property of the company.[7] Thus it has been said that an administrator may exercise any power which would have been available to the directors prior to the appointment of the administrator.[8]

5.004 As well as their different functions, the differing status of office-holders also affects their powers. Whereas a trustee in bankruptcy has the powers of a legal owner with respect to the assets of the bankruptcy estate that actually vest in them (albeit that those assets are held for the benefit of the bankruptcy estate, and not their personal benefit), a liquidator or administrator is in the position of an agent with respect to the company over which they are appointed, which continues to exist as an entity even in administration/liquidation.[9] Thus questions can arise as to whether a corporate office-holder is purporting to act or contract in their own capacity or on behalf of the company.

5.005 This chapter considers a number of important aspects of office-holder powers, highlighting the differences and similarities between them. The focus is on bankruptcies, liquidations and administrations as the types of insolvency procedure where it is most likely that a claim will be brought. This is not to say that the office-holder could not make a claim in other types of procedure, but such cases are unusual.

B. MAKING CLAIMS

1. Introduction and standing

5.006 An important power of any office-holder is the ability to bring claims for the benefit of the insolvent company or the bankruptcy estate. Not only does this power support their function of getting in and realising the assets, but in many cases the office-holder themself also stands to benefit from such litigation because there will often be no other assets out of which to pay their fees.

5.007 Claims available to the office-holder in insolvency can be loosely divided into two broad categories:

---

7 IA 1986 Sch B1 paras 59(1) and 59(3) which further provides that a person dealing with the administrator of a company in good faith and for value need not inquire whether the administrator is acting within his powers.

8 *Denny v Yeldon* [1995] 1 BCLC 560 at 564A–F: an administrator was permitted to amend a company's pension scheme trust deed.

9 *In re Anglo-Moravian Hungarian Junction Ry Co* (1875) 1 Ch D 130; *Knowles v Scott* [1891] 1 Ch 717; *Butler v Broadhead* [1975] Ch 97 at 108. In exercising their functions under Sch B1 administrators act as agents of the company, but the statutory agency is of a design peculiar to its purpose. However, the status of the administrator as agent means that an administrator can have no greater power than the company itself as principal under the scope of the company's objects clause in its memorandum of association: see *Re Home Treat Ltd* [1991] BCLC 705 at 706I–707B.

(1)   claims which belong to the office-holder, for the benefit of the estate, and which arise under IA 1986 as a result of the onset of an insolvency process (which shall be referred to in this chapter as 'office-holder claims'[10]); and

(2)   claims that are assets of the company or assets which form part of the bankruptcy estate. This might include debt and other contractual claims, claims for damages for breach of tortious, contractual, statutory or fiduciary duty and claims for restitution or return of goods.

As the former type of claim is a creature of statute, the office-holders' standing to bring such a claim is thus expressly provided for (or not, as the case may be) in the relevant provision. These types of claim are brought in the office-holders' capacity in that particular role and in their own 'official name'.[11]   **5.008**

The position with regard to the latter type of claim depends on the type of insolvency process. In bankruptcy, causes of action which are assets in the bankruptcy estate automatically vest in the trustee.[12] The trustee in bankruptcy is therefore able to bring such claims in their official name.   **5.009**

By contrast, on liquidation, the assets of the insolvent company (including causes of action) do not vest automatically in the liquidator.[13] Instead the liquidator in a compulsory liquidation can apply for and obtain a vesting order in respect of all or part of the company's property of whatsoever description in order to bring and defend legal proceedings in respect of the vested property in their own official name.[14] However, a liquidator does have the express power to bring or defend any action or other legal proceeding in the name and on behalf of the company[15] (as, indeed, does an administrator[16]), so in practice applications for such vesting orders are very rare.   **5.010**

2. Types of claim

(a) Claims falling within the bankruptcy estate

Personal insolvency differs from corporate insolvency in that it involves an individual who will continue to exist after their discharge. As such, the law must draw a line between what current and future property should be available for a bankrupt's creditors and what should be left to the bankrupt to enable bankrupts to support themselves and any dependants.   **5.011**

---

10   And are dealt with in subs. 2(e) below at para 5.032.

11   That is, X as Liquidator, Trustee in Bankruptcy, or Administrator of Y.

12   See IA 1986 s306.

13   See *John Mackintosh & Sons Ltd v Bakers Bargain Stores (Seaford) Ltd* [1965] 1 WLR 1182. In *Ayerst v C & K (Constructions) Ltd* [1976] AC 167 the House of Lords held that on a winding up the company is divested of the beneficial interest in its property, and only the legal title remains vested in the company. This view was endorsed by the Privy Council in *Cambridge Gas Transport Corporation v Official Committee of Unsecured Creditors of Navigator Holdings plc* [2006] UKPC 26 [2007] 1 AC 508. However, in *Commissioner of Taxation v Linter Australia Ltd (In Liquidation)* [2005] HCA 20 a majority of the Australian High Court declined to follow *Ayerst* and held there is no change in ownership of a company's assets on liquidation (Kirby J dissenting).

14   IA 1986 s145.

15   Ibid Sch 4 para 4.

16   Ibid Sch 1 para 5.

5.012   Not every asset belonging to a debtor who is made bankrupt is automatically transferred to their trustee in bankruptcy to realise for the benefit of their creditors. By way of example, the bankrupt is permitted to keep such clothing, bedding, furniture, household equipment and provisions as are necessary for satisfying their basic domestic needs and those of their family.[17] The IA 1986 uses the concept of the 'bankruptcy estate'[18] to refer to those assets which do automatically vest in the trustee immediately on his appointment taking effect and without any conveyance, assignment or transfer.[19] The estate will also include any 'after-acquired property' to which the bankrupt becomes entitled during the period in which the bankrupt remains undischarged.[20] There is no equivalent concept in liquidation or administration.[21]

5.013   The definition of bankruptcy estate in IA 1986 s283 encompasses all choses in action.[22] However, the courts have long recognised, seemingly as a matter of policy, that certain causes of action can be said to be personal to the bankrupt such that they do not vest in their trustee in bankruptcy.

5.014   In 1849, Lord Mansfield stated the position thus:[23]

> The right of action does not pass where the damages are to be estimated by immediate reference to pain felt by the bankrupt in respect of his body, mind or character, and without immediate reference to his rights of property. Thus it has been laid down that the assignees cannot sue for breach of promise of marriage, for criminal conversation, seduction, defamation, battery, injury to the person by negligence, as by not carrying safely, not curing, not saving from imprisonment by process of law.

5.015   Much like the proverbial elephant, claims that fall within this category are perhaps easier to identify than to define. Causes of action which the court has confirmed *are* personal to the bankrupt, and which therefore fall outside the bankruptcy estate and do not vest in the trustee in bankruptcy once appointed include:

(i)   reputational claims, including damages for loss of reputation[24] or for slander;[25]
(ii)   actions for assault or other bodily harm;[26]
(iii)   claims for social security benefits in the nature of income;[27]
(iv)   claims for pain, suffering and loss of amenity, or for medical negligence giving rise to personality change;[28]

---

17   IA 1986 s283(2)(a).
18   The definition of the bankrupt's estate is in IA 1986 s283.
19   IA 1986 s306.
20   Ibid s307. See paras 5.021–5.023 below.
21   Indeed, the problem of determining which causes of action do and do not vest in the office-holder does not arise in the corporate context, since none of an insolvent company's assets vest automatically in the liquidator/administrator.
22   The definition of 'property' in IA 1986 s436(1) includes things in action.
23   *Beckham v Drake* (1849) 2 HL Cas 579 at 604.
24   *Wilson v United Counties Bank Ltd* [1920] AC 102.
25   *Re Wilson ex p Vine* (1878) 8 Ch D 364.
26   *Heath v Tang* [1993] 4 All ER 694.
27   *Mulvey v SS for Social Security* [1997] BPIR 696, considered in *SS for Work and Pensions v Payne* [2011] UKSC 60, [1998] BPIR 224.
28   *Davis v Trustee in Bankruptcy of the Estate of Davis* [1998] BPIR 572.

(v)   a claim for damages for professional negligence in respect of conduct which gave rise to the bankruptcy;[29]

(vi)   some claims under the Employment Rights Act 1996, such as for reinstatement or re-engagement consequent on an unfair dismissal.[30]

Interestingly, Peter LJ observed in *Cork v Rawlins*[31] that there is no reported authority **5.016** supporting the proposition that a contractual claim (as opposed to a statutory claim or claim for breach of tortious duty) is capable of remaining vested in the bankrupt,[32] pursuant to what he described as the 'common law exception' to the statutory definition of property within a bankrupt's estate.[33]

In *Cork*, the bankrupt had suffered an injury which left him unable to work. He made a claim **5.017** in respect of two whole life insurance policies, each providing for a benefit if he became permanently disabled. The claim was accepted by the insurers after he had been made bankrupt. His trustee applied for a declaration that the sums formed part of the bankrupt's estate in bankruptcy and so vested in the trustee and were divisible amongst his creditors. The judge granted the declaration at first instance. The bankrupt appealed on the ground that the claim to benefits under the policies was peculiarly personal to him because his disablement must be assumed to impact on his ability to provide for and maintain himself and his family. He contended that the circumstances giving rise to the payment were so inherently tied up with the pain and suffering of the insured or his person that it is wholly inequitable and contrary to the principles underpinning IA 1986 that such monies should be appropriated by the trustee for the creditors.

Peter LJ held that the policy monies, being a contractual entitlement, did not relate to or **5.018** represent or compensate for loss or damage to the bankrupt personally, nor were they measured by such loss or damage. Payment was merely triggered by the permanent disablement being proved, such that:[34]

> To my mind it would involve a considerable extension of the common law exception from the bankrupt's estate to include within that exception an asset whose only connection with the pain and suffering of the bankrupt is that his disablement is the contractual contingency on which the moneys assured have become payable. If, for social reasons or otherwise, it is thought desirable that the exception should be extended, in my opinion it is for Parliament, not for the courts, to make that extension.

(b) Hybrid claims

Where a single cause of action comprises both personal and non-personal heads of loss (e.g. a **5.019** claim for medical negligence which comprises separate heads of claim for both pain and suffering and loss of earnings) the single cause of action vests in the trustee, but the trustee

---

29   *Mulkerrins v PriceWaterhouseCoopers* [2003] UKHL 41, [2003] 1 WLR 1937.
30   *Grady v Prison Service* [2003] EWCA Civ 527 [2003] 3 All ER 745. This is to be contrasted with a claim for wrongful dismissal, which is an action for damages for breach of contract and will vest in the bankruptcy estate: *Grady* at [22].
31   [2001] EWCA Civ 202, [2001] Ch 792.
32   [2001] Ch 792, 799.
33   *Cork* at 798.
34   *Cork* at 800.

holds the proceeds of the personal element of the claim on a constructive trust for the bankrupt and accounts to them for any damages recovered under that head.[35]

5.020 Alternatively, the trustee in bankruptcy could reverse the position by choosing to assign the cause of action to the bankrupt on the basis that they account to the trustee in bankruptcy for any damages received in respect of the non-personal heads of the claim.[36]

(c) After acquired property and income

5.021 A trustee in bankruptcy has the power to claim 'after acquired property'[37] (i.e. property which has been acquired by or been devolved on the bankrupt since the commencement of the bankruptcy) by serving a written notice on the bankrupt. Title to such property vests in the trustee in bankruptcy upon service of a request in writing on the bankrupt.[38] Title to the property will however have relation back to the time at which the property was acquired by, or devolved upon, the bankrupt,[39] subject to a defence of an interim purchaser who acquires the property in good faith, for value and without notice of the bankruptcy.[40] If the bankrupt's discharge is extended beyond the default period of one year,[41] such property will potentially continue to vest in the trustee in bankruptcy, thereby underscoring the penal nature of such suspensions.

5.022 A trustee in bankruptcy can also apply for an 'income payments order'[42] or seek to make an 'income payments agreement'[43] claiming the whole or a portion of the bankrupt's income for a period of up to three years.[44] But the court shall not make an income payments order the effect of which would be to reduce the income of the bankrupt below what appears to the court to be necessary for meeting the reasonable domestic needs of the bankrupt and his family.[45] Such an application must be made before the discharge of the bankrupt.[46]

5.023 By their nature, the above powers are exclusive to personal insolvency.[47]

---

35 See *Ord v Upton* [2001] 1 All ER 193, *Hayes v Butters* [2014] EWHC 4557 (Ch), [2015] BPIR 287 and *Hayes v Willoughby* (unreported) 22 July 2015.

36 But see paras 5.075–5.076 below for the possible costs consequences to an office-holder of assigning causes of action.

37 IA 1986 s307.

38 Ibid s307(1). However, the trustee must serve the notice within 42 days of becoming aware of the after acquired property unless the court provides otherwise: IA 1986 s309(1)(a).

39 Ibid s307(3).

40 Ibid s307(4)(a). This protection therefore mirrors the status granted to 'Equity's Darling' in respect of innocent transferees of other types of property: Land Registration Act 2002 s29; Companies Act 2006 s859H.

41 Under ibid s279(3).

42 Ibid s310.

43 Ibid s310A.

44 Ibid s310(6).

45 Ibid s310(2).

46 Ibid s310(1A)(b).

47 Note there is also a similar power to seek the vesting, by notice, of items (such as tools of trade, or household effects), under IA 1986 s308, if the item has a realisable value in excess of the cost of a reasonable replacement, subject to application of funds to purchase such a replacement. However this is a little used section and so is not discussed further here.

(d) Company claims

By contrast, liquidators and administrators have the power to bring any claim which belongs to **5.024**
the company on its behalf.

Until the introduction of changes made by the Small Business, Enterprise and Employment **5.025**
Act 2015 ('SBEEA 2015'), a liquidator of a company in compulsory liquidation had to obtain
the sanction of the court or the liquidation committee before taking certain actions, including
bringing legal proceedings on behalf of the company.[48] In the leading case, *Re Greenhaven
Motors Ltd*,[49] it was made clear that the court would give weight to the views of an impartial
liquidator, but the decision was ultimately that of the court, who would take into account the
interest of the creditors (but might discount the views of creditors influenced by extraneous
considerations). For liquidators' decisions which did not require sanction, the decision to be
taken had been entrusted to the liquidators' commercial judgement as to the insolvent estate's
best interests. The requirement for a liquidator in a compulsory liquidation to obtain sanction
to bring legal proceedings was abolished by SBEEA with effect from 26 May 2015.[50]

By contrast no sanction was generally required in a voluntary liquidation and there is no **5.026**
provision requiring sanction in administration or administrative receivership. However administrators should generally manage the affairs, business and property of the company in
accordance with the proposals approved by creditors, and thus where litigation is contemplated, should give consideration to having this approved as part of the proposals.[51] Given the
latitude that was given to IPs prior to the amendment brought about by SBEEA 2015 s120, it
is perhaps unsurprising that the amendment was introduced.

The mirror image of the latitude that is given to IPs as to when they choose to commence **5.027**
litigation means that office-holders may find that any application to the court may be met with
a judicial response that the matter is generally one for the IP, and not for the court.[52] The test
will therefore be whether pursuing the particular claim falls within the range of decisions which
a reasonable office-holder could reasonably make.[53]

Re Longmeade concerned a liquidators' application for directions[54] regarding a potential legal **5.028**
claim by the company in liquidation against the Department of Business, Innovation and
Skills[55] which could significantly increase the return to creditors if successful. A litigation
funder offered to fund the claim and cover adverse costs orders, eliminating financial risk to the
company, in return for a share of damages. However, over 99 per cent by value of the
company's creditors opposed the claim being pursued. HMRC (the majority creditor) did not
wish to support litigation against a government department, while companies in the same
group as the company wished to close the insolvency proceedings quickly.

---

48   Pursuant to IA 1986 s167(1).
49   [1999] 1 BCLC 635.
50   SBEEA 2015 s120.
51   IA 1986 Sch B1 para 68.
52   *In re Longmeade Ltd (in liquidation)* [2016] EWHC 356 (Ch).
53   Ibid at [67], [69], [71].
54   See generally on applications for directions paras 5.089–5.119 below.
55   Now the Department of Business, Energy and Industrial Strategy.

5.029   Snowden J held that the removal of the need to obtain sanction did not change the courts' existing approach to liquidators' exercise of powers not requiring sanction, and the established principles should be applied to the post-26 May 2015 regime concerning commencement of proceedings by a company in compulsory liquidation. He therefore summarised the position as follows:[56]

(i)   a decision by liquidators appointed by the court as to whether to commence proceedings in the name of the company is essentially a commercial decision which the liquidators are entrusted to take without obtaining sanction from the court or the liquidation committee;

(ii)   in taking that decision, the liquidators should act in what they believe to be the best interests of the insolvent company and all those who have an interest in its estate;

(iii)   the liquidators may, but are not obliged to, consult the creditors (or contributories) who have an interest in the estate;

(iv)   the liquidators should normally give weight to the reasoned views of the majority of such creditors (or contributories), provided that they are uninfluenced by extraneous considerations;

(v)   if all those who are interested in the insolvent estate are fully informed and are unanimously of the same view, the liquidators should ordinarily give effect to their wishes;

(vi)   the court should not generally become involved in giving directions to liquidators as to how to make commercial or administrative decisions; and

(vii)   the court should not generally interfere with a commercial or administrative decision of liquidators after the event, unless it is a decision that was taken in bad faith or was a decision that no reasonable liquidator could have taken.

5.030   While recognising that the question whether to litigate was one for the commercial judgment of the liquidators, Snowden J did give his own view (which he expressed in terms of providing some 'reassurance' to the liquidators) that if there remained one or more creditors, even for comparatively small amounts, who would lose the opportunity for a materially increased distribution if the claim were not to be pursued (given the positive advice received by counsel and the fact that it appeared that the majority of creditors were pursuing their own agendas), a decision that the claim should be pursued at no financial risk would be within the range of decisions that a reasonable liquidator could properly take.[57]

5.031   He further observed that:[58]

I do not think that the comment in the Explanatory Notes to the Small Business Enterprise and Employment Bill that liquidators, *'should not undertake actions that are likely to have a negative financial impact on the estate. Such conduct may give rise to disciplinary concerns which may be addressed the regulatory system'* should be read out of context or be taken to indicate that liquidators must always adopt the alternative that has the lowest risk of loss to the insolvent estate. The overriding requirement is for liquidators to exercise their professional judgment in what they believe to be the best interests of creditors. It is obvious that they should not voluntarily do something that is likely (ie more probable than not) to result in loss to the estate. But that does not mean that they cannot properly run some risk of loss: otherwise no liquidator could ever embark upon litigation without a 100% costs indemnity from a third party.

---

56   *Re Longmeade* at [66].
57   Ibid at [71].
58   Ibid at [73].

(e) Office-holder claims

5.032 Claims which arise only as a result of the entry into an insolvency process (by contrast to claims which are assets of the company, or were assets of the bankrupt and which form part of the bankruptcy estate upon the bankruptcy order being made) include, in respect of liquidation, administration and bankruptcy:

(i)   claims in respect of transactions entered into at an undervalue;[59]

(ii) claims in respect of preferences;[60]

(iii) claims in respect of transactions defrauding creditors (this type of claim may also be available to 'victims' of the transaction other than the office-holder).[61]

5.033 And in respect of both liquidation and (from 1 October 2015) administration:[62]

(i)   fraudulent trading claims;[63]

(ii) wrongful trading claims;[64]

(iii) extortionate credit transactions.[65]

5.034 While the above claims are all available to an administrator, litigation is often not the top, or first, priority in administration, since administrators are mainly concerned at the outset with seeking to rescue or sell the business.

5.035 Any sums recovered in respect of these office-holder claims form part of the insolvency estate for the benefit of the general unsecured creditors. Because the claims do not come into existence until the appointment of the office-holder, any recoveries made cannot be the subject of a charge created before the insolvency process commenced.[66]

(f) Restitutionary claims

5.036 In addition, restitutionary claims may arise as a result of the transaction avoidance provisions in the IA 1986, most notably claims to recover property alienated from the company or bankruptcy estate as a result of transactions which took place between presentation of the

---

59   IA 1986 s238 in respect of administration and liquidation; IA 1986 s339 in respect of bankruptcy.

60   Ibid s239 in respect of administration and liquidation; ibid s340 in respect of bankruptcy.

61   Ibid s423; IA 1986 s424(2).

62   Ibid s246ZA. See also ibid s246ZB (in respect of wrongful trading) introduced by SBEEA 2015 s117. Small Business, Enterprise and Employment Act 2015 (Commencement No 2 and Transitional Provisions) Regulations 2015, SI 2015/1689) paras 15–17.

63   Ibid s213.

64   Ibid s214.

65   Ibid s244.

66   *Re Oasis Merchandising Services Ltd* [1998] Ch 170. Although this case was decided in the corporate context, the same principles would seem equally applicable to bankruptcy. Note that this principle is codified for administrations and liquidations commencing on or after 1 October 2015 in respect of floating charge recoveries from actions in relation to fraudulent trading, wrongful trading, transactions at an undervalue, preferences and extortionate credit transactions: IA 1986 s176ZB.

winding up or bankruptcy petition and the making of the order in either case.[67] Property which is recouped as a result of a restitutionary claim can be caught by existing charges over company assets.

(g)   The summary procedure for misfeasance under IA 1986 s212

5.037   IA 1986 s212 provides a summary procedure to the liquidator (as well as the Official Receiver ('OR'), or any creditor or contributory[68]) for bringing claims where a director or officer[69] of the company, or a person who has acted as liquidator or administrative receiver of the company,[70] has 'misapplied or retained, or become accountable for, any money or other property of the company, or been guilty of any misfeasance or breach of any fiduciary or other duty in relation to the company'.[71]

5.038   The reference to 'other duty' is in principle wide enough to allow s212 to be used to bring tortious proceedings for negligence,[72] provided the duty is owed to the company or, in the case of an office-holder, to the body of creditors as a whole.[73] The duty must be owed in the defendant's relevant capacity. For instance, a misfeasance action would not be available to recover a simple debt due from a former company secretary to the company, because the obligation to repay did not arise from a duty owed in his capacity as company secretary.[74] A classic example of a misfeasance claim is for breach of a director's duty under CA 2006 ss171–177, which codified the common law and equitable duties of directors into seven identifiable duties. Claims brought under IA 1986 s212 (by reference to CA 2006 ss171–177) are often brought in respect of misapplications of company money or property.[75]

---

67   IA 1986 s127 in liquidation; IA 1986 s284 in bankruptcy.

68   Ibid s212(3). Note contributories may only apply if they obtain the leave of the court: IA 1986 s212(5).

69   An 'officer' of the company includes directors (including *de facto* directors, but apparently not shadow directors): *Holland v Revenue and Customs and Another* [2010] UKSC 51. Note however that IA 1986 s212(1)(c) also catches anyone who 'is or has been concerned, or has taken part, in the promotion, formation or management of the company'. Company secretaries and managers are included: IA 1986 s251. The term 'Officer' in IA 1986 s212(1)(a) might also include a company's auditor: *Re London and General Bank* [1895] 2 Ch 166 (CA); *Re Thomas Gerard & Sons* [1968] Ch 455), but not other professional advisers such as its solicitors (*Re Great Western Forest of Dean Coal Consumers Co* (1886) 31 Ch D 496) or bankers (*Re Imperial Land Co of Marseilles* (1870) LR 10 Eq 298).

70   IA 1986 s212(1)(b). Note that s212 does not apply to administrators: *Irwin v Lynch* [2010] EWCA Civ 1153. This is to be contrasted with the position for administrative receivers. The reason for this is unclear, although it was suggested by Lloyd LJ in *Irwin* at [4] that this may be due to the administrator not normally remaining in office long. After the commencement of the corporate liquidations provision of Part 10 of the Enterprise Act 2002 ('EA 2002') on 15 September 2003, proceedings for misfeasance against administrators must now be brought under Sch B1 para 75. The position of monitors is unclear, as they remain officers of the court, but are probably not officers of the company. There is a standalone provision for applications to be brought against monitors in IA 1986 sA42, but the statutory intention appears to be that monitors will not be ordered to pay compensation: sA42(4)(c).

71   IA 1986 s212(1).

72   *Re D'Jan of London Ltd* [1993] BCC 646.

73   *Oldham v Kyrris* [2003] EWCA Civ 1506. The duty is indirectly owed to creditors where the company is insolvent or in a state of dubious solvency: CA 2006 s172(3); *BTI 2014 LLC v Sequana SA* [2019] EWCA Civ 112 at [210]–[220]. An appeal to the Supreme Court is outstanding. For an overview of CA 2006 s172, see Keay 'Office-holders and the duty of directors to promote the success of the company' (2010) 23(9) *Insolv Int* 129–34.

74   *Re Etic Ltd* [1928] Ch 861.

75   Such claims are essentially brought to get in the assets of the company, or their monetary substitute. Query also whether IA 1986 s234 gives office-holders this power (and which includes administrators within its ambit, unlike s212), though typically s234 is used to recover physical property where ownership is not in dispute (though it has been found that it is

The court may, on such an application, examine the conduct of the respondent and compel **5.039**
him to:

(a)   repay, restore or account for the money or property or any part of it, with interest at such
      rate as the court thinks just; or
(b)   contribute such sum to the company's assets by way of compensation in respect of the
      misfeasance or breach of statutory duty as the court thinks fit.[76]

It is important to note that s212 is purely procedural in effect. It does not provide any new **5.040**
cause of action, but does allow an office-holder a summary route for breach of established
obligations and duties there identified.[77] The description of the procedure as a summary
remedy is somewhat misleading. Although the text of IA 1986 s212(3) states that '[t]*he court
may ... examine into the conduct of the person falling within subsection (1)*',[78] the practice that has
developed is that it will trigger a claim in the Insolvency and Companies Court.[79] For this
same reason, administrators can also bring claims that might be brought by a liquidator,
although they cannot make use of the mechanism in s212 for so doing.[80] As a further result,
the limitation period will be that applicable to the underlying claim.[81] Where the misfeasance
is also potentially actionable under another provision of IA 1986, a claim for misfeasance may
be brought even if the alternative claim is unavailable because of the passage of time.[82]

Further, any recovery from a claim brought pursuant to IA 1986 s212 will form part of the **5.041**
assets of the company, as the chose in action existed prior to the insolvency. Accordingly,
where a creditor or contributory brings a s212 claim, they must pay any compensation
recovered to the office-holder (subject to any contrary agreement). Further, recoveries may be
covered by a prior charge.

---

    not so limited and may be used to resolve disputes as to ownership: see e.g., *Re Cosslett (Contractors) Ltd* [1998] 495
    (relating to construction site plant and equipment).

76 Apparently not including future or consequential loss: *Re Coniston Hotel (Kent) LLP (in liquidation)* [2013] EWHC 93
    (Ch).

77 *Top Brands Ltd v Sharma* [2014] EWHC 2753 (Ch), [2015] 1 BCLC 546.

78 The wording suggests that the procedure is similar to a public examination under IA 1986 ss133 or 290.

79 Curiously this also means that an application needs only to be made under Form IAA and supported by a witness
    statement, rather than for Particulars of Claim to be filed and served in compliance with CPR Parts 6, 7 and 16. It is
    however common practice for draft Points of Claim to be exhibited to the first witness statement in support of the
    application, and for them to stand as Points of Claim (usually by order of the court at the first directions hearing).

80 The practical result of this is that it would appear administrators should rely on CPR Part 7 for bringing such claims, at
    least where they are for 'pure' misfeasance claims and not brought alongside other related claims, such as preference or
    TUV claims. This would also seem to give rise to a much greater liability for court fees for administrators than
    liquidators. It is suggested that where the claim is 'mixed' (i.e., with misfeasance and office-holder claims), the company
    in administration can be added as an applicant to the action and the streamlined procedure under Form IAA can be
    used.

81 *Goldfarb (liquidator of Eurocruit Europe Ltd) v Poppleton* [2007] EWHC 1433 (Ch), [27]. This will most usually be six
    years from the breach of duty.

82 See, e.g., *Re Palmier plc (in liquidation)* [2009] EWHC 983 (Ch) where a IA 1986 s212 claim against a director for
    granting what was effectively a preference was valid even though a preference claim could not have been successful, since
    the preference was not made at a 'relevant time' and thus was effectively time-barred.

3. Limitation periods

(a) Introduction

5.042 After a long delay it may become unjust to allow claims to be brought, and the policy that '[l]*ong dormant claims have often more of cruelty than of justice in them*' is just as applicable to insolvency claims as it is to other areas of law.[83] It is '*a policy of the Limitation Acts that those who go to sleep upon their claims should not be assisted by the courts in recovering their property*' and '*there shall be an end of litigation, and that protection shall be afforded against stale demands*'.[84] A detailed treatment of limitation periods is beyond the scope of this book and the reader is referred to specialist texts in that respect.[85] However, there are two areas which are worthy of mention, and some discussion, in relation to limitation periods when considering the liabilities of IPs. The first relates to limitation periods which IPs might seek to raise by way of defence to a claim brought against them.[86] The second relates to the limitation period applicable to claims they might make, which is the subject of this chapter, and which is considered further below, under the following headings: (b) existing causes of action; (c) office-holder claims; and (d) misfeasance claims. These are worth considering, as the failure to have regard to them could result in a liability on the part of the IP to compensate for the lost opportunity to bring any claim which became statute-barred during the IP's time in office. Such liabilities are considered further in Chapter 6 below, but it is considered useful to consider the main limitation periods initially here in brief terms, in the context of making of claims.

5.043 Claims brought by a claimant against a company in liquidation will not expire by reason of the further passage of time, provided that the limitation period had not already expired before the commencement of the insolvency.[87] The reason originally given for this principle appears to have been that, once the time for the distribution of assets in the liquidation had come to pass, it would not prejudice the creditors generally to allow another creditor to come in and prove.[88] Whether this principle still holds good in circumstances where such a claim may be brought for the purposes of the Third Parties (Rights Against Insurers) Act 1930 is perhaps open to doubt, but it represents the current state of the law.[89] The principle, known as the *General Rolling Stock* principle, applies whether the liquidation is compulsory or voluntary.[90] But it probably does not apply in administrations, at least until the administration becomes a distributing administration. It would therefore seem to be an independent issue from the stay (or 'moratorium') on claims being brought against the company,[91] although both aspects can be viewed as part and parcel of the emphasis on insolvency proceedings being collective proceedings. If a company enters into liquidation, is dissolved, and then restored back into liquidation, the company will usually be deemed to have been in liquidation for the period of

---

83   *A'Court v Cross* 3 Bing. 329.

84   *RB Policies at Lloyd's v Butler* [1950] 1 KB 76.

85   See, e.g., McGee, *Limitation Periods* (8th edn, 2018).

86   Considered in Chapter 8 below. See paras 8.014–8.033.

87   *Re Art Reproduction Co Ltd* [1952] Ch 89.

88   *In re General Rolling Stock Co* (1871–1872) L.R. 7 Ch App 646, 649.

89   *FSCS v Larnell (Insurances) Ltd* [2005] EWCA Civ 1408 at [39]. Claims made the Third Parties (Rights Against Insurers) Act 2010 may be brought directly against the relevant insurer, without the company being restored to the register.

90   For example, *Larnell*, ibid.

91   Since no such stay applies automatically in the case of CVL, whereas a moratorium will exist for claims against a company in administration. However, the court can, on application, depart from these default positions.

the intervening dissolution, and so the *General Rolling Stock* principle will apply as if the company had not been dissolved.

(b) Existing causes of action

(i) Some basic limitation periods

This paragraph, and the next few paragraphs, are intended to introduce the reader to some of **5.044** the basic limitation periods and concepts in relation to the most common causes of action. In relation to debt claims, the relevant period is generally six years from the date when the cause of action accrues.[92] In relation to judgment debts, no action can be brought on a judgment six years after it became enforceable.[93] Note however that liquidation or bankruptcy proceedings are not *'an action upon judgment'* and are consequently not subject to any limitation period.[94] In relation to simple contract claims, the period is generally six years from the date of the breach of contract relied upon.[95] So far as contracts made by deed are concerned, these are actions on a 'specialty'[96] and generally the period runs from 12 years from breach.[97] In relation to tort claims, the period is generally six years from the date loss was first suffered as a result of the tortious conduct.[98] However, such a period may be extended by reason of the fact that the damage suffered is latent damage and where relevant knowledge is not acquired at the date of loss.[99] In relation to personal injury claims the period is ordinarily three years (though again there is scope for this to be extended, in certain discretionary circumstances).[100]

(ii) Statutory claims

In relation to claims based on a statutory provision, the limitation period in relation to a claim **5.045** to recover a sum of money is generally six years from the accrual of the cause of action,[101] or, where the claim is a claim on a specialty, the limitation period is 12 years.[102]

(iii) Claims against directors

In the case of a claim by a company against one of its directors for breach of a director's **5.046** obligations to act with skill and care, the normal limitation period is six years from the date of

---

92 Limitation Act 1980 ('LA 1980') s5, but see also s6 which contains additional rules which apply to certain loan contracts.
93 Ibid s24.
94 *Ridgeway Motors (Isleworth) Ltd v ALTS Ltd* [2005] EWCA Civ 92. A winding-up petition based on a judgment debt is not an *'action upon a judgment'* within the meaning of s24 of the LA 1980: see Mummery LJ at [29]. It was explicitly recognised in *Ridgeway Motors* at [35] that the same principle applies to a bankruptcy petition. Although this may seem counterintuitive, it followed from the decision of *Lamb (W T) & Sons v Rider* [1948] 2 KB 331, [1948] 2 All ER 402, CA. That case was cited in the Report of the Law Reform Committee on Limitation of Actions (1977) (Cmnd 6923), which was in turn enacted by Parliament in the LA 1980, and apparently constrained the House of Lords from holding otherwise in *Lowsley v Forbes (trading as L E Design Services)* [1999] 1 AC 329 (HL) (in relation to a garnishee order). This exception to the LA 1980 therefore has a significant pedigree.
95 LA 1980 s5.
96 A specialty has been said to be 'an archaic word of somewhat imprecise meaning'. It includes contracts and other obligations in documents under seal, and also, traditionally, obligations arising under statute (Franks, *Limitation of Actions* (1959)).
97 LA 1980 s8.
98 Ibid s2. Loss being required to complete the cause of action.
99 Ibid s14A.
100 Ibid ss11, 33.
101 Ibid s9(1).
102 Ibid s8.

breach; that is on the basis that such claims are treated, for limitation purposes, as being analogous to claims in tort or for breach of a contract between the director and the company. In respect of claims for breach of fiduciary duty, which arise from the fact that a director is in a 'trustee-like' position in relation to the company and the company's assets, such claims are treated, for limitation purposes, as breach of trust claims, in relation to which, see the following paragraphs.

(iv)   Breach of trust claims

5.047   A claim by a beneficiary for breach of trust (which does not involve fraud or the recovery of trust property) is subject to a limitation period of six years, with time running from accrual of the cause of action, which is usually the date of breach.[103] A claim to recover land, by contrast, is subject to a 12-year limitation period.[104]

5.048   In the event that a breach of trust is fraudulent, or, alternatively, that the cause of action is based on fraud, no limitation period prescribed by the LA 1980 will apply to the claim. Such claims, in effect, have no limitation period. This is to be contrasted with claims where there has been fraud, concealment, or mistake which otherwise prevents the claimant from becoming aware of the claim. In such cases, time running is postponed until the claimant has discovered the fraud, concealment or mistake (as the case may be) or could with reasonable diligence have discovered it.[105]

5.049   In certain cases, an IP may wish to bring a claim *in personam* (albeit arising from or connected with a breach of trust) against a third party who is not the trustee or company director, e.g. a claim for dishonest assistance or a claim for knowing (or unconscionable) receipt of trust property. Such claims are subject to the LA 1980, and in particular a six-year limitation period.[106] In *Williams v Central Bank of Nigeria*,[107] a case in which the claims against the bank included claims based on dishonest assistance and knowing receipt, the Supreme Court decided that the bank had a good limitation defence under the LA 1980, and in so doing, it rejected an assertion that the claim came within LA 1980 s21(1)(a).[108]

5.050   The application of LA 1980 s21 in the context of a claim brought by an IP against company directors was considered by the Supreme Court in *Burnden Holdings (UK) Ltd v Fielding*.[109] The case reached the Supreme Court on a summary judgment application made by defendant directors in the face of a claim from an IP which relied on a number of causes of action, including allegations of breach of directors' duties in undertaking a specific transaction. Initially, the IP did not allege fraud against the directors, but, by the time the summary judgment application reached the Supreme Court, an allegation of fraud had been introduced. The relevant transaction at issue in the case was a distribution *in specie* by the company of a share it held in a subsidiary to a separate newco which, in turn, transferred it through a variety of corporate vehicles until a proportion of the shareholding of the relevant subsidiary was sold

---

103   LA 1980 s21(3).
104   Ibid s15.
105   Ibid s32.
106   Ibid s21(3).
107   [2014] UKSC 10.
108   *Williams* has been followed in *Rashid Nasrullah* [2018] EWCA Civ 2685.
109   [2018] UKSC 14, [2018] AC 857.

to a third party. The defendant directors relied upon LA 1980 s21(1)(b). At first blush, and given that the share had travelled through a number of corporate vehicles without ever being owned by the directors, it was a credible defence. Lord Briggs, giving the judgment of the Supreme Court, held that LA 19808 s21(1)(b) did not apply because, as company directors, they were to be treated as the fiduciary stewards of the company's assets, and were therefore to be treated as though they were in possession of the company's property from the outset.

(v)   Cross-over claims – unlawful loans

In *Brown v Button*[110] the High Court considered the limitation period for a claim under IA **5.051** 1986 s212 by the liquidators of a company against the former directors, regarding loans that were unlawful under s330 of the Companies Act 1985 ('CA 1985').[111] The court held that a claim against a director to repay an unlawful loan under s330 had no statutory limitation period, as the claim was treated as one for breach of trust. However, claims based on joint liability under CA 1985 s341(2)(b)[112] must be brought within six years from the date of the relevant transaction.[113]

(c)   Office-holder claims

(i)   Introduction

IA 1986 enables an IP to commence a variety of different claims against third parties, either as **5.052** a result of events occurring in the run-up to the opening of insolvency proceedings, or to realise the debtor's assets in which third parties may have an interest.[114] An IP is able to bring a claim to reverse a transaction which was entered into by the debtor in the period leading up to insolvency (so-called 'avoidance claims'). In a corporate insolvency, an IP is able to make claims in connection with the actions of a director of the company and others insofar as their conduct comes within the provisions of IA 1986 dealing with fraudulent trading or wrongful trading, or simply for breach of duty (misfeasance). In a bankruptcy case, in which the major asset is often the bankrupt's interest in a matrimonial home, the IP is able to apply to the court for orders for possession and sale of the debtor's home. Each of those different claims is subject to a limitation period of some form, which is explored next.

(ii)   Transaction avoidance claims

A claim by an IP, whether in a personal or corporate insolvency context, that a transaction **5.053** entered into by a debtor was a transaction at an undervalue, and for appropriate relief under IA 1986[115] is subject to the LA 1980. The limitation period which applies to the claim will be either a six-year period or a 12-year period, depending on whether the claim is for monetary relief or for some other non-monetary relief (such as setting aside a transaction).[116] It could be said that this is a somewhat arbitrary distinction, because in many cases the relief sought may

---

110   [2011] EWHC 1034 (Ch).
111   See now CA 2006 ss197–203.
112   See now CA 2006 s213(3), (4).
113   LA 1980 s9.
114   See paras 5.032–5.035 for further discussion of the nature of office-holder claims.
115   IA 1986 ss238–241, 339–342.
116   *Re Priory Garage (Walthamstow) Ltd* [2001] BPIR 144. This is on the basis that either LA 1980 ss8 or 9 will apply.

be in the alternative,[117] and the relief sought by the applicant may be different from that which is granted.[118] Nevertheless, the position in relation to preference claims is the same, and applies whether it is in the context of corporate or personal insolvency; the limitation period is six years (in the case of a claim which seeks monetary relief) or 12 years (in a case in which the relief sought is not monetary).[119] In determining whether a claim made by an IP is for monetary or non-monetary relief, a court can be expected to seek to determine the substance or essential nature of the relief being sought by the IP. The cause of action accrues on the making of the relevant insolvency order, or the opening of the relevant insolvency proceedings.[120] Claims under IA 1986 s423 are also subject to a limitation period, which, in common with transaction at an undervalue claims or preference claims is either six years or 12 years depending on the relief that is sought.[121] Where a claim is brought by an IP, the cause of action accrues when the relevant insolvency proceedings commenced.[122]

(iii)   *Fraudulent and wrongful trading claims under IA 1986 ss213 and 214*

5.054   A claim in a corporate insolvency for fraudulent trading or for wrongful trading is also subject to a limitation period under the LA 1980. In the case of fraudulent and wrongful trading, the limitation period is six years, and the cause of action accrues when the company goes into the relevant insolvency process.[123]

(iv)   *Possession and sale of the matrimonial home by a trustee in bankruptcy*

5.055   In most cases in which it is sought to realise a bankrupt's interest in a matrimonial home and it is necessary to have recourse to the court, a trustee in bankruptcy will apply to court under s14(1) of the Trusts of Land and Appointment of Trustees Act 1996 ('TOLATA 1996') as a person with an interest in property subject to a trust of land.[124] In such cases, the IA 1986 displaces the criteria more commonly applied in such applications[125] in favour of the criteria contained in IA 1986 s335A.[126] Prior to the EA 2002, there was no bar on allowing cases to remain dormant and taking no action to realise the bankruptcy estate's interest in the debtor's former home until years later, at which point the property would typically have increased in value, and the sale of the property could take effect notwithstanding the bankrupt's discharge. In order to correct this perceived injustice, EA 2002 s261 introduced s283A into the IA 1986. The section creates a 'use it or lose it' period of three years commencing with the date of the

---

117   A common order sought is delivery up of company property or, in the alternative, a personal order for the value of the same property.
118   IA 1986 ss241, 342.
119   *Re Priory Garage (Walthamstow) Ltd* [2001] BPIR 144.
120   It is not dependent on the appointment of the IP as office-holder.
121   LA 1980 ss8 or 9: see *Hill v Spread Trustee Co Ltd* [2006] EWCA Civ 542, [2007] 1 All ER 1106, [2007] 1 BCLC 450.
122   *Hill v Spread Trustee Co Ltd*, ibid.
123   *Re Farmizer (Products) Ltd, Moore v Gadd* [1997] 1 BCLC 589, [1997] BCC 655, CA and *Re Overnight Ltd* [2010] BCC 787.
124   If the property is solely owned by the bankrupt, then it is unnecessary to have recourse to TOLATA, and instead, a trustee in bankruptcy can simply apply to the court for appropriate directions under IA 1986 s363: *Holtham v Kelmanson* [2006] BPIR 1422.
125   TOLATA 1996 s15.
126   IA 1986 s335A(3) provides that, after a year has passed after the real property vested, there is a presumption that the interests of creditors will outweigh all other interests, and the property will be sold. The interests of the bankrupt are irrelevant (IA 1986 s335A(2)(c)) and the threshold for *'exceptional circumstances'* under s335A(3) is a high one indeed: see the summary in *Dean v Stout* [2004] EWHC 3315 (Ch), [2005] BPIR 1113 at [6]–[11] (Lawrence Collins J).

bankruptcy after which the bankrupt's interest in the matrimonial home will revest in the debtor.[127] In order to prevent the interest revesting in the bankrupt, it is necessary for the trustee in bankruptcy to take action, most commonly by applying for possession or sale of the relevant property.[128] It is important to note that the section is only engaged when the property was, at the date of the bankruptcy order, the sole or principal residence of the bankrupt, the bankrupt's spouse or civil partner, or a former spouse or civil partner of the bankrupt.[129]

(d) Misfeasance claims

As already noted in paragraphs 5.040 and 5.051 above, the important point to have in mind in relation to misfeasance claims is that whilst they may be brought by office-holders in their own name, they are causes of action which already existed before appointment and so limitation periods are calculated from before the appointment. This is a not uncommon area of potential risk for IPs, particularly where they are not the first office-holder(s) appointed.

5.056

(e) Extensions of time – concealment and LA 1980 s32

In three categories of cases, it is possible that the running of time against a claimant may be postponed.[130] The first type of cases are cases in which the action is based on the fraud of the defendant.[131] The second category of cases are those in which a fact that is relevant to the claimant's cause of action has been deliberately concealed from him or her, by the defendant.[132] The final category of cases are those in which the claim is for relief from the consequences of a mistake.[133] In each of those three categories, times does not run against a claimant until the claimant either has discovered the fraud, concealment or mistake, or could, with reasonable diligence, have discovered it. In this context, 'reasonable diligence' involves some consideration of whether the claimant acted as an ordinary prudent person would in the circumstances.[134]

5.057

4. Securing funding/ATE Insurance

(a) Introduction

A perennial question that faces office-holders is how to fund the issue or continuance of a claim in the context of an insolvency, where the company or bankruptcy estate has insufficient assets to meet its own costs of proceedings and/or any adverse costs awarded to the other side. This is a particular issue where office-holders litigate in their own name, since they will be personally liable as a party to the litigation for the costs[135] (subject to any right of indemnity

5.058

---

127 IA 1986 s283A(2).
128 Ibid s283A(3)(b) or (c). IA 1986 s283A(3) specifies other means by which the proverbial clock can be stopped.
129 Ibid s283(A)(1). The section only applies to interests in dwelling houses vested in the bankrupt at the start of bankruptcy, and not to an interest capable of being recovered under IA 1986 s339: *Stonham v Ramrattan* [2011] EWCA Civ 119, [2011] 4 All ER 392.
130 LA 1980 s32.
131 Ibid s32(1)(a).
132 Ibid s32(1)(b). It is to be noted that a deliberate breach of duty in circumstances in which it is unlikely to be discovered for some time will amount to deliberate concealment of the facts involved in the breach of duty: s32(2).
133 Ibid s32(1)(c).
134 *Peco Arts Inc v Hazlitt Gallery Ltd* [1983] 1 WLR 1315.
135 As to which, see paras 6.110–6.116 on IPs' potential liability for costs.

from the assets of the company or the bankruptcy estate).[136] By contrast, if a corporate office-holder brings litigation in the company's name, the office-holder does not generally have a personal liability for costs, unless they might be said to be acting in their own rather than the company's interests, in which case this conduct might attract a third-party costs order.[137] However, claims by an insolvent company may well be met with an application by the respondent for security for costs.[138]

5.059   In order to fund the claim, the office-holder may consider the following options, some of which are considered in further detail later in this chapter:

(i)   Entering into a conditional fee arrangement ('CFA');
(ii)   Obtaining funding from creditors (who may lend the company or office-holder money to fund the claim directly and/or agree to indemnify them against the risk of adverse costs);
(iii) Assigning whole or part of the claim;
(iv)   Bringing in a professional litigation funder;
(v)   Entering into a damages-based agreement ('DBA');
(vi)   Insurance. The bankrupt or company may have had Before the Event legal expenses insurance ('BTE') which will pay for the cost of pursuing the claim. BTE is more common in respect of individuals who often have this type of insurance as part of their household insurance or as an extra with their bank account or credit card. Alternatively, the office-holder may wish to consider After the Event insurance ('ATE'), which may be procured to cover their or the company's own costs, the other side's costs of the claim or both.

5.060   It should be noted that, where there is a dispute between the office-holder and the creditors as to which funding option to take, resolution may be sought by the office-holder applying to the court for directions (or by a creditor applying to challenge his decision).

(b)   CFAs in insolvency

5.061   Solicitors and barristers may agree to enter into a CFA.[139] The most common arrangement is that the solicitor or barrister will receive nothing unless they achieve 'success' (as defined in the agreement itself). 'Success' is usually defined as being contingent on an outcome whereby (i) the IP becomes entitled, whether pursuant to a decision of the court or agreement between the parties, to the relief defined in the CFA for the purposes of 'success' and (in a case where the IP's entitlement to that relief is pursuant to a decision of the court) (ii) the opposing party is not allowed to appeal against the court decision, or has not appealed in time, or has entered into a settlement agreement. Other definitions of 'success' encountered may also be contingent on recovery of assets in the estate. If 'success' is achieved, the base fee plus any percentage

---

136   See paras 6.117–6.118.
137   See paras 6.119–6.123 on non-party costs orders, and *Dymocks Franchise Systems (NSW) Pty Ltd v Todd* (Costs) [2004] UKPC 39 at [29].
138   One of the grounds for applying for security for costs pursuant to the Civil Procedure Rules ('CPR') is that: 'the claimant is a company or other body (whether incorporated inside or outside Great Britain) and there is reason to believe that it will be unable to pay the defendant's costs if ordered to do so': CPR r25.13(2)(c).
139   CFAs are exempt from the 'cab rank' rule that otherwise mandates barristers to accept instructions: Bar Standards Board Handbook (version 4.4), rC30.8; gC91.

'uplift' will be payable. The maximum uplift chargeable is 100 per cent.[140] Other disbursements (such as court fees, copying charges and expert fees) will still need to be met in the usual way.

While a CFA means litigation can be run with fewer up-front costs, where a claim is successful **5.062** the success fees can significantly increase the overall costs payable and reduce the recoveries available to creditors. Although the losing party can be ordered to meet the base costs, success fees are no longer recoverable in this way for CFAs.[141]

Where the costs payable to the successful legal team exceed any recoveries actually made in the **5.063** litigation and there are insufficient funds in the estate to meet those costs, the terms of the CFA may impose personal liability on the office-holder to pay any shortfall in respect of the legal costs and uplift. This point came before the court in *Stevensdrake Ltd v Hunt.*[142] In that case the IP was appointed as liquidator of a company, principally to investigate the conduct of its previous administrators, and engaged the claimant solicitors to act in relation to litigation brought against the former administrators. The liquidator and solicitors entered into a CFA, the significant provisions of which were that:

(i)   The liquidator would be 'personally responsible for any payments that [he] may have to make under [the] agreement. Those payments are not limited by reference to the funds available in the liquidation.'

(ii)   'As with costs in general, the liquidator remain[ed] ultimately responsible for paying [the solicitor's] success fee'; and

(iii) 'Success' meant obtaining an order requiring the former administrators to the misfeasance action to contribute to the assets of the insolvency company. The definition of success was not qualified by reference to the ultimate recovery of funds in satisfaction of such an order.

The liquidator eventually settled the litigation with the former administrators, but did not **5.064** recover the full settlement sum (due to one of them becoming insolvent). Despite the lack of recovery, the settlement itself constituted 'success' under the terms of the CFA, and the solicitor sued the liquidator for their fees, and applied for summary judgment on the claim.

Chief Master Marsh granted summary judgment in favour of the solicitors on part of the claim **5.065** (that relating to counsel's fees). On appeal, the liquidator argued that, as a matter of construction, he should be taken to have entered into the CFA on behalf of the insolvent

---

140   Conditional Fee Agreements Order 2013/689 Art 3.

141   Success fees ceased to be recoverable from the other side in litigation generally from 1 April 2013: Legal Aid, Sentencing and Punishment of Offenders Act 2012 ('LASPO 2012') ss44 and 46. Insolvency proceedings were initially exempt from this change, but that exemption came to an end on 6 April 2016: Legal Aid, Sentencing and Punishment of Offenders Act 2012 (Commencement No 12) Order 2016 (SI 2016/345). Although there is no authority on this point yet, if the courts treat the application of s46 of LASPO to insolvency proceedings in the same way as its application to 'non exempt' proceedings when it first came into force (which seems likely), then a success fee payable under a CFA may still be recoverable from the other side if the CFA was entered into before 6 April 2016 and either (i) the agreement was entered into specifically for the purposes of the provision of advocacy or litigation services in connection with the matter that is the subject of the proceedings in which the costs order is made, or (ii) advocacy or litigation services were provided under the agreement in connection with that matter before 6 April 2016.

142   [2015] EWHC 1527 (Ch), [2016] BCC 485.

company, and not in his personal capacity, relying on *Stewart v Engel*.[143] He submitted that the use of the word 'responsibility' (as opposed to 'liability') in the CFA denoted an obligation to ensure that the fees were paid, should there be funds available to do so, and did not impose a direct obligation on him to pay. HHJ Purle QC did not agree with those submissions, and determined that the liquidator's argument he had not been the client lacked reality.[144] While the assumption was that a liquidator did not contract personally, the plain words of the CFA could not be ignored.

5.066 However, the liquidator was permitted to amend his defence to the remainder of the solicitor's claim for their own fees. By that amended defence, the liquidator averred that while CFAs will contain terms that success in the litigation triggers a liability to pay the fees, there is a recognised and established practice in the field of insolvency litigation against estates where there are few or no assets of value that solicitors and counsel in fact will not enforce their strict legal rights but instead provide their legal services on terms that they will become entitled to payment only out of recoveries made in the litigation, and to the extent that there are insufficient recoveries, the entitlement to payment will abate pro rata.

5.067 The liquidator further averred estoppel by convention as, on previous engagements, the solicitors had agreed to be paid on the recoveries basis and ongoing correspondence indicated that continued to be their common understanding post-CFA, and also undue influence, negligence and breach of fiduciary duty on the part of the solicitors, for not highlighting that the CFA imposed personal liability.

5.068 At trial,[145] HHJ Simon Barker QC rejected the assertion that the general practice adopted between IPs and lawyers dealing with contentious matters in nil asset estates was that the lawyers would only be paid out of recoveries, but accepted, on the unusual facts of this case, that the agreement contained an implied term that the liquidator was not personally liable for the solicitors' basic costs and uplift under the CFA (since, although this finding might superficially seem at odds with the principles governing the construction of and implication of terms into a contract, the volume and quality of the evidence that the liquidator and the solicitors actually both understood that the solicitors would be paid on the recoveries basis made any other conclusion impossible). The Court of Appeal[146] overturned this aspect of the decision, applying the orthodox principle that terms could not be implied which negated the express terms of the written agreement between the parties.[147]

5.069 Nevertheless, on the facts, the Court of Appeal upheld the judge's alternative finding that the liquidator was protected on this occasion by estoppel by convention, based on the relationship and history of dealing between the liquidator and the solicitors, both prior and subsequent to

---

143 [2000] BCC 741. There the Court of Appeal held that, when considering a liquidator's liability under a contract entered into in the course of his appointment, the starting point was that he contracted on behalf of the company to which he was appointed, and did not incur personal liability in doing so.

144 *Stevensdrake v Hunt* at [23].

145 *Stevensdrake Ltd v Hunt (No 2)* [2016] EWHC 342 (Ch), [2016] BCC 515.

146 [2017] EWCA Civ 1173.

147 See e.g., *BP Refinery (Westernport) Pty Ltd v Shire of Hastings* (1977) 180 CLR 266 at [282]–[283], approved in *Marks and Spencer plc v BNP Paribas Securities Services Trust Co (Jersey) Ltd* [2015] UKSC 72.

entry into the CFA. The outcome therefore remained practically the same, notwithstanding the different juridical route adopted by the Court of Appeal.

The case provides a salutary tale for practitioners to ensure they are extremely clear with their **5.070** clients as to the effect of a CFA where this departs drastically from the terms that governed their previous dealings.

HHJ Simon Barker QC's postscript to his first instance judgment is also notable:[148] **5.071**

> This has been a trial in which an elephant has been lurking in, or at least peering through the glass panelled doors into, the courtroom. The issues as presented and decided have not called for consideration of or a decision upon whether the arrangements that SH insists upon in few- or nil-asset estate cases offend the indemnity principle, the essence of which is that if a solicitor expressly or impliedly agrees that the firm will not in any circumstances charge the client no costs are recoverable from the other party ... There is a public interest in there being a practical means by which insolvency practitioners are able to obtain the assistance of lawyers to advise and represent them in the pursuit of misfeasant and dishonest officers and former office-holders in nil-asset estate cases where no creditor is willing to provide an indemnity, and it is the case that litigation funding is evolving, but at present the indemnity principle remains the law.

Notwithstanding the lurking doubts created by those words, it ought to be possible to **5.072** construct a funding agreement which does not offend against the indemnity principle. Indeed the CPR expressly allow for costs being recoverable notwithstanding that the client is liable to pay their own legal representative's fees and expenses only to the extent that sums, in that respect, are recovered from the other side, whether by way of costs or otherwise.[149]

(c) Creditor funding

Creditors may fund litigation by the office-holder or company, but often creditors are loath to **5.073** 'throw good money after bad'. Further, because of the *pari passu* principle, any recoveries made as a result of the litigation are shared amongst the creditors. The interest of each creditor in the fruits of the litigation may therefore be insufficient to warrant them risking further funds, even on a claim with reasonable prospects. Further, there is a risk that a creditor who funds litigation might be susceptible to a third-party costs order, particularly if they are seen to be running the litigation behind the scenes.[150]

It should be noted that just because a creditor is willing to fund litigation does not mean that **5.074** the office-holder is obliged to pursue it. The office-holder must consider the likely benefit to creditors overall. The preferable approach might be for the office-holder to agree to assign the cause of action to the creditor who wishes to fund its pursuit.[151]

---

148 *Stevensdrake Ltd v Hunt (No 2)* [2016] EWHC 342 (Ch), [2016] BCC 515 at [135]. See also *Absolute Living Developments Ltd v DS7* [2018] EWHC 1432 (Ch).
149 See CPR r44.1(3) (following the amendments made by the Civil Procedure (Amendment) Rules 2014 (SI 2014/407)).
150 See paras 6.119–6.123 below on non-party costs orders, and 5.077–5.083 below on litigation funders.
151 Note that a liquidator may not generally purport to assign his right to conduct proceedings in the name of the company, as this right is non-assignable: *Ruttle Plant Ltd v Secretary of State for the Environment (No 3)* [2008] EWHC 238 (TCC).

(d) Assignment and costs

5.075 If the cause of action is assigned to a creditor or other third party outright (e.g., for cash consideration), the IP or company will not be liable for the costs of any action taken by the assignee. By contrast, if the cause of action is assigned to a creditor or third party in return for a share of the proceeds, there remains a risk that a third-party costs order could be made against the IP or company because they retain an interest in the proceedings. The prudent IP would be wise to seek an indemnity from the assignee or the benefit of an insurance policy to cover this eventuality.

5.076 Alternatively, it is possible for an office-holder to retain the cause of action (and thus control of the litigation) but assign a share of its proceeds to a creditor or other third party in exchange for funding. It should be noted that this arrangement potentially exposes the assignee to a risk of a costs order as a third-party litigation funder.

(e) Litigation funders

5.077 Professional litigation funding is a growth area and models of funding are evolving. In the UK, there are more specialist litigation funding companies than in any other jurisdiction. England and Wales is the first and only jurisdiction to have a Code of Conduct for litigation funding, authored and enforced by the Association of Litigation Funders ('ALF'). Historically English law set its face against arrangements under which litigation was funded by third parties, such 'maintenance' or 'champerty' being contrary to public policy on the ground that involvement of interested third parties might sully the purity of justice. The modern view, however, recognises the reality of the need for litigation funding, and the current approach generally appears to be that a funding agreement will not be void save for cases where there is an element of impropriety, such as undue control by the funder, disproportionate profits or tangible risks to justice in terms of inflated claims or distortion of evidence.[152]

5.078 Most current litigation funding models involve the funder agreeing to fund all or part of the costs of the litigation (which might also include funding any order made for security for costs) in return for a fee payable from the fruits of the litigation (which might be a percentage of the amount recovered, a multiple of the funding actually deployed or reserved for the case, or some hybrid of the two, or a simple investor rate of return on funds deployed or reserved). Under most agreements the fee is contingent upon recoveries being made. A funding agreement may also include an indemnity from the funder for any adverse costs awarded.

5.079 A funder who has acquired an interest in the proceedings may be made liable for the other side's costs of proceedings. Until recently it was thought that this was usually only to the same extent as it had funded the cost of the losing litigant, unless the funding arrangement was champertous. This was known as the 'Arkin Cap' after *Arkin v Borchard Lines Ltd*,[153] in which a commercial funder that had funded the claimant's expert evidence in the sum of £1.3M in exchange for a percentage of recoveries if the claim was successful was ordered to contribute

---

152   See, e.g., *R (Factortame) v Secretary of State* [2002] EWCA Civ 932.
153   [2005] EWCA Civ 655.

£1.3M to the cost of the defendants when the claim failed. The court in *Arkin* made clear that its decision was confined to cases where the funding agreement was not champertous.[154]

The Arkin cap has since been criticised.[155] In *Bailey v GlaxoSmithkline UK Ltd*[156] the court **5.080** held that the Arkin cap was just one factor for the court to consider when deciding what level of security for costs to order against a litigation funder pursuant to CPR r25.14. Foskett J held that, since an order for security for costs does not fetter the court's discretion as to what costs award to make at the end of the case, ordering security for costs against a litigation funder in excess of the Arkin cap was appropriate.[157] He noted there would be no injustice if the cap were ultimately applied as the additional money which had been provided as security could simply be returned to the funder. Applications for security for costs against litigation funders are becoming more common. In *Wall v RBS*[158] the court held that it had power under CPR r25.14(2) to order a claimant to disclose the name and address of any third party who was funding the litigation in return for a share of the proceeds, in order to facilitate the defendant's application for security for costs against that funder. Further, in *Re Hellas Telecommunications (Luxembourg)*[159] the court ordered the respondent liquidators to disclose the identity of the funders to the litigation and the terms on which funding was provided so as to enable the defendants to make an effective application for such security, but limited the disclosure to a narrow group of individuals who would be required to give undertakings to the court that the information would not be disclosed to others or used for other purposes, in order to protect the interest of the liquidators (as there was a possibility that some of the funders were also creditors).

The stability of the Arkin Cap was brought further into doubt by the decision of Snowden J in **5.081** *Davey v Money (Costs)*.[160] The decision continued the trend in the authorities in adopting a robust and critical approach to the cap, particularly in light of developments in the market for litigation funding. Acknowledging the broad discretion available under Senior Courts Act 1981 s51, Snowden J observed that the Arkin Cap was not intended to be applied automatically, and other factors such as: (i) the association of the funder with the litigant; (ii) the likely inability of that litigant to meet any costs order made against her; and (iii) the funder's financial interest in the recoveries of the litigation outweighed the application of the Arkin Cap. Snowden J's decision was upheld by the Court of Appeal,[161] which considered that, while the Arkin Cap was by no means 'redundant', it was not a 'binding rule', the decision as to what (if any) costs order to make against a commercial funder being, ultimately, discretionary. However, it is suggested that those factors identified by Snowden J will be likely to arise in most cases where a professional funder is involved. Consequently, it seemed that in practice *Davey v Money* marked the end of the Arkin cap's application, and certainly marked the end of

---

154   At [43].
155   Sir Rupert Jackson recommended that litigation funders should face potential liability for the full amount of adverse costs without limitation to the amount of their investment (subject to judicial discretion) in his Review of Civil Litigation Costs (the 'Jackson Report', 21 December 2009) but there are to date no proposals to implement this recommendation.
156   [2017] EWHC 3195 (QB) (Foskett J).
157   Security for costs was ordered at the level of £1.75m, as compared with the funding commitment of £1.2m.
158   [2016] EWHC 2460 (Comm).
159   [2017] EWHC 3465 (Ch).
160   [2019] EWHC 997.
161   Chapelgate Credit Opportunity Master Fund Ltd v Money [2020] EWCA Civ 246.

it being applied routinely. Nevertheless, there remain instances where the court may make an order in line with the Arkin cap even after *Davey v Money*.[162] For example, Zacaroli J considered it was appropriate to do so in *Burnden UK Ltd v Fielding*.[163]

5.082 It should be noted that third-party funders (and even their parent companies) can be made liable for costs on an indemnity basis even where they are not personally responsible for the matters which gave rise to the order being made on the indemnity basis; since a funder chooses which claims to back, it cannot disassociate itself from the conduct of those claims, and a costs order can be made against a person who, in reality will receive the benefit of the litigation (such as a parent company) even if they are not a party to the funding arrangement.[164]

5.083 In practice, the issue of potential liability for adverse costs is often dealt with by funders making offers conditional on sufficient ATE being purchased to cover the adverse costs risk.

(f) Damages based agreements

5.084 Further, DBAs are now allowed in most civil litigation in England and Wales.[165] Solicitors who agree to act under a DBA essentially become litigation funders, self-funding the work carried out on behalf of the client in exchange for a share in the fruits of the litigation. A further market evolution (the advent of DBA insurance with deferred contingent premiums) makes these arrangements far more palatable to solicitors, who can insure part of their fees in the event of a loss or low value outcome.

(g) After the event insurance ('ATE') and security for costs

5.085 ATE insurance is an extremely useful way for an IP to limit their own risk in litigation, provided it can be obtained in a sufficient sum and for a reasonable premium. Premiums are often staged so they increase over the life of the litigation, in order to remain proportionate with the costs incurred. It is usually also possible to obtain a contingent premium which is only payable in the event of success, but it is no longer possible to reclaim an ATE premium from the other side in successful litigation,[166] and thus the premium will reduce recoveries to creditors. ATE providers will usually wish to be assured, by means of a written opinion from solicitors or counsel, that the claim has sufficient merit for them to agree to insure it, and will require updates on prospects of success throughout the litigation where there are key developments in the case, and in particular where there is a material change in the merits.

5.086 The major advantage of ATE is removing the risk of adverse costs if the case is lost, but it may also have a part to play in defeating a defendant's application for security for costs, although the

---

162 For example, where the funder has covered the costs associated with a discrete element of the case only, e.g. instructing experts, as was the fact pattern in Arkin.

163 [2019] EWHC 2995 (Ch).

164 See *Excalibur Ventures LLC v Texas Keystone Inc* [2014] EWHC 3436 (Comm) in which two funders, and their parent companies, were held jointly and severally responsible to pay the successful defendant's costs on an indemnity basis in an unsuccessful claim relating to interests in oil fields in Kurdistan, which was objectively hopeless.

165 With effect from 1 April 2013: LASPO 2012.

166 ATE premiums ceased to be recoverable from the other side in litigation generally from 1 April 2013: LASPO ss44 and 46. See fn 141 above.

courts have reached differing views on this, and the cases turn on the facts of the case and the wording of the relevant policy. This is illustrated in the leading case of *Premier Motorauctions Ltd v PricewaterhouseCoopers* where at first instance Snowden J took the view that the ATE policy was such that there was no real risk of avoidance, but the Court of Appeal took a different view.[167] Subsequent cases, including those outside the immediate insolvency context, have not always taken the same approach.[168] It remains an open question as to whether a person who arranges a deed of indemnity or such other security as may be required may be able to recover those costs, notwithstanding the fact that ordinarily an ATE premium is not recoverable.[169]

However, it should also be noted that ATE may also function as a bar to settlement in some **5.087** cases, since the premium will erode the recoveries actually available for the creditors. It may also be unaffordable or not available in marginal cases, which nevertheless have merit. In those circumstances the office-holder may wish to take advantage of the ability to bring claims in the name of a company without having to provide for security (using, e.g., IA 1986 s212). In other cases, the office-holder may prefer to bring a claim in the name of the company and seek to resist an order for security for costs. In *Absolute Living Developments Ltd (in liquidation) v DS7 Ltd*[170] a claim was brought with the benefit of funding support from lawyers (acting on a conditional fee basis), an ATE policy was not available (or not available at a suitable price) and there were no other sources of funding available. The respondents applied for security for costs, but the court declined to order security. Marcus Smith J placed emphasis on the fact that the IP should not be expected to expose themselves personally, and had satisfied him that other funding sources were not reasonably available.[171] In addition, claims may be brought in the name of both the IP and the company. In those circumstances the resources and assets of the IP may be relevant to any application against the company as co-claimant.[172]

(h) Office-holders' fees and expenses

It should be noted that office-holders' fees and expenses of investigating and bringing a claim **5.088** are not ordinarily recoverable as damages in the litigation, and will need to be accounted for out of the assets of the company or the bankruptcy estate, or any recoveries made in the litigation.[173] A litigation funder may agree to cover some or all of these costs as part of a funding package.

---

167 *Premier Motorauctions Ltd (in liquidation) v PricewaterhouseCoopers and Lloyds Bank* [2017] EWCA Civ 1872 on 23 November, allowing an appeal against the decision of Snowden J ([2016] EWHC 2610 (Ch), [2017] 4 All ER 243).

168 See, e.g., *Bailey v GlaxoSmithkline UK Ltd v Managed Legal Solutions Ltd* [2017] EWHC 3195 (QB) and see also *UK Trucks Claim Ltd v Fiat Chrysler Automobiles NV* [2019] CAT 26 (unrep'd, 28 October 2019).

169 There does not appear to be any authority which has considered whether the cost of arranging a deed of indemnity to an ATE policy, in order to meet an application for security, is recoverable post-LASPO. It might be thought that in principle it should be, applying, by analogy, cases such as *ENE KoS 1 Ltd v Petroleo Brasileiro SA (No 2)* [2009] EWHC 1843 (Comm) at [76]–[96], upheld in the Court of Appeal in [2010] EWCA Civ 772 at [55] (appealed on a different point to the Supreme Court). However, this may be difficult to reconcile with the wording in LASPO and therefore remains open for argument.

170 [2018] EWHC 1432 (Ch).

171 Ibid, at [34]–[35].

172 See the decision in *Holyoake v Candy* [2016] EWHC 3065 (Ch), where Nugee J accepted that if a co-claimant might be liable for costs, then their asset position may become relevant.

173 *Re Ralls Builders (in liquidation)* [2016] EWHC 1812 (Ch). See paras 3.023–3.028 above on office-holder's remuneration. A possible exception to this may arise where the losses claimed is based on avoidance of an insolvency procedure.

C. APPLICATIONS TO COURT FOR DIRECTIONS

1. Introduction

5.089 An important, and sometimes overlooked, power of an office-holder is to apply to the court for directions. This can provide a useful gateway for an IP to seek to avoid liability, though, as appears below, it is not a panacea.

5.090 Table 5.1 sets out the relevant statutory provision granting this power in respect of each type of insolvency proceeding:

Table 5.1   Statutory provisions for applications for directions

Type of insolvency proceeding	Office-holder (or third party)	Statutory provision
Administration	Administrator	Paragraph 63, Schedule B1, IA 1986
	Creditor	Although there is no express provision for a creditor to apply for directions, there is authority for a creditor to do so under the court's general power to exercise control over administrators as officers of the court in *Re Mirror Group (Holdings) Ltd*[174]
Compulsory liquidation	Liquidator	Section 168(3), IA 1986
	Creditor or contributory	Section 167(3), IA 1986
Voluntary liquidation	Liquidator, creditors and contributories	Section 112, IA 1986
Company voluntary arrangement	Supervisor	Section 7(4)(a), IA 1986
	Creditor or third party	Section 7(3), IA 1986
Receivership	Receiver and those who appointed the receiver	Section 35, IA 1986
Bankruptcy	Trustee in bankruptcy	Section 303(2), IA 1986
	Bankrupt, creditor or third party	Section 303(1), IA 1986
Individual voluntary arrangement	Supervisor	Section 263(4), IA 1986
	Debtor, creditor or third party	Section 263(3), IA 1986

5.091 By an application for directions the court is asked to make an order directing how an issue should be dealt with, to assist the parties where the IP is unsure how to proceed or if a dispute has arisen. The benefits of making such an application are obvious; the IP is able to proceed in the knowledge that their actions have been effectively approved by the court. However, such an

---

174   [1992] BCC 972.

application is not to be used as a mere rubber-stamping exercise. Nor should such applications be made where the IP effectively surrenders their discretion to the court.

Applications for directions are governed by different sections of the IA 1986 depending on the insolvency process, and each will be considered in turn in this section. It is important to note, however, that the courts have generally applied the tests in a similar way, often citing authority relating to one of the other provisions in coming to a decision. The words of Neuberger J (as he then was) in *Re T&D Industries plc (in administration)*,[175] give a flavour of the stance that will be taken by the court when an office-holder asks for guidance on how to act:[176] **5.092**

> My decision tends to emphasise the fact that a person appointed to act as an administrator may be called upon to make important and urgent decisions. He has a responsible and potentially demanding role. Commercial and administrative decisions are for him and the court is not there to act as a sort of bomb shelter for him.

An application may be required or desirable, subject to the issues identified below, in order to determine issues about the validity of security registered against the company's assets and the extent to which they are enforceable, the remuneration of the office-holder (although this may not be available to all office-holders), or other complex issues of law that arise, such as jurisdictional challenges. **5.093**

2. Scope

(a) Administrators[177]

The administrator is a professional person expected to exercise professional and commercial judgment. As such, the court is unlikely to be persuaded to make a direction where the administrator is doing no more than effectively attempting to surrender their discretion. Neither will the court interfere or be drawn into the day-to-day running of the administration,[178] or give directions on matters with which it is the administrator's responsibility to deal.[179] **5.094**

Thus the court will not normally interfere with a commercial decision made by an administrator unless the decision is wrong at law, or is clearly unfair to a particular creditor or person dealing with the company,[180] or is tainted by any collateral purpose (such as might amount to 'a fraud on the power'). The administrator must have properly considered their proposals to be for the benefit of those for whom they act. **5.095**

However, the administrator may apply to the court where, although clearly a matter within the administrator's powers, the proposed course is of a *'significant nature'* such that it would be **5.096**

---

175 [2000] 1 WLR 646, [2000] 1 All ER 333, [2000] 1 BCLC 471 at 657.
176 See also *Re Longmeade Ltd (in liquidation)* [2016] EWHC 356 (Ch).
177 Sch B1 para 63.
178 See *Re Lehman Brothers International (Europe) (in administration)* [2008] EWHC 2869 (Ch).
179 See *RAB Capital plc v Lehman Brothers International (Europe)* [2008] EWHC 2335 (Ch).
180 See *Re C E King Ltd* [2000] 2 BCLC 297 and *Re Zegna III Holdings Inc* [2009] EWHC 2994 (Ch), [2010] BPIR 277.

appropriate to seek the directions from the court. In *Re Nortel Group (Global Settlement)*,[181] the proposed settlement involved the administrations of some 19 companies across Europe and their claims in relation to their Canadian parent company. HHJ Hodge QC made clear that the court need only be satisfied that the exercise of the administrator's power was both '*rational and a decision honestly reached*'.[182]

5.097 The subjects upon which an administrator may apply to the court for directions are not circumscribed beyond the very wide description of their being 'in connection with his functions'.[183]

5.098 Although the Insolvency (England and Wales) Rules 2016 ('IR 2016') do not contain any express provisions for expense claims to be made and determined, there is no doubt that Sch B1 para 63 enables an administrator to apply for directions from the court if they are in any doubt as to what qualifies as an expense.[184]

5.099 It is also now accepted that the court can use its powers to give directions under paragraph 63 to both: (i) assist administrators in ascertaining which liabilities of the company properly rank as administration expenses; and (ii) authorise administrators to distribute the property of the company to unsecured creditors who rank lower in order of priority in the statutory waterfall without regard to any claims for administration expenses that have not been made by a specified date.[185] In such cases the discretionary question as to whether the court should give directions is whether it is just to do so, balancing both the interests of those who might have expenses claims against the need to efficiently conclude the insolvency process.[186]

5.100 In *Re Nortel Networks UK Ltd (No 2)* and *Re Nortel Networks SA (in administration)*[187] the court made orders that administrators could inform potential claimants for expense claims in the administrations to notify the administrators by a specified 'bar date' of their claim. Late expense claims after that date would not be extinguished, but would only be paid to the extent that the administrators had any unreserved funds available after making distributions to unsecured creditors.

5.101 However, the court does not have the jurisdiction to make directions that would illegitimately extinguish the right of creditors or vary the statutory waterfall; or amount to judicial legislation.[188]

---

181   [2016] EWHC 2769 (Ch).
182   See also *Tamlin v Edgar* [2011] EWHC 3949 (Ch).
183   *Re Collins & Aikman Europe SA* [2006] EWHC 1343 (Ch), [2006] BCC 861 (Lindsay J).
184   See *In re Nortel GmbH* [2013] Bus LR 1056; *Re London Bridge Entertainment Partners* [2019] EWHC 2932 (Ch) (payments to replenish a deposit not covered by *Lundy Granite* principle).
185   *In re Nortel Networks UK Ltd (No 2)* [2017] EWHC 1429 (Ch), [2018] Bus LR 206 at 222 (Snowden J) and *Re Nortel Networks SA (in administration)* [2018] EWHC 1812 (Ch), [2018] 7 WLUK 369.
186   See also *In re R-R Realisations* [1980] 1 WLR 805 and *In re WW Realisation 1 Ltd* [2012] 1 BCLC 405.
187   [2017] EWHC 1429 (Ch) and [2018] EWHC 1812 respectively.
188   See the observations of Lord Neuberger PSC in *In re Nortel GmbH* at [115]–[127] and also in *Lehmans Waterfall* [2017] 2 WLR 1497 at [13].

(b) Liquidators

(i) Compulsory liquidation[189]

The court will not generally become involved in giving directions to liquidators as to how to make commercial or administrative decisions.[190] An obvious example of this is where a liquidator is required to make a decision on proof of debt. In such cases, there is a clearly defined process within the IR 2016 for the liquidator to adjudicate on the proof of those claims and for parties to appeal that decision and, as a result, is unlikely to be a matter on which the court will give directions. **5.102**

However, a liquidator might properly seek guidance from the courts before adjudicating on a creditor's claim for voting purposes where they seek assistance on a point of law, particularly in an area of developing jurisprudence, such as whether or not a given claim should be treated as liquidated or unliquidated.[191] **5.103**

Further, the court will take a pragmatic approach to conflicts and will decide what to do as and when the issue of possible conflict arises.[192] The use of the directions procedure in IA 1986 s168(3) is the appropriate route to use in such circumstances.[193] **5.104**

(ii) Voluntary liquidation[194]

The court has a discretion and may refuse to permit proceedings under this provision where some other procedure is more appropriate.[195] It has also been said that an application for directions under IA 1986 s112 in a voluntary liquidation will only be entertained where its purpose is a legitimate purpose of the liquidation.[196] It seems the test to be applied is whether the direction would 'be conducive to both the proper operation of the process of liquidation and to justice between all those interested in the liquidation'.[197] In *Kean v Lucas*[198] the court refused an application by a liquidator for directions that would have prevented a meeting which the requisite number of creditors sought to vote for the liquidator's removal for failing to meet this test. **5.105**

---

189 IAA 1986 s168(3).

190 *Re Longmeade Ltd (in liquidation)* [2016] EWHC 356 (Ch), [2016] All ER (D) 259 (Feb).

191 See *Day v Haine* [2007] EWHC 2691 (Ch), [2007] BPIR 1470, [2008] ICR 452.

192 Possible solutions include the appointment of conflict liquidators (*Re Arrows Ltd* [1992] BCC 121) or the joint instruction of counsel by the administrators of each of the relevant companies to advise on the merits and propose a way forward (*Re TPS Investments (UK) Ltd* [2018] EWHC 360 (Ch)). See Oulton and Shah, 'Claims against administrators: some causes, the import of recent cases and the approach of the courts' (2019) 32(3) *Insolv Int* 96–100.

193 *Re Angel Group Ltd* [2016] 2 BCLC 509.

194 IA 1986 s112.

195 See *Re Stetzel Thomson & Co Ltd* (1988) 4 BCC 74.

196 *IRC v Mills* [2003] EWHC 2022 (Ch).

197 HHJ Cooke in *Autobrokers Ltd v Dymond* [2015] EWHC 2691 (Admin), [2017] BCC 291 at [8], citing *Re Barings plc; Hamilton v Law Debenture Trustees Ltd* [2001] 2 BCLC 159.

198 [2017] EWHC 250 (Ch), [2017] BCC 311.

5.106   IA 1986 s112 also confers a discretion to order disclosure.[199] Where the liquidator uses the procedure to obtain a collateral advantage it will not act as a complete bar to the court's discretion.[200] However, s112 should not be invoked to create an equivalent right to that under some other, more appropriate procedure, for example, section IA 1986 s236, which would otherwise be unavailable to a party.[201]

5.107   The court confirmed, in *Re Central A1 Ltd; Rubin v Cohen*,[202] that it had jurisdiction on an application for directions to determine a dispute as to reasonableness or necessity regarding fixed fees charged by accountants for work undertaken in relation to statements of affairs and meetings of creditors of a large number of companies to enable them to be placed into creditors' voluntary liquidation.

(c)   Receivers

5.108   IA 1986 s35 enables a receiver to apply for directions. This has been interpreted to include guidance on remuneration.[203] Usually, however, the provision has been used for the receiver, or their appointor, to apply to the court for directions in the event of legal uncertainty arising. For example, in *Re Cheyne Finance plc*[204] directions were given on what would amount to an insolvency event as defined in the trust deed and accordingly what payments the receivers should make and when. In *Bank of Ireland v Edeneast Ltd*,[205] the court again took a wide view of the power to give directions making a retrospective appointment of a receiver, although it should be noted that this case involved a court appointed receiver and manager.

(d)   Trustee in bankruptcy

5.109   Either the trustee or the official receiver may apply to the court for directions in relation to any particular matter arising under the bankruptcy pursuant to IA 1986 s303(2). The proposed course of action must be for the benefit of the estate and the court is likely to defer to the trustee's view on this issue.[206]

5.110   In general, therefore, the court will usually be reluctant to give directions to a trustee where a professional judgment needs to be made, even on difficult questions.[207] The court is also unlikely to give directions on the day-to-day administration of the estate, save in cases of serious irregularity or wholly unreasonable conduct.[208] As it was put in *Re a Debtor (No 400 of*

---

199   *Inland Revenue v Blueslate* [2003] EWHC 2022 (Ch) and confirmed in *Re Sustainable Wealth Investments (UK) Ltd* [2015] EWHC 1674. The court, again, will only make such a direction where it was just and beneficial to do so, *Sunwing Vacation Inc v E-Clear (UK) plc* [2011] EWHC 1544 (Ch), [2011] 6 WLUK 27.
200   *Re Movitex Ltd* [1992] BCC 101.
201   See *Re McHale (James) Automobiles Ltd* [1997] 1 BCLC 273, [1997] BCC 202, ChD and followed in *MG Rover Dealer Properties Ltd v Hunt* [2013] BCC 698, [2012] BPIR 590.
202   [2017] EWHC 220 (Ch), [2017] BCC 69.
203   See *Re Therm-a-Stor Ltd* [1996] 1 WLR 1338, [1997] BCC 301 and *Munns v Perkins* [2002] BPIR 120.
204   [2007] EWHC 2402 (Ch), [2008] BCC 182.
205   [2013] NIQB 95.
206   *Re Omar (a bankrupt)* [1999] BPIR 1001.
207   See e.g., *Parker v Nicholson* [2015] EWHC 3881 (Ch), [2015] All ER (D) 278 (Nov).
208   See *Re a Debtor (No 400 of 1940)* [1949] Ch 236 and *Osborn v Cole* [1999] BPIR 251.

1940):[209] 'It is the right and duty of the trustee to realise that which vests in him to the best advantage, and it is for him alone to decide ... how best the realisation may be made.'

A good example of this approach is the case of *In Re Chinn*[210] in which Registrar Barber **5.111** refused to give directions to a trustee on whether to admit a proof of debt, characterising such an application as cautious and seeking 'bomb shelter' protection from the court.[211]

Examples of successful applications for directions include *Buchler v Al-Midani (No 3)*[212] where **5.112** an order was made preventing the bankrupt from taking steps in foreign proceedings and *Donaldson v O'Sullivan*[213] where a trustee in bankruptcy was appointed under a block transfer order.[214] Ultimately, this provision allows a trustee to apply to the court for guidance on a difficult matter so that the court can make appropriate orders to take the bankruptcy forward, for example to determine the competing jurisdictions of the bankruptcy court and the First-tier Tax Tribunal.[215]

The test to be applied under IA 1986 s303(2) is the same as that under s303(1).[216] Section **5.113** 303(1) allows the bankrupt, any of his creditors, or any other person who is dissatisfied by an act, omission or decision of the trustee of a bankrupt's estate to apply to the court, which may confirm, reverse or modify any act or decision of the trustee or give directions or make any other such order as it thinks fit.

Importantly, unlike other provisions in this part, Ferris J held in *Re Peri*[217] that IA 1986 s303 **5.114** did not give the court jurisdiction to determine questions of renumeration but that this was a matter that ought properly to be regulated by IA 1986 s363 and the IR 2016.

(e) Supervisors

(i) CVA[218]

In *Re Alpa Lighting Ltd,*[219] Nourse LJ confirmed that the only power conferred on the court **5.115** pursuant to IA 1986 s7(4)(a) is to give directions in relation to any particular matter arising *under* the voluntary arrangement. Thus, the arrangement must still be subsisting before the court may make directions. Further, it was said (*obiter*) that there was no authority that a power to give directions under an instrument, whether it be a voluntary arrangement under the IA 1986, a trust instrument, or other such instrument, that such a discretion included a power to amend the instrument. This is in contrast to the decision of Hoffmann J (as he then was) in

---

209 *Ex parte the Debtor v Dodwell (the Trustee)* [1949] 1 Ch 236, 241 (Harman J).
210 (unrep'd, 10 November 2015).
211 See also the cases of *Leon v York-o-Matic* [1966] 3 All ER 277 and *Re Greenhaven Motors Ltd* [1997] BCC 547 (the enunciation of the test being approved by the Court of Appeal) but which are directed more at applications made by the bankrupt rather than the office-holder.
212 [2006] EWHC 170 (Ch), [2006] BPIR 881.
213 [2008] EWCA Civ 879.
214 But see now IR 2016 rr12.35–12.38.
215 *Ariel v Revenue and Customs Commissioners, Re Halabi* [2016] BPIR 373 (Registrar Derrett).
216 *Re Michael* [2010] BPIR 418.
217 [2002] EWHC 799 (Ch), [2002] BPIR 961.
218 Under IA 1986 s7(4)(a).
219 [1997] BPIR 341.

Re FMS Financial Management Services Ltd,[220] where he directed that shareholders not included under the arrangement should be treated as creditors and be given the benefit of the scheme, with the consequence that the other creditors received a substantially smaller dividend. This case was not overturned in *Re Alpa* but distinguished on the basis that the arrangement in *Re FMS* was still subsisting at the time of the application. It is nevertheless difficult to reconcile with the *obiter* comments of Nourse LJ. In both *Re Beloit Walmsley Ltd*[221] and *Re A Block Transfer by Kaye*[222] HHJ Pelling QC took the position that *FMS* ought not to be followed. The comments of Norris J in *Re Hellard and Goldfarb (Joint Supervisors of Pinson Wholesale Ltd)*[223] that *FMS* makes it possible 'that what is effectively a variation may be brought about, provided that it is not an actual variation of the approved proposal' seem somewhat contrived and unpersuasive. However, what is clear is that IA 1986 s7(4)(a) gives the court a jurisdiction to make directions as to supervisor renumeration.

(ii) IVA[224]

5.116 The relevant provision for IVA supervisors is IA 1986 s263(4), which is applied in the same way as s7(4)(a) applies to CVA supervisors. Thus, on an application under IA 1986 s263(4), the court is not able to vary the IVA.[225] Whether the court is able to investigate the level of remuneration claimed by a supervisor of an IVA is not certain, but the Court of Appeal suggested in *King v Anthony*[226] that this would fall within its jurisdiction under IA 1986 s263. Further, given the similarity of approach taken by the court in respect of CVAs and IVAs, and the readiness of the court to give directions on renumeration in *Re Hellard*, it seems likely that this would also be the case under s263(4) should the circumstances so require it.

5.117 It has been held, but only at County Court level, that IA 1986 s263(4) was never intended to provide the court with the power to resolve matters of civil jurisdiction between the supervisor and some third party.[227]

3. Commercial decision – when not to apply to court

5.118 The courts generally defer to the professionalism of office-holders in conducting their affairs. To make an application for directions before making a decision which the Rules require an office-holder to make, for example, whether to admit or reject a creditor's proof, would not only be misconceived but is likely to avoid the costs protections afforded to them under IR 2016 r14.9[228] and may leave, for example, a trustee vulnerable to a personal costs order being made against them. As a result, it is likely to be both more time and cost efficient for the office-holder to make the decision that they are empowered to do. However, the court will only rarely seek to intervene in a decision that has been made that calls for commercial and administrative judgment. Applications made by other parties appealing the decision of an

---

220   (1989) 5 BCC 191.
221   [2008] EWHC 1888 (Ch), [2008] BPIR 1445.
222   [2010] EWHC 692 (Ch), [2010] BPIR 602.
223   [2008] BCC 112.
224   IA 1986 s263(4).
225   See the discussion of *Re Alpa* above and also *Raja v Rubin* [1999] BPIR 575.
226   [1999] BPIR 73.
227   *Re Section 263(4) of the Insolvency Act 1986* [1994] 9 WLUK 132 County Court (Truro); Bhogal v Knight [2018] EWHC 2952 (Ch).
228   Previously IR 1986 r6.94(5).

office-holder have high thresholds that afford a great degree of protection, both personally and in terms of costs. This includes situations where an office-holder makes a reasonable decision based upon evidence available to them at the time but the position subsequently changes when further evidence comes to life, particularly where the office-holder has already requested such information, in the context of a supervisor.[229] It may often be quicker and cheaper for an office-holder to make a decision and then respond to any challenge which is likely to be more focused on a particular issue.

However, parties should also not be tempted to see such applications as a backdoor route to remedies that would otherwise be available under a different procedure as this is likely to lead to an adverse costs order. If a more appropriate procedure is available, then that route should be taken. **5.119**

D. DEALING WITH PROPERTY

1. Real property

A liquidator and administrator have the express power to sell or otherwise dispose of the property of the company.[230] An administrative receiver appointed under a debenture is deemed to have the powers specified in Schedule 1 to the IA 1986 (i.e. the same powers as an administrator).[231] **5.120**

A trustee in bankruptcy has the power to sell any part of the property comprised in the bankruptcy estate and to make any arrangement as may be thought expedient with respect to any claim arising out of or incidental to the bankrupt's estate.[232] The effect of the vesting of the bankruptcy estate in a trustee is that, where the legal title is vested, they can deal with the estate as legal owner. Where the property is held on trust, only the beneficial title vests in the trustee and they can exercise their rights as a beneficiary of the trust. **5.121**

The largest asset to be realised in most bankruptcies will be real property; usually the family home where the bankrupt is a homeowner, and perhaps some additional rental properties. Where the property is solely owned, the matter is straightforward. The trustee in bankruptcy can apply to the Land Registry to have the property registered in his name and can convey the property without recourse to the bankrupt. Where the property is occupied, the trustee will usually apply to the court for an order for possession and will generally also ask for an order for sale at the same time, as well as other consequential orders, which the court can grant under its general power of control in IA 1986 s363.[233] **5.122**

---

229   See *Re Linfoot (A Debtor)* [2018] EWHC 2952 (Ch).
230   IA 1986 Schs 1 and 4.
231   Ibid s42. See Annexes I and II.
232   Ibid s314 Sch 4 paras 9 and 9B.
233   *Holtham v Keltmanson* [2006] BPIR 1422.

5.123 Where the property is jointly owned, the trustee can apply for an order for sale, just as the bankrupt can, under TOLATA 1996 s14.[234] In practice most trustees will wait for a year from their appointment before making such an application, as when an application for sale is made after the end of the period of one year beginning with the first vesting of the bankrupt's estate in a trustee, the court shall assume, unless the circumstances of the case are exceptional, that the interests of the bankrupt's creditors outweigh all other considerations.[235] The interests of the bankrupt will never be relevant to the exercise of the court's discretion,[236] and the threshold for *'exceptional circumstances'* is a high one.[237] If there are exceptional circumstances, the court can also decide to postpone the sale (rather than order it immediately).

5.124 During the period between the bankruptcy order having been made and the sale of the property, the non-bankrupt owner may have been paying the mortgage. Upon the division of the proceeds of sale, credit should normally be given by the trustee to the non-bankrupt owner for the proportion of the mortgage payments (both capital and interest[238]) which is attributable to the bankrupt's liability under the mortgage.

5.125 The court will often order a sum of money to be paid by the non-bankrupt co-owner to the trustee as an occupation rent. It seems such a rent can be payable even in cases where the bankrupt continues to reside in the property post-bankruptcy order.[239] It has been the usual practice of the court to allow, from the date of bankruptcy, any credit due for the interest element of mortgage payments to be set off against the liability of the co-owner to pay an 'occupation rent' to the trustee in bankruptcy, to avoid the necessity of expensive and protracted inquiries and accounts,[240] although 'if the trustee in bankruptcy insists on strict accounts being taken, then he is entitled to do so, at least unless it can be seen in advance that

---

234 Other considerations in TOLATA 1996 s15 are however replaced by IA 1986 s335A.

235 IA 1986 s335A(3).

236 Ibid s335A(2)(c).

237 *Dean v Stout* [2005] EWHC 3315 (Ch), [2005] BPIR 1113 at [6]–[11] (Lawrence Collins J).

238 *In re Gorman* [1990] 1 WLR 616 (Vinelott J).

> I can see no reason why, if an account is taken, the party paying the instalments should not be entitled to set a due proportion of the whole of the instalments paid against the share of the other party. The mortgagee will normally have a charge on the property for principal and interest and a right to possession and sale to enforce his charge. The payment of instalments due under the mortgage operates to relieve the property from the charge and gives rise to an equitable right of contribution by the co-owner who has not paid his due proportion of the instalments.

239 See *Re Byford* [2003] EWHC 1267 (Ch), [2003] BPIR 1089 and *French v Barcham* [2008] EWHC 1505 (Ch), [2009] 1 WLR 1124 at [35] (Blackburne J):

> When a trustee in bankruptcy has been appointed of the estate of a co-owner so that that co-owner's interest vests in the trustee, but the other co-owner remains in occupation of the property, application of the principle will ordinarily, if not invariably, result in the occupying co-owner having to account to the trustee of the beneficial interest to which the bankrupt co-owner was formally entitled for an occupation rent. This is because it is not reasonable to expect – even if it were otherwise practicable for him to do so – the trustee in bankruptcy to exercise the right of occupation attaching to the interest in the property that vested in him on his appointment as trustee of the bankrupt co-owner. If it could be shown that the occupying co-owner was given by the trustee to understand that no occupation rent would be charged or was unaware of, and had no reasonable means of discovering, the other co-owner's bankruptcy, the court might take the view that it would not be just to require the occupying co-owner to pay an occupation rent. But short of such circumstances it is difficult to see why the occupying co-owner should not be charged an occupation rent.

> See also *Davis v Jackson* [2017] EWHC 698 (Ch) where the property was acquired jointly by the bankrupt and his wife but it was only intended to be a home for her.

240 *In re Gorman* [1990] 1 WLR 616.

the amounts are likely to be so similar that the taking of the two accounts would be a waste of time and the costs would outweigh any possible advantage to be gained thereby'.[241] The account and setting-off is not an exact science, and if arguments present themselves as to a shift in common intention giving rise to a common intention constructive trust,[242] it may be more economical for those matters to be 'set off' in the same way.

2. Assigning claims

All office-holders have the power to assign claims vested in them or the insolvent company, provided that the claim is capable of assignment.[243] The office-holder, as an officer of the court, has to satisfy himself as to the viability of the cause of action, especially if it is being assigned back to the bankrupt, or to the directors of the company, which might expose the defendant to vexatious litigation. **5.126**

Office-holders are therefore permitted to make such assignments back to the director or bankrupt, but must exercise care when doing so, and as a matter of practice would be well advised not to do so unless clear and certain benefits are likely to be obtained for the creditors.[244] **5.127**

These sorts of considerations mean the office-holder is not necessarily obliged to assign a cause of action to the highest bidder, for instance if the only offer is derisory and seeking other offers would be an unjustifiable expense.[245] **5.128**

---

241 *Re Pavlou* [1993] 1 WLR 1046, 1051C–D (Millett J), 'In such a case the court might well impose its own solution of directing the interest element in the mortgage instalments to be set off against the use and occupation without any further inquiry.'

242 As described and identified in e.g., *Stack v Dowden* [2007] UKHL 17.

243 IA 1986 s246ZD, introduced by SBEEA 2015 s118, enables corporate 'office-holder' claims to be assigned. The assignment of the particular claim must also not be prohibited (i) by contractual terms, (ii) by statute or public policy, (iii) because it is a purely personal contract or covenant, or (iv) because assignment would adversely affect the obligor.

244 *Re Papaloizou* [1999] BPIR 106, 112 (Browne-Wilkinson J) (*obiter*):

   At best the transaction here was very close to the line of what is permissible ... I think trustees should exercise their power to take such a step with great circumspection. It must not be forgotten that by so doing they are enabling the bankrupt to conduct possibly vexatious litigation against third parties who will have no effective remedy in costs against him, since all his assets have been vested in the trustee. There may be cases in which this is an appropriate course to adopt, for example if immediate substantial assets are made available for the creditors. But in general the policy of the bankruptcy legislation is for the trustee – and not any one else – to get in the assets of the bankrupt and for that purpose to decide whether causes of action should be pursued, if necessary with funds provided for that purpose by the creditors in the bankruptcy. Before abdicating this responsibility by putting the bankrupt back in the saddle, the trustee should bear in mind the consequences to the other parties in litigation of so doing. My present view is that it should not be done unless clear and certain benefits are obtained for the creditors.

   See also *Re Shettar* [2003] EWHC 220 (Ch); [2003] BPIR 1055 at [21]–[24] and *Cummings v Official Receiver* [2004] All ER (D) 328.

245 *Khan v Official Receiver* [1997] BPIR 109 where the Court of Appeal refused a bankrupt permission to appeal against a district judge's decision not to compel the official receiver to assign him a potential cause of action against his former solicitors for £100 which he was prepared to increase to £1,000. Cf. the decision in *Hamilton v Official Receiver* [1998] BPIR 602 where the OR was compelled to assign a cause of action which could have been worth c £500,000 for £1,000. In Laddie J's view, the refusal to accept a reasonable and indeed the only offer on the table for an asset which the receiver had no interest now in realising was perverse. He seemed to be influenced by the fact that the cause of action might be worth a substantial sum.

3. Pre-packs

5.129 There was initially some controversy as regards the power to effect a 'pre-packaged' sale of a business, effectively at the same time as an administrator was appointed.[246] The three main concerns troubling practitioners were whether they needed court sanction, whether administrators unlawfully fettered their discretion by doing so, and whether conflicts could be effectively managed. The first two concerns were effectively answered by the two first instance decisions of *T & D Industries plc*[247] (pre-EA 2002) and *Transbus International Ltd* (post-EA 2002).[248]

5.130 The last issue, that of potential for conflict and transparency, has remained a concern. The position was improved by the introduction of SIP 16. The purpose of this SIP was to ensure that creditors are informed of the reasons why an IP decided on a pre-packaged sale.[249]

4. Onerous property

(a) What constitutes onerous property

5.131 Both liquidators and trustees in bankruptcy (but not administrators or administrative receivers) have a statutory power to disclaim 'onerous' property.[250] This enables office-holders to discard property which is considered to be a burden, thus limiting the exposure of the insolvent estate to any ongoing liability in respect of that property. Anyone suffering loss as a consequence of disclaimer may prove as an unsecured creditor in the estate in respect of compensation for the loss, but has no other remedy.[251]

5.132 For the purpose of disclaimer, 'onerous property' consists of:

(1) *Any unprofitable contract*: this is a contract the satisfactory performance of which would prejudice the office-holder's obligation to realise the assets comprised in the insolvent estate and make a distribution to creditors within a reasonable time. It is not enough that the contract is fiscally disadvantageous or that if he were to disclaim the trustee could get a better deal. It must have the potential to interfere with the swift administration of the insolvency in a way detrimental to the interests of the creditors.[252] Thus a contract cannot normally be disclaimed if it requires no future performance by the office-holder.[253]

---

246   For a historical discussion as to the position before and after the EA 2002 see Sims and Cranston, 'Pre-packs: recent law and practice' (Seminar paper, 16 April 2007). Accessible online at: https://www.guildhallchambers.co.uk/files/Pre-packs_RecentLaw&Practice_HS&PeterCranston.pdf (accessed 24 April 2020).

247   [2000] 1 WLR 646 (Neuberger J).

248   [2004] EWHC 932 (Ch), [2004] 1 WLR 2654 (Lawrence Collins J).

249   See further paras 6.178–6.181 below, and in particular on the Pre-Pack Pool.

250   See IA 1986 ss178 (liquidation) and 315 (bankruptcy).

251   IA 1986 ss178(6) (liquidation) and 315(5) (bankruptcy). See Frieze, 'Control of the insolvency practitioner' (2010) 23(8) *Insolv Int* 126–7.

252   *Manning v AIG Europe UK Ltd* [2006] EWCA Civ 7, [2006] Ch 610.

253   *In re SSSL Realisations (2002) Ltd; Squires v AIG Europe (UK) Ltd* [2006] EWCA Civ 7, [2006] Ch 610 (CA).

(2) Any other property[254] of the company or in the bankrupt's estate that is:

    (i) Unsaleable or not readily saleable (and the question of whether property is readily saleable is a matter to be determined by the trustee in bankruptcy and the court will only intervene if the decision to disclaim is perverse or has been exercised in bad faith); or

    (ii) Such that it might give rise to a liability to pay money or perform any other onerous act.

(b) When can an office-holder disclaim?

It should be noted that the liquidator or trustee can disclaim onerous property: **5.133**

(i) even if they have previously exercised rights of ownership in relation to it (including taking possession of it or trying to sell it);[255] and

(ii) at any time, unless a person interested in the property has served a 'notice to elect' on the liquidator or trustee in which case they have 28 days from receipt of the notice to disclaim. If the liquidator or trustee does not disclaim within the 28-day period, he loses the right to do so,[256] unless he obtains an extension of the 28-day time limit (which can be obtained retrospectively).[257]

But:

(i) The disclaimer must relate to the whole of the property – the liquidator or trustee cannot disclaim part and keep the remainder;

(ii) A liquidator may not disclaim any property that is subject to a financial collateral arrangement; and

(iii) A trustee in bankruptcy may not disclaim, unless he obtains the court's permission:

    (a) property he has claimed as 'after acquired property' under IA 1986 s307;

    (b) property claimed by the trustee as personal property of the bankrupt exceeding reasonable replacement value under IA 1986 s308; or

    (c) tenancies that vest in the trustee under IA 1986 s308A.

(c) Effect of disclaimer

Disclaimer (when properly exercised[258]) determines, from the date of the disclaimer, the rights,   **5.134** interests and liabilities of the insolvent company or the bankrupt and his estate in or in respect

---

254 In the context of IA 1986, property is defined extremely broadly as all money, goods, things in action, land and every description of property wherever situated, obligations and every description of interest, whether present or future or vested or contingent, arising out of or incidental to property: IA 1986 s436. Indeed *'it is hard to think of a wider definition of property'*: *Bristol Airport plc v Powdrill* [1990] Ch 744 at [759] (Sir Nicholas Browne-Wilkinson). It is likely to be sufficiently wide to include cryptoassets, which are likely to be recognised as a species of property by the courts of England and Wales: see 'Legal statement on cryptoassets and smart contracts' (UK Jurisdiction Taskforce, November 2019).

255 IA 1986 ss178(2) (liquidation) and 315(1) (bankruptcy).

256 IA 1986 ss178(5) (liquidation) and 315(1)(b) (bankruptcy).

257 IA 1986 ss178(5)(b) and 376, IR 2016 r1.3 and Sch 5 to the IR 2016.

258 The procedure, including the prescribed contents of the notice of disclaimer and to whom it should be delivered, can be found in IR 2016 r19.2.

of the property disclaimed. In bankruptcy, it also discharges the trustee in bankruptcy from all personal liability in respect of that property as from the commencement of their appointment.

5.135 The most commonly disclaimed property is leases. Disclaimer of a lease extinguishes the liability between landlord and tenant such that the tenant's liability to pay rent ends, as does the landlord's right to receive it.[259] The landlord instead has a right to prove in the insolvency as a creditor for the amount of the loss suffered. In assessing damages for a landlord, usual breach of contract principles apply, such that the loss is, usually, the rents and other payments which would have been due under the lease for the balance of the lease period, less the amount the lessor will or is likely to receive from re-letting, discounted for early payment.[260]

5.136 Disclaimer of a leasehold interest does not take effect unless a copy has been served on every person claiming under the bankrupt as underlessee or mortgagee and either (1) no application has been made for a vesting order within 14 days beginning with the day on which the last notice was served; or (2) where such an application has been made the court orders that the disclaimer is to take effect.[261]

5.137 The disclaimer of property in a dwelling house does not take effect until the disclaimer has been served (so far as the trustee is aware of their addresses) on every person in occupation of or claiming a right to occupy the property and either (1) no application has been made for a vesting order within 14 days beginning with the day on which the last notice was served; or (2) where such an application has been made the court orders that the disclaimer is to take effect.[262]

5.138 Disclaimer does not affect the rights and liabilities of any other person, except so far as necessary for the purpose of releasing the insolvent company or bankrupt, bankrupt's estate and trustee from any liability.[263] Thus:

(i) Disclaimer of freehold property will not determine mortgages or tenancies in respect of the land;[264]

(ii) Disclaimer in respect of a contract will not divest a counterparty of any right which they have already acquired by reason of the contract.[265] For example the purported disclaimer of contracts for the sale of land comprised in the bankrupt's estate (which immediately transfers the equitable interest in the land) cannot be disclaimed unless the interest to which the contract relates has also been disclaimed;

(iii) Disclaimer will not terminate the obligations of any party in relation to the disclaimed property or contract apart from those owed to the bankrupt, such that co-obligors,

---

259 Australian authority suggests this is so, even if the company or bankrupt was the landlord, not the tenant. Disclaimer extinguishes the tenant's interest in the property: *Re Wilmott Forests Ltd* [2013] HCA 51 (High Court of Australia).
260 *Re Park Air Services plc* [1999] BCLC 155 (HL).
261 IA 1986 ss179 (liquidation) and 317 (bankruptcy).
262 Ibid s318.
263 Ibid ss178(4) (liquidation) and 315(3) (bankruptcy).
264 See *Scmlla Properties Ltd v Gesso Properties (BVI) Ltd* [1995] BCC 793.
265 See *Capital Prime Properties plc v Worthgate Ltd (in liquidation)* [2000] BCC 525.

guarantors and other persons who have otherwise covenanted in respect of the performance of a disclaimed contract remain bound by their obligations notwithstanding disclaimer.[266]

Disclaimed property vests in the Crown as *bona vacantia* or, in the case of freehold land, by **5.139** escheat (subject to any vesting order being made in favour of another party). Thus, where the bankrupt's interest in the matrimonial home is disclaimed, it does not by means of that disclaimer revert to the bankrupt.[267]

(d) Challenging a disclaimer and vesting orders

Any disclaimer by a liquidator or trustee is presumed valid and effective unless it is proved that **5.140** they were in breach of their duties relating to the giving of notice of disclaimer or otherwise under the provisions of the IA 1986 or the IR 2016 relating to disclaimer.[268] A breach of these provisions does not lead to automatic invalidity, instead there is no longer a presumption of validity.[269] A decision by a liquidator or trustee to disclaim property is one made as a result of the exercise of their powers of management and administration of the estate, and contributories or creditors have a statutory mechanism to challenge the exercise of these powers.[270] Alternatively, if the liquidator or trustee are in doubt as to the proper course of action, they can apply for directions from the court. When a notice of disclaimer has been issued by a liquidator or trustee, a party may apply to the court for an order vesting the property in that party if they:

(i)   claim an interest in the disclaimed property (which must be a proprietary interest, a mere financial interest in acquiring the property will be insufficient);[271]

(ii)   have a liability in respect of the disclaimed property that is not discharged by the disclaimer; or

(iii) following disclaimer of a dwelling house by a trustee in bankruptcy only are an individual who, at the start of the bankruptcy, was in occupation or entitled to occupy the dwelling house.[272]

Such an application must be made within three months of the applicant becoming aware of the **5.141** disclaimer or receiving a copy of the notice, whichever occurs first.[273]

The court's discretion whether to make a vesting order is at large. There is no statutory **5.142** guidance, but it has been said that, in the absence of some competing applicant, and in the

---

266   See *Hindcastle Ltd v Barbara Attenborough Associates Ltd* [1997] AC 70; *Shaw v Doleman* [2009] EWCA Civ 279, [2009] BCC 730, [2009] BPIR 945.

267   Although the interaction between disclaimer and IA 1986 s283A (the 'use it or lose it' provision) in relation to the family home has yet to be explored by the court. See *Young v Official Receiver* [2010] EWHC 1591 (Ch), [2010] BPIR 1477 at [35].

268   See IR 2016 r19.10.

269   *Hunt v Conwy CBC* [2013] EWHC 1154 (Ch), [2013] BPIR 790.

270   See paras 4.021–4.027.

271   See *Lloyds Bank SF Nominees v Aladdin Ltd (in liquidation)* [1996] 1 BCLC 920 and *Re Ballast plc* [2006] EWHC 3189 (Ch), [2007] BCC 620. This means also that a trustee in bankruptcy has no standing to apply for a vesting order in respect of property that they had earlier disclaimed: *Sleight v The Crown Estate Commissioners* [2018] EWHC 3489 (Ch).

272   IA 1986 ss181 (in liquidation) and 320 (in bankruptcy).

273   IR 2016 r19.11.

absence of some good reason to the contrary, the court ought ordinarily to exercise its discretion in favour of a qualifying application, at least in relation to disclaimer of a freehold.[274]

E. DECISION-MAKING AND DELEGATION

5.143   As already discussed in paragraph 4.015 above, the duties of an IP are non-delegable. That does not mean however that the IP does not have the power to delegate decision-making, simply that they remain liable for any breaches of duties. For further guidance in relation to delegation by IPs to others such as their staff, sub-contractors, other IPs (including joint IPs) or specialists see the *Insolvency Guidance Paper: Control of Cases*.[275] This makes clear that the IP must be satisfied that the work delegated to more junior staff is conducted in a proper and efficient manner, appropriate to the case. Liability may arise for an IP where they do not organise suitable delegation or instruction of another professional.[276] Or, perhaps, where they instruct an inappropriate agent who fails to have the correct specialism.[277]

F. DISCLOSURE

1. Introduction

5.144   In the corporate context, office-holders[278] have a duty to consider the books and records of a company and a corresponding right to take possession of the books and records of the company. Where any person has in his possession or control any property, books, papers or records to which the company appears to be entitled, the court may require that person to pay, convey, surrender or transfer the property, books, papers or records to the office-holder.[279]

5.145   A trustee in bankruptcy has a like obligation to take possession of all books, papers and other records which relate to the bankrupt's estate or affairs and which belong to him or are in his possession or under his control (including any which would be privileged from disclosure in any proceedings)[280] and the bankrupt has a corresponding obligation to deliver up those documents to the trustee.[281]

5.146   The purpose of these provisions is obvious. The office-holder needs to be in a position to understand the affairs of the insolvent to perform their functions of getting in and distributing the estate to creditors. A separate question arises as to how long an IP should retain records for, having regard to their obligations under the General Data Protection Regulation ('GDPR').

---

274   *Hunt v Conwy CBC* [2013] EWHC 1154 (Ch), [2013] BPIR 790.
275   See https://www.gov.uk/government/publications/control-of-cases-insolvency-practitioner-guidance-paper/insolvency-guidance-paper-control-of-cases (July 2005, accessed 10 May 2020).
276   The claim in *Medforth v Blake* [2000] Ch 16 might be said to illustrate this – it was usual commercial practice to obtain discounts for the pig feed but the receivers failed to do so. Presumably if they had engaged a suitable agent, that agent would have done so.
277   See, e.g., *Brewer v Iqbal* [2019] EWHC 182 (Ch).
278   Applicable to administrators, administrative receivers, liquidators and provisional liquidators: IA 1986 s234(1).
279   IA 1986 s234(2).
280   Ibid s311(1).
281   Ibid s312(1).

2. Privilege

However, recent developments in the case law relating to privilege has made trustees in **5.147** bankruptcy think twice about what documentation they are able to disclose to other interested parties and/or the court or rely on as evidence in support of claims they wish to make on behalf of the company or bankruptcy estate. A full discussion of the doctrine of privilege is outside the scope of this work, but we seek to set out a very brief introduction to legal professional privilege in this section, in order to provide context for the discussion below of when an office-holder may find their hands tied in relation to disclosure of even key documents by an assertion of privilege.

Legal professional privilege is the name given to the right to resist the compulsory disclosure of **5.148** certain documents. There are two distinct types of legal professional privilege: 'legal advice privilege' attaches to communications between a lawyer and their client which contain legal advice (and can apply whether or not litigation is pending/contemplated). 'Litigation privilege' attaches to documents which were created for the dominant purpose of obtaining information or advice in connection with actual or contemplated litigation. The court is not permitted to draw adverse inferences from the failure to disclose a privileged document.

Legal professional privilege cannot be claimed unless the evidence in question is confidential. **5.149** It follows that a privileged document that has ceased to be confidential (because, e.g., it has been made available to the general public on a website) can no longer be the subject of a claim for privilege, and no privilege can be asserted in public documents. As Simler J observed in *Shepherd v Fox Williams LLP*:[282]

> It is well established that a document which would otherwise be privileged does not lose the quality of confidentiality necessary to attract privilege simply because it has been seen by someone other than the lawyer and client. The critical question is whether the document and its information remain confidential in the sense that it is not properly available for use. If a document has been made generally available, confidence and therefore privilege will be completely lost. However documents communicated to a third party in circumstances expressly or impliedly preserving confidentiality against the rest of the world are unlikely to lead to the privilege being lost.

Where legal advice is given to joint clients, those clients will be entitled to joint privilege. **5.150**

Privilege can be waived, for instance by deploying the privileged material in court or disclosing **5.151** it to another party (either voluntarily or inadvertently). Once waived, it cannot be revived. Joint privilege cannot be waived by one joint client without the other's consent; but one joint client cannot claim privilege against another joint client in respect of communications which are subject to joint privilege.[283]

There is no legal professional privilege in respect of documents which are themselves part of an **5.152** iniquitous proceeding or in communications made in order to obtain advice for the purpose of carrying out an iniquity. This 'iniquity exception' applies to criminal and civil cases, and not only in cases of fraud but also more generally where wrongdoing or iniquity is considered

---

282 [2014] EWHC 1224 (QB) at [50].
283 *Shore v Bedford* (1843) 5 M. & G. 271.

sufficient to set aside privilege: *Barclays Bank plc v Eustice*.[284] The context of that decision was a claim under IA 1986 s423 (transactions defrauding creditors), and there was a strong prima facie case that the defendant had entered into a transaction at an undervalue for the purpose of prejudicing the interests of a secured creditor. The Court of Appeal held that such purpose was 'sufficiently iniquitous for public policy to require that communications between him and his solicitor in relation to the setting up of these transactions be discoverable'.

(a) Personal insolvency

5.153 In *Crescent Farm (Sidcup) Sports Ltd v Sterling Offices Ltd*[285] Goff J held that where a vendor of land had obtained legal advice relating to the validity of third-party rights claimed over the land before selling it, the buyer, as the successor in title to the land, also succeeded to and was entitled to assert the vendor's privilege in the legal advice which related to the land. That proposition has since become known as 'the *Crescent Farm* principle'.

5.154 For some time it was believed, following *Re Konigsberg (a Bankrupt)*[286] (a case decided under the Bankruptcy Act 1914 ('BA 1914')) that the *Crescent Farm* principle applied also in personal insolvency cases such that a trustee succeeded to privilege belonging to the bankrupt. In *Konigsberg*, a firm of solicitors had provided advice to a married couple in relation to the transfer of their jointly owned matrimonial home into the wife's sole name. The husband was subsequently adjudged bankrupt and his trustee in bankruptcy sought a declaration that the transfer of the matrimonial home was void by virtue of BA 1914 s42. The wife sought to exclude evidence of the communications with the solicitors on the basis that those communications were the subject of joint privilege which had not been waived.

5.155 Peter Gibson J (as he then was) concluded that the wife was not entitled to assert privilege against the trustee, stating:[287]

> Important and desirable though I recognise it is to maintain the principle of legal professional privilege I can see no sufficient reason to treat the trustee as a third party for that purpose. The rule recognises that joint clients cannot maintain privilege against each other and as the privilege of the bankrupt had devolved on to the trustee who is entitled to obtain the privileged information from the bankrupt, in my judgment it is appropriate to treat the trustee as being in the shoes of the bankrupt for the purpose of privilege in proceedings against the joint client. It would be very odd if the trustee,

---

284 [1995] 1 WLR 1238 at 1249C–G. There has been some discussion as to whether this case goes too far, and the exception should be restricted to cases of dishonesty. In *McE v Prison Service of Northern Ireland* [2009] UKHL 15, [2009] 1 AC 908 at [109], Lord Neuberger expressly left open the question of whether *Eustice* was correctly decided. The Court of Appeal considered the fraud exception in *Z v Z (Legal Professional Privilege: Fraud Exception)* [2018] 4 WLR 52, it being argued that Haddon-Cave J (as he then was) had wrongly applied an *'iniquity'* test rather than a *'dishonesty'* test, at first instance. The Court of Appeal decided not to resolve the question of the appropriate test, but observed at para 57 that:

> it is not easy to see why the actual decision in *Eustice* in relation to section 423 of the Insolvency Act 1986 and in *C v C (Privilege)* in relation to section 37 of the Matrimonial Causes Act 1973, should be questioned, whatever criticisms there may be of some of the reasoning.

This was based on the decision in *Williams v Quebrada Railway, Land & Copper Co* [1895] 2 Ch 751.
285 [1972] Ch 553.
286 [1989] 1 WLR 1257.
287 At 1267E–F.

entitled as he is to, and possessing, the information, cannot use it in the performance of his duties in seeking to recover the bankrupt's property.

The decision in *Konigsberg* was expressly followed by Stanley Burnton QC (as he then was) in **5.156** *Re Cook*,[288] which held that the power and right to waive legal professional privilege in relation to the estate and affairs of a bankrupt pass to the trustee in bankruptcy in the same way as the bankrupt's assets and the right to possession of books, papers and records. In reaching that decision, the court did not draw any distinction between the effect of IA 1986 s306 (i.e., the transfer of the beneficial ownership of assets from the bankrupt to the trustee in bankruptcy) and s311(1) (which entitles the trustee to take possession of certain documents).

However, in *Avonwick Holdings Ltd v Shlosberg*[289] the Court of Appeal took a different view. **5.157** Following the making of the bankruptcy order, the solicitors who acted for the petitioning creditor were then instructed to act on behalf of the bankrupt's trustees in bankruptcy. The trustees exercised their power under IA 1986 s311(1) to take possession of the bankrupt's books, papers and other records, which were then passed to, and reviewed by, the solicitors for the purpose of enabling the creditor to use the documents in conspiracy proceedings against the bankrupt. When he discovered this, the bankrupt applied for an order directing the solicitors to cease to act for the creditor on the basis they had seen his privileged information.

Some of the documents related to an asset of the bankrupt (earlier litigation which had resulted **5.158** in a county court judgment in his favour) and were subject to the sole privilege of the bankrupt. It was presented to the court at first instance as common ground between the parties that the privilege in those documents vested in the trustee as successor to title in the assets under the *Crescent Farm* principle. At first instance,[290] Arnold J expressed doubt as to whether this was correct, but nevertheless accepted the proposition on the basis that it was not disputed. The remainder of the documents related to the liabilities of the bankrupt and were subject to the joint privilege of the bankrupt and his company. The key issue for determination was whether the benefit of the bankrupt's privilege in these documents vested in his trustees as part of his estate. Arnold J held it did not.

The trustees appealed to the Court of Appeal. The trustees argued that: (i) the documents were **5.159** property and thus any associate privilege had devolved on them as successors in title under the *Crescent Farm* principle; (ii) the privilege itself was 'property' which vested in them on their appointment taking effect; and (iii) it is a necessary implication of IA 1986 s311 that trustees are entitled to use privileged documents for the purpose of their functions and powers.[291]

The Court of Appeal rejected those arguments, holding that: **5.160**

---

288   [1999] BPIR 881.
289   [2016] EWCA Civ 1138, [2017] Ch 210.
290   [2016] EWHC 1001 (Ch).
291   By IA 1986 ss311(1) and 312(1), the trustee has an obligation to take possession of all books, papers and other records which relate to the bankrupt's estate or affairs and which belong to him or are in his possession or under his control (including any which would be privileged from disclosure in any proceedings) and the bankrupt has a corresponding obligation to deliver up those documents to the trustee.

(i) privilege is not property of a bankrupt which automatically vests in the trustee in bankruptcy. Privilege is a fundamental doctrine and the bankrupt could only be deprived of the benefit of it if the Insolvency Act expressly so provides (which it does not) or it is a necessary implication of the express language of its provisions (which it is not);

(ii) the decision in *Konigsberg* was incorrect insofar as it was considered that privilege devolved on the trustee in bankruptcy; and

(iii) whilst IA 1986 s311(1) entitles the trustee in bankruptcy to take possession of documents which include privileged information for the overriding function of getting in, realising and distributing the bankrupt's estate, and to look at the documents to obtain information relevant to those matters, the provision does not entitle the trustee to waive the bankrupt's legal professional privilege in taking steps against third parties for the benefit of the bankrupt's estate.

5.161 The Court of Appeal's decision in *Shlosberg* was extremely controversial, but it was soon followed by the High Court in *Leeds v Lemos*.[292] There the trustees argued that the decision in *Shlosberg* confirmed that a bankrupt's privilege in documents that relate to assets (but not liabilities) of the bankrupt's estate devolves upon the trustee.

5.162 Having carefully analysed the decisions in *Shlosberg*, HHJ Hodge QC (sitting as a judge of the High Court) concluded that the Court of Appeal had in fact overruled *Konigsberg* for all purposes, that the *Crescent Farm* principle has no continuing application in bankruptcy cases and, accordingly, that a trustee in bankruptcy does not automatically step into the shoes of a bankrupt in relation to privileged documents even if they affect assets of the bankrupt and the privilege belongs solely to the bankrupt.

5.163 The trustee had also argued that the bankrupt could be ordered to waive his privilege pursuant to IA 1986 ss333 and 363 since: (i) s333 imposes an obligation upon a bankrupt to cooperate with his trustees in the fulfilment of their functions to the extent that the trustees may reasonably require; and (ii) s363(2) enables the court with supervisory jurisdiction over the bankruptcy to compel such compliance, the Bankruptcy Court can compel a bankrupt to waive his privilege. HHJ Hodge QC rejected that argument on the basis that the right to privilege is such a fundamental principle that only an express power in s363(2) itself would confer jurisdiction to order waiver of privilege and that even if the court did have such jurisdiction, it was difficult to envisage any circumstances in which the court would exercise it.

5.164 It is expected that this case will have serious repercussions within the industry, which are yet to be fully worked out. In *Lemos* itself, the trustee gave the following five practical examples of ways in which he alleged that the proper administration of bankruptcy estates would be hampered by a finding (ultimately made) which meant that a trustee could not waive privilege without the consent of the bankrupt:

(i) trustees will be unable to disclose details of their investigations to any creditors who are funding the bankruptcy process where such details would reveal information contained within privileged documents, which might impact on the creditor's willingness to continue to provide support;

---

292 [2017] EWHC 1825 (Ch), [2018] Ch 81.

(ii)   trustees might also be unable to disclose relevant privileged information to third-party funders who might otherwise be interested in funding a claim in relation to the bankrupt's estate;

(iii) when interviewing any third party, trustees will be unable to refer to any information contained in privileged documents which will hamper their ability to question the third party effectively;

(iv)   if asked to adjudicate on a creditor claim, and the trustees have seen privileged documentation which proves that a creditor's claim is wholly or partly without basis, they might be unable to evidence the reasons why they are rejecting that claim, or to defend any appeal against their decision; and

(v)   if a privileged document reveals an asset in the bankruptcy estate, trustees will be unable to use that document to further their investigations into that asset, and accordingly that could prevent that asset from being realised for the benefit of the bankrupt's creditors.

It should be noted that, whilst trustees are prima facie prevented from taking any steps which **5.165** would have the effect of waiving the bankrupt's right (solely or jointly) to privilege that does not mean that the trustees cannot derive any useful benefit from the privileged information. If, for instance, a privileged communication reveals the existence of a previously unknown bankruptcy asset, this will set off an investigation which stems from (but crucially does not involve the disclosure of) the privileged communication. Further, any communications which tend to show wrongdoing may fall within the 'iniquity exception' discussed above at paragraph 5.152.

(b) Corporate insolvency

In a corporate insolvency process the company remains a legal entity until it is dissolved, but it **5.166** passes into the effective control of the office-holder. Therefore, the company's privilege, while remaining with the company, is effectively in the control of the office-holder who has the power to assert or waive it.

(c) Common interest

It should be noted that third parties may be able to claim to have a common interest with the **5.167** party claiming privilege, such that the third party is entitled to see documents which would otherwise be privileged.

Thus a shareholder in a company is entitled to see all documents obtained by the company in **5.168** the course of the administration of its affairs, including legal advice, on the basis of common interest,[293] unless the legal advice relates to actual or contemplated litigation between the shareholder and the company. However, although a 'direct shareholder' in a company is entitled to see legal advice given to that company on the ground of common interest, it has been held that there was no reason to extend that basic rule all the way up the chain of holding

---

293   *Arrow Trading and Investments v Edwardian Group Ltd* [2004] EWHC 1319 (Ch). In *Sharp v Blank* [2015] EWHC 2681 (Ch), Nugee J clarified that the foundation of the general rule is that a company taking advice on the running of its affairs (and paying for it out of the company's assets) cannot assert a privilege against the shareholders who have indirectly paid for it.

companies despite the steady dilution of that common interest. Accordingly, a direct share-holder in a company could not share the material with its own shareholders.[294] However, common interest privilege has also been held to apply between companies in the same group, including parent companies and subsidiaries.[295]

5.169 In *Singla v Stockler*,[296] the claimant liquidator had retained the defendant solicitors to act for him in proceedings he brought in his capacity as liquidator, funded by the principal creditor in the liquidation. The liquidator terminated his retainer with the defendant, whereupon the creditor instructed the defendants to bring a claim against the liquidator. This prompted the liquidator to seek injunctions restraining the defendants from acting for the creditor and restraining them from disclosing to the creditor any communications with him. The liquidator's claim was struck out on the basis he had no arguable case for breach of confidence because there had been a common interest between him and the creditor.

5.170 The liquidator's appeal was dismissed by Briggs J (as he then was).[297] He was at pains to point out that the relationship between a liquidator pursuing claims and a principal creditor and funder of those claims did not, of itself, create a common interest to displace the usual obligation of confidence by solicitors to their client. The test was to ask whether the liquidator's ordinary expectation that the defendants would treat their communications as confidential had been displaced either by agreement or by the mutual conduct of the liquidator, the creditor and the defendants. Here there was no agreement, but the routine transmission by the defendants to the creditor of ordinarily confidential and privileged materials, with the liquidator's full knowledge, gave rise to the 'strongest inference' that the ordinary obligation of confidence had been displaced by the parties' mutual conduct.

G. THE RULE IN *EX PARTE JAMES*

5.171 The principle in *ex parte James* (derived from the nineteenth century case of *Ex parte James; In re Condon*[298]) has already been discussed to some extent in Chapter 4, in the context of duties, at paragraphs 4.041–4.045. It has been described as a well-established principle providing a means by which the court can control the conduct of its officers.[299] Administrators, liquidators in a compulsory winding up, and trustees in bankruptcy are all officers of the court and subject to this jurisdiction. The rule requires an office-holder to act with equity and utmost fairness, even to the point of not standing upon his strict legal rights if the result would be inequitable.

5.172 In *ex parte James* itself, a bankrupt paid to his trustee in bankruptcy monies on the basis he thought that he was legally required to as a result of his bankruptcy. In fact he was not. At that

---

294 *BBGP Managing General Partner Ltd v Babcock & Brown Global Partners* [2010] EWHC 2176 (Ch).

295 See *USP Strategies plc v London General Holdings Ltd* [2004] EWHC 373 (Ch) at [14]. It seems that the principle applied to the common interest of two separate parties must apply with at least equal force to a single interest shared by a company and its wholly owned subsidiary jointly.

296 Order of Deputy Master Mark (unrep'd, 28 October 2011): see [2012] EWHC 1176 (Ch) at [1].

297 [2012] EWHC 1176 (Ch).

298 (1874) LR 9 Ch App 609.

299 In *Re Lehman Brothers International (Europe) and Lomas v Burlington Loan Management Ltd* [2015] EWHC 2270 (Ch) (Richards J) at [174].

time, money paid under a mistake of law was not recoverable, but the Court of Appeal directed that its officer should not stand on his strict legal rights but should return the funds, notwithstanding that the effect was to deprive the creditors of funds which would otherwise be available for distribution among them. The rationale for the principle was that, although irrecoverable at law, the officer of the court could not in all conscience retain the money, given the circumstances in which it had been paid. It would amount to an unjust enrichment of the estate.

James LJ stated the principle thus: 5.173

> [a] trustee in bankruptcy is an officer of the Court. He has inquisitorial powers given him by the Court, and the Court regards him as its officer, and he is to hold money in his hands upon trust for its equitable distribution among the creditors. The Court, then, finding that he has in his hands money which in equity belongs to someone else, ought to set an example to the world by paying it to the person really entitled to it. In my opinion the Court of Bankruptcy ought to be as honest as other people.

A more modern statement of principle was given in *Re Clark (a Bankrupt)*[300] where Walton J   5.174
set out four conditions that needed to be satisfied before the rule could be exercised against a trustee in bankruptcy, namely:

(i)   '... there must be some form of enrichment of the assets of the bankrupt by the person seeking to have the rule applied';
(ii)   '... except in the most unusual cases the claimant must not be in a position to submit an ordinary proof of debt';
(iii)   'if in all the circumstances of the case, an honest man who would be personally affected by the result would nevertheless be bound to admit: "It's not fair that I should keep the money; my claim has no merits", then the rule applies so as to nullify the claim which he would otherwise have;' and
(iv)   '... the rule ... applies only to the extent necessary to nullify the enrichment of the estate; it by no means necessarily restores the claimant to the status quo ante'.

Although the principle was first developed and exercised in mistaken payment cases, subse-   5.175
quent cases have applied it in other circumstances and it cannot now be said to be confined to particular categories of case. In *Re Nortel GmbH*,[301] Lord Neuberger stated the rule, although *obiter*, in broad terms: it would apply where it would be unfair for an office-holder to take full advantage of their legal rights as such, the court will order them not to do so.

The rule has been criticised as an anomaly, but it is still regularly relied upon and (more   5.176
irregularly) applied in cases where the bankruptcy estate or company would otherwise be in receipt of an unjustified windfall. For criticism of the rule, see paragraphs 4.041–4.045 above.

For example, in *Re Young*[302] Chief Registrar Baister held that the rule applied where it was   5.177
accepted that the trustee in bankruptcy would not have had a claim but for a verbal agreement

---

300   [1975] 1 WLR 559.
301   [2013] UKSC 52, [2014] AC 209 at [122].
302   [2017] BPIR 1116.

made by the respondent who had done so without legal advice. As a result, to enforce that agreement would have resulted in a windfall to the estate of a wholly unjustified nature.[303]

5.178   In *Hieber v Duckworth*,[304] the applicant had succeeded in setting aside a Tomlin order made between herself, the liquidator and the company on the basis of undue influence and duress applied by her husband, but in any event it was held that the case met the conditions in *ex parte James* – it would have been unfair for the liquidator to rely on his strict legal rights under the Tomlin order given the circumstance in which the applicant came to be a party and the result would be an unjustified enrichment to the company.

5.179   More controversially, in *Evans v Carter* while the rule did not operate as a defence because there was no unfairness, HHJ Hodge QC held[305] that the bankrupt was entitled to credit for the fact that she had expended legal costs in fighting the appeal. How such a decision was reached is uncertain – the estate had not been enriched by the legal costs which were not paid to the estate. This appears to have been a decision made on the facts to mitigate the harshness of his decision to the bankrupt but it remains to be seen whether such an approach will be sidelined or seen as an extension to the operation of the rule.

5.180   In Australia the rule appears to have been applied more flexibly, without the need to establish unjust enrichment. For example, in *Re Associated Dominions Assurance Society Pty Ltd*,[306] an employee of a company in liquidation had a two-year limitation period to bring a claim for payment in lieu of long service leave. The employee relied upon the liquidator's indication they would seek directions from the court and therefore did not make an application in the usual way. By the time the liquidator made the application for directions, more than two years had elapsed and the employee was out of time irrespective of the outcome of the application. The High Court of Australia applied the principles in *ex parte James* to disregard the passing of limitation. More recently, the rule in *ex parte James* has been reinvigorated in *Lehman Brothers Australia*, where a mistake common to both the creditor and office-holders in the drafting of certain 'claims determination deeds' was held to be a sufficient basis to prevent the office-holders relying on their strict rights.[307]

5.181   An office-holder might well find it beneficial to seek directions from the court on how to proceed when the circumstances likely to give rise to such a claim have been identified thus avoiding potentially costly and protracted litigation.

---

303   But compare with an earlier case, *Green v Satsangi* [1998] BPIR 55, where the court found that the trustee might have acted unfairly but not wrongly.
304   (unreported, 20 June 2017, Ch D).
305   [2017] EWHC 2163 (Ch) at [54].
306   (1962) 109 CLR 516.
307   *Lehman Brothers Australia Ltd v MacNamara* [2020] EWCA Civ 321.

H. PRIVATE AND PUBLIC EXAMINATIONS

1. Private examinations

Office-holders'[308] investigations are assisted immeasurably by the power to apply to the court   **5.182**
to examine a person[309] who has demonstrated a reluctance to cooperate voluntarily. The
relevant statutory provisions are contained in IA 1986 s236 in the case of companies and s366
in respect of bankrupt individuals.[310] These provisions allow the court to require the
respondent to submit an account of their dealings with the insolvent, produce documents or
attend for an examination before the court.

The purpose of these apparently wide-reaching investigative powers was described by Lord   **5.183**
Slynn in *Re British & Commonwealth Holdings plc* as follows:[311]

> In my opinion, although there may be some difference in the wording of these sections, the position
> under section 236 of the Insolvency Act 1986 is broadly the same as that under section 268 of the
> Companies Act 1948 as explained by Buckley J. in *In re Rolls Razor Ltd* [1968] 3 All ER 698, 700, in
> a passage subsequently approved by the Court of Appeal in *In re Esal (Commodities) Ltd* [1989] BCLC
> 59, 64:
>
>> 'The powers conferred by section 268 are powers directed to enabling the court to help a
>> liquidator to discover the truth of the circumstances in connection with the affairs of the
>> company, information of trading, dealings, and so forth, in order that the liquidator may be able,
>> as effectively as possible, and, I think, with as little expense as possible ... to complete his
>> function as liquidator, to put the affairs of the company in order and to carry out the liquidation
>> in all its various aspects, including, of course, the getting in of any assets of the company
>> available in the liquidation. It is, therefore, appropriate for the liquidator, when he thinks that he
>> may be under a duty to try to recover something from some officer or employee of a company,
>> or some other person who is, in some way, concerned with the company's affairs, to be able to
>> discover, with as little expense as possible and with as much ease as possible, the facts
>> surrounding any such possible claim.'

---

308   In this context, this definition includes a provisional liquidator, liquidator, administrator, administrative receiver, trustee
or, in compulsory liquidation or bankruptcy, and the OR (whether as liquidator or trustee). The power is not available to
any of: a nominee of a voluntary arrangement, a contributory, or a creditor.

309   The respondent in the case of an application pursuant to IA 1986 s236 can be any officer of the company, any person
known or suspected to have in his possession property of the company or supposed to be indebted to the company, and
any person the court thinks capable of giving information concerning the promotion, formation, business, dealings,
affairs or property of the company: IA 1986 s236(2). Obvious and frequent targets are directors, debtors, shareholders,
accountants and auditors, solicitors and bankers. In the case of an application under IA 1986 s366 the respondent can be
the bankrupt, any current or former spouse or civil partner, any person known or suspected to have in his possession
property of the bankrupt or supposed to be indebted to the bankrupt, and any person the court thinks capable of giving
information concerning the bankrupt's dealings, affairs or property. Persons include corporations (in which case
compliance is by a proper officer). There is some doubt whether ss236 and 336 can be used to order someone outside the
jurisdiction to be examined in the jurisdiction, quite apart from the difficulties in enforcing such an order.

310   Further IA 1986 s251N empowers the official receiver to apply for examination in respect of individuals who have
obtained debt relief orders.

311   [1993] AC 426, 438 (HL). A case on IA 1986 s236, but the reasoning is equally applicable to s366.

5.184   It should also be noted that in *Re Pantmaenog Timber Co Ltd*[312] the House of Lords held that a liquidator's functions were not limited to the recovery and distribution of the company's assets, but extended to the investigation of both the causes of the company's failure and the conduct of its directors in the wider public interest of ensuring appropriate action is taken against those engaged in commercially culpable conduct in the management companies. As such, IA 1986 s236 could be invoked to gather information for the purposes of disqualification proceedings.

5.185   The burden of establishing that it is a proper case to make an order rests upon the office-holder, although, as the independent person whose duty it is to investigate the affairs of the insolvent, the court will usually attach significant weight to their views.

5.186   In exercising its discretion whether to make an order the court is undertaking a balancing exercise between the competing interests of an office-holder in requiring information and/or documents and the degree of 'oppression' to the person sought to be examined ('the examinee'). The court is conscious of the need not to impose an unnecessary and unreasonable burden on the examinee, and relevant factors include the nexus between the company/bankrupt and the examinee,[313] the inconvenience and the burden of work upon an examinee which would be caused by an order being made and their potential exposure to future claims.[314] As a general rule an order for an oral examination will be regarded as more oppressive than an order to produce documents.

5.187   Legitimate purposes for seeking an order include to enable an office-holder to trace known assets or identify previously held assets and what has happened to them, to reconstitute accounting or other business records and to obtain information from third parties to enable contracts to be completed.

5.188   The court will however not allow an office-holder who intends to litigate to obtain an advantage over the proposed target which would not otherwise exist in the usual litigation process, by using the provision to obtain or bolster evidence against the intended defendant. The possibility of bringing, or the fact that a decision has been made to commence, proceedings or the existence of extant proceedings are all relevant factors (although not necessarily determinative) to the question of whether oppression to an examinee is outweighed by the legitimate requirements of an office-holder.[315]

5.189   The court is also alive to prevent an office-holder using their powers to obtain the benefit of contracts without making payment. For example, in *Cowlishaw v O&D Building Contractors*

---

312   [2004] 1 AC 158.

313   Thus it is generally easier to obtain an order against a company officer, including auditors who are treated as officers of a company, and a bankrupt than a third party: *Re Seagull Manufacturing Co Ltd (in liquidation)* [1993] Ch 345 at 358. The more distant a respondent from the insolvent the more likely an order will be oppressive.

314   See e.g., *Cloverbay Ltd (joint administrators) v Bank of Credit and Commerce International SA* [1991] Ch 90, [1991] 1 All ER 894 (Browne-Wilkinson V-C), approved in *British & Commonwealth Holdings plc v Spicer & Oppenheim* [1993] AC 426.

315   See e.g., *Shierson v Rastogi* [2002] EWCA Civ 1624 at [39] (Peter Gibson LJ):

> … it is oppressive to require a defendant accused of serious wrongdoing to provide what amount to pre-trial depositions and to prove the case against himself on oath. But that oppression may be outweighed by the legitimate requirements of the liquidator.

Ltd[316] HHJ Cooke refused to order the disclosure of documents which would otherwise have been unavailable to the insolvent by reason of non-payment, saying:[317]

> The benefit to the administration of obtaining these documents is in my judgement outweighed by the unfairness to the respondent of being required to produce them, in circumstances in which the respondent is a stranger to the companies in administration and (perhaps indirectly) a substantial unsecured creditor which will go unpaid as a result of that administration. But for the insolvency the respondent would have been under no obligation to provide any of the documents to the companies in administration and, particularly, that purpose and effect of the order sought is to obtain the benefit of the work done by the respondent in performance of his contract, without the payment which the companies in administration ought to have made for that work.

It should be noted that the use which the office-holder may make of evidence obtained under these sections is limited to fulfilling their statutory functions. Thus in *Barlow Clowes Gilt Managers Ltd*[318] the court refused liquidators permission to disclose voluntarily to defendants in criminal proceedings transcripts of interviews conducted by the liquidators after the interviewees had been threatened with compulsory examination under IA 1986 s237. The disclosure would have been for purposes collateral to the liquidation and foreign to those for which the information was obtained.[319] Further, in *First Tokyo Index Trust v Gould*[320] the Court of Session refused to allow liquidators to disclose transcripts of evidence, obtained by them under IA 1986 ss236 and 237, to a third party contemplating its own private litigation.   **5.190**

2. Public examinations

The OR has the ability to make an application to court for the public examination of a bankrupt at any time before their discharge.[321] Similar provisions apply in a compulsory liquidation and extend to the examination of any person who is or has been an officer of the company, has acted as liquidator, administrator, receiver or manager of the company, or has taken part in the promotion, formation or management of the company.[322] The examination takes place in a public court under oath.[323] The parties who may ask questions of the examinee include the OR, the trustee or liquidator, and any creditor who has submitted a proof of debt.[324] Failure to attend a public examination without reasonable excuse renders the examinee   **5.191**

---

316 [2009] EWHC 2445 (Ch).
317 At [42].
318 [1992] Ch 208 (Millett J).
319 On the other side of the coin, it should be noted that IA 1986 s433 prevents any statement provided by a person under compulsion from being used by the prosecution against that person in subsequent criminal proceedings.
320 [1996] BPIR 406.
321 IA 1986 s290(1).
322 Ibid s133(1).
323 IR 2016 rr10.103(1) in bankruptcy and 7.105(1) in a compulsory liquidation.
324 IA 1986 ss290(4) and 133(4) contain the full list.

in contempt of court and liable to arrest.[325] Given the serious consequences, public examinations tend to be used in cases of failure on the part of the bankrupt or a company officer to cooperate with the OR, often after a number of requests for interview have been made to no avail.[326]

I. REMUNERATION

1. The right to charge for work done

5.192 The IR 2016 deal with remuneration principles for office-holders in Part 18 chapter 4.[327] They apply to administrators, liquidators and trustees in bankruptcy (but not provisional liquidators or interim receivers).[328] Further, a revised version of SIP 9 applies to all existing and future insolvency appointments.[329] The SIP aims to ensure that the fees and expenses charged by IPs and their associates are fair and reasonable reflections of the work necessarily and properly undertaken and that those responsible for approving payments of these fees and expenses have sufficient information to make an informed judgment about whether they are reasonable.

5.193 An administrator, liquidator or trustee in bankruptcy is entitled to receive remuneration for the work that they and their staff undertake,[330] though it should be noted that they are not entitled to retain remuneration if the assets are insufficient to pay other expenses ranking higher.[331] The basis of the remuneration may be fixed on (i) the time cost basis, (ii) the asset value basis (being some percentage of the value of the property with which the administrator has to deal, or the assets which are realised, distributed or both by the liquidator or trustee) or (iii) a fixed fee basis,[332] or a combination of these.[333] In arriving at the determination of the basis upon which remuneration is to be fixed for administrators, liquidators and trustees in bankruptcy, regard must be had to the complexity (or otherwise) of the case, any respects in which, in connection with the company's or bankrupt's affairs, there falls on the office-holder, any responsibility of an exceptional kind or degree; the effectiveness with which the office-holder appears to be carrying out, or to have carried out, the office-holder's duties; and the value and nature of the property with which the office-holder has to deal.[334]

5.194 Before the basis is fixed, the administrator, liquidator (other than in a MVL) or trustee in bankruptcy, must deliver to the creditors information as to the work the office-holder proposes to undertake, and details of the expenses they consider will be, or are likely to be, incurred.[335]

---

325   IA 1986 ss290(5) and 364(2)(e) in relation to a bankrupt and ss134(1) and 134(2)(a) in compulsory liquidation.
326   However, one-half of the creditors (and in a compulsory liquidation, three-quarters of the contributories) has the ability to request that the OR makes an application for public examination: IA 1986 ss290(2) and 133(2).
327   IR 2016 rr18.15–18.38.
328   Ibid r18.15.
329   'Payments to insolvency office-holders and their associates' (effective from 1 December 2015).
330   IR 2016 r18.16(1).
331   See the discussion in Chapter 6 below at paras 6.240 to 6.248 and the discussion in para 6.241 of *Re Salters Hall School* [1998] BCC 503.
332   IR 2016 r18.16(2).
333   Ibid r18.16(3).
334   Ibid r18.18(9).
335   Ibid rr18.16(6), (7).

Further, if they propose to take all or any part of the remuneration on a time cost basis, they must also deliver to the creditors an estimate of fees.[336]

As to how remuneration is fixed, each process is dealt with in turn below.   **5.195**

(a) Administration

In an administration, it is for the creditors' committee (if there is one) to fix the basis of the   **5.196**
administrator's remuneration,[337] but if it fails to do so (or there is none in existence), then the
creditors must be asked to do so by a decision procedure[338] (or only the secured and/or
preferential creditors, if the administrator has delivered a paragraph 52(1)(b) statement that
there is insufficient property for a distribution to be made to unsecured creditors).[339] Where
the committee and the creditors have both failed to fix the remuneration, the administrator
must apply to court for the court to fix it if within the first 18 months of their appointment.[340]

(b) Compulsory liquidation

In a compulsory liquidation, it is for the committee to determine the basis of remuneration,[341]   **5.197**
but if they fail to do so or if there is none, then the basis of remuneration may be fixed by a
decision of the creditors by a decision procedure.[342] If the liquidator has requested the creditors
to fix the basis of remuneration and they have not done so or more than 18 months have
elapsed from the liquidator's appointment, the liquidator is entitled to a sum arrived at using
the formula in IR 2016 r18.22(2). There remains considerable doubt, on the basis of the rules
as they are currently drafted, as to whether it is possible to go to creditors for approval after 18
months (and it would appear there is currently no reported authority on the point).[343] It may
be said that this rule is only intended to operate as a default rule when there has been no
creditor or committee approval, but if that is so then it is difficult to understand why there is an
18-month cut-off, and the rule is not expressed simply to provide that scale rates apply until
such time as such approval has been given. This may suggest that the better view is the
18-month cut-off is indeed intended to have consequences and encourage requests for
remuneration to be made well in advance of this deadline in compulsory liquidations and
bankruptcies. This would also be more consistent with the imperative language used, requiring
applications to be made within 18 months (such as in CVLs; see paragraph 5.199 below).
Nevertheless, even if the 18-month period has expired, it might still be open for an extension
of time application to be made.[344]

It should be noted that, where either (a) a company which is in administration moves into   **5.198**
liquidation under para 83(1) of Sch B1 and the administrator becomes the liquidator; or (b) a

---

336   IR 2016 r18.16(4).
337   Ibid r18.18(2).
338   Ibid r18.18(3).
339   Ibid r18.18(3).
340   Ibid r18.23.
341   Ibid r18.20(2).
342   Ibid r18.20(3).
343   There is probably a residual power of the court to fix remuneration at any time: see *Re Colgate* [1986] Ch 439 (a decision
      under the BA 1914).
344   See Sch 5 para 3: the provisions of CPR r3.1(2)(a)(b) (the court's general powers of management) apply so as to enable
      the court to extend or shorten the time for compliance with anything required or authorised to be done by IR 2016.

winding-up order is made immediately upon the appointment of an administrator ceasing to have effect and the court under IA 1986 s140(1) appoints as liquidator the person whose appointment as administrator has ceased to have effect, the basis of remuneration fixed under IR 2016 r18.18 for the administrator is treated as having been fixed for the liquidator.[345]

(c)   CVL

5.199 In a CVL, it is for the committee to determine the basis of remuneration,[346] but if it fails to do so or there is none, then the basis of remuneration may be fixed by a decision of the creditors by a decision procedure. Where the committee and the creditors have both failed to fix the remuneration, the liquidator must apply to court for the court to fix it if within the first 18 months of their appointment.[347] As noted in paragraph 5.197 above, however, there remains doubt as to whether this right is lost if 18 months have expired before the application is made and whether such a problem may be overcome with an extension of time application.

(d)   MVL

5.200 In a members' voluntary liquidation, it is for the company in general meeting to determine the basis of remuneration.[348] If the company does not do so, the liquidator must apply to court for the court to fix it if within the first 18 months of their appointment.[349] The liquidator must deliver at least 14 days' notice of such an application to the company's contributories, or such one or more of them as the court may direct; and the contributories may nominate one or more of their number to appear, or be represented, and to be heard on the application.[350]

(e)   Bankruptcy

5.201 In bankruptcy, it is for the committee to determine the basis of remuneration,[351] but if it fails to do so or there is none, then the basis of remuneration may be fixed by a decision of the creditors by a decision procedure.[352] If the trustee has requested the creditors to fix the basis of remuneration and they have not done so or more than 18 months have elapsed from the trustee's appointment, the trustee is entitled to a sum arrived at using a formula in IR 2016 rr18.22(2) and (3). This is the same set of rules as apply to compulsory liquidations, notwithstanding that there is no direct reference to trustees in bankruptcy in those rules. There is probably also a residual power under IA 1986 s363 for the court to fix remuneration even if the 18-month period has lapsed.[353]

(f)   Re-consideration

5.202 In each case an office-holder may also need to refer back to the company, the creditors' committee, the creditors or the court (depending on who fixed their remuneration in the first

---

345   IR 2016 r18.20(4).
346   Ibid r18.20(2).
347   Ibid r18.23.
348   Ibid r18.19.
349   Ibid r18.23.
350   Ibid r18.23(4).
351   Ibid r18.20(2).
352   Ibid r18.20(3).
353   *Re Colgate* [1986] Ch 439 (a decision under the BA 1914).

place) to re-consider their remuneration. Circumstances where such reference may be made include where they seek to increase the amount, or to change the basis due to a material and substantial change in circumstances or they have exceeded or are likely to exceed their fees estimate.[354]

(g)   Joint office-holders

Where there are joint office-holders, they may agree between themselves as to how the   **5.203**
remuneration should be apportioned between them.[355] If the joint office-holders disagree, they can refer the dispute to the creditors' committee or to the creditors for settlement by a decision procedure. Alternatively, they may refer the dispute to the court for settlement by order.[356]

2.   The right to an indemnity from the insolvency estate

Office-holders who litigate in their own names (whether as Claimant/Applicant or Defendant/   **5.204**
Respondent)[357] and are the subject of a costs order will be personally liable for those costs in the same way as any other litigant. However, they will ordinarily be entitled to recoup those costs from the assets of the company or the bankruptcy estate (if there are any), although the court may deprive him of that right in appropriate cases. The restriction of the right to recoup is ordinarily limited to cases where the office-holder has acted unreasonably, negligently or otherwise improperly.[358] One such example is *Autobrokers v Dymond*,[359] where HHJ Cooke ordered that liquidators who had unsuccessfully sought to resist the calling of a creditors' meeting to consider their removal were not entitled to an indemnity from the estate for their costs. The other side of the coin is that it will be wholly improper for office-holders to use the assets of the estate to protect their own reputation.[360]

Where the office-holder is dealing with trust assets, which do not form part of an insolvent   **5.205**
estate, the court may, in some circumstances, allow insolvency office-holders to recover their fees and expenses in dealing with trust property and to be paid from the trust property itself (known as the Berkeley Applegate principle),[361] notwithstanding that the trust property is not an asset of the company within the meaning of IA 1986 s107.[362] The *Berkeley Applegate*

---

354   See IR 2016 rr18.24–18.28.
355   This will usually be done by way of a memorandum, agreement or protocol entered into by the joint office-holders on their appointment (it matters not what the document is described as).
356   IR 2016 r18.17.
357   By contrast, where an office-holder brings proceedings in the name of the company, any costs order made is against the company and the office-holder will not normally be personally liable to pay (unless there are grounds to make a third-party costs order).
358   See e.g., *Smurthwaite v Simpson* [2006] BPIR 1504; *Capitol Films Ltd v Cobalt Pictures Ltd* [2010] EWHC 3223 (Ch); *Re Wedgwood* [2012] EWHC 1974 (Ch).
359   [2015] EWHC 2691 (Admin).
360   *Re Dalnyaya Step llc (No 2)* [2017] EWHC 3153 (Ch) at [82].
361   After the leading case of *Re Berkeley Applegate (Investment Consultants) Ltd (no 2)* [1989] Ch 32, (1988) 4 BCC 279. See summary of the authorities in *Gillan v HEC Enterprises Ltd* [2016] EWHC 3179 (Ch) at [71]–[89].
362   All payments made to a company will usually be the property of the company, even if the payee's subjective intentions may have been for the property to be held on trust for some other specified purpose: *Re Arms (Multiple Sclerosis Research) Ltd* [1997] 1 WLR 877. The statutory scheme is generally inflexible, and it will not usually be possible for the office-holder to usurp or alter that scheme, even if conscience would seem to require a different result: see *Re Stanford International Bank Ltd* [2019] UKPC 45 at [40]. However, the dividing line between what will be an attempt to re-order

jurisdiction is therefore an exception to the rule that office-holders must be paid out of the assets of the company. The jurisdiction is entirely within the court's discretion,[363] although will be sparingly exercised.[364] A useful guide may be whether certain claims or assets would have been established or identified but for the work of the office-holders.[365] In such cases, it seems to follow that there is no injustice for creditors to bear the cost of obtaining the asset if they are to gain the benefit of a part of the assets realised.[366] The converse is that where office-holders have not performed work in relation to a trust asset,[367] or where the work would have been done anyway, the jurisdiction is less likely to be engaged.[368] It is in principle possible for such claims to be compromised, and IPs must be careful that where deeds of settlement are entered into, such claims are not unintentionally compromised.[369] Applications under the *Berkeley Applegate* principle must properly identify the work done.[370] Office-holders should not assume that they will be entitled to rely on the *Berkeley Applegate* principle at a later stage in the process, and may in appropriate cases make an application for directions at an earlier stage or else undertake the work 'on risk'.[371] The court may similarly permit office-holders to be paid from property subject to a fixed or floating charge where the chargee has not appointed a receiver.[372]

3. Priority of costs and expenses

(a) Bankruptcy

5.206 The trustee in bankruptcy's costs and expenses which are properly chargeable or incurred by the Official Receiver or the trustee in:

(i) preserving, realising or getting in any of the assets of the bankrupt

(ii) or otherwise relating to the conduct of any legal proceedings which the OR or the trustee has power to bring (whether the claim on which the proceedings are based forms part of the bankrupt's estate or otherwise) or defend are recoverable from the bankrupt's estate in priority to any distribution to creditors (indeed, they are at the very top of the list in IR 2016 r10.149).

---

the statutorily mandated scheme of distribution, and situations where the rule in *ex parte James* will bind the conscience of the office-holder, will not always be clear.

363 *Green v Bramston* [2010] EWHC 3106 (Ch).

364 *Berkeley Applegate* at 290.

365 *Re Telesure Ltd* [1997] BCC 580 at 583. This might be interpreted as an extension of the general principle that office-holders are entitled to be remunerated for the work they do: see IR 2016 r18.16(1).

366 The same principle applies to administrators who, when taking office after former administrators find they must administer and execute the terms of a statutory charge under Sch B1 para 99(4). In *Re Sports Betting Media Ltd* re [2007] EWHC 2085 (Ch), [2008] BCC 177, Briggs J held at [10]–[11] that it seemed correct as a matter of 'common sense, justice and equity' right that the beneficiaries of such a charge should have to pay collectively a reasonable sum towards the cost of having it executed in their favour against the company's assets.

367 Such as work that related to the interests of unsecured creditors: *Re HEC Enterprises Ltd* at [102].

368 *Tom Wise Ltd v Fillimore* [1999] BCC 129 at 133F.

369 *Green v Bramston* [2010] EWHC 3106 (Ch). The claim was not so compromised in that case.

370 *Re HEC Enterprises Ltd* at [106].

371 *Re HEC Enterprses Ltd* at [32]–[33], citing *Re Lehman Brothers International (Europe) Ltd (No 2)* [2010] Bus LR 480 at [86].

372 *Re Leyland DAF Ltd, Buchler v Talbot* [2004] UKHL 9; see *Re MF Global* [2013] EWHC 1655 (Ch) at [44].

(b) Liquidation

A liquidator's costs and expenses which are properly chargeable or incurred by the liquidator in preserving, realising or getting in any of the assets of the company or otherwise in the preparation, conduct or assignment of any legal proceedings, arbitration or other dispute resolution procedures, which the liquidator has power to bring in the liquidator's own name or bring or defend in the name of the company or in the preparation or conduct of any negotiations intended to lead or leading to a settlement or compromise of any legal action or dispute to which the proceedings or procedures relate are payable also out of the assets of the company available for the payment of general creditors (and are also at the very top of the list of priority).[373] **5.207**

It should be noted that, in liquidation, costs of litigation that exceed £5,000 may not be recovered from assets subject to a floating charge unless they have been approved by the charge holder or the court under the procedure set out in IR 2016 rr6.44 to 6.48 (in respect of a CVL) or rr7.111 to 7.116 (in a compulsory liquidation). **5.208**

An adverse costs order will be payable out of the assets of the company in priority to all other claims (including the liquidator's remuneration and his own legal costs)[374] although this does not extend to the direct costs of realising the assets to pay the costs order.[375] **5.209**

(c) Administration

In an administration, costs and expenses properly incurred by the administrator in performing the administrator's functions are also an expense of the administration (and are at the top of the list of priority for payment of the expenses of the administration in IR 2016 r3.51(2)). IR 2016 r3.51(3) however enables the court, if the assets are insufficient to satisfy the liabilities, to vary the order of priority for payment of expenses, but must be satisfied there is a good or sufficient reason to do so.[376] **5.210**

An administrator's remuneration and expenses are 'charged on and payable out of property of which he had custody or control immediately before cessation [of his appointment as administrator]'.[377] This includes property that the administrator is entitled to control or take into custody, and an administrator does not actually have to have taken steps to enforce such rights for the relevant property to come within paragraph 99(3)(a).[378] However, it does not include payments to be paid to the insolvent company where that company had since been dissolved since the payments were not a product of assets formerly in the administrators' control and the former administrators could not act as the company's representative in accepting the payments.[379] **5.211**

---

373 See IR 2016 rr6.42(4) in respect of creditors' voluntary liquidation and 7.108(4) in compulsory liquidation.
374 *Re Pacific Coast Syndicate* [1913] 2 Ch 26; *Re MT Realisations Ltd* [2003] EWHC 2895.
375 *Re Movietex* [1990] BCC 491.
376 *Irish Reel Production Ltd v Capitol Films Ltd* [2010] EWHC 180 (Ch), [2010] BCC 588 at [10] (Briggs J). Relevant considerations are whether the administrator has been misfeasant, or has made a serious mistake or blunder in the conduct of the administration.
377 IA 1986 Sch B1 para 99(3)(a).
378 *Re MK Airlines Ltd* [2012] EWHC 1018 (Ch).
379 *Walker v National Westminster Bank Plc* [2016] EWHC 315.

5.212 The charge is registrable as an agreed notice against registered property under the Land Registration Act 2002.[380]

5.213 Enforcement of the charge is not dealt with by statute, but it is suggested that the administrator may apply for enforcement of the charge by an order for sale under the court's inherent jurisdiction.

---

380   LRA 2002 ss29, 30. It will therefore have priority under s32(1): *Whitfield v Al Jaber* [2013] EWHC 3925 (Ch).

Part III

OFFICE-HOLDER LIABILITY

6

BREACHES OF DUTY

A. INTRODUCTION

6.001 The main focus of this chapter is on claims for breach of duty on the part of the IP, giving rise to civil liability. Whilst, in order to establish liability, a claimant, or applicant, will ordinarily need to prove a causative link to losses sustained by reason of that breach of duty, those topics are addressed in Chapter 7 below.[1] In addition, any generic defences there may be to such claims for civil liability, beyond defences based on the contention that there has been no breach of duty, are considered in Chapter 8 below.

6.002 In many instances claims against IPs are akin to professional negligence claims against professionals in other fields.[2] If this is so the IP will be under a duty to exercise the professional care and skill to be expected of a competent IP in carrying out the function in question.[3] In

---

1 A possible exception to this being a breach of contract claim relating to services provided outside the IP's statutory duties, which may give rise to a claim for nominal damages even if substantial loss may not be proven.

2 These are given extensive treatment in other well-known texts such as *Jackson & Powell on Professional Liability* (8th edn, 2016, with supplements to 2019). Accountants are considered as a category of professional (in Chapter 17) but IPs are not given any particular attention.

3 For a recent endorsement of this approach by the Supreme Court, see *MacDonald v Carnbroe* [2019] UKSC 57 (Lord Hodge JSC) at [38], referring to *Hague v Nam Tai Electronics Inc* [2008] UKPC 13, [2008] BCC 295; *Kyrris v Oldham*

other instances, there are features of claims which share more in common with claims against directors, and other office-holders of companies.[4] In yet others, the IP may be said to incur strict liability if they act beyond or in contravention of their statutory powers.[5] As discussed further below, the precise standard and duties expected of an IP are heavily influenced by the functional context for the claim, as are the remedies and destination of any recoveries (considered further in Chapter 7 below).

This chapter starts by considering the different routes to a claim and the question of standing. **6.003** Then the different classes of claim are considered, including both personal and class claims. The nature of the decision-making, or acts in question, are considered in general terms when assessing liability risk. The role played by expert evidence in assessing liability is also considered. Then, there is a more extensive consideration of the different situations in which claims arise, in Section F below. This is looked at on the basis of functional categories which typically arise across the range of work IPs carry out, looking at the path of those cases in broadly chronological order, from cradle to grave. The situations in which liabilities of an office-holder arise are various, but in many cases they may be said to fall within the three overarching functions of an IP to 'get in', 'realise' and 'distribute'. An IP may also engage in activities pre-appointment, which are considered in the context of advisory liability, below.

B. CIVIL LIABILITY IN GENERAL

1. Introduction

As discussed in Chapter 4 above, IPs, once appointed in a corporate context, owe duties to the **6.004** company, or more precisely, the creditors and members of that company (ordinarily, as a whole). In exceptional cases, following appointment they may also owe duties to third parties. Liabilities owed to the company, and in particular its creditors and members, arise as a result of the statutory duties imposed upon the office-holder by the scheme of the legislation, with some of those duties (but not all) being fiduciary in nature. This has been explained, in the context of a winding up order, in the following terms:[6]

> The making of a winding-up order divests the company of the beneficial ownership of its assets which cease to be applicable for its own benefit. They become instead subject to a statutory scheme for distribution among the creditors and members of the company. The responsibility for collecting the assets and implementing the statutory scheme is vested in the liquidator subject to the ultimate control of the court. The creditors do not themselves acquire a beneficial interest in any of the assets, but only have a right to have them administered in accordance with the statutory scheme.

[2003] EWCA Civ 1506, [2004] BCC 111; and *Lightman & Moss on the Law of Administrators and Receivers of Companies* (6th edn, 2017), para 12-042.

4 Typically when an IP is engaging in trading activities, considered further at Section F.7 below.

5 There is some debate as to whether such claims are based on a subjective requirement, but there may be certain categories of claim, see, e.g., in relation to distributions in MVLs discussed in Section F.9 below, where it may be said the liability is strict.

6 *Mitchell v Carter* [1997] 1 BCLC 673 (Millett LJ) at 686, citing *Ayerst (Inspector of Taxes) v C & K (Construction) Ltd* [1976] AC 167.

6.005   Liabilities to third parties tend to arise as a result of the IP entering into contractual relations with those parties,[7] usually in relation to pre-appointment services, or otherwise as a consequence of their assuming responsibility (in a legal sense) to those third parties.[8] Where such post-appointment liabilities arise (and insofar as they were properly incurred) the office-holder may have a right of recoupment out of the insolvency estate in respect of those liabilities. The value of such a right being dependent upon there being sufficient realisations within the estate for the office-holder to benefit from the right of recoupment.

6.006   The majority of claims brought against an office-holder are likely to arise as a result of their breach, or alleged breach, of duties owed to the company and/or creditors and be in the nature of class claims. This is considered further in Section C below. In such circumstances, the benefit of any recoveries brought will be for the company or the bankruptcy estate and will be distributed in accordance with the statutory scheme. In most cases, the proper approach to commencing proceedings against an office-holder for breach of duties owed to the company will be under the misfeasance provisions the scope and extent of which are addressed immediately below. These provisions confer upon interested parties standing to bring proceedings for causes of action that would, ordinarily,[9] otherwise be properly vested in the company or otherwise in the trustee themselves as trustee of the bankruptcy estate. In this regard there is at least some similarity with the concept of a derivative claim whereby the applicant for permission (if successful) will have a statutory entitlement to cause the company to bring proceedings in the name of the company and for the company's benefit rather than for that of the applicant.

2.   Routes for claimants to claim

(a)   Introduction

6.007   In seeking to impose civil liability on an office-holder, the prospective claimant/applicant can (in some cases) proceed by way of Part 7 proceedings.[10] However, in most instances the better approach will be to bring proceedings under the Insolvency Act 1986 ('IA 1986') by way of an application within the relevant insolvency proceedings. The principal procedural mechanism for bringing such proceedings are the misfeasance provisions which are found at IA 1986 s212 (liquidators and administrative receivers) and IA 1986 s304 (trustees in bankruptcy), with paragraph 75 of Schedule B1 to the IA 1986 making similar provision in respect of administrators. These mechanisms are addressed below.

(b)   IA 1986 Section 212 – Liquidators; Administrative Receivers

6.008   IA 1986 s212 provides a summary remedy against (amongst others) liquidators and administrative receivers of insolvent companies. Additionally, it has been suggested that the wording in s212(1)(c) is broad enough to extend to a CVA supervisor although there appears to be no

---

7   For example, *A & J Fabrications Ltd v Grant Thornton* [1998] 2 BCLC 227.

8   For example, *Prosser v Castle Sanderson Solicitors (a firm)* [2002] EWCA Civ 1140, [2003] BCC 440.

9   Of course, after appointment, particularly in an insolvent liquidation scenario, in no real sense is the claim a company claim; instead it is a claim on behalf of those interested in the proper administration of the statutory scheme.

10   Under Part 7 of the Civil Procedure Rules ('CPR').

reported decision on the point.[11] As originally enacted, the provision also provided a remedy as against administrators. However, from 15 September 2003, Schedule 17 paragraph 18 to the Enterprise Act 2002 ('EA 2002') amended IA 1986 s212 so that it ceased to apply to administrators. At the same time, Schedule 16 EA 2002 came into effect providing a separate provision dealing with administrator's misfeasance which is now found at paragraph 75 of Schedule B1.

IA 1986 s212 is solely procedural in effect.[12] It does not provide any new cause of action,[13] **6.009** rather it provides a more efficient means[14] by which a claim can be dealt with in the existing insolvency proceedings rather than by issuing fresh proceedings. The provision does not create new or additional obligations or duties, rather it provides the route of recourse for breach of established obligations and duties identified within the section.[15] As a result, the limitation period will be that applicable to the underlying claim.[16]

The provision applies where the respondent 'has misapplied or retained, or become account- **6.010** able, for any money or other property of the company, or been guilty of any misfeasance or breach of fiduciary duty or any other breach of duty'.[17] This formulation is broader than that used in the Companies Act 1985 ('CA 1985'), and preceding legislation, which applied where the relevant person had 'misapplied or retained or become liable or accountable for any money or property of the company, or been guilty of any misfeasance or breach of trust in relation to the company'. This is significant in that the words 'or any other breach of duty' (as found in s212) are broad enough to apply to a breach of a duty of care by a liquidator, thereby bringing common law negligence, or negligent breaches of statutory duty, within the scope of the provision.[18]

Although IA 1986 s212 is more commonly relied upon by liquidators to bring proceedings **6.011** against former directors, s212(1)(b) lists liquidators and administrative receivers as potential respondents to a claim. Indeed, it seems that s212 proceedings may even be instituted by one joint liquidator against another.[19]

The provision (and its predecessors) have been relied upon to bring proceedings against **6.012** liquidators in the following contexts (with varying degrees of success):

---

11 Sealy and Milman, *Annotated Guide to the Insolvency Legislation* (23rd edn, 2021), 234.

12 *Re Canadian Land Reclaiming & Colonizing Co* (1880) 14 Ch D 660 at 670, 28 WR 775, 42 LT 559; *Cohen v Selby* [2001] 1 BCLC 176, 183 at [20]; *Re Paycheck Services 3 Ltd*; *Revenue and Customs Commissioners and another v Holland* [2010] UKSC 51, [2011] 1 All ER 430 at [55].

13 *Re City Equitable Fire Insurance Co Ltd* [1925] Ch 407; *Re Paycheck Services 3 Ltd*; *Revenue and Customs Commissioners and another v Holland* [2010] UKSC 51, [2011] 1 All ER 430 at [55].

14 *Cavendish Bentinck v Fenn* (1887) 12 App Cas 652.

15 *Top Brands Ltd v Sharma*; *Re Mama Milla* [2014] EWHC 2753, [2015] 2 All ER 581 at [38].

16 *Goldfarb (liquidator of Eurocruit Europe Ltd) v Poppleton* [2007] EWHC 1433 (Ch), [2007] 2 BCLC 598 at [27].

17 IA 1986 s212(1).

18 *Re Centralcrest Engineering Ltd* [2000] BCC 727; *Re D'Jan of London Ltd* [1993] BCC 646; and cf. *Re B Johnson & Co (Builders) Ltd* [1955] Ch 634.

19 *Re Miranda Coal & Iron Co* (1892) 11 NZLR 640.

- Misapplication of trust monies by a liquidator arising out of his settling an unmeritorious claim with a third party.[20]
- Allowing the company to continue to trade without the sanction of the court or liquidation committee (as required by IA 1986 s167) and allowing the company to continue to trade when it was clear that the liquidator should have realised the company's assets very quickly after her appointment.[21]
- In breach of trust, or otherwise negligently, the liquidator making a payment to third parties in respect of a claim to which there was a defence.[22]
- Making payment to a contributory, prior to the company's liabilities having been satisfied in full and in circumstances where there were insufficient assets available in the liquidation to discharge the company's remaining liabilities.[23]
- Liquidator failing to provide for equal ranking and payment of all preferential claims.[24]
- The adoption of an incorrect application made under the Town and Country Planning Act 1947.[25]
- Hasty sale of a company by administrators[26] resulting in an alleged sale at an undervalue.[27]
- Failure of a liquidator to ensure that his co-liquidator paid the proceeds of sale of a property into the liquidation account.[28]

6.013 As to claims against administrative receivers, historically, s212 (and its predecessors) provided no relief as against administrative receivers, it having been held that an administrative receiver was neither an 'officer' nor a 'manager' for the purposes of what was CA 1948 s333 (now IA 1986 s212).[29] However, following the coming into force of the EA 2002, and the reformulation of IA 1986 s212(1)(b), administrative receivers are expressly referred to as potential respondents to such an application.[30]

6.014 Claims under s212 are derivative in that (ordinarily, and subject to the question of timing referred to below) the party relying upon the provision can only bring proceedings arising out of a cause of action vested in the company and not those vested in individual creditors or third parties.[31] By extension and unlike other statutory rights of action arising under IA 1986,[32] a party commencing proceedings under s212 ordinarily is doing so in the right of the company, rather than for the benefit of the general body of creditors. As a consequence, any contribution (less the costs of bringing the action) will, or may (depending on their wording and the nature

---

20 *Re Home & Colonial Insurance Co* [1930] 1 Ch 102.
21 *Re Centralcrest Engineering Ltd* [2000] BCC 727.
22 *Re Windsor Steam Coal Co* [1929] 1 Ch 151.
23 *Re A.M.F. International Ltd.* [1996] 1 WLR 77.
24 *Lord Advocate v Liquidators of Purvis Industries Ltd* 1958 SC 338.
25 *Re B Johnson & Co (Builders) Ltd* [1955] Ch 634.
26 The claim was brought prior to the coming into force of Sch 17 para 18 EA 2002 which resulted in IA 1986 s212 being amended to remove administrators from the ambit of the provision.
27 *Re Charnley Davies Ltd* [1990] BCC 605.
28 *Re Gold Co of Southern India*, unrep'd (*The Times*, 3 March 1883).
29 *Re B Johnson & Co (Builders) Ltd* [1955] Ch 634.
30 This has the consequence of reversing the effect of the decision of the Court of Appeal in *Re B Johnson & Co (Builders) Ltd.*
31 *Re Ambrose Tin & Copper Mining Co* (1880) 14 Ch D 390; *Re Hill's Waterfall Estate and Gold Mining Co* [1896] 1 Ch 947.
32 For example, IA 1986 s214.

of the claim in question), be caught by any charges that third parties have over the company's present and future property.[33]

In *Re Oasis Merchandising Services Ltd (in liquidation)* Gibson LJ contrasted the causes of action **6.015** that might be brought under IA 1986 s212 with the causes of action arising under ss213 and 214, with the latter causes of action being personal to the liquidator and therefore assignable with causes of action under s212 being property of the company and therefore (under the law as it then stood) not being capable of assignment. In doing so he observed that:[34]

> ... a right of action against directors for misfeasance which the liquidator (amongst others) can enforce under s 212 of the 1986 Act and the fruits of such an action are property of the company capable of being charged by a debenture, because the right of action arose and was available to the company prior to the winding up.

It should be noted this was in the context of a claim against a director. Where a claim is **6.016** brought against a liquidator in respect of matters arising out of their conduct in the winding up, the cause of action will not have arisen prior to the commencement of the winding up but at some point thereafter. Application of Gibson LJ's analysis, and that of Millett LJ in *Mitchell v Carter*, referred to in paragraph 6.004 above, would suggest that the fruits of such an action will not necessarily inure for the charge holder, but instead, and depending on the nature of the claim, for the general body of creditors, in accordance with the statutory scheme (as is the case where proceedings are brought for fraudulent or wrongful trading). However, the position may be different if the claim relates to an asset which was, before any insolvency procedure commenced, an asset of the company which was charged to a third-party debenture holder. If so, the better view is that the making of the winding-up order should not of itself (and subject to the terms of the charge instrument) affect the charge holder's entitlement under the charge, with the only question being whether the recoveries in question are (or were) property of the company and therefore capable of being caught by the charge. This is consistent with the notion that the IA 1986 is not (ordinarily) intended to affect the rights of secured creditors.[35]

In addition to any substantive defence that a respondent office-holder may have to a claim **6.017** under IA 1986 s212, he may also be able to raise procedural defences, including (in appropriate cases) challenging the standing of the applicant.[36] Further, the relief available to an applicant is discretionary in nature and a respondent may seek to rely upon that discretion as well as (potentially) the ability of the court to grant relief pursuant to the Companies Act 2006 ('CA 2006') s1157. These points are considered further in Chapter 8 below.[37]

Relief under s212(3) is discretionary and the court can exercise its discretion to reduce or **6.018** otherwise limit the amount which it orders a respondent to contribute.[38] In addition CA 2006

---

33   *Re Anglo–Austrian Printing and Publishing Co* [1895] 2 Ch 891.
34   *Re Oasis Merchandising Services Ltd (in liquidation)*; *Ward v Aitken and others* [1997] 1 BCLC 689, 698–9.
35   See principles 1 and 3 in the 10 principles discussed in *Goode on Principles of Corporate Insolvency Law* (5th edn, 2018).
36   See also paras 6.208 and 6.037 below. See Chapter 8 below on the question of defences more generally.
37   Paras 8.060–8.075.
38   *Re Sunlight Incandescent Lamps* (1900) 16 TLR 535l; *Re Loquitur Ltd, Inland Revenue Commissioners v Richmond* [2003] EWHC 999 (Ch), [2003] 2 BCLC 442.

s1157 provides that in proceedings for negligence, default, breach of duty or breach of trust against, inter alia, an officer of the company, where it appears to the court hearing the case that the officer or person is or may be liable but that he acted honestly and reasonably, and that having regard to all the circumstances of the case (including those connected with his appointment) he ought fairly to be excused, the court may relieve him, either wholly or in part, from his liability on such terms as it thinks fit. This raises the question of whether the liquidator or administrative receiver is an 'officer' for the purposes of s1157. In *In Re Home Treat Ltd* Harman J placed reliance upon the decision of Parker J in *Re X Co Ltd*[39] and held that an administrator was an officer and therefore entitled in principle to rely upon s1157. However, HHJ Behrens in *Rawnsley and Canal Dyeing Company Ltd (in liquidation) v Weatherall Green & Smith North Ltd* held that it was 'seriously arguable that a liquidator is not within the ambit of s 1157' albeit without the benefit of citation of the earlier authorities.[40] The conflict has now been resolved in *Re Powertrain Ltd (in liquidation)* where Newey J reviewed the above authorities and concluded that a liquidator could be granted relief under CA 2006 s1157.[41]

6.019 In *Re Loquitur Ltd* counsel were agreed that in addition to the power of the court to grant relief under what was then s727 of CA 1985 (now CA 2006 s1157), s212(3) IA 1986 confers a further discretion on the court to determine precisely what or how much the director should be ordered to restore to the company so as to do what is just in all the circumstances.[42] In those circumstances, Etherton J (as he then was) held that notwithstanding the fact that CA 1985 s727 was not engaged on the facts, it would nevertheless be appropriate to limit the amount which should be paid by the defendants under IA 1986 s212(3).[43] It has subsequently been questioned whether the discretion existing under s212(3) is 'intended to provide a further mechanism for relieving from liability based on broad and ill-defined ideas of fairness' in circumstances where s727 CA 1985 (now CA 2006 s1157) provides an express power upon the court to relieve in well-defined circumstances.[44] The proper ambit of the discretion was confirmed on appeal to the Supreme Court where Lord Hope held that the discretion given by s 212(3) is as to the order that would be appropriate once liability has been established, not to grant relief against liability.[45]

6.020 Finally, it has been held that a liquidator is not entitled to be indemnified or otherwise seek relief under ss30 and 68 of the Trustee Act 1925 ('TA 1925').[46]

6.021 The orders which the court can make on an application under IA 1986 s212 are set out in s212(3) and are as follows:

---

39 [1907] 2 Ch 92.
40 [2009] EWHC 2482 (Ch).
41 [2015] EWHC 3998 (Ch), [2017] 1 BCLC 95 at [13].
42 *Re Loquitur Ltd, Inland Revenue Commissioners v Richmond* [2003] EWHC 999 (Ch), [2003] 2 BCLC 442 at [245].
43 Ibid at [247].
44 *Re Paycheck Services 3 Ltd* [2008] EWHC 2200 (Ch), [2008] 2 BCLC 613 [232]. See also, more recently, the decision of Deputy ICCJ Schaffer in *Re DCL Hire* [2018] EWHC 3457 (Ch), where a deduction was made relying on *Re Loquitur* but which was questioned, on appeal, by Mann J: see [2019] EWHC 2086 at [25].
45 *Re Paycheck Services 3 Ltd; Revenue and Customs Commissioners and another v Holland* [2010] UKSC 51, [2011] 1 All ER 430 at [51]. See also the decision of Rimer LJ in the Court of Appeal [2009] EWCA Civ 625, [2009] 2 BCLC 309 at [110].
46 *Re Windsor Steam Coal Co* [1929] 1 Ch 151.

- An order to repay, restore or account for any money or property of the company or any part of it, with interest at such rate as the court thinks just; or
- An order to contribute such sum to the company's assets by way of compensation in respect of the misfeasance or breach of fiduciary or other duty as the court thinks just.

In addition, the relief ordered should go no further than that required to compensate the company for the loss arising out of the conduct which gave rise to the breaches of the relevant duty by the respondent and the court is not entitled to disregard causation.[47] **6.022**

An office-holder (and any other respondent) is unable to assert a right of set-off in respect of any liability owed to them by the company on an application under s212, misfeasance not constituting a 'dealing' thereby meaning that the requirement for mutual dealings cannot be satisfied.[48] **6.023**

Section 212 (as well as the other misfeasance provisions) does not impose additional liabilities on the respondent. Rather they provide a more efficient procedural basis for obtaining relief within the insolvency proceedings. The application should be made by way of an application notice[49] and accompanying witness statement. Where the complexity of the application merits it, direction should be sought for the parties to file points of defence and points of claim. In an unreported decision of Snowden J in 2019 in *Re Money Worries Ltd* it was held that where the court has ordered pleadings, they replaced any previous witness statements and had to be read in isolation. A further procedural point which should be noted is that where a liquidator has been released,[50] IA 1986 s212(4) requires that an applicant under IA 1986 s 212(3) must obtain the leave of the court. This point is addressed in greater detail at paragraph 6.039 below. **6.024**

(c) Para 75 of Sch B1 IA 1986 – Misfeasance by administrators

As noted above, prior to the coming into force of EA 2002, IA 1986 s212 applied to administrators. On the coming into force of EA 2002 paragraph 18 of Schedule 17 of that Act had the effect of removing all references to 'administrator'. At the same time, Schedule 16 EA 2002 introduced a new provision which addressed misfeasance by administrators which is now contained within paragraph 75 of Schedule B1 IA 1986. **6.025**

Differences between the pre- and post-EA 2002 regimes are modest. However, they include the fact that it is no longer necessary for the company to be in liquidation prior to a claim being brought. Additionally, paragraph 75 Schedule B1 IA 1986 also applies to a person who 'purports to be an administrator' as well as a person who *is* an administrator.[51] Further, paragraph 75(3) Schedule B1 requires an applicant to set out the conduct complained of by reference to the conduct set out in that provision. **6.026**

---

47   *Cohen v Selby (Re Simmon Box (Diamonds) Ltd)* [2001] 1 BCLC 176; *Re Continental Assurance Co of London plc* [2001] BPIR 733.

48   *Re Anglo-French Co-operative Society Ex p Pelly* (1882) 21 Ch. D 492; *Manson v Smith (liquidator of Thomas Christy Ltd)* [1997] 2 BCLC 161.

49   Usually by way of an Insolvency Act Application Notice (Form IAA).

50   See IA 1986 ss173 and 174.

51   Sch B1 IA 1986 para 75(1).

6.027 As with IA 1986 s212, the provision is procedural in nature and the applicant must allege conduct of the type set out in sub-paragraph (2) of the provision which is cast in similarly broad terms to the conduct set out in IA 1986 s212(1). In order to succeed on a claim under paragraph 75 a claimant will need to show that there has been a breach of a relevant duty and it must be shown that the breach has caused loss.[52] Any recovery inures for the benefit of the company and not an individual creditor or contributory.[53]

6.028 Those with standing to make an application under paragraph 75 Schedule B1 IA 1986 include: the official receiver; the administrator of the company; the liquidator of the company; a creditor; and a contributory.[54] In order to establish standing under the provision, a creditor will need to show that they have a sufficient interest in the relief that is sought.[55] This test is unlikely to be met where the applicant is pursuing the litigation as a nominee of a third party or where the litigation is being funded and directed by a third party.[56] A former creditor and shareholder whose property has vested in their trustee in bankruptcy will be neither a creditor nor a shareholder and will therefore lack standing to bring proceedings under the provision.[57]

6.029 Given the similarity with IA 1986 s212 (and the fact that, prior to 2003, s212 applied to administrators) reference should also be made to the text preceding this heading and the various authorities cited there.

6.030 Examples of the provision being relied upon include:

- Allegations that administrators had, inter alia, conducted a 'light touch' administration; failed to exercise independent judgment; and sold property at an undervalue.[58]
- Sale of the company's assets at an undervalue to a company incorporated for the purpose of acquiring the assets of the company in the administration combined with undue deference to the views of the director.[59]
- Drawing down of monies from a funder for the purpose of paying administrators' remuneration where the funding deed provided for the monies to be applied for payment of the administrators' remuneration.[60]
- Alleged failure by administrators to take steps to obtain further funding from the LLP's bankers and an allegation that the administrators were parties to a pre-determined arrangement to enable a third party to acquire a hotel at an undervalue.[61]

---

52 *Berntsen v Tait (Re Coniston Hotel (Kent) LLP)* [2014] EWHC 1100 (Ch) at [52] (citing *Re Simmon Box (Diamonds) Ltd* [2002] BCC 82).

53 *Re Coniston Hotel* [2013] EWHC 93 (Ch), [2013] 2 BCLC 405.

54 Sch B1 para 75(2) IA 1986.

55 *Re Coniston Hotel* [2014] EWHC 1100 (Ch), [2014] 4 WLUK 289 [52] (citing: *Cavendish Bentinck v Thomas Fenn* (1887) 7 App Cas 652; *Deloitte & Touche v Johnson* [1999] 1 WLR 1605; *Jameel v Dow Jones & Co Inc* [2005] EWCA Civ 75, [2005] QB 946).

56 *Brake v Lowes* [2020] EWHC 538 (Ch) at [24].

57 *Fabb v Peters, Alpa Industries Ltd, CKE Engineering Ltd v Andrew Philip Peters, William Kenneth Dawson, Greig Mitchell, Deloitte LLP* [2013] EWHC 296 (Ch), [2013] BPIR 264.

58 *Davey v Money* [2018] EWHC 766 (Ch).

59 *Brewer v Iqbal* [2019] EWHC 182 (Ch), [2019] 1 BCLC 487.

60 *Katz v Oldham* [2018] EWHC 540 (Ch), [2019] BCC 48

61 *Re Coniston Hotel (Kent) LLP* [2013] EWHC 93 (Ch), [2013] 2 BCLC 40; *Berntsen v Tait* [2015] EWCA Civ 1001.

- Alleged duty of care owed to unsecured creditors in circumstances where there was no special relationship between the administrators and those creditors.[62]

(d) IA 1986 s304 – Liability of trustees in bankruptcy

Section 212 IA 1986 and paragraph 75 of Schedule B1 to IA 1986 find their analogue in **6.031** personal insolvency in IA 1986 s304. The provision creates a framework for claims brought for the benefit of the bankruptcy estate. It is concerned with, and confined to, acts or omissions on the part of the trustee that have caused loss or damage to the estate.[63] It applies where the court is satisfied that:[64]

(a) the trustee of a bankrupt's estate has misapplied or retained, or become accountable for, any money or other property comprised in the bankrupt's estate; or
(b) that a bankrupt's estate has suffered any loss in consequence of any misfeasance or breach of fiduciary or other duty by a trustee of the estate in the carrying out of his functions.

Section 304(1) makes clear that liability arising under this provision is in addition to and not in **6.032** replacement of, any liability otherwise arising. Accordingly, s304 extends to any claim for any common law or other duty not falling within the express terms of the provision.[65] As with s212 and paragraph 75 Schedule B1 IA 1986, the provision is procedural in nature and does not give rise to any new cause of action. Accordingly, the applicable limitation period will be that relating to the underlying claim.[66]

The formulation is similar to the provisions addressed above and the inclusion of the words 'or **6.033** other duty' indicate that the provision extends to conduct which is negligent.[67] Similarly, as with the corporate provisions, any recoveries made under the provision will be for the benefit of the bankruptcy estate.[68] Accordingly, it will only be where the bankruptcy is a 'surplus bankruptcy' that the bankrupt will have a personal interest in the outcome of proceedings under IA 1986 s304.[69]

IA 1986 s299(5) provides that upon release, the trustee will be discharged from all liability **6.034** both in respect of acts or omissions in the administration of the estate and otherwise in relation to his conduct as trustee. However, the provision expressly retains the court's power to make an order under IA 1986 s304 post-release.

Examples of attempted applications or claims under IA 1986 s304 include the following: **6.035**

---

62 *Charalambous v B&C Associates* [2009] EWHC 2601 (Ch), [2009] 43 EG 105 (CS).
63 *Oraki v Bramston* [2017] EWCA Civ 403, [2018] 3 WLR 569 at [214].
64 IA 1986 s304(1).
65 *Oraki v Bramston* [2017] EWCA Civ 403, [2018] 3 WLR 569 at [216].
66 Cf. *Re Goldfarb (liquidator of Eurocruit Europe Ltd) v Poppleton* [2007] EWHC 1433 (Ch), [2007] 2 BCLC 598 at [27].
67 See by analogy *Re D'Jan of London Ltd* [1993] BCC 646 and *Re Centralcrest Engineering Ltd* [2000] BCC 727. See also *McAteer v Lismore* [2012] NICh 7, [2012] BPIR 812 at [5] for adoption of this approach by the High Court of Justice in Northern Ireland.
68 IA 1986 s304(1).
69 Ibid s330(5).

- A claim for breach of contract was a personal claim which fell outside the scope of IA 1986 s304 whilst the remaining claims had been the subject of prior litigation.[70]
- In a surplus bankruptcy, permission was refused to bring proceedings under IA 1986 s304 in relation to the trustee's decision to accept a proof of debt from the petitioning creditor and the trustee's remuneration and expenses, save that limited permission was given in respect of those expenses which related to an application for possession and sale which was the subject of a 'costs cap'.[71]
- Notwithstanding the fact that it was strongly arguable that an order providing for the vesting of the benefit of a cooperation agreement in the trustee should not have been made, there had been no misapplication of assets under IA 1986 s304 and neither could the rule in *ex parte James*[72] turn what was not a misapplication of estate funds into something which was.[73]

6.036 An application can be made under the provision by the official receiver; the Secretary of State; a creditor; or the bankrupt.[74] However, where bankrupts wish to make the application, they first need the leave of the court. See further paragraph 6.046 below.[75]

3. Standing

(a) Section 212

6.037 IA 1986 s212(3) lists those with standing to apply under the provision as being: the liquidator; the official receiver; creditors;[76] and contributories. Accordingly, administrators do not have standing to bring proceedings under IA 1986 s212, although they can bring proceedings in the name of the company outside the s212 route.[77] There does not appear to be any good reason for this distinction, given the modern role of administrations extends far beyond 'old-style' breathing-space administrations.

6.038 Creditors can bring proceedings (which include those who have taken assignment of claims[78]) as of right. Contributories require the court's leave but do not need to show that they will benefit from any order that the court may make on the application.[79] From the perspective of a successor office-holder, the benefit of a contributory bringing proceedings is that they will bear the burden of much of the risk and expense of the proceedings, albeit that the price is a loss of control by the office-holder. A party does not become a contributory by reason of them being

---

70 *Reynard v Fox* [2018] EWHC 2141 (Ch), [2018] 8 WLUK 78.

71 *Helen Irene Borodzicz; Borodzicz v Horton, Re* [2015] Lexis Citation 286, [2016] BPIR 24.

72 Discussed further in Chapter 4 at paras 4.041–4.045 above.

73 *Green v Satsangi* [1998] 1 BCLC 458, [1998] BPIR 55.

74 IA 1986 s304(2).

75 Which refers to *Oraki v Bramston* [2015] EWHC 2046 (Ch), [2016] 3 WLR 1231 at [164] and see: *McGuire v Rose* [2013] EWCA Civ 429, [2014] BPIR 650.

76 See, e.g., *Top Brands Ltd v Sharma* [2014] EWHC 2753, [2015] 2 All ER 581; *Re Centralcrest Engineering Ltd* [2000] BCC 727 and generally: *Re Loquitur* [2003] EWHC 999 (Ch), [2003] BCLC 410.

77 *Irwin v Lynch* [2010] EWCA Civ 1153, [2011] 1 WLR 1364.

78 *Mullarkey v Broad* [2007] EWHC 3400 (Ch), [2008] 1 BCLC 638.

79 IA 1986 s212(5) and cf. *Re Rica Gold Washing Co* (1879) 11 Ch D 36.

liable to contribute to the company under an order made under IA 1986 ss213 or 214,[80] nor on an order made under IA 1986 s212.[81]

Once the liquidator has had their release, no application can be made without the leave of the **6.039** court.[82] In order to obtain leave, the applicant will need show (i) a reasonably meritorious cause of action and (ii) that the grant of permission is reasonably likely to benefit the estate.[83] The above factors are not however exhaustive and other considerations may be taken into account.[84]

A claim cannot be brought directly following presentation of a winding-up petition. A **6.040** claimant must wait until a winding-up order has been made.[85] It may however be the case that a court will grant permission retrospectively by analogy with the approach taken in *Gresham International Ltd v Moonie*.[86]

(b) Para 75 Sch B1

Paragraph 75(2) of Schedule B1 IA 1986 lists those who have standing to make an application **6.041** under that provision as being: the official receiver; the administrator; a creditor; and a contributory. A creditor is only likely to pursue an application under paragraph 75 Schedule B1 IA 1986 where he has a personal interest in the outcome of the application.[87]

Unlike under IA 1986 s212, there is no requirement for a contributory to obtain the leave of **6.042** the court.[88] However, similar to IA 1986 s212(4), when the administrator has been discharged under paragraph 98 of Schedule B1, the application can only be made with the leave of the court.[89] In order to obtain leave, the applicant will again need to show (i) a reasonably meritorious cause of action and (ii) that the grant of permission is reasonably likely to benefit the estate.[90] The above factors are not however exhaustive and other considerations may be taken into account.[91] However, the court will be slow to deny permission where the claim is reasonably meritorious.[92] In *Re One Black Friars Ltd*, Mr William Trower QC held that the permission requirement served a different purpose under paragraph 75 to that under IA 1986 s304. Under the former it was said to arise out of the need to provide protection to the administrator who no longer has the assets of the company in his possession whilst under s304, the court's concern is to prevent vexatious litigation.[93] However, in both *Katz v Oldham* and *AM Holdings Ltd v Batten* the court took the view that the policy considerations were the same

---

80   Ibid s79(2).
81   *Re AMF International Ltd* (No 2) [1996] 1 WLR 77, 82; *Burnden Group Holdings Ltd v Hunt* [2018] EWHC 463 (Ch).
82   IA 1986 s212(4).
83   *Parkinson Engineering Services plc v Swan* [2009] EWCA Civ 1366, [2010] 1 BCLC 163.
84   *Re Parkinson Engineering Services plc* at [34].
85   *Wightman v. Bennett* [2005] BPIR 470 at 473.
86   [2009] EWHC 1093 (Ch), [2010] Ch 285.
87   *Berntsen v Tait* [2015] EWCA Civ 1001 at [65].
88   Cf. IA 1986 s212(5).
89   Para 75(6) of Sch B1 to IA 1986.
90   *Katz v Oldham* [2016] BPIR 83 at [7]. See also: *AM Holdings Ltd v Batten* [2018] EWHC 934 (Ch) at [35].
91   *Katz v Oldham* at [7]; *Re Parkinson Engineering Services* [2009] EWCA Civ 1366, [2010] BCLC 163 [34]; *McGuire v Rose* [2013] EWCA Civ 429, [2014] BPIR 650 at [25].
92   *AM Holdings Ltd v Batten* [2018] EWHC 934 (Ch) at [38].
93   *Re One Black Friars Ltd* [2018] EWHC 901 (Ch), [2018] 4 WLUK 412 at [22]–[23].

under s304 and paragraph 75, namely the avoidance of vexatious litigation.[94] It seems probable that both policy considerations are relevant and the emphasis to be placed on each, is to be determined on a case-by-case basis, with little conflict between the two considerations being evident in any event.

(c) IA 1986 s304

6.043 Section 304(2) sets out those who may apply for an order under the section as being: the official receiver; the Secretary of State; a creditor of the bankrupt; and the bankrupt himself. The provision also states that leave of the court will be required where (i) the application is made by the bankrupt[95] and (ii) where the trustee has had their release under IA 1986 s299.

6.044 When determining whether to grant leave to a bankrupt to bring proceedings under IA 1986 s304 the bankrupt will need to prove (as with applications post-release/discharge under IA 1986 s212 and para 75 of Sch B1) (i) a reasonably meritorious cause of action and (ii) that the grant of permission is reasonably likely to benefit the estate.[96] These factors are not exhaustive.[97] With regard to the first requirement, it has been said that when regard is had to the underlying case law it is 'clear that an applicant has a high hurdle to overcome to obtain permission to challenge decisions of a trustee'.[98] The application can be made by the bankrupt even where there will be no surplus within the meaning of s330(5).[99] However the existence of a surplus (or otherwise) is likely to be material to the question of permission even if its absence is not determinative.[100]

6.045 An applicant will also need permission if the trustee has had his release and it seems that the court will adopt a similar approach to granting leave.[101] As with paragraph 75[102] (and presumably s212), where there is a reasonably meritorious claim, the court is likely to be slow to refuse permission. Whilst caution is to be exercised when transposing principles gleaned under paragraph 75 (and s212) to s304, part of the reason for such caution is the propensity for bankrupts to engage in vexatious litigation.[103] Where the claim is reasonably meritorious it seems unlikely that the proposed litigation will be vexatious.

6.046 As was observed by Proudman J in *Oraki v Bramston* at first instance, it is the bankruptcy court which is the court to give permission for an application under s304(1), and not the court in

---

94 *AM Holdings Ltd v Batten* at [37]; *Katz v Oldham* at [10]–[11].

95 It has been noted elsewhere that this requirement is consistent with the fact that as an ordinary matter of law, the bankrupt has no right of action in respect of property vested in his trustee (*Muir Hunter on Personal Insolvency* [3-920]). Cf. *Heath v Tang* [1993] 1 WLR 1421.

96 *Brown v Beat* [2002] BPIR 341; *McGuire v Rose* [2013] EWCA Civ 429, [2014] BPIR 650; *Helen Irene Borodzicz; Borodzicz v Horton, Re* [2015] Lexis Citation 286, [2016] BPIR 24; cf. *Re Hellyer (a Bankrupt)* [1998] BPIR 695 at 696C.

97 *Katz v Oldham* [2016] BPIR 83 at [7]; *Re Parkinson Engineering Services* [2009] EWCA Civ 1366, [2010] BCLC 163 at [34]; *McGuire v Rose* [2013] EWCA Civ 429, [2014] BPIR 650 at [25].

98 *Helen Irene Borodzicz; Borodzicz v Horton, Re* [2015] Lexis Citation 286, [2016] BPIR 24 at [40], see also *Frosdick v Fox* [2017] EWHC 1737 (Ch), [2018] 1 WLR 38 at [65].

99 IA 1986 s304(2).

100 *McGuire v Rose* [2013] EWCA Civ 429, [2014] BPIR 650 at [13].

101 *Helen Irene Borodzicz; Borodzicz v Horton, Re* [2015] Lexis Citation 286, [2016] BPIR 24.

102 *AM Holdings Ltd v Batten* [2018] EWHC 934 (Ch) at [38].

103 *Re One Black Friars Ltd* [2018] EWHC 901 (Ch), [2018] 4 WLUK 412 at [22]–[23].

which the proceedings are being pursued, with the relevant definitions being found in IA 1986 ss385 and 373(3).[104]

4. No immunity from suit

It is also worth briefly noting here that in general terms when an IP carries out their statutory **6.047** functions they risk a potential claim if they fail to exercise reasonable skill and care in doing so; see Chapter 4 above.[105] There is no general immunity from suit by reason of their involvement in statutory proceedings or by reason of their discharge of statutory functions.[106] However, there is one potential exception in the case of monitors, who will not be ordered to pay compensation.[107] This stands in contrast with nominees under the pre-existing 'small company' moratorium procedure, for whom no such carve-out was given.[108]

C. CLAIMANTS: CLASS AND PERSONAL CLAIMS

1. Different types of claimant

(a) Introduction

There is a distinction to be drawn between claims made by individuals against office-holders **6.048** and those which are of a class nature. Where an office-holder, or IP, owes duties to an individual creditor (or a third party) personally (e.g., where there is a special relationship which results in a duty of care, or where some other tortious or contractual relationship exists) the prospective claimant will be entitled to bring proceedings in the ordinary way. Where the company is being wound up and there is (ordinarily) no such duty owed to an individual creditor, the prospective claimant will need to rely upon the various statutory mechanisms discussed above and any recovery will be for the benefit of the company, or creditors as a class, which in many cases will mean that any recovery will be for the benefit of secured creditors.

An office-holder will owe duties to the company, and the creditors as a class, as a result of the **6.049** effect of the many provisions within the insolvency legislation which confer powers and impose duties upon them as an incident of their office. As discussed further below, there is a narrow

---

104 *Oraki v Bramston* [2015] EWHC 2046 (Ch), [2015] BPIR 1238 at [164] (citing: *McGuire v Rose* [2013] EWCA Civ 429, [2014] BPIR 650).

105 Paras 4.026–4.033.

106 The decision of the Court of Appeal in *Mond v Hyde* [1999] QB 1097, to the effect that the official receiver is immune from suit must be viewed as being restricted to its own facts (liability for alleged negligent statements made by the OR to the trustee) and its correctness must now be questioned in the light of the general retreat from blanket immunities for those involved in the conduct of proceedings such as advocates (see *Arthur J S Hall & Co (a firm) v Simons* [2002] 1 AC 615) and experts (see *Jones v Kaney* [2011] UKSC 13, [2011] 2 AC 398). Compare also with the decision of Edis J in *Sebry v Companies House* [2015] EWHC 115 (QB), [2015] 4 All ER 681, [2016] 1 WLR 2499, [2015] 1 BCLC 670. In *Sebry*, Companies House was found to be liable for damages arising from wrongly indicating that Mr Sebry's company was subject to a winding-up petition and was in liquidation. Permission to appeal was granted, with the appeal listed for hearing in March 2017, but no decision of the Court of Appeal was reported and it is inferred the appeal did not proceed.

107 IA 1986 sA42(4)(c). Whether this apparent immunity applies only to actions under this section or to monitors in general remains an open question.

108 Ibid Sch A1 para 27(3).

category of cases where there may be personal liability to an individual creditor in relation to distributions. Separately, an office-holder may voluntarily acquire, or assume, duties to third parties as a result of their entering into contractual relations with those parties or otherwise as a consequence of an assumption of legal responsibility. The circumstances in which they will do so will however be rare, as is illustrated by *Fraser Turner Ltd v PricewaterhouseCoopers LLP*,[109] considered further below.

6.050 Additionally, liability may be involuntary in circumstances where that liability arises by way of court order, with orders for costs being of particular note in this regard.

(b)   The company, creditors and shareholders

6.051 As noted in paragraph 6.004 above, on a winding up, individual creditors and members of the company do not have proprietary interest in the assets of the company. As explained by Millett LJ (as he then was) in *Mitchell v Carter, Re Buckingham International plc* above, they only have a right to have the assets administered in accordance with the statutory scheme.[110]

6.052 It follows that, as a general rule, an office-holder owes no duty to individual creditors in relation to the conduct of administration of the company[111] in much the same way as a director of a company does not owe a duty to individual shareholders.[112] That is subject to the fact that if it can be established that the relevant office-holder assumed responsibility to an individual creditor or member in such a way as to create a 'special relationship' with that individual, the assumption of responsibility is capable of giving rise to duties becoming owed to them.[113] The test for an assumption of responsibility is an objective one, where 'the primary focus is on things said or done by the Officeholder in dealings with the individual creditor, judged in the light of the relevant contextual scene, with the primary focus on exchanges which cross the line'.[114] In *Peskin v Anderson* Mummery LJ summarised the position (in the context of a solvent company) as follows:[115]

> The fiduciary duties owed to the company arise from the legal relationship between the directors and the company directed and controlled by them. The fiduciary duties owed to the shareholders do not arise from that legal relationship. They are dependent on establishing a special factual relationship between the directors and the shareholders in the particular case …
>
> Fiduciary relationships, such as agency, involve duties of trust, confidence and loyalty. Those duties are, in general, attracted by and attached to a person who undertakes, or who, depending on all the circumstances, is treated as having assumed, responsibility to act on behalf of, or for the benefit of, another person. That other person may have entrusted or, depending on all the circumstances, may be treated as having entrusted, the care of his property, affairs, transactions or interests to him.

---

109   [2018] EWHC 1743 (Ch), upheld on appeal in *Fraser Turner Ltd v PricewaterhouseCoopers LLP* [2019] EWCA Civ 1290.

110   *Mitchell v Carter, Re Buckingham International plc* [1997] 1 BCLC 673 at 684 (citing *Ayerst (Inspector of Taxes) v C & K (Construction) Ltd* [1975] 2 All ER 537, [1976] AC 167).

111   *Kyrris v Oldham* [2003] EWCA Civ 1506, [2004] 1 BCLC 305 at [141] and [163].

112   *Peskin v Anderson* [2001] I BCLC 372, cf. *Williams v Natural Life Health Foods* [1998] 1 WLR 830; CA 2006 s172.

113   *Fraser Turner Ltd v PricewaterhouseCoopers LLP* [2019] EWCA Civ 1290 at [70] citing *Williams v Natural Life Health Foods* [1998] 1 WLR 830.

114   Ibid.

115   *Peskin v Anderson* [2001] BCC 874 (CA) at [34] (see also *Bristol & West Building Society v Mothew* [1998] Ch 1, 16–18).

In the important case of *Kyrris v Oldham*, the Court of Appeal cited the above extracts with **6.053** approval and applied identical principle in the context of a company in administration with Jonathan Parker LJ holding:[116]

> Given the nature and scope of an administrator's powers and duties, I can for my part see no basis for concluding that an administrator owes a duty of care to creditors in circumstances where a director would not owe such a duty to shareholders. In each case the relevant duties are, absent special circumstances, owed exclusively to the company.

The fact that duties are owed exclusively to the company, precludes individual creditors being **6.054** able to proceed against the office-holder personally (absent a special relationship) and instead their remedy is to commence proceedings against the individual office-holder for the benefit of the company under the various statutory provisions found with the insolvency legislation.[117] Whilst the decision in *Kyrris v Oldham* was given in the context of administration, the principle will apply with equal force in both liquidations[118] and bankruptcies and to breaches of both a duty of care as well as fiduciary duties.[119]

An assumption of responsibility giving rise to a duty can occur in a variety of ways. Whilst **6.055** there are limited examples in the context of companies or individuals in insolvency proceedings, directors of solvent companies have been found to have assumed responsibility to third parties in a number of different contexts. Examples include:

- Directors who had acquired shares from shareholders in order to sell them to a third party had made themselves agents for the shareholders, and hence were accountable for the profits they had made.[120]
- A fiduciary duty was owed where the oldest of three brothers, who was the only director of the company, bought out his younger brothers who held preference shares.[121]

The circumstances in which an IP will be found to have assumed a responsibility to an **6.056** individual outside the statutory scheme, after appointment, will be very rare. So, in *Fraser Turner Ltd v PricewaterhouseCoopers LLP* above, an administration case, the mere fact that a creditor informed an office-holder of alleged royalty rights and that, in the creditor's view, they should be drawn to the attention of any proposed purchaser so that they would be honoured by such proposed purchaser, did not mean that an IP was under a duty to do so. On appeal, the Chancellor noted that:[122]

> All that happened here was what happens in hundreds of administrations every year. A creditor brought its particular problem to the attention of the administrator, who listened politely and said he would look into it. No promises were made, nor are any alleged. All that is alleged is that Mr Turner believed that the Administrators would do as he had asked. If he did so believe (and we must accept what he says at face value at this stage of the case), he was, I am afraid to say, commercially naïve. It

---

116 *Kyrris v Oldham* [2003] EWCA Civ 1506, [2004] 1 BCLC 305.
117 For example, IA 1986 ss212, 304 and para 75 of Sch B1.
118 *Hague v Nam Tai Electronics* [2008] UKPC 13, [2008] BCC 295 at [13].
119 *Kyrris v Oldham* [2003] EWCA Civ 1506, [2004] 1 BCLC 305 at [143].
120 *Allen v Hyatt* (1914) 30 TLR 444.
121 *Platt v Platt* [1999] 2 BCLC 745.
122 [2019] EWCA Civ 1290 at [72].

was the duty of the Administrators in acting for London Mining to achieve the best realisation of its assets for the benefit of all the creditors ... .

6.057 That said, the position is somewhat different pre-appointment. In that scenario contractual relations may also give rise arise to an assumption of responsibility, albeit one that takes effect by force of the underlying contract. In *A & J Fabrications Ltd v Grant Thornton*[123] Jacob J accepted that creditors who had made payment to the defendant firm of £5,000 with a view to an employee or employees of that firm being appointed as liquidator had entered into a contract with that firm. Accordingly, the creditor's remedy was, at least arguably, not limited to bringing proceedings under IA 1986 s212 against the liquidators for the benefit of the general body of creditors. In addition, they were also able to sue the firm on the contract with there being nothing inconsistent in the liquidators owing duties to the company and the employing firm owing contractual obligations to the appointing creditor.[124]

6.058 There is also some suggestion in earlier authorities to the effect that duties were owed to individual creditors personally in the context of the distribution of dividends, and there is a certain logic in that, or at least the notion that such claims are personal rather than class ones. In both *Pulsford v Devenish*[125] and *James Smith & Sons (Norwood) Ltd v Goodman*[126] it was held that the liquidators were liable to individual creditors personally for breach of statutory duty on claims brought following the dissolution of the companies. However, the Court of Appeal in *Kyrris v Oldham*[127] took a restrictive view of the effect of those decisions and found that the dissolution of the companies was 'crucial'[128] or otherwise 'highly relevant'[129] and held (with reference to *Pulsford v Devenish*) that if:

> ... dissolution [had] not occurred, then as I read [Farwell J's] judgment he would have concluded that the creditors could not have brought their claim. At all events, it does not follow from his decision that they could have done.[130]

6.059 The effect of the decision in *Kyrris v Oldham* was described by Mr Mark Cawson QC (sitting as a Deputy High Court Judge) in *Lomax Leisure Ltd (in liquidation) v Miller* as being that pre-dissolution such a 'claim would ordinarily only be capable of being brought as a misfeasance claim under s 212'.[131] However, no guidance is given there as to what (if anything) would take such a claim outside the 'ordinary'. Whilst dissolution may open the possibility of a claim being brought by a creditor against the office-holder in relation to the treatment of dividends, it does not provide a route for an individual creditor to attack a decision of the office-holder relating to the administration of the company.[132] Instead, the company will need to be restored to the register and proceedings brought in the usual way. The remedy ought,

---

123 [1998] 2 BCLC 227.
124 Ibid at 230; *Kyrris v Oldham* [2004] 1 BCLC 305 at [152].
125 [1903] 2 Ch 625.
126 [1936] Ch 216, [1935] All ER 697.
127 *Kyrris v Oldham* [2003] EWCA Civ 1506, [2004] BCC 111.
128 Ibid at [155].
129 Ibid at [160].
130 Ibid at [155].
131 [2007] EWHC 2508 (Ch), [2008] 1 BCLC 262 at [34(4)].
132 *Fraser Turner Ltd v PricewaterhouseCoopers LLP* [2018] EWHC 1743 (Ch) at [69] (upheld on appeal: [2019] EWCA Civ 1290).

nevertheless, still to be a personal one, otherwise the creditor who has wrongly missed out on a distribution would not receive compensation for being missed (and on this hypothesis, as a result of the misfeasance of the IP).

It is also important to remember, however, that a creditor is unable to enforce a personal **6.060** entitlement to a distribution, prior to dissolution, against an office-holder. Rather, their remedy lies in an application to court for the office-holder to pay the dividend under IR 2016 r14.45,[133] with similar provision existing in the context of personal bankruptcy at IA 1986 s325(1). It is questioned, therefore, whether the distinction between dissolution and pre-dissolution cases is a valid one, but the safer option for a complainant will be to make an application under s212, where they are able to do so.

One further exception to the general principle that the office-holder owes no duty to individual **6.061** creditors is where the creditor holds security. In such circumstances, a liquidator or other office-holder who distributes assets without paying or providing for preferential claims may be personally liable to those creditors for breach of statutory duty.[134]

(c) The bankrupt

The question of whether the trustee could owe duties to the bankrupt personally was addressed **6.062** by Proudman J at first instance in *Oraki v Bramston*. The judge held that as a matter of fact, the complaints were unsustainable which was dispositive of the claim. As to the question of whether duties were owed to the bankrupt, the judge first observed that in the ordinary case the trustee's duties are owed to the creditors as a group[135] before going on to hold that there was no common law duty in negligence which went beyond the statutory duties owed to the bankrupt.[136] The judge did however accept that in circumstances where the bankruptcy was likely to give rise to a surplus then there was a statutory duty owed to the bankrupt arising out of IA 1986 s330(5).[137]

On appeal, the Court of Appeal (David Richards LJ giving the leading judgment) dismissed **6.063** the appeal holding that on the facts, there had been no breach of duty on the part of the trustee, and the acts and omissions relied upon had caused no loss.[138] However, Richards LJ did express disagreement with Proudman J on the legal question of whether duties were owed to the bankrupt beyond those found in the Act and held that 'section 304 cannot be read as excluding any liability on the part of a trustee to a bankrupt, save as expressly provided by the section'.[139]

In particular, the Court of Appeal found it relevant that: (i) IA 1986 s304 is 'concerned with, **6.064** and confined to, acts or omissions on the part of the trustee that have caused loss or damage to

---

133   Cf. IA 1986 s325(2) in bankruptcy.
134   *IRC v Goldblatt* [1972] Ch 498; *Re HIH Casualty & General Insurance Ltd.* [2005] EWHC 2125 (Ch), [2006] 2 All ER 671 at [121].
135   *Oraki v Bramston* [2015] EWHC 2046 (Ch), [2016] 3 WLR 1231 at [24].
136   Ibid at [34].
137   Ibid at [34] (citing Hoffmann LJ (as he then was) in *Heath v Tang* [1993] 1 WLR 1421, 1422G).
138   *Oraki v Bramston* [2017] EWCA Civ 403, [2018] 3 WLR 569 at [207], [224]–[225].
139   Ibid at [217].

the estate';[140] (ii) whilst 'it is perfectly understandable that the bankrupt should need leave before he can apply under the section *for the benefit of the estate*. That does not explain why a trustee cannot in any circumstance owe an enforceable duty to the bankrupt in respect of loss or damage caused not to the estate but to the bankrupt personally';[141] and (iii) the provision itself contains the words 'without prejudice to any liability arising apart from this section'.[142]

6.065 The Court of Appeal's determination in this regard was strictly *obiter*[143] and intentionally limited with the consequence that the nature and extent of the duties owed by a trustee to the bankrupt awaits authoritative judicial determination.

2. Impact of release

(a) Bankruptcy

6.066 Upon removal, or upon their vacating their office, the trustee will obtain their release in accordance with, and at the time provided by, subsections 299(1)–(4). The effect of the trustee's release is then provided for by IA 1986 s299(5) as follows:

> Where the official receiver or the trustee has his release under this section, he shall, with effect from the time specified in the preceding provisions of this section, be discharged from all liability both in respect of acts or omissions of his in the administration of the estate and otherwise in relation to his conduct as trustee.

> But nothing in this section prevents the exercise, in relation to a person who has had his release under this section, of the court's powers under section 304.

6.067 It follows that upon obtaining their release, the trustee will cease to be legally responsible for their acts or omissions arising out of their conduct of the bankruptcy save where the act or omission is capable of giving rise to liability under IA 1986 s304 (and subject to the following observations).

6.068 The consequences of release were described by Chief Registrar Baister in *Re Borodzicz* as being '*far reaching*'.[144] As set out in the judgment of the Chief Registrar, Walton J in *In re Munro, ex parte Singer v Trustee in Bankruptcy* explained the intention behind the provision in the following terms:[145]

> What is in my judgment crystal clear is that upon a true construction of section 93(3), which interestingly does not ever appear to have been previously construed, although the proviso thereto was construed in *In re Harris, Ex parte Hasluck* [1899] 2 QB 97, it appears to me that the intention of that subsection, and it is a very right, proper and wholesome intention, is to wipe the slate completely clean so far as the trustee is concerned, so that he may thereafter pay no thought to the previous course of his actions as the trustee in bankruptcy.

---

140   Ibid at [214].
141   Ibid at [216].
142   Ibid.
143   Cf. *Birdi v Price* [2018] EWHC 2943 (Ch), [2019] 3 All ER 250 at [96].
144   *Helen Irene Borodzicz; Borodzicz v Horton, Re* [2015] Lexis Citation 286, [2016] BPIR 24 at [43].
145   *In re Munro and Another, ex parte Singer v Trustee in Bankruptcy* [1981] 1 WLR 1358 at 1362G (as cited in *Helen Irene Borodzicz; Borodzicz v Horton, Re* [2015] Lexis Citation 286, [2016] BPIR 24).

In *In re Munro*, the court was addressing s93(3) of the Bankruptcy Act 1914 ('BA 1914') **6.069**
(the statutory predecessor of IA 1986 s299(5)) but as was observed in *Re Borodzicz* whilst the
wording is different, the thrust and effect of the provision is the same[146] albeit that the
exclusion for applications made under IA 1986 s304 militates against the absolute terms set out
by Walton J. Nevertheless, Chief Registrar Baister held that Walton J's '... judgment is
nonetheless a clear expression of the purpose of release that must be as good today ... as it was
when he made it in the context of the Bankruptcy Act'.[147]

It has also been argued that Walton J overstated the position under the BA 1914 in that under **6.070**
the law as it then stood a trustee remained at risk of an application to revoke the
release.[148] Nevertheless, it has been held that neither criticism serves to detract from Walton J's
approval of the policy of minimising the scope for claims against a former trustee.[149]

In *Oraki v Bramston*, David Richards LJ observed that s304 was 'concerned with, and confined **6.071**
to, acts or omissions on the part of the trustee that have caused loss or damage to the estate'.[150]
It follows that a bankrupt will be unable to contour around the prohibition upon bringing
claims post-release provided by s299(5) where they are seeking to recover in respect of losses
suffered by them personally by relying upon IA 1986 s304. However, that does not necessarily
mean that after the trustee has had their discharge, that no claim can be brought against them
other than under IA 1986 s304.[151] In this regard David Richards LJ adverted to some difficult
and untested questions which may arise.[152]

First he postulated the scenario whereby in the course of realising an asset, a negligent or even **6.072**
fraudulent mis-statement was made by the trustee to a third party who subsequently relied
upon it. In such a scenario, s304 would not be engaged, the third party lacking standing,[153] the
trustee not having misapplied property comprised in the bankruptcy estate[154] and the
bankruptcy estate not having suffered loss. It appears that David Richards LJ had doubts as to
the correctness of counsel's submission on behalf of the trustee that the third party would have
no remedy as against the trustee.

Second, David Richards LJ noted that the provision could, on one view, operate to provide a **6.073**
complete defence in circumstances where the trustee obtained his release after the commencement of proceedings, an outcome that he considered to be surprising. Although not cited to
the court, the correctness of the trustee's position (in a rather different context) seems to have
been accepted in *Hotel Company 42 The Calls Ltd* (albeit without detailed consideration on the
point) where HHJ Purle QC (sitting as a judge of the High Court) declined to grant the
administrators' discharge under paragraph 98 of Schedule B1 in circumstances where proceedings challenging the administrators' remuneration had been commenced by a shareholder

---

146   *Helen Irene Borodzicz; Borodzicz v Horton, Re* [2015] Lexis Citation 286, [2016] BPIR 24 at [43].
147   *Re Horton* at [55].
148   *Birdi v Price* [2018] EWHC 2943 (Ch), [2019] 3 All ER 250 at [94].
149   Ibid at [94].
150   *Oraki v Bramston* [2017] EWCA Civ 403, [2018] 3 WLR 569 at [214].
151   Ibid at [214].
152   Ibid at [220].
153   IA 1986 s304(2).
154   Ibid s304(1)(a).

and director of the company under paragraphs 74 and 75 of Schedule B1. Whilst those parts of the action constituted under paragraph 75 would have survived the court giving the administrators their discharge,[155] it is implicit in the decision of HHJ Purle QC that he considered that those parts of the action founded on paragraph 74 would not (or at least might not) have survived and declined to grant discharge accordingly.[156] A similar approach was adopted in *Barclays Mercantile Business Finance Ltd v Sibec Developments Ltd* where Millett J (as he then was) held that it was 'unthinkable that the administrators should be released while there is a proper claim against them which is outstanding and which ought to be tried'.[157]

6.074 Whilst Richards LJ did not consider it valuable to express *obiter* views on these difficult questions, there is at least some suggestion that IA 1986 s299(5) may not afford a complete post-release defence to all claims other than those brought by way of IA 1986 s304.

6.075 Whilst the questions remain unresolved, the apparent potential for injustice caused to third parties is only one consideration. This needs to be weighed against the fact that upon vacating office, a trustee will cease to hold the assets of the estate from which (where appropriate) he may be able to obtain an indemnity and who may no longer hold the papers and records of the bankrupt. As was held by Judge Eyre QC (sitting as a judge of the High Court) in *Birdi v Price* the question is one for Parliament with IA 1986 being taken to set out its concluded position:[158]

> There are strong policy considerations in favour of giving redress to those whose property is wrongfully seized by trustees in bankruptcy. There are also strong policy considerations in favour of drawing a line in respect of claims against Officeholders and in favour of enabling those Officeholders to proceed on the footing that no claim will be made following a release. The question as to where the balance lies between those competing considerations is a matter for Parliament and it is to be taken as having set out the concluded position in the Act.

6.076 A further consideration is that in appropriate circumstances, a trustee's release may be set aside by order of the court as was in fact the case in *Re Munro*, thereby depriving the trustee retrospectively of the protection provided by IA 1986 s299(5).

(b)   Corporate insolvency

6.077 The means by which a liquidator can obtain their release are as set out in IA 1986 ss173 (in a voluntary winding up) and 174 (in a winding up by the court). The consequences which flow from their release are set out in ss173(4) and 174(6). The provisions are in broadly similar terms and provide in effect that from the date of release the liquidator (or in the case of a compulsory winding up, the official receiver, a liquidator or a provisional liquidator) is 'discharged from all liability both in respect of acts or omissions of his in the winding up and otherwise in relation to his conduct as Liquidator or Provisional Liquidator'.

---

155   See: para 98(4)(b) of Sch B1 IA 1986.
156   *Hotel Company 42 The Calls Ltd* [2013], re (Whitfield v Al Jaber) EWHC 3925 (Ch) at [32].
157   [1992] 1 WLR 1253, 1260.
158   *Birdi v Price* [2018] EWHC 2943 (Ch), [2019] 3 All ER 250 at [102].

However, that formulation is subject to the important statutory caveat that nothing in either **6.078** provision 'prevents the exercise, in relation to a person who has had his release under this section, of the court's powers under section 212'. IA 1986 s212(4) retains a further important procedural safeguard, namely that the power to apply for relief under s212 in relation to a person who has acted as liquidator of the company is only exercisable, with the leave of the court, after the liquidator has had his release. The net effect of the provisions is that following release, any claim against a liquidator can only be brought by misfeasance proceedings under s212 and then only with the court's permission.

The principles applicable to the grant of permission are discussed at paragraphs 6.039–6.045 **6.079** above but in summary, the applicant will need show (i) a reasonably meritorious cause of action and (ii) that the grant of permission is reasonably likely to benefit the estate.[159] The above factors are not however exhaustive and other considerations may be taken into account.[160]

A similar regime is found in the case of administration where paragraph 98(1) of Schedule B1 **6.080** provides that where a person ceases to be the administrator of a company, he is discharged from liability in respect of any action of his as administrator.

The extent of the administrator's discharge is qualified by paragraph 98(4) which makes clear **6.081** that the statutory discharge of liability applies only to liability which accrued prior to that discharge and (importantly) that the discharge is without prejudice to the court's powers under paragraph 75 Schedule B1 (i.e., for misfeasance). It will be apparent therefore that no right of challenge to the administrator's conduct under paragraph 74 will survive discharge under paragraph 98.

Discharge does not take effect upon the cessation of office but upon the occurrence of the **6.082** relevant event listed at IA 1986 s98(2). Of particular importance is s98(2)(c), which states that in any case the court can specify the date on which the discharge takes effect. The court's usual practice is to fix a date 28 days after the administrator or administrators have filed the final report in accordance with IR 2016 r3.59[161] thereby allowing a period of time to permit investigations to be conducted by the liquidator into the administrator's handling of the administration.[162] The reason that it will usually be right to order such a discharge was explained by Sales J in *Re Hellas Telecommunications (Luxembourg) II SCA*[163] as being that:

> the administrator will no longer retain in his hands the assets of the company out of which he is entitled to meet any liability properly incurred by him, so that it is unfair to leave him on risk generally. In so far as there is a good arguable case against him of improper conduct or misfeasance, that can be proceeded with after the discharge is given, in accordance with para 98 of Sch B1 read with para 75.

---

159 *Re Parkinson Engineering Services plc* [2009] EWCA Civ 1366, [2010] BCLC 163.
160 Ibid at [34].
161 Cf. *Re Hellas Telecommunications (Luxembourg) II SCA* [2011] EWHC 3176 (Ch), [2013] 1 BCLC 426 at [96].
162 *Re Angel Group Ltd* [2015] EWHC 3624 (Ch), [2016] 2 BCLC 509 at [38].
163 *Re Hellas Telecommunications (Luxembourg) II SCA* [2011] EWHC 3176 (Ch), [2013] 1 BCLC 426 at [96].

6.083 Whilst it is open to the court to order a longer period (and theoretically even an indefinite suspension[164]) such extension is the exception with a period of three months (subject to further application) appearing to be the limit on the authorities as they stand.[165]

3. Personal liability to third parties

(a) Introduction

6.084 Paragraph 69 of Schedule B1 expressly provides that in exercising his functions under that Schedule, the administrator acts as the company's agent. Similarly, a liquidator will generally act as the company's agent.[166] However, that is not to say that all acts undertaken by an office-holder will be in the capacity of agent.

6.085 In *In re Southern Pacific Personal Loans Ltd* the court was invited to determine, inter alia, whether the joint liquidators of the company were data controllers for the purposes of the Data Protection Act 1998 s1(1). In addressing that question the court observed that some of the duties of a liquidator are undertaken by them as principal including by way of example the receipt and adjudication on proofs of debt.[167] Equally, there are many respects in which a liquidator will act as agent of the company in liquidation in circumstances where the company continues to exist as a separate legal entity notwithstanding its entry into liquidation.[168] As the court observed, that distinction can be illustrated by the legal proceedings which can be brought at the behest of the liquidator with some types of claim being brought by the company and others by the office-holder personally:

> The different capacities in which a liquidator may act are illustrated by legal proceedings which may be brought. A company in liquidation may commence or defend legal proceedings in its own name. If it does so it is the company which is the party and not the liquidator. In instructing lawyers to act on behalf of the company in such proceedings, the liquidator acts as the agent of the company. It is for that reason that security for costs may be ordered against a company in liquidation which brings proceedings. This may be contrasted with those proceedings brought by the liquidator in his own name, as provided by various provisions of the Insolvency Act 1986, such as sections 212–214 and 238–239. In those cases it is the liquidator himself who is the party and ordinarily security for costs will not be ordered against him.

6.086 When entering into a contract, it will be a matter of construction of the relevant contract to determine whether it is the company, the office-holder, or both who are parties to the agreement. In *Stewart v Engel*, HHJ Jack QC described the position as follows:[169]

---

164 See *Re Angel Group Ltd* [2015] EWHC 3624 (Ch), [2016] 2 BCLC 509 where relief in such expansive terms was sought and refused.

165 See *Re Exchange Travel (Holdings) Ltd* [1993] BCLC 887; *Re Angel Group Ltd* [2015] EWHC 3624 (Ch), [2016] 2 BCLC 509 at [39].

166 *Stewart v Engel* [2000] 2 BCLC 528, 533.

167 *In re Southern Pacific Personal Loans Ltd* [2013] EWHC 2485 (Ch), [2014] Ch 426 at [19].

168 Ibid at [21].

169 *Stewart v Engel* [2000] 2 BCLC 528, 533.

... the general position is that a liquidator contracts as the agent of the company and does not incur personal liability. He may, however, as may any agent, contract on terms which show that he *is* undertaking a personal liability. The contract in question must be examined to see whether that is so.

This analysis accords with well-established principle[170] and is subject to any equitable defence that an office-holder may have to the claim including by way of estoppel.[171] Similarly, describing an office-holder 'as administrator' in proceedings does not mean that they are being sued in their capacity as an agent of the company and any judgment entered in those proceedings will be against the office-holder personally.[172] Whilst it is possible for the parties to impose personal liability on the office-holder, such instances are rare and a well advised office-holder will take care to ensure that such liability is excluded or indemnified.[173] **6.087**

Whilst IPs will rarely be personally liable under a contract, the scheme of the IA 1986 does provide contractual counterparties with protection. First, the expenses following the entry of the company into administration or liquidation (as the case may be) are payable and not provable.[174] Further, where the company is in administration, paragraph 59(3) of Schedule B1 IA 1986 provides statutory confirmation of the fact that a person who deals with the administrator of a company in good faith and for value need not enquire whether the administrator is acting within his powers.[175] Additionally, upon the cessation of the administrator's appointment, liabilities arising out of contracts entered into by the administrator will become charged on and payable out of the property of which the former administrator had custody and control immediately before the cessation of the IP's office.[176] That statutory charge takes priority over that enjoyed by the former administrator under IR 2016 r99(3).[177] The provision is silent as to how the charge is to be enforced and the precise manner of enforcement awaits authoritative determination.[178] However, in *Walker v National Westminster Bank plc*, it was held that the rights of the statutory chargee in relation to the assets are limited to enforcement through the court, and do not extend to enabling the chargee to deal with the assets direct as a legal owner could.[179] **6.088**

The liquidator or administrator's position can be contrasted with that of an administrative receiver, with the latter being personally liable on contracts which they enter into whether in their own name or in that of the company.[180] The stringency of that position is ameliorated to some extent by the statutory entitlement of the administrative receiver to an indemnity out of **6.089**

---

170 For example, *Stead, Hazel & Co v Cooper* [1933] All ER 770.
171 *Stevensdrake v Hunt* [2017] EWCA Civ 1173, [2017] 4 Costs LR 781.
172 *Wright Hassall LLP v Morris* [2012] EWCA Civ 1472, [2012] BPIR 1310.
173 On which, see paras 8.082–8.085 below.
174 They will normally outrank the provable debts in the insolvency: see IR 2016 rr3.51, 6.42 and 7.108.
175 Cf. CA 2006 s39 and general principles on agency.
176 Para 99(4) Sch B1 IA 1986.
177 Ibid.
178 *Hosking v Slaughter and May (a firm)* [2016] EWCA Civ 474, [2016] 3 Costs LR 617 at [33].
179 [2016] EWHC 315 (Ch) [2017], 1 BCLC 124 at [29].
180 Except insofar as the contract otherwise provides: IA 1986 s44(1)(b).

the assets of the company[181] with their being unlikely to incur liabilities unless they are satisfied that there are sufficient assets to enable those liabilities to be met in any event.[182]

6.090 Unlike a liquidator or an administrator, the property of the bankrupt vests in the trustee personally in accordance with IA 1986 s306 with there being no question of the trustee acting in an agency capacity. As a result, he will be personally liable for any contract which he enters into with third parties even if for the benefit of the bankruptcy estate.[183] Further, he can acquire personal liability in the case of contracts entered into by the bankrupt prior to the making of the bankruptcy order where he loses the right to disclaim the contract in circumstances where: (i) a person interested in the contract has applied in writing to the trustee to decide whether he will disclaim the contract and (ii) a period of 28 days has elapsed without a notice of disclaimer under IA 1986 s315 having been given.[184] In this context, it seems that the word 'contract' in s316(2) does not extend to a lease.[185]

(b)   Tort

6.091 By analogy with company directors, a liquidator or administrator who makes fraudulent representations to third parties will be liable in deceit irrespective of whether he makes the representations on behalf of the company.[186] In order to be personally liable to a third party, the IP will need to have directed or procured the commission of the tortious act.[187] Further, it will need to be established that the office-holder personally assumed responsibility to the claimant in order for a duty to arise.[188]

6.092 Where office-holders deal with property of a third party without authorisation of the court, they may be personally liable to that third party in the tort of conversion or trespass.[189] That is subject to the ability of IPs to relieve themselves of liability by way of the statutory defences provided within the insolvency legislation. In the case of an administrator, administrative receiver, liquidator or provisional liquidator, the office-holder can rely upon IA 1986 s234(3)–(4); in the case of an interim receiver, s287(4); and in the case of a trustee in bankruptcy, s304(3).

6.093 In order to invoke the statutory defence, the office-holder will need to establish that at the time of seizure or disposal the IP believed, and had reasonable grounds for believing, that he or she was entitled (whether in pursuance of an order of the court or otherwise) to seize or dispose of the property.[190] Where that defence is made out and insofar as any loss caused was not attributable to his own negligence, the office-holder will: (i) not be liable for any loss or

---

181   Ibid s44(1)(c).

182   *Lipe Ltd v Leyland DAF Ltd (in administrative receivership)* [1994] 1 BCLC 84, 88.

183   Cf. *Re Lister* [1926] Ch 149.

184   IA 1986 s316(2).

185   *Re ABC Coupler and Engineering Co Ltd (No 3)* [1970] 1 All ER 650 at 669.

186   *Standard Chartered Bank v Pakistan National Shipping Corp (Nos 2 and 4)* [2003] 1 AC 959 at [22] and [40]; *Stone & Rolls Ltd (in liquidation) v Moore Stephens (a firm)* [2009] UKHL 39, [2009] 3 WLR 455; *Knowles v Scott* [1891] 1 Ch 717.

187   *MCA Records Inc v Charly Records Ltd* [2001] EWCA Civ 1441, [2003] 1 BCLC 93.

188   *Williams v Natural Life Health Foods Ltd* [1998] 2 All ER 577, [1998] 1 BCLC 689; *Partco Group Ltd v Wragg* [2002] EWCA Civ 594, [2002] 2 BCLC 323.

189   *Hachette UK Ltd v Borders (UK) Ltd* [2009] EWHC 3487 (Ch) at [3].

190   IA 1986 ss234(3)(b), 287(4)(b) and 304(3)(b).

damage resulting from the seizure or disposal of the property; and (ii) be entitled to exert a lien on the property, or the proceeds of its sale, for such of the expenses of the insolvency as were incurred in connection with the seizure or disposal.[191]

Notwithstanding the broad definition of property found at IA 1986 s436, the Court of Appeal in *Welsh Development Agency v Export Finance Co Ltd*[192] held that the references in the various provisions to seizing property can only apply to tangible property, and do not apply to choses in action.[193] The significance of this is perhaps limited in circumstances where a claim cannot be brought in conversion in respect of intangible property.[194]   **6.094**

Further, it is to be noted that the protection conferred by the provisions is limited to loss or damage resulting from the seizure or sale of the property and there seems no reason in principle why the owner of the property would be precluded from commencing proceedings for the recovery of the property or the proceeds of sale. Examples of the defence being relied upon include where liquidators sold equipment in circumstances where they were justified in believing that equipment to be property of the company[195] and where a trustee in bankruptcy disposed of tools and associated equipment in circumstances where he had reasonable grounds for believing that the equipment formed part of the bankruptcy estate.[196] In the latter instance, HHJ Eyre QC[197] explained the circumstances in which the protection would arise in the following terms:[198]   **6.095**

> … the sub-section gives a defence to a trustee who has acted on the basis of a belief held genuinely and formed on reasonable grounds provided that the trustee does not then act carelessly when judged by reference to the standard of a competent trustee. It does not limit the potential liability for a wrongful seizure of goods to cases where a freestanding duty of care exists as between the trustee and the owner of the chattels.

The judge then found that the trustee did have reasonable grounds for believing that the equipment formed part of the bankruptcy estate and in the absence of any negligence on his part, he was entitled to the statutory protection.[199]   **6.096**

Where proceedings are brought against an IP personally in the tort of inducing a breach of contract or in conspiracy, it is open to the office-holder to rely upon the rule in *Said v Butt*.[200] The rule provides that where a director of a company has caused the company to act in breach of contract he will not be liable provided that he acted *bona fide* in the course of his duties as a director. In *Welsh Development Agency v Export Finance Co Ltd*[201] the rule was applied by the Court of Appeal in the context of a receiver appointed under a debenture and in the case of   **6.097**

---

191   Ibid ss234(4), 287(4) and 304(3).
192   [1992] BCLC 148.
193   Ibid at 171.
194   *OBG Ltd v Allan* [2007] UKHL 21, [2007] 2 WLR 920.
195   *Euromex Ventures Ltd v O'Connell* [2013] EWHC 3007 (Ch).
196   *Birdi v Price* [2018] EWHC 2943 (Ch), [2019] 3 All ER 250.
197   Sitting as a High Court Judge.
198   *Birdi v Price* [2018] EWHC 2943 (Ch), [2019] 3 All ER 250) at [76].
199   Ibid at [77]–[78].
200   [1920] 3 KB 497, [1920] All ER 232.
201   [1992] BCLC 148.

Lictor Anstalt v MIR Steel UK Ltd it was common ground between the parties that the rule is of equal application where the company is in administration and the administrator is the subject of the proceedings[202] with that concession being accepted by David Richards J (as he then was) as being correct.[203] Where the contract in question is one with whom the company is not in a contractual relationship (referred to as a tripartite situation in *Welsh Development Agency v Export Finance Co Ltd*) it seems that the office-holder will not be able to rely upon the rule.[204]

6.098 IPs may also be liable if they commit other torts. In recent years IPs have faced an increased number of claims based on economic torts, including allegations of being involved with others (typically lenders who have appointed them) in unlawful means conspiracies. To date such claims have either been struck out before trial, or have not continued to trial,[205] or have generally been unsuccessful at trial.[206]

(c) Liabilities arising pre-appointment

6.099 Once appointed, the IP's duties are owed to the creditors as a class absent special circumstances, as noted above. However, IPs may perform more than one function. Following their appointment, they perform their statutory functions in the manner prescribed by the relevant legislation and owe duties as discussed elsewhere. Additionally, it is not uncommon for IPs to perform a private function in advising a debtor as to the available insolvency procedures. In this latter role, the IP may owe contractual and tortious duties to the debtor.[207] It is fair to say however that those liabilities (if they exist) tend to arise in relation to or arising out of pre-appointment dealings.

6.100 In *Prosser v Castle Sanderson Solicitors (a firm)*[208] the Court of Appeal reversed a first instance decision that the nominee of an IVA who had failed to properly advise the debtor during a short adjournment of a creditors meeting convened to consider the debtor's proposal for an individual voluntary arrangement under Pt VIII of IA 1986 did not owe the debtor a duty of care. Clarke LJ accepted that the courts should be careful not to impose duties upon nominees or chairmen of creditors meetings when they are acting in that capacity.[209] However, it did not follow that all acts undertaken by a nominee or supervisor were undertaken in that role. On the facts of the case the court accepted that the IP had not acted in his capacity as nominee during the short adjournment. Further, in circumstances where the IP had not given the debtor any

---

202   *Lictor Anstalt v MIR Steel UK Ltd* at [38].
203   Ibid at [54].
204   *SCI Games Ltd v Argonaut Games plc* [2005] EWHC 1403 (Ch) (not cited in *Lictor Anstalt v MIR Steel UK Ltd*).
205   For examples of such a claim being struck out before trial see: *Fraser Turner Ltd v PricewaterhouseCoopers LLP* [2018] EWHC 1743 (Ch) at [69] (upheld on appeal [2019] EWCA Civ 1290); and *AM Holdings Led v Batten* [2018] EWHC 934 (Ch). For an example of a case which did not run to trial see (in the context of an interim application for security for costs) *Premier Motorauctions Ltd (in liquidation) v PricewaterhouseCoopers and Lloyds Bank* [2017] EWCA Civ 1872, allowing an appeal against the decision of Snowden J ([2016] EWHC 2610 (Ch), [2017] 4 All ER 243).
206   See *Davey v Money* [2018] EWHC 766 (Ch) at [771].
207   For example, *Pitt v Mond* [2001] BPIR 624. See also: *A & J Fabrications Ltd v Grant Thornton* [1998] 2 BCLC 227 and *Clydesdale Financial Services Ltd v Smailes* [2009] EWHC 1745 (Ch), [2009] EWHC 3190 (Ch), [2009] BCC 810 at [52].
208   [2002] EWCA Civ 1140, [2003] BCC 440.
209   *Prosser v Castle Sanderson* at [66].

indication that he was acting *qua* nominee and not in his capacity as an adviser, it was fair, just and reasonable to impose a duty upon him.[210] Finally, Clarke LJ held as follows:[211]

> I do not think that this view creates difficulties for nominees or chairmen of creditors' meetings. It merely emphasizes the importance of their making it clear to the debtor in what capacity they are acting at any time, which in my opinion is very desirable.

With the above in mind, IPs may be well advised to ensure, insofar as is practicable, that debtors are fully aware of the capacity in which they are acting when engaging with debtors and their officers at the different stages of the insolvency process. Some further examples where claims have been brought in this respect are considered in Section F below. **6.101**

(d) Personal liabilities in respect of real property comprised in the insolvency estate

Where the bankrupt is a tenant, the term vests in his trustee upon the making of the bankruptcy order and the trustee (as assignee) becomes personally responsible for the rent and under the covenants contained in the lease[212] albeit subject to a right of indemnity out of the bankruptcy estate.[213] In addition, it may be possible for the trustee to treat rent and other payments as expenses of the bankruptcy. **6.102**

Where the trustee disclaims the lease, any personal liability will be discharged from the date of the commencement of his trusteeship.[214] However, disclaimer of the lease where the trustee is in occupation (which is perhaps unlikely in the modern context) will not insulate him from any obligation to pay rates as the obligation to make such payments arises from a combination of statute and occupation of premises and not the lease itself.[215] Where the trustee does retain property for the benefit of the bankruptcy, it seems likely that any liability for rates would be an expense in the bankruptcy and payable as such.[216] **6.103**

Where the insolvent estate includes a solely-owned tenanted property or properties, the trustee will become landlord of the property or properties upon appointment. Where a property is jointly owned, legal title will remain with the legal owners as the legal title cannot be severed[217] and the legal owners will remain the landlord of the property. It will therefore be the legal owners and not the trustee who retain the legal rights and responsibilities associated with the property. **6.104**

---

210 Ibid at [67].
211 Ibid at [68].
212 *Re Solomon, ex p Dressler* (1879) 9 ChD 252; *Wilson v Wallani* (1880) 5 Ex D 155, 163; *Titterton v Cooper* (1882) 9 QBD 473.
213 *Lowrey v Barker* (1880) 5 Ex D 170, 173.
214 IA 1986 s315(3)(b); *Schofield v Hincks* (1888) 37 WR 157.
215 *In Re Lister; ex p Bradford Overseers and Bradford Corporation* [1926] Ch 149.
216 Cf. *Re Toshoku Finance UK plc* [2002] UKHL 6, [2002] 1 BCLC 598 at [34] and see *Pillar Denton Ltd v Jervis* [2014] EWCA Civ 180, [2014] 2 All ER (Comm) 826.
217 *Re McCarthy (a bankrupt)* [1975] 1 WLR 807, 809. This is to be contrasted with the position of co-owners who hold property as joint tenants in law and in equity, where the bankruptcy will sever the joint tenancy.

6.105 In the case of solely owned property and where the property is unoccupied by tenants, the trustee *qua* landlord is likely to owe a duty of care to third parties who are visitors[218] as well as to trespassers.[219] In addition (and irrespective of whether the property is tenanted) the trustee may owe duties to third parties under s3 and/or 4 of the Defective Premises Act 1972. Therefore, a trustee will wish to review all insurance policies and ensure that proper insurance is put in place.

6.106 Additionally, the trustee will need to give notice in writing of the statutory assignment[220] to all tenants of the property[221] with a failure to do so without good reason giving rise to a summary offence punishable by a fine of up to £2,500.[222]

6.107 Where the property is let under an assured shorthold tenancy, the burden of the covenants of the lease (as well as the benefit) will pass to the trustee under the statutory assignment.[223] As such, the trustee will need to: (i) allow the tenant quiet enjoyment of the property;[224] (ii) hold the deposit in a government authorised tenancy deposit scheme;[225] (iii) ensure that the repairing obligations (express or implied under s11 of the Landlord and Tenant Act 1985) are complied with; (iv) ensure an annual gas safety check;[226] and (v) ensure compliance with electrical and fire safety legislation.

4. Costs claims and liabilities

(a) Procedural basis

6.108 The scheme of the insolvency legislation makes only limited provision for the costs consequences of litigation which is as set out at Chapter 8 of Part 12 of IR 2016. By IR 2016 r12.41(3), Parts 44 and 47 of the CPR apply to costs with those costs being defined as including 'charges' and 'expenses'.[227] Although IR 2016 r12.1 provides that the CPR apply for the purposes of proceedings under Parts 1–11 of the IA 1986 with any necessary modifications that is subject to the requirement that the provisions of the CPR are not disapplied by or inconsistent with IR 2016. It follows that not all of the costs provisions contained in the CPR (save for those under Parts 44 and 47) are necessarily operative, even in circumstances where costs may otherwise be in the insolvency process.[228] It should also be borne in mind that not all proceedings which an IP may become involved in are insolvency proceedings and where that is the case, the provisions of IR 2016 will be of no application.[229]

---

218   Occupiers Liability Act 1954 s2.
219   Ibid s1.
220   See: Landlord and Tenant (Covenants) Act 1995 s11.
221   Landlord and Tenant Act 1985 s3.
222   Ibid s3(3).
223   Landlord and Tenant (Covenants) Act 1995 s 3(1)(b).
224   *Markham v Paget* [1908] 1 Ch 697.
225   Housing Act 2004 s213.
226   Gas Safety (Installation and Use) Regulations 1998 reg 36.
227   IR 2016 r12.41(2).
228   *LF2 Ltd v Supperstone* [2018] EWHC 1776 (Ch), [2019] 1 BCLC 38 at [78] ff.
229   *Bannai v Erez* [2013] EWHC 4287 (Comm), [2014] BPIR 1369 at [5].

(b) Office-holder as respondent

Of particular interest to IPs is IR 2016 r12.47 which provides (in summary) that where an **6.109** office-holder is made a party to proceedings on the application of another party, they are not personally liable for the costs unless the court otherwise directs.[230] This provision may be seen as statutory recognition of the principle articulated in *In Re London Metallurgical Co* where it was held that the general rule is that the costs (in that case) of a liquidator who was a respondent to proceedings within the insolvency were to be paid out of the assets of the company and it would only be in exceptional circumstances that the liquidator would be personally responsible for them.[231] Subsequently it has been said that the court will only impose liability under r12.47 in a 'special case' or where there is 'good reason' to do so[232] and it retains a jurisdiction to order that the successful party's costs be treated as an expense of the insolvency.[233] In *Promontoria (Chestnut) Ltd v Craig* it was held that the administrator's decision to remove receivers appointed by the fixed charge holder at the outset of the administration was unreasonable and constituted grounds for departing from the normal rule as articulated in IR 2016 r12.47. As a result, an order was made that the respondent administrators bear the costs of the application personally and otherwise than as an expense of the administration.[234]

(c) Office-holder as applicant/claimant

When IPs cause a company to bring or maintain proceedings against a third party, they will **6.110** not be a party to the claim and it will only be in exceptional circumstances that they will incur personal liability for costs under a non-party costs order.[235] Where proceedings are instigated (or continued) by an insolvent company, the defendant's remedy is to seek an order for security for costs with there being no scope for argument that the proceedings constitute an abuse of process as a result of the claimant's inability to meet an adverse costs order.[236]

Although an order for costs is discretionary, IPs who commence (or adopt) proceedings in **6.111** their own names are, as a general rule, personally liable for the costs of those proceedings (albeit subject to an indemnity from the insolvency estate)[237] save where there is statutory provision to the contrary.[238] The fact that the office-holder is the official receiver does not alter the position.[239] The costs payable under an order made against an office-holder personally are

---

230   In the case of an appeal against a proof of debt the position is confirmed by IR 2016 r14.9(2); in respect of an application on grounds that the office-holder's remuneration is excessive by IR 2016 r18.36(6).

231   *In Re London Metallurgical Co* [1895] 1 Ch 758, 763.

232   *Re Mordant (a bankrupt)* [1995] 2 BCLC 647; cf. *Fielding v Hunt* [2017] EWHC 406 (Ch) [2017], 2 Costs LO 191 at [19].

233   *In re National Wholemeal Bread and Biscuit Co* [1892] 2 Ch 457; *Re Mordant (a bankrupt)* ibid; *Fielding v Hunt* ibid at [20].

234   *Promontoria (Chestnut) Ltd v Craig* [2017] EWHC 2405 (Ch) at [70]–[71].

235   *Metalloy Supplies Ltd (in liquidation) v MA (UK) Ltd* [1997] 1 All ER 418 at 423 and see: *Fraser v Province of Brescia Steam Tramways Co* (1887) 56 LT 771; *Van Den Hurk v R Martens & Co Ltd* [1920] 1 KB 850.

236   *Metalloy Supplies Ltd (in liquidation) v MA (UK) Ltd* [1997] 1 WLR 1613, 1618–9.

237   *In Re Wilson Lovatt & Sons Ltd* [1977] 1 All ER 274, 285 (liquidation); *BPE Solicitors v Gabriel* [2015] UKSC 39, [2015] AC 1663 [4] and [10] (bankruptcy).

238   For example, IR 2016 r10.105(2) (on an application by the official receiver for the public examination of a bankrupt pursuant to s290 IA 1986); IR 2016 r10.164 (costs in criminal bankruptcy proceedings not to be borne by the official receiver).

239   *Re W Powell & Sons* [1896] 1 Ch 681; *Ferrao's Case* (1874) 9 Ch App 355.

not expenses incurred in the winding up and are not payable as such,[240] instead, the office-holder will need to seek an order from the court seized with the insolvency proceedings for recoupment from the assets of the insolvency estate. The same principles apply in circumstances where the office-holder commences or adopts proceedings and subsequently discontinues those proceedings.[241]

6.112 However, where an application is made by a trustee pursuant to IA 1986 s303 (and presumably on any other application by an office-holder for directions) it seems that there is no hard and fast rule but that the court's practice is to order that the costs be payable by the estate.[242] That is subject to the observation that the costs will need to have been reasonably incurred and in circumstances where the office-holder is adopting a neutral stance, consideration will need to be given to the nature of representation at the hearing.[243] An IP who briefs leading counsel to appear on such a hearing (at least in circumstances where their actions are unlikely to be subject to criticism and there is no other special reason for instructing leading counsel) does so at the risk of such costs being irrecoverable either in those proceedings or by way of recoupment.[244] If the IP is dissatisfied with the first instance decision on an application for directions in the proceedings and decides to appeal it then the proceedings relating to the appeal are distinct proceedings for the purposes of costs[245] and the office-holder may be deemed to have gone from 'being a neutral seeker of directions towards the role of a litigation combatant'.[246] In such circumstances, the court will have to consider the matter in the round and may be more likely to make a personal costs order against the IP in the event of dismissal.

6.113 Where proceedings are extant prior to the appointment of an IP, it is for the office-holder to determine whether to adopt the proceedings. If they decide not to, the proceedings will be stayed or dismissed if the insolvent is the claimant. If the insolvent is the defendant, the proceedings will (in most cases) be stayed under the Act.[247] In the case of a company, the IP will (save for exceptional circumstances) acquire no personal liability if the proceedings are adopted as the party to those proceedings remains the company, albeit that a successful defendant's costs may be ordered to be paid in priority to the IP's remuneration thereby potentially having the same effect albeit by indirect means.[248]

6.114 Where the party to proceedings (pre-appointment) was an individual, the assets of that individual vest in the trustee upon their appointment pursuant to IA 1986 s306 and the trustee becomes a party to those proceedings personally[249] on an order under CPR r19.2, or otherwise

---

240   *Re MT Realisations Ltd* [2003] EWHC 2895 (Ch), [2004] 1 All ER 577 [19]; *Re Floor Fourteen Ltd, Lewis v IRC* [2001] 2 BCLC 392 at 405.

241   *Re Walker Windsail Systems Ltd; Walker v Walker* [2005] EWCA Civ 247, [2005] 1 All ER 272.

242   See para 8.051 below. *Re Tully* [2017] NICh 18 at [20]; *Re Lehman Brothers International (Europe) (in administration)* [2018] EWHC 924 (Ch) (Hildyard J) at [6]–[7].

243   Cf. *BNY Corporate Trustee Services Ltd v Eurosail-UK 2007–3BL plc and others* [2011] EWCA Civ 227, [2011] 2 BCLC 1 at [105].

244   *Re Wedgwood Museum Trust Ltd (in administration); Young v Attorney General* [2012] EWHC 1974 (Ch).

245   *BPE Solicitors v Gabriel* [2015] UKSC 39, [2015] AC 1663 at [16].

246   *Re Tully* [2017] NICh 18 at [24].

247   For example, under IA 1986 ss285(1) and (2).

248   *Norglen v Reeds Rains* [1998] 1 BCLC 176, 191.

249   *BPE Solicitors v Gabriel* [2015] UKSC 39, [2015] AC 1663 at [9].

he will be considered as having waived the irregularity of not obtaining such an order by adopting the action and taking steps in furtherance of it.[250]

Prior to the decision of the Supreme Court in *BPE Solicitors v Gabriel* a trustee who adopted proceedings ran the risk of being exposed to the entirety of the costs of the claim including those incurred prior to their appointment.[251] This is no longer good law and a trustee who adopts a claim will not be exposed to an adverse costs order in respect of earlier proceedings within the same action in the courts below.[252] Further, it would appear that a trustee's liability for costs in the same proceedings prior to his adoption of those proceedings is a matter for the court's discretion.[253] The rationale behind the law as it stood prior to the decision in *BPE Solicitors v Gabriel* was (at least in part) that a costs order made after an individual had been declared bankrupt would not be provable in the bankruptcy, the discretionary character of a costs order meaning that it was not a contingent liability until the order had actually been made.[254] In *Re Nortel GmbH (in administration)*[255] the Supreme Court had clarified that such an analysis was not correct. In those circumstances, 'freed of the baggage of earlier misconceptions', the Supreme Court found it possible to revisit the issue as a matter of principle and clarified the law as stated above. **6.115**

Notwithstanding the decision in *BPE Solicitors v Gabriel* it remains the case that a trustee will be at risk of a personal costs order in the event that they adopt the proceedings. Where there are sufficient assets within the bankruptcy estate to give them the necessary comfort to continue (or commence) proceedings this may be of limited concern. However, it remains the case that where (as is often the case) there is a risk that the bankruptcy estate is insufficient to meet prospective litigation liabilities, a trustee is likely to look to obtain sufficient ATE cover, seek to assign the cause of action on such terms as they may be able to obtain[256] and/or look to the creditors for an indemnity.[257] Similar considerations are likely to arise in liquidation, not least because of the possibility that a successful defendant may be paid their costs in priority to those of the office-holder.[258] **6.116**

(d) Right of recoupment

Where an IP is the subject of an adverse costs order he is entitled to be recouped out of the insolvency estate in circumstances where he has acted *bona fide*.[259] However, costs payable by an office-holder personally are not payable as an expense and an office-holder does not have an **6.117**

---

250 *Trustee of the Property of Vickery (a bankrupt) v Modern Security Systems Ltd* [1998] 1 BCLC 428, 434.

251 *Borneman v Wilson* (1884) 28 Ch D 53.

252 *BPE Solicitors v Gabriel* [2015] UKSC 39, [2015] AC 1663 at [12].

253 Ibid at [15].

254 Ibid at [13] (citing *In re Bluck, ex p Bluck* (1887) 57 LT 419; *In re British Gold Fields of West Africa* [1899] 2 Ch 7; *In re A Debtor (No 68 of 1911)* [1911] 2 KB 652; *In re Pitchford* [1924] 2 Ch 260; *Glenister v Rowe* (Costs) [2000] Ch 76).

255 *Nortel GmbH (in admin), Re Lehman Brothers International (Europe) (in admin) (Nos 1 and 2)* [2013] UKSC 52, [2014] AC 209.

256 It should be noted that assignment does not remove the possibility of the opposing party seeking a non-party costs order from the assignor in appropriate circumstances. Cf. *Hunt v Aziz* [2011] EWCA Civ 1239; *Hamilton v Official Receiver* [1998] BPIR 602; *Osborn v Cole* [1999] BPIR 251.

257 *Re Angerstein, ex p Angerstein* (1873–74) LR 9 Ch App 479.

258 *Norglen v Reeds Rains* [1998] 1 BCLC 176, 191.

259 *Pitts v La Fontaine* (1880) 6 App. Cas. 482. See also para 5.204 above.

unfettered right to recoup his costs of unsuccessful litigation.[260] The precise source of the court's power to order that the office-holder be recouped out of the insolvency estate is unclear[261] and has been suggested to arise by way of the court's inherent jurisdiction[262] or otherwise in equity as expenditure incurred by a fiduciary.[263]

6.118 The question of entitlement to recoupment falls to be determined in the court seized with the insolvency proceedings and not the court in which the substantive proceedings have been dealt with (if different).[264] The court's jurisdiction to deprive an IP of their entitlement to recoupment is discretionary[265] and should only be exercised where there has been a degree of unreasonableness on the part of the IP[266] meaning that their conduct 'has fallen below the standard of a reasonable insolvency practitioner acting reasonably'.[267] When determining whether to deprive an IP of the right to recoupment out of the insolvency estate, the test is not whether the expenditure was properly incurred but whether it would be just to make the order.[268] Whilst misconduct by the IP is likely to give rise to them being unable to recoup an adverse costs order from the insolvency estate[269] mere negligence can also give rise to loss of the right.[270] Further, where the actions of the IP cannot be said to have been designed to advance the interests of the holder of a floating charge or the unsecured creditors, justice is likely to require they should not be entitled to recoupment.[271]

(e) Non-party costs order

6.119 Where proceedings are brought by a company whilst acting by its office-holder, that office-holder will not be a party to those proceedings. Nevertheless, they may become liable for costs by way of a non-party costs order. The court's jurisdiction to make such an order arises as a result of s51 of the Senior Courts Act 1981[272] with the procedure for doing so set out in CPR r46.2. Guidance as to that procedure was provided by the Court of Appeal in *Symphony Group plc v Hodgson* which in summary requires:[273] (i) the applicant should warn the non-party at the earliest opportunity of the possibility that they might seek to apply for costs against them; (ii) that an application for payment of costs by a non-party should normally be determined by the trial judge; (iii) the fact that the trial judge in the course of their judgment had expressed

---

260   *Re R S & M Engineering Co Ltd, Mond v Hammond Suddards* [1999] 2 BCLC 485, 495, [2000] Ch 40, 52.

261   *Lewis v IRC* [2001] 3 All ER 499.

262   Ibid at [41].

263   *Re Exchange Travel (Holdings) Ltd (in liquidation) (No 3); Katz v McNally* [1997] 2 BCLC 579.

264   *Re Wilson Lovatt & Sons Ltd* [1977] 1 All ER 274, 286.

265   *Re Capitol Films Ltd (in administration)* [2010] EWHC 3223 (Ch), [2011] 2 BCLC 359 at [100] (citing *Mond v Hammond Suddards* [2000] Ch 40 as affirmed in *Lewis v IRC* [2001] 2 BCLC 392).

266   *Re Wedgwood Museum Trust Ltd (in administration); Young v Attorney General* [2012] EWHC 1974 (Ch) at [27].

267   *Nutting (as joint trustees of the Estate of Benya Meain Khaliq (a bankrupt)) v Khaliq* [2012] EWCA Civ 1726, [2013] BPIR 340 at [32].

268   *Re MC Bacon Ltd (No 2)* [1990] BCLC 607, 615.

269   For example, *Re Capitol Films Ltd (in administration)* [2010] EWHC 3223 (Ch), [2011] 2 BCLC 359 at [101] (citing *Re Wilson Lovatt & Sons Ltd* [1977] 1 All ER 274) albeit that in the latter case the court did not determine whether the liquidator should be deprived of that right and left the question to be determined by the winding-up court should it be required to do so.

270   *Re Silver Valley Mines* (1882) 21 Ch D 381 and cf. *In re Beddoe; Downes v Cottam* [1893] 1 Ch 547, 562.

271   *Re Capitol Films Ltd (in administration)* [2010] EWHC 3223 (Ch), [2011] 2 BCLC 359 at [111] and see *MC Bacon Ltd (No 2)* [1990] BCLC 607, 615–16.

272   *Aiden Shipping Co Ltd v Interbulk Ltd* [1986] AC 965.

273   [1994] QB 179, 19; *The White Book* (2020 edn, vol 1) at [46.2.2].

views on the conduct of the non-party, does not constitute bias nor the appearance of bias; (iv) generally, a non-party funding proceedings by an insolvent company solely or substantially for his own financial benefit should be liable for the costs in the event of failure. But non-party costs orders will not invariably be made in such cases, particularly where the funder is a director or liquidator acting in the interests of the company rather than his own; and (v) a non-party should not ordinarily be liable for costs which would in any event have been incurred without the non-party's involvement in the proceedings, although the position may be different where a number of non-parties have acted in concert.

The court has jurisdiction to order an IP (as a non-party) to pay the costs of an action **6.120** personally, but it will only be in exceptional cases that the jurisdiction will be exercised.[274] The word '*exceptional*' generally has the meaning 'no more than outside the ordinary run of cases where parties pursued or defended claims for their own benefit and at their own expense',[275] although in cases involving IPs it will be rare indeed. The ultimate question is whether it is just to make the order.[276] Impropriety on the part of an office-holder is not a prerequisite for a non-party costs order against an office-holder although it is a powerful factor in the exercise of the court's discretion.[277] Further, the fact that the IP may stand to benefit as a result of their being an enhancement of realisations from which to discharge their professional fees in the event of success does not turn the IP into the real party to litigation.[278]

This analysis reflects the powerful public interest in office-holders being able satisfactorily to **6.121** carry out the duties which the statutory scheme confers on them.[279] It is also reflective of the fact that a defendant to proceedings is adequately protected by the court's jurisdiction to order security for costs.[280] In this regard, where IPs are instituting proceedings in the name of the company, they are likely to seek ATE cover with a view to heading off any security for costs application. Subject to arguments on inadequacy of the policy[281] and stifling,[282] the obtaining of such a policy will: (i) allow the proceedings to be prosecuted by the company notwithstanding its impecuniosity; and (ii) provide adequate protections to the defendant.

It is not an abuse of the process of the court or in any way improper or unreasonable for an **6.122** impecunious claimant to bring proceedings which are otherwise proper and *bona fide* while lacking the means to pay the defendant's costs if they should fail.[283]

---

274 *Aiden Shipping* [1986] AC 965, 980.
275 *Dolphin Quays Developments Ltd v Mills* [2008] EWCA Civ 385, [2008] 1 WLR 1829 at [72]; *Dymocks* [2004] 1 WLR 2807 at [25].
276 *Dolphin Quays Developments Ltd* [2008] EWCA Civ 385, [2008] 1 WLR 1829 at [72] and [74].
277 *Hunt v Aziz* [2011] EWCA Civ 1239 at [16]; *Dolphin Quays Developments Ltd* [2008] EWCA Civ 385, [2008] 1 WLR 1829 at [65].
278 *Hunt*, ibid; *Dolphin Quays Developments Ltd*, ibid at [79].
279 *Eastglen Ltd v Grafton* [1996] BCC 900.
280 *Metalloy Supplies Ltd (in liquidation) v MA (UK) Ltd* [1997] 1 WLR 1613, 1618; *Eastglen Ltd v Grafton* [1996] BCC 900.
281 E.g., *Premier Motorauctions Ltd (In Liquidation) v PricewaterhouseCoopers LLP* [2017] EWCA Civ 1872, [2018] 1 WLR 2955, though see paras 5.085 to 5.087 for cases which have not followed this approach.
282 For example, *Absolute Living Developments Ltd (in liquidation) v DS7 Ltd* [2018] EWHC 1432 (Ch).
283 *Metalloy Supplies Ltd (in liquidation) v MA (UK) Ltd* [1997] 1 WLR 1613, 1619.

6.123   It is unclear as to whether the receiving party will need to establish a causative link between (i) the conduct complained of and giving rise to the order and (ii) the costs incurred. In *Tradition (UK) Ltd v Ahmed*, Mr Andrew Simmonds QC[284] found guidance in the analogous jurisdiction of wasted costs orders being made against solicitors and held that such an order is intended to be compensatory and not punitive in effect and determined that it was necessary to establish that the conduct complained of caused the costs to be incurred.[285] However, in the earlier case of *Total Spares & Supplies Ltd v Antares SRL* (not cited in *Tradition UK Ltd*) Richards J found guidance in the decision of Lord Phillips MR (as he then was) in *Arkin v Borchard Lines Ltd*[286] and held that whilst causation will often be a vital factor, there may be cases where, in accordance with principle, it is just to make an order for costs against a non-party who cannot be said to have caused the costs in question.[287] It is suggested that this more nuanced approach is both in accordance with the authorities and is correct in principle in circumstances where (as indicated above) the 'ultimate question' is whether it is just to make the order.[288]

(f)   Indemnity costs orders

6.124   Where an IP is subject to a claim then they will incur costs in defending themselves. Ordinarily they will benefit from professional indemnity insurance. However, that may be subject to an excess, and so an IP may be interested in seeking to recover all of their costs in the event they manage to defeat a claim brought against them. This is not the usual order a court will make in a claim. However, where the integrity or reputation of an IP is challenged, those circumstances may justify the court awarding an indemnity cost order, which will result in the IP having a better chance of recovering a greater proportion (if not all) of their costs.[289]

D.   NATURE OF DECISION OR ACTS

1.   Commercial role and realism

6.125   The decision-making process engaged in by an IP, and the duties this gives rise to, have already been considered in Chapter 4 above at paragraphs 4.022–4.025. The court has repeatedly recognised that office-holders have to make commercial judgments and that it should not interfere with these or be called upon to make such decisions itself.[290] This also includes the method adopted of valuing a company, where a range of possible valuation methodologies may be available.[291]

---

284   Sitting as a Deputy High Court Judge.
285   *Tradition (UK) Ltd v Ahmed* [2008] EWHC 3448 (Ch) at [24] (citing *Ridehalgh v Horsefield* [1994] Ch 205 and *Harmony Carpets v Chaffin-Laird* [2000] BPIR 61).
286   [2005] EWCA Civ 655, [2005] 3 All ER 613.
287   *Total Spares & Supplies Ltd v Antares SRL* [2006] EWHC 1537 (Ch) at [54].
288   *Dolphin Quays Developments Ltd v Mills and others* [2008] EWCA Civ 385, [2008] 1 WLR 1829 at [72].
289   See *Two Right Feet Ltd (in liquidation) v National Westminster Bank plc* [2017] EWHC 1745 (Ch), [2017] 6 Costs LR 735 at [61]–[62].
290   *Mitchell v Buckingham* [1998] 2 BCLC 369; *T & D Industries plc* [2000] 1 WLR 646; *Mahomed v Morris* [2000] 2 BCLC 536; *Transbus International Ltd* [2004] 2 BCLC 550; *DKLL Solicitors v Revenue and Customs Commissioners* [2007] EWHC 2067 (Ch), [2008] 1 BCLC 112.
291   Smith and King, 'How insolvency practitioners value a business'(2015) 28(2) *Insolv Int* 20–24.

Errors of judgment are not per se compatible with negligence, as is more classically illustrated in medical negligence cases.[292] **6.126**

In short, where the action in question is really a judgment call for the IP based on commercial reality and experience the court will be slow to interfere. Nor can such a scenario be readily addressed by asking what a reasonably competent IP would do, though in some instances, consideration of the *Bolam* test, considered next, may be instructive. **6.127**

There are limits to the mantra, however, that there can be no liability for commercial judgments or decision-making. There are a number of instances, as discussed further in Section F below, where commercial decisions have been found to be wanting. A recent example of this can be found in the case of *Brewer v Iqbal*[293] where the IP conducted a negligent undervalue sale, seemingly involving the wrong choice of agent. The chosen agent, Edward Symmons, were not experts in selling a very specialised asset and hence there was a sale at undervalue. This is considered further in Section F.5 below, but provides a useful illustration of the limits of the commercial judgement argument. **6.128**

2. The standard

The standard of skill and care which a court will expect of a professional is assessed by reference to other members of the same profession. As noted in paragraph 6.002 above, the IP will be under a duty to exercise the professional care and skill to be expected of a competent IP in carrying out the function in question.[294] The Insolvency Code of Ethics in force from 1 January 2009 to 30 April 2020[295] identifies one of the fundamental principles an IP must follow, in relation to professional competence and due care, in the following terms:[296] **6.129**

> An *Insolvency Practitioner* has a continuing duty to maintain professional knowledge and skill at the level required to ensure that a client or employer receives competent professional service based on current developments in practice, legislation and techniques. An *Insolvency Practitioner* should act diligently and in accordance with applicable technical and professional standards when providing professional services.

The observations in paragraph 2 of the Code are also worth having in mind in this context, which emphasises the IP's responsibility for their employees and agents working in their practice, and provides that: 'Although, an *insolvency appointment* will be of the *Insolvency Practitioner* personally rather than his *practice* he should ensure that the standards set out in this Code are applied to all members of the *insolvency team*.' This can cause difficulties to IPs. They **6.130**

---

292 See *Ashcroft v Mersey Regional Health Authority* [1983] 2 All ER 245 and *Sidaway v Bethlem Royal Hospital* [1984] 1 All ER 1018 at 1023.

293 [2019] EWHC 182 (Ch).

294 See the Scottish case of *MacDonald v Carnbroe* [2019] UKSC 57 (Lord Hodge JSC) at [38], referring to *Hague v Nam Tai Electronics Inc* [2008] UKPC 13, [2008] BCC 295; *Kyrris v Oldham* [2003] EWCA Civ 1506, [2004] BCC 111; and *Lightman & Moss on the Law of Administrators and Receivers of Companies* (6th edn, 2017), para 12-042.

295 A copy of which is published at https://www.gov.uk/government/publications/insolvency-practitioner-code-of-ethics (accessed 20 December 2019), and which has been adopted by all IPs RPBs effective from 1 January 2009. A new code is then in force from 1 May 2020, though it is in substantially the same terms as the Code in place before. It can also be accessed online, including via the ICAEW website.

296 Code of Ethics, Part 1 para 4(c).

are expected to delegate to junior staff at lower charge out rates (and their fees would be criticised otherwise) yet the IP remains personally responsible if the staff member makes a mistake.[297] The Code may therefore provide useful justification to the IP for remuneration requests, since they may point out they have a duty to ensure that any delegation is in relation to work which the member of staff is competent to perform, and will still require more senior supervision.

6.131 The contemplated test, as referred to in the Code above, is substantially the same as what is often referred to as the *Bolam* principle, based on the direction given in a medical negligence case in *Bolam v Friern Hospital Management Committee*.[298] The same applies in an insolvency context.[299] There are some qualifications to that standard as it applies to negligence issues in an insolvency context. In determining whether an IP has fallen below the standard, it is very relevant to consider that in many insolvencies, an IP will not have ready funds at his disposal (e.g., for the purposes of availing himself of legal advice) and time will often be short. This is considered in the different situations in which claims may arise, in Section F below. Therefore, the standards practised by insolvency practitioners and informed by their lack of funds will be relevant to any claim.

6.132 That said, it should not be assumed that the courts will always accept the standards practised widely in a profession. In a conveyancing context liability was imposed notwithstanding evidence that the conduct reflected common practice, because the court considered the practice was unreasonable.[300] Whilst the courts will not always articulate this expressly, they may be attracted by the idea a particular result could and should have been achieved whether or not an ordinarily skilled practitioner can be found who will say they (and others) would not have done so. And as noted in the context of failures of investigation, considered further in Section F below, industry guidance now spells out that lack of funds is not an excuse for a certain level of investigation.

6.133 In the last couple of years there has been a shift away from the use of the *Bolam* test in professional negligence cases where the duty of care encompasses a duty to explain risks. This has been considered further in Chapter 4 at paragraphs 4.029–4.033 above. In summary here, in *Montgomery v Lanarkshire Health Board*,[301] the Supreme Court eschewed the *Bolam* test in the context of a doctor's duty to explain risks associated with treatment to a patient to whom advice is given, because this was not a matter of purely professional judgment. This was recognised in a conveyancing negligence case in Northern Ireland.[302] So too in the context of risk warnings in the context of the provision of financial services by Kerr J in *O'Hare v Coutts & Co*.[303] Kerr J cited the decisions in *Montgomery* and *Baird*, and noted that, in the context of investment advice too, there must be proper dialogue and communication between adviser and

---

297 Essentially a form of vicarious liability, although it might be better characterised as a species of non-delegable duty (the IP having been personally appointed): see *Woodland v Essex CC* [2013] UKSC 66.
298 [1957] 1 WLR 582.
299 *Re Charnley Davies Ltd (No 2)* (Millett J) [1990] BCLC 760.
300 See *G & K Ladenbau (UK) Ltd v Crawley & De Reya* [1978] 1 WLR 266; *Edward Wong Finance Co v Johnson, Stokes & Master* [1984] AC 296.
301 [2015] UKSC 11.
302 See *Baird v Hastings* [2015] NICA 22.
303 [2016] EWHC 2224 (QB).

client. He concluded that: 'I do not think the required extent of communication between financial adviser and client to ensure the client understands the advice and the risks attendant on a recommended investment, is governed by the *Bolam* test.'[304] This might be relevant to the standard of care to be expected by the IP acting in an advisory capacity pre-appointment, but the underlying reasoning by Kerr J in *O'Hare v Coutts & Co* goes beyond that.

In drawing his conclusion, Kerr J pointed out that the relevant regulatory regime (there the **6.134** Conduct of Business Rules Sourcebook ('COBS')) was strong evidence of what the common law requires,[305] and a duty to explain in terms not dissimilar to the *Montgomery* formulation is found in the COBS rules.[306] He considered the content of those rules would be very difficult to square with the application of a conventional *Bolam* approach, as they do not include reference to a responsible body of opinion within the profession.[307] He was not swayed by the defendant's submission that there were differences between the medical and financial contexts; how much to say to a client was not a question to be decided according to whether the adviser acted in accordance with a practice accepted as proper by a responsible body of persons skilled in the giving of financial advice, because expert evidence tended to indicate that there is little consensus in the financial services industry about how the treatment of risk appetite should be managed by an adviser, and, as in the medical context, the extent of required communication with the client should not depend on the attitude of the individual adviser.[308]

It is perhaps unsurprising that, in cases where there are comprehensive regulations which **6.135** prescribe in detail what is required when undertaking particular tasks, a professional who fails to comply with these regulations should be held to have failed to exercise reasonable skill and care without reference to the general body of professional opinion. The editors of Jackson and Powell point out that: 'In this way regulations and codes of conduct and guidelines can require a profession to achieve a higher standard than is currently being achieved and so effect a change in the required standard.'[309] With a growing trend amongst professional bodies to publish written standards which reflect the best practices of the profession, it is an open question how far in the future the 'codification' of professional standards will overtake the *Bolam* test.

These latter observations are of particular relevance to IPs, who are heavily regulated. This has **6.136** already been considered in Chapter 2 above. In summary here, however, only a licensed IP may be appointed in relation to formal insolvency procedures. All qualified IPs must be licensed and regulated by a recognised professional body (a 'RPB'). Currently, there are five RPBs. Each is required to have proper procedures in place to ensure that a complaint made against an IP it authorises is properly investigated. IPs are required to comply with Statements of Insolvency Practice (SIPs), have regard to 'Dear IP' letters, and act in accordance with their RPB's codes and guidance. Whether or not an IP has complied with guidance set out in the relevant SIP (such as, e.g., the disposal of an asset to a connected person under SIP 13), a Dear IP letter or their code will be very persuasive, if not always determinative, of a negligence

---

304 At [204].
305 Citing *Loosemore v Financial Concepts (a firm)* [2001] Lloyds Rep PN 235 (HHJ Jack QC), 241 per; and *Green v Royal Bank of Scotland (Financial Conduct Authority intervening)* [2014] Bus LR 168 (Tomlinson LJ) at [18].
306 See in particular rr2.2.1(1) and 2.2.2(1)(b); r4.2.1(1); rr9.2.1, 9.2.2, 9.2.3 and 9.2.6 of COBS.
307 [2016] EWHC 2224 (QB) at [208]–[209].
308 Ibid at [204]–[205].
309 *Jackson & Powell on Professional Liability* (8th edn) at para 2–012.

claim.[310] It is well established that 'the skill and care to be expected of a reasonably competent financial advisor ordinarily includes compliance with the relevant regulatory rules'.[311]

6.137 Moreover, in certain respects, the liability which the IP is fixed with may be said to be strict, rather than based on a breach of a duty of skill and care. This may arise where the allegation is that they have acted outside their powers, effectively in breach of trust and/or in breach of their fiduciary duties. This is discussed further when considering distributions in Section F below.[312]

6.138 Overall, it is important to keep in mind the functions being discharged by the IP when considering whether the conduct fell below a particular standard. The duties have to be considered in the context of the appointment and the purpose and objectives of the appointment.

3. Time of assessment

6.139 The IP's conduct is to be assessed at the time of the act or omission. Similarly, the standard against which an IP's conduct and acts are assessed is the standard which prevailed at the time of the relevant conduct, not at the time when (no doubt many years down the line) the court comes to assess that conduct.[313]

E. ROLE OF EXPERT EVIDENCE

1. Introduction

6.140 A key issue which faces those who are considering bringing a professional negligence claim, including claims against an IP, is whether it is necessary to obtain expert evidence. By expert evidence, we mean the opinion of a fellow competent professional as to whether or not the conduct in issue fell below the standard of care to be expected from an ordinarily competent practitioner carrying out the task in question. Experts will often talk in terms of what they might, or might not have done themselves, although that is not in fact the correct test.[314]

6.141 Given the prevalence of the use of expert evidence to bolster weak cases,[315] and the risk of proliferation as to costs, there is now a restriction on the use of expert evidence in proceedings in the following terms: the court has a duty to restrict expert evidence *'to that which is reasonably required to resolve the proceedings'*.[316] The court will not normally need evidence, for example, that the process adopted in selling real property was inadequate.[317]

---

310   For a useful recent briefing paper on the regulation of insolvency practitioners see: http://researchbriefings.parliament.uk/ResearchBriefing/Summary/SN05531#fullreport 10.
311   *Shore v Sedgwick Financial Services Ltd* [2007] EWHC 2059 (QB) (Beatson J).
312   Although see also the decision of the Supreme Court in *AIB Group (UK) plc v Mark Redler & Co* [2014] UKSC 58.
313   *Pitt v Mond* [2001] BPIR 624, 639.
314   See *Midland Bank Trust Co Ltd v Hetts Stubbs & Kemp* [1979] 1 Ch 384, 402.
315   See, e.g., the case of *Gumpo v Church of Scientology* [2000] CP Rep 38.
316   CPR r35.1.
317   *Devon Commercial Property Ltd v Barnett* [2019] EWHC 700 (Ch).

This has been interpreted as requiring a three-step test by Warren J in *British Airways plc v* **6.142**
Paul Spencer:[318]

> ... it is necessary to look at the pleaded issues and, unless and until a particular issue is excluded from
> consideration under CPR 3.1(2)(k), the court must ask itself the following important questions:
>
> (a) The first question is whether, looking at each issue, it is necessary for there to be expert
> evidence before that issue can be resolved. If it is necessary, rather than merely helpful, it
> seems to me that it must be admitted.
> (b) If the evidence is not necessary, the second question is whether it would be of assistance to the
> court in resolving that issue. If it would be of assistance, but not necessary, then the court
> would be able to determine the issue without it (just as in *Mitchell* the court would have been
> able to resolve even the central issue without the expert evidence).
> (c) Since, under the scenario in (b) above, the court will be able to resolve the issue without the
> evidence, the third question is whether, in the context of the proceedings as a whole, expert
> evidence on that issue is reasonably required to resolve the proceedings. In that case, the sort
> of questions I have identified in para 63 above will fall to be taken into account. In addition, in
> the present case, there is the complication that a particular piece of expert evidence may go to
> more than one pleaded issue, or evidence necessary for one issue may need only slight
> expansion to cover another issue where it would be of assistance but not necessary.

Pulling the other way, are cases such as the decision of Coulson J in *Pantelli Associates Ltd v* **6.143**
Corporate City Developments Number Two Ltd where it was suggested that in the professional
negligence context, it is expected that input will need to be obtained from an expert prior to
making any allegation against that professional that their conduct has fallen below that of a
fellow professional.[319] The judge even went so far as to suggest it might be an abuse of process
if the claimant had not obtained such evidence when they issued, since they would not properly
be able to sign a statement of truth suggesting the competency had fallen below expected
standards without such evidence. This may be going too far, at least in many cases involving
claims against IPs, and particularly in cases involving breaches of fiduciary duty, which the
court is generally able to adjudicate upon without the need for such evidence.

A subsequent office-holder contemplating a claim against a former office-holder may be **6.144**
tempted to think that they could form a view themselves, and that it would be sufficient for
them to articulate that view before the court in evidence. However, the hunter might find
themselves become the hunted in those circumstances, since it is well-established that an IP
cannot act as an expert in his or her own cause.[320]

Thus the general rule in professional negligence claims against an IP is that an expert opinion **6.145**
from an independent third party should be obtained before a decision is made to commence
proceedings. This is reflected in most of the well-known cases, such as in *Charnley Davies*

---

318 [2015] EWHC 2477 (Ch) at [68].
319 [2010] EWHC 3189 (TCC) at [16]–[19].
320 See *Re Colt Telecom Group plc (No 2)* [2002] EWHC 2815 (Ch) at [80], where it was made plain on conventional
grounds that a liquidator cannot be his own expert in adversarial litigation. See to similar effect *Re Continental Assurance
Co of London plc* [2001] BPIR 733 at [327].

(No 2),[321] where each side relied on an IP expert. So too in *Pitt v Mond*.[322] But like all good general rules there are some exceptions.

6.146 Both the general rule and one possible exception to it is illustrated in the following passage from the judgment of Butler Sloss LJ in *Sansom v Metcalfe Hambleton and Co*:[323]

> In my judgment, it is clear, from both lines of authority to which I have referred, that a court should be slow to find a professionally qualified man guilty of a breach of his duty of skill and care towards a client (or third party), without evidence from those within the same profession as to the standard expected on the facts of the case and the failure of the professionally qualified man to measure up to that standard. It is not an absolute rule … but, unless it is an obvious case, in the absence of the relevant expert evidence the claim will not be proved.

2. Where expert evidence may not be required

6.147 There are a number of areas or situations where expert evidence is not appropriate, or may not be required.

(a) The plain and obvious case

6.148 The plain and obvious case is alluded to by Butler Sloss LJ in *Sansom v Metcalfe Hambleton and Co* above. In all areas of commercial and professional negligence litigation, there may sometimes arise a plain and obvious case, for example involving missed time limits.

6.149 In addition, parties sometimes seek to adduce expert evidence when in reality the issues are issues of fact which require no expert evidence.[324]

(b) Novel situations

6.150 The conduct of a professional may come to be criticised in entirely novel situations, where, by definition, no evidence of the adoption of any particular practice or standard is available in any event. This is exemplified by the medical case of *AB v Tameside & Glossop Health Authority*.[325] The issue was as to the way in which a competent health authority ought to alert patients, who had come into contact with a health worker diagnosed as HIV positive, that there was a risk they may have been infected. The authority chose to alert patients by means of a letter. A number of patients claimed to have experienced psychological injury as a result of being informed in this manner. It was contended that a prudent authority would have communicated the information via general practitioners or through health workers experienced in providing counselling. While the Court of Appeal accepted that the standard of care was set by *Bolam*, it had to conclude that the *Bolam* test was of no assistance because of the entirely novel facts and the absence of any respectable body of medical opinion supporting any particular practice as to the appropriate method for disclosing such matters to the public.

---

321 [1990] BCC 605.
322 [2001] BPIR 624.
323 [1998] PNLR 542 (CA), 549.
324 See *Re ISG Group Ltd (No 2)* [2003] BPIR 597, concerning a removal application of a liquidator and SIP 13.
325 (1997) 8 Med L R 91.

(c) Where the practice followed is unreasonable

Simply because a practice is routinely followed, and may be even be supported by expert **6.151** evidence, will not always carry the day. This is exemplified by the House of Lords decision in another medical case, *Sidaway v Governors of Royal Bethlem Hospital*.[326] This involved consideration of the scope of duty on the part of the doctor to warn as to the risks of a particular type of treatment, a matter already discussed above. Lord Bridge indicated:

> even in a case where, as here, no expert evidence in the relevant medical field condemns the non disclosure as being in conflict with accepted and responsible medical practice, I am of opinion that the Judge might in certain circumstances come to the conclusion of a particular risk was so obviously necessary to an informed choice on the part of the patient that no reasonably prudent medical man would fail to make it.[327]

This analysis explains the decision in *Edward Wong Finance Co Ltd v Johnson Stokes & Master*[328] where the defendant's solicitors handed over completion money to the vendor's solicitor in exchange for an undertaking that suitable security would be provided within ten days. No such security was in the event forthcoming and the vendor's solicitors defaulted on the undertaking. The transaction thus carried on was on the evidence conducted entirely in accordance with normal conveyancing procedures prevalent in Hong Kong. This notwithstanding, the Privy Council held the risk inherent in this style of completion was foreseeable and readily avoidable. It concluded there could only be an affirmative answer as to whether the defendant firm was negligent in not foreseeing and avoiding the risk.

(d) Where there is adequate text book learning or standard practitioner guidance as to the practice to be followed

Expert evidence is unlikely to be needed from an accountant on the meaning and interpretation **6.152** of standard accountancy documents, such as SIPs.[329]

(e) Two final words of warning

There are other areas where the courts may conclude expert evidence is not required. Typically, **6.153** this occurs in solicitors' negligence cases, and a judge will consider that they do not need another lawyer to tell them whether or not something falls below the standards to be expected of a reasonably competent lawyer. It is just possible that an experienced Chancery Judge, or ICC Judge, might form a similar view where the question is whether or not an IP has followed a provision in the IA 1986 or a rule. But a word of warning if that is the case: such an enquiry might be suggestive that in fact the best case to be advanced is not a professional negligence case, requiring it to be shown that due skill and care has not been followed, but instead that an office-holder may have acted outside their permitted powers, and strictly liable for the consequences.[330]

---

326 [1985] AC 871.
327 Ibid at 900E.
328 [1984] AC 296.
329 See *Re ISG Group* Ltd (No 2) [2003] BPIR 597, which concerned SIP 13 in its then form, and see also *LHS Holdings v Laporte* [2001] EWCA Civ 278.
330 See, e.g., in the context of a distribution in an MVL the decision in *Re AMF International Ltd* [1995] 2 BCLC 529, referred to in Section F.9 below.

3. Conclusion

6.154 That said, the advantages of obtaining expert evidence, and in particular an advisory expert opinion from a third-party IP, will usually outweigh the disadvantages and will be a prudent investment. If the evidence is not necessary, and instead the expert remains in the shadows, it is likely to help inform the manner in which evidence and submissions are presented. And if the expert opinion proves to be both wrong and negligently so then the estate will have the ability to hold that expert to account for losses suffered by that negligence.

F. CATEGORIES OF CLAIM

6.155 Most of the situations in which liabilities may arise for IPs are heavily influenced by the statutory context, and in particular the offices they hold, whether as liquidator, administrator, trustee in bankruptcy, nominee or supervisor. For the purposes of this section we consider some specific instances in which claims have been made against IPs, in relation to work they have performed, across a range of different offices. The cases provide insight into the potential risk areas for IPs carrying out the same functions in the same office. An obvious example being a case concerning an alleged sale of an asset at undervalue by a liquidator will provide useful guidance for an allegation against another liquidator in relation to asset realisation failings.[331] They also provide insight into how a claim may be made, or defended, for a different office, where the same or similar functions are being discharged. For example, a liquidator undervalue case will provide helpful insight in relation to an allegation concerning a trustee's failure in seeking to realise an asset, although there are some differences in approach so far as a trustee is concerned.[332] The cases also provide a signpost to how the law may develop incrementally from established precedent, incrementalism being much favoured by the courts where novel situations arise.[333] This may be particularly helpful in the light of the new restructuring plan procedure brought into force under CIGA 2020, largely modelled on principles of the US Chapter 11 Bankruptcy Code.[334] The situations or categories which are considered below are taken in broadly chronological order, in the sense that they seek to trace through some of the potential risk areas in the order in which an IP may face them when introduced to

---

331 For a useful discussion of IP Liability from a functional perspective see the Guildhall Chambers seminar paper, 'IP Liability – An Overview', Nicholas Briggs and Philip May, April 2008, which this section draws on and develops, together with another more recent Guildhall Chambers seminar paper, 'Claims Against Insolvency Office-Holders for Professional Negligence', Hugh Sims QC and Stefan Ramel, February 2017.

332 It has recently been held by Snowden J at [383]–[384] in *Davey v Money; Dunbar Assets plc v Davey* [2018] EWHC 766 (Ch) that an administrator does not owe the more onerous duties of a trustee selling property. See further discussion in relation to this case in paras 6.192–6.199 below.

333 The Supreme Court has recently re-emphasised the importance of using incrementalism when ascertaining whether a duty of care may be owed in novel circumstances, and in the context of an alleged advisory duty in the common law context has encouraged focus on the question of assumption of responsibility: see *Steel v NRAM* [2018] UKSC 13. In *Steel* Lord Wilson emphasises that the necessary assumption of responsibility would arise where (a) the alleged adviser must reasonably foresee that the other party would rely on their advice and (b) the other party must reasonably so rely.

334 CA 2006 Part 26A, and in particular the introduction of the 'cross class cram-down' in CA 2006 s901G(1); cf. US Bankruptcy Code: 11 U.S.C. §1129. See the government's response to the consultation on insolvency and corporate governance, published by the Insolvency Service on 26 August 2018, and referred to at https://www.gov.uk/government/news/new-tools-to-improve-rescue-opportunities-for-financially-distressed-companies. See also 'Coronavirus: changes to insolvency rules to help businesses' (House of Commons Briefing Paper No. 8877, 31 March 2020) (accessed on 12 May 2020).

a potential new instruction before or outside an appointment, then on appointment and then during the course of their appointment.

1. Advice

(a) Introduction

An IP typically faces a potential claim for negligent advice in relation to advice given before **6.156** their appointment, although they may incur liability after appointment if they continue to provide advice, or receive a fresh instruction to provide advice in a non-office-holder capacity. An example of the latter is the IP's advice and assistance being sought to provide an exit solution. There are several noteworthy examples of potential liability for pre-appointment advice, or advice outside the statutory office.

(b) Pre- and post-IVA advice to debtor

One situation is that of a debtor seeking advice before formally entering an insolvency process **6.157** (including a voluntary arrangement). The IP may, depending on the existence and the terms of their retainer, owe a debtor a tortious duty of care.[335] Considering the latter in more detail here, *Prosser v Castle Sanderson* was a professional negligence claim brought by an individual against his former solicitor and an IP who had become the supervisor of his IVA. The allegations of negligence concerned the advice (or, more accurately, the lack thereof) given to the debtor during the course of a break taken after the relevant creditors' meeting to consider the IVA proposals had begun. At first instance, HHJ Hegarty QC had found that, in relation to the events which occurred during that break, the IP did not owe a duty of care. His decision was reversed by the Court of Appeal who held that the IP did owe a duty of care. The reasoning is apparent from this passage in the judgment (Clarke LJ):[336]

> ... The judge said that it was a fine line. I have reached a different conclusion from the judge on this point. I agree that the courts should be careful not to impose duties upon nominees or chairmen of creditors' meetings when they are acting in that capacity. However, to my mind Mr Sleight was not acting in that capacity during the discussion with the appellant and Mr Addlestone during the short adjournment. He was acting in precisely the same capacity as he had when he gave advice in the period before the meeting. Moreover, it was advice on the very same questions, namely what options were available to the appellant.

> ... In the absence of a clear indication to the appellant that he was no longer acting in that capacity but as nominee or chairman it would be fair, just and reasonable to impose a duty upon him. Indeed, to my mind he was then acting pursuant to the contract just as he had been before ... .

The Court of Appeal accepted that it should be careful not to impose duties upon nominees or **6.158** chairmen of creditors' meetings when they were acting in that capacity, but it emphasised that it was important for a nominee or chairman of a creditors' meeting to make clear to a debtor in

---

335   *Pitt v Mond* [2001] BPIR 624 and *Prosser v Castle Sanderson*.
336   Ibid at [66]–[67].

what capacity they were acting at any time. After all, they were the professional. So, on the facts it was held to be appropriate to impose a duty of care,[337] though there was no causal loss.

(c) Pre-receivership advice

6.159 A similar situation arose in the corporate context in *Wade v Poppleton & Appleby (a firm)*.[338] The principal claimant, Mr Wade, had built up an engineering business, structured via a holding company and a trading company. Mr Wade was a director of both companies and the major shareholder (with his wife). The companies encountered trading difficulties with a contractor and two days before the appointment of receivers approached the defendant firm to seek their advice. The claimants wished to avoid an insolvency process and sought the assistance and advice of the defendants in that objective, which was ultimately unsuccessful. The bank subsequently appointed the defendants as receivers, and the claimants brought a negligence claim against the defendants, alleging negligent advice before their appointment as receivers. David Richards J (as he then was) concluded, having regard to the circumstances of the initial engagement, that a duty was owed both to the Wades personally as well as to the companies in question. However, the allegations of breach ultimately failed on their facts and for causation reasons. The advice and service that the IPs were requested, and required, to provide did not go further than advising on the approach to the bank, preparing a letter to the bank on behalf of the holding company, and giving advice from an insolvency perspective on the offer of finance from the lender of last resort. Having regard to the very short time period involved, and the limited nature of their instructions, the defendants were not able, and could not have been expected, to carry out an independent business review or be expected to perform any wider investigations. Nor was it accepted there was any realistic counterfactual prospect of additional or alternative funding being made available, which would have averted the appointment.

(d) Independent business reviews

6.160 A more recent case, in which an allegation of negligence in the context of work carried out during an independent business review ('IBR'), is *Premier v PwC & Lloyds*.[339] This has been reported in the context of interim applications on the question of security for costs, but it provides a further example of potential liabilities for IPs in the advisory context. The allegation of negligence against the accountancy firm in question related to the work they carried out before the company entered into insolvent administration. In particular this focused on advisory work they gave shortly before, and during, an IBR process. That IBR process was itself a process which the firm advised the companies to follow in order to procure support from their bank for further funding. The firm also advised on the funding need before and during the IBR process. The allegations were defended and the case settled before trial. The case provides an example, however, where a firm of IPs may be liable for advisory work in the context of pre-insolvency advice. It also shows that where the IP is appointed to conduct the IBR by the customer, and the

---

337 Reliance on the earlier decision in *King v Anthony* [1998] 2 BCLC 517, where it was held that a person acting as a supervisor under IA 1986 s263 did not owe individual creditors a duty of care because when so acting he was an officer of the court, was unsuccessful.

338 [2003] EWHC 3159 (Ch), [2004] 1 BCLC 674.

339 [2016] EWHC 2610 (Ch), [2017] 4 All ER 243 (Snowden J) and the subsequent decision in the Court of Appeal [2017] EWCA Civ 1872.

bank, an issue may arise as to the scope of the duties owed and to whom they were owed. That question gave rise to a triable issue of fact in the case of *Premier*.

(e) Exit advice

The final situation worth considering here is advice and/or assistance given to the person or **6.161** company in question to assist them in exiting from the insolvency process. Such a claim was made in the case of *Demarco v Perkins*.[340] The claimant was a bankrupt who retained the second defendant firm (the first defendant being a partner in that firm) to obtain an annulment via an IVA with his creditors. That route was only open to an undischarged bankrupt and so any IVA had to be established before the date of automatic discharge, in March 2000. That was not achieved and the opportunity for an annulment by that route was lost. Proceedings were issued by the claimant against the defendants for negligence in the advice and assistance they provided to the claimant. The judge at first instance found the defendants liable for negligence. The case is perhaps better known for its observations on the appropriate general and special damages to be awarded for the breach, and the rejection of the notion that the claimant should be awarded special damages for the loss of chance of obtaining an annulment under a different statutory route. Nonetheless it provides an example of negligence for work other than as an office-holder, and an illustration of another potential risk category.

2. Conflicts

(a) Introduction

It is undoubtedly the case that an office-holder will owe fiduciary duties[341] and a breach of **6.162** those duties, by reason of the office-holder being in a position of conflict, may give rise to a claim. Such a conflict may arise due to prior engagement by the IP before appointment, which may be said to give rise to a material professional relationship and a conflict. A classic example of where this may arise is explored in the context of pre-packaged sales, and the obligations under SIP 16, and this is considered further in section 3 below. If an IP, such as an administrator, has a conflict of interest, then they should consider whether to resign.[342] An administrator may resign because the further discharge of the duties of administrator is prevented or made impractical by a conflict of interest.[343]

Moreover, the office-holder will be expected to comply with the ethical guidelines laid down **6.163** by his or her RPB.[344] A failure to comply with the IP's code of ethics, may result in regulatory action and disciplinary sanctions for the IP. All RPBs have now signed up to a single code of ethics, the Insolvency Code of Ethics ('the Code of Ethics' or 'the Code'). We will consider the version here which was effective from 1 January 2009 to 30 April 2020, and this provides a useful framework against which to test allegations of conflict, of an IP.[345] Moreover, breaches

---

340   [2006] EWCA Civ 188, [2006] BPIR 645.

341   See the observations of Arden LJ *In Re Stanford International* [2011] Ch 33 at 97B, and see also para 4.012 above.

342   In the case of administrators, under para 87 of Sch B1.

343   IR 2016 r3.62(1)(c)(i)

344   The RPB's being themselves subject to regulatory oversight by the Insolvency Service, Insolvency Practitioner Regulation Section ('IPRS'). See paras 2.005–2.012.

345   A copy of the Code of Ethics is published at https://www.gov.uk/government/publications/insolvency-practitioner-code-of-ethics (accessed 20 December 2019), and which has been adopted by all IPs RPBs effective from 1 January

of the Code may also point to wider professional failings and lack of competence and due care leading to wider liability in negligence, going beyond simply regulatory liabilities. But some care is required with the question of conflicts of interest and a lack of impartiality: it is possible that an IP may have a conflict and be in breach of the Code of Ethics but still carry out a competent and reasonably careful job. In those circumstances, whilst they may be exposed to regulatory sanction, they are unlikely to be liable for professional negligence liabilities to third parties, or under a misfeasance action, unless some separate and additional head of loss is identified.

(b)   Code of Ethics

6.164   Considering a potential breach of the Code of Ethics in more detail here, as noted in the paragraph immediately above an office-holder, such as administrator, will be licensed by an RPB, all of which have signed up to the Code. The codes of ethics go back some years, including back to 2002 so any claim which is now being considered is likely to be covered by a professional code. Since 2002 the code was revised a number of times: on 1 January 2004 and then again on 1 January 2009 and finally with effect from 1 May 2020. The 2004 Code adopted five 'Fundamental Principles' which were intended to provide a framework for the IP's conduct. The Code of Ethics effective from 1 January 2009 uses the same approach. In this text we will mainly focus on the Code in force from 1 January 2009 to 30 April 2020. It is worth noting that the Code applies to both work leading to an appointment and work carried out during the appointment:[346]

> This Code applies to all *Insolvency Practitioners*. *Insolvency Practitioners* should take steps to ensure that the Code is applied in all professional work relating to an *insolvency appointment*, and to any professional work that may lead to such an *insolvency appointment*.

6.165   The Introduction to the Code states that the spirit, as well as the strict terms, of the code should govern an insolvency practitioner's conduct. Paragraph 3 provides that: 'It is this Code, and the spirit that underlies it, that governs the conduct of *Insolvency Practitioners*.' It goes on to set out five 'Fundamental Principles'. One of those five fundamental principles has already been considered and referred to in paragraphs 6.129 and 6.130 above. The two which are of most relevance to conflict allegations are the first two:

(a) Integrity

An *Insolvency Practitioner* should be straightforward and honest in all professional and business relationships.

(b) Objectivity

An *Insolvency Practitioner* should not allow bias, conflict of interest or undue influence of others to override professional or business judgements.

---

346   2009 to 30 April 2020. The version in place from 1 May 2020 is in similar terms, and can be found online (e.g., at https://www.icaew.com/-/media/corporate/files/technical/ethics/insolvency-code-of-ethics.ashx?la=en) (accessed 12 May 2020).

346   Code, para 2.

The second of these, objectivity, is likely to be the most common principle to be applied to the situations in which an insolvency practitioner works and where there is a potential conflict issue.

As is common with many modern professional codes, the Code adopts a 'framework approach' **6.166** under which practitioners can identify actual or potential threats to objectivity and whether there are any safeguards that might be available to offset them.[347] The Code also usefully sets out the application of the framework to specific situations.[348] An impairment to objectivity is most likely to come from a conflict of interest, and may arise from either (a) a 'self-interest threat' or (b) a 'self-review threat'.

These are described in the following manner:[349] **6.167**

(a) Self-interest threats: which may occur as a result of the financial or other interests of a *practice* or an *Insolvency Practitioner* or of a *close or immediate family* member of an *individual within the practice*;
(b) Self-review threats: which may occur when a previous judgement made by an *individual within the practice* needs to be re-evaluated by the *Insolvency Practitioner* ....

The assessment of conflicts of interest, and whether there are any safeguards which exist or can **6.168** be put in place to manage them must be undertaken, not just at the beginning of a prospective assignment, but also throughout the period of the appointment. The IP is required to take reasonable steps to identify circumstances which could pose a conflict, and gives the following three examples:[350]

(a) An *Insolvency Practitioner* has to deal with claims between the separate and conflicting interests of entities over whom he is appointed.
(b) There are a succession of or sequential *insolvency appointments* (see section H).
(c) A significant relationship has existed with the *entity* or someone connected with the *entity* (see also section A).

The Code encourages safeguards to be used to reduce threats.[351] A concept central to the Code **6.169** is what is now described as a 'significant relationship' (previously described as a 'material professional relationship'). The Code states that: 'the principle of objectivity may be threatened if any *individual within the practice*, the *close or immediate family* of an *individual within the practice* or the *practice* itself, has or has had a professional or personal relationship which relates to the *insolvency appointment* being considered'.[352] In order to identify the level of the threat the Code sets out a number of factors to take into account, including the nature and impact of previous work during an earlier relationship with the same entity. The 2004 Code defined a 'material professional relationship' ('MPR') as arising:

---

347   Ibid para 5.
348   Ibid Section H.
349   Ibid para 10.
350   Ibid para 31.
351   Ibid paras 32 and 25.
352   Ibid para 41.

Where a practice, or subject to the provisions of paragraph xix (below), a principal or employee of the practice is carrying out, or has during the previous three years carried out, material professional work for that client. Material professional work would include the following: a) where a practice or person has carried out, or has been appointed to carry out, audit work for a company or individual to which the appointment is being considered; or b) where a practice or person has carried out one or more assignments, whether of a continuing nature or not, of such overall significance or in such circumstances that a practitioner's objectivity in carrying out a subsequent insolvency appointment might be, or be seen to be, impaired.

The Code defines a "Significant" relationship in the following terms:[353]

An *Insolvency Practitioner* may encounter situations in which no or no reasonable safeguards can be introduced to eliminate a threat arising from a professional or personal relationship, or to reduce it to an acceptable level. In such situations, the relationship in question will constitute a significant professional relationship ('Significant Professional Relationship') or a significant personal relationship ('Significant Personal Relationship'). Where this is case the *Insolvency Practitioner* should conclude that it is not appropriate to take the *insolvency appointment*.

6.170 The 2004 Code went on to provide that:

A material professional relationship with a company or individual (as referred to in paragraphs (ii) to (iv) below) includes any material professional relationship with companies or entities controlled by that company or individual or under common control, where the relationship is material in the context of the company or individual; to whom appointment is being sought or considered.

So, an MPR could also arise according to the 2004 Code:

where a practice or person has carried out professional work for any director or shadow director of a company of such a nature that a practitioner's objectivity in carrying out a subsequent insolvency appointment in relation to that company could be or could reasonably be seen to be prejudiced.

In forming views as to whether an MPR exists, practitioners are required by the 2004 Code to:

have regard to existing or previous relationships with firms with which they are, or have been associated which might impair, or appear to impair, their objectivity, including relationships whereby they or their firm are held out by name, association or other public statements as being part of a national or international association.

The 2004 Code requires that: 'A practitioner should take reasonable steps prior to his acceptance of any insolvency appointment to ascertain whether any of the above work has been performed.'

6.171 It is likely that this would also be so under the Code. The Code also, considers certain specific circumstances or examples where prior professional work might result in a conflict, including in relation to audit work and also work carried out by the IP as an investigating accountant.[354]

---

353   Ibid para 47.
354   Ibid paras 79 and 80.

The Code also contains some specific prohibitions in relation to the manner in which **6.172** appointments are obtained. In particular in Section E, the Code provides that:[355]

> The special nature of *insolvency appointments* makes the payment or offer of any commission for or the furnishing of any valuable consideration towards, the introduction of *insolvency appointments* inappropriate. This does not, however, preclude an arrangement between an *Insolvency Practitioner* and an employee whereby the employee's remuneration is based in whole or in part on introductions obtained for the *Insolvency Practitioner* through the efforts of the employee.

The Code also reminds IPs of the importance of record-keeping in the following terms: **6.173**

> It will always be for the *Insolvency Practitioner* to justify his actions. An *Insolvency Practitioner* will be expected to be able to demonstrate the steps that he took and the conclusions that he reached in identifying, evaluating and responding to any threats, both leading up to and during an *insolvency appointment*, by reference to written contemporaneous records.

This burden is similar to other professionals, and indeed is reflected in the case law: the courts will frequently find against a professional where they do not have any record to back them up.[356]

(c) Conduct of administrators and alleged material (or significant) professional relationship

An unreported example of an alleged breach of the Code of Ethics (which focused on the 2002 **6.174** Code but which also considered more recent versions of the code) arose in *Re Our Price Entertainment Ltd (in liquidation)*[357] where the liquidators brought misfeasance proceedings in 2011 and 2012 against the former administrators in relation to their conduct of the administration (mainly in 2003). The liquidators alleged that the administrators had failed to investigate the validity of floating charges granted by the company to a debenture holder (called 'CAM') dated 19 September 2003, and in particular failed: to consider whether the company was insolvent at the time of the creation of those floating charges; to give any or any proper consideration to the fact that the company received no money, goods or services at the same time or after the creation of the said floating charges, or any other value, for the purposes of IA 1986 s245(2); and to take any steps to set aside the said floating charges or otherwise challenge CAM's rights to any payment thereunder. The payment out to CAM was therefore challenged on a number of bases but a substantial part of the complaint related to the objectivity failings on the part of the administrators, which were alleged to lie at the heart of the problem.

In particular it was alleged that the administrators' firm had had a number of prior dealings **6.175** with the company – referred to as 'Entertainment' to distinguish it from other group entities – as well as other group and associated entities. It was alleged that those relationships constituted material (or significant) professional relationships, including that the firm had carried out corporate finance work for the holding company as well as the company, including in relation to a sale of the holding company to another group company which was said to involve unlawful

---

355 Ibid para 43.
356 That a client's version of events will, in the absence of any contemporaneous note supporting any contrary version of events, generally be preferred, is shown in the following solicitor's negligence cases: *Robins v Meadows & Moran* [1991] 29 EG 145; *Morton v Harper Grey Easton* (1995) 8 BCLR (2d) 53.
357 Unreported, case no 1627 of 2005; see also *Sisu Capital Fund Ltd v Tucker* [2005] EWHC 2170 (Ch), [2006] BCC 463.

and improper financial assistance, and that the firm also undertook a monitoring role for the holdings and group entities with regard to the company. It was also alleged that one of the administrators had a personal relationship with the director and involvement in the formation of financials between the debenture holder (CAM) and the company and other group entities, which it was alleged caused self-review and self-interest threats. In short it was alleged that the administrators should have determined they could not have accepted the appointment and should have resigned as soon as they became aware of the extent of the conflict issues arising. The case settled before trial, but provides an illustration of a situation where the IP may face a liability risk arising from allegations of conflicts.

6.176 Another area where allegations of conflict have been raised concern the payment of sums as consideration for the introduction of IP appointments. As noted above, and by reference to Section E of the Code, this is inappropriate. It is even more inappropriate if it is undisclosed and involves payments made from realisations, which is an allegation which has surfaced in some unreported cases which the writers have been instructed in relation to.

(d)   Conflicts and removal applications

6.177 Before turning to the question of pre-packs, it is worth noting that the question of conflicts also arises frequently in the context of removal applications,[358] and that such removal applications may be linked to or a pre-cursor to a wider liability claim. This is considered in more detail in Part 1, Chapter 3, above. For a helpful recent review of the jurisdiction to remove, and appoint 'conflict' administrators, including on an interim basis see the decision in *Re Zinc Hotels (Holdings) Ltd.*[359] In that case, which concerned a removal application under paragraph 88 of Schedule B1 and for other relief under paragraphs 74 and 75 of Schedule B1, the court held it did have jurisdiction to appoint an interim 'conflict' administrator (finding that power in para 7 of Sch B1), but declined to do so in favour of the applicant shareholders on the facts, noting the facts were somewhat different from the typical reported cases (such as in the context of pre-packs), and notwithstanding the complaint that the office-holders had close relationships with the secured creditor.

3.   Pre-packs

(a)   Definition

6.178 A pre-packaged sale or 'pre-pack' may be defined as follows: 'An arrangement under which the sale of all or part of a company's business or assets is negotiated with a purchaser prior to the appointment of an administrator, and the administrator effects the sale immediately on, or shortly after, his appointment.'[360]

(b)   Introduction of SIP 16

6.179 The legality of such a procedure in administrations is now well-established but it has caused much public controversy, particularly where pre-packs involve sales back to entities associated

---

358   Sch B1 para 88.
359   [2018] EWHC 1936 (Ch). See also Oulton and Shah, 'Claims against administrators: some causes, the import of recent cases and the approach of the courts' (2019) 32(3) *Insolv Int* 96–100.
360   This is the definition contained in SIP 16.

with the directors who presided over the insolvency which led to the pre-pack.[361] According to the Insolvency Service the rise in pre-packs substantially coincided with the introduction of the new style of administration (following the introduction of reforms under the EA 2002).[362] This meant that administration became the insolvency procedure of choice for many insolvent companies, since the reforms rendered it possible for assets to be distributed to creditors by administrators, so that a winding up can be avoided. That said, administrations and in particular pre-packaged administrations remain a minority procedure, though it gathers the majority of bad press. In order to provide some protection against abuse of pre-packs the Insolvency Service introduced SIP 16 on 1 January 2009.[363]

(c)   SIP 16 and revisions

This SIP sets out the standards required of IPs when carrying out pre-packs and a contraven- **6.180** tion of it may lead to a liability risk for the IP in question. The principal object of SIP 16 is to provide creditors with better and quicker access to information in order to enable them to understand and if appropriate challenge the proposals or resolutions sought and/or pursued by the administrators. Following a review by Teresa Graham CBE (the 'Graham Review'), SIP 16 was revised and a new SIP introduced from 1 November 2015. The revised SIP requires enhanced disclosure of information to creditors and directors. In particular IPs are also required to advise the company that any valuations should be carried out by appropriate independent valuers who hold adequate professional indemnity insurance. An IP is also required to make connected parties aware of the ability to approach the Pre-pack Pool service for an independent view on the proposed transaction.[364] It remains to be seen whether the current version of SIP 16 remains intact following the implementation of further proposed reforms.[365]

---

361   As Prof Fletcher described it in 'Spreading the gospel: the mission of insolvency law, and insolvency practitioners, in the early 21st century' (2014) 7 *JBL* 523–40 at 526:

> when it comes to concluding a rapid sale of assets and businesses to internal buyers without any open marketing, and without the necessity of obtaining prior endorsement of the creditors, many of whom are destined to go uncompensated, questions are bound to be asked regarding the professional judgment and probity of the IP selected to serve as administrator. Particularly when, as is so often the case, the administrator is selected and appointed by the very persons who are destined to acquire the assets at a price previously agreed with the selfsame IP prior to being clothed with the powers of office concluding a rapid sale of assets and businesses to internal buyers without any open marketing, and without the necessity of obtaining prior endorsement of the creditors, many of whom are destined to go uncompensated, questions are bound to be asked regarding the professional judgment and probity of the IP selected to serve as administrator. Particularly when, as is so often the case, the administrator is selected and appointed by the very persons who are destined to acquire the assets at a price previously agreed with the selfsame IP prior to being clothed with the powers of office.

362   See the Insolvency Service Report on the First Six Months of Operation of SIP 16, published in 2009. The latest statistics are published by the Insolvency Service at: https://www.gov.uk/government/organisations/insolvency-service.

363   See Parkhouse and Scott, 'A Fair Deal?' (2009) 159 *NLJ* 421. The article describes SIP 16 as a step in the right direction of placating the critics of pre-packs.

364   The administrator should include one of the following in the SIP 16 statement: (i) a statement that the Pre-Pack Pool has been approached by the connected party, or not; (ii) a statement that the administrator has requested a copy of the opinion given by the Pool member. If an opinion is made by the Pre-Pack Pool and is provided by the connected party to the administrator, a copy of that opinion is to be included within the SIP 16 statement, clearly stating the date of that opinion.

365   Further reform of SIP 16 was being considered at the end of 2017 but the government's response to the consultation on insolvency and corporate governance, published by the Insolvency Service on 26 August 2018, did not recommend a further re-write of SIP 16 and instead appear to focus on enhancing measures to be able to pursue directors. However, on 8 October 2020 the government published draft regulations for reform of pre-packs involving sales to connected entities. In summary, the draft regulations only apply to sales which take place within 8 weeks of a company entering

(d) Challenges

6.181   Notwithstanding, and perhaps in part facilitated by some of these reforms, pre-packs continue to provide a fertile ground for challenge. A recent example of this arose in the context of a removal application heard in the Companies Court in *Re Ve Interactive; Ve Vegas Investors IV LLC v Shinners*.[366] The Companies Court granted the creditors' application to remove the administrators of the company and to replace them with new administrators.[367] It was held that the new administrators should be appointed to investigate potential claims against the company's directors and/or a professional services firm, relating to a pre-pack sale of the company's business and assets, and that the respondents ought to have concluded, from the date of their appointment or soon thereafter, that they, as members of that same firm, were conflicted and could not carry out the necessary investigations. See also *Clydesdale Financial Services Ltd v Smailes*[368] which also concerned a pre-pack sale.[369]

4.   Investigations

(a) Introduction

6.182   The duty of investigation is considered in further detail in Part II, Chapter 4, paragraphs 4.056–4.059 above. What follows is a brief summary to set the context for discussion of investigatory liabilities.

(b) SIP 2

6.183   It is the core function of any office-holder that they investigate the affairs of the company, or the estate (in the case of a trustee in bankruptcy) over which they are appointed. In the case of a liquidator they have a duty to investigate the affairs of the company, including its promotion and formation and the conduct of its business in the past, including the conduct of its officers. The duty is positive and they have to undertake the investigation exercising reasonable skill and care. SIP 2, introduced in May 2011, emphasises and outlines the positive investigatory duties owed by liquidators and administrators. This recognises that investigatory functions should be proportionate (para 4), but irrespective of a lack of funds there are certain key initial actions, which are emphasised at paragraphs 9 –11, and which contemplate basic initial enquiries must be performed in all cases:

> 9. Notwithstanding any shortage of funds, an office holder should consider the information acquired in the course of appraising and realising the business and assets of a company, together with any

---

administration. The draft regulations are not limited to pre-packs – they concern any substantial disposal of the company's assets within the 8 week period which begins when the company enters administration. The draft regulations will apply where there is a disposal in administration of all or a substantial part of a company's assets. An administrator will be unable to dispose of property of a company to a person connected with the company within the first 8 weeks of the administration without either (i) the approval of creditors or (ii) an independent written report. The connected party purchaser will be required to obtain the written report and the provider of it must be independent of the connected party purchaser, the company and the administrator and must meet certain eligibility requirements.

366   [2018] EWHC 186 (Ch).

367   In fact, the administrators chose to step down part-way through the hearing of the application. However, this did not prevent Registrar Jones from handing down a reasoned judgment: see at [39].

368   [2009] BCC 810 (David Richards J) at [30].

369   See also *Sisu Capital Fund Ltd v Tucker* [2006] BCC 463 (Warren J) at [82]–[90] where the question of conflicts and removal was considered in more detail (though *Sisu Capital* was not focussed on pre-packs).

information provided by creditors or gained from other sources, and decide whether any further information is required or appropriate. The office holder should make enquiries of the directors and senior employees, by sending questionnaires and/or interviewing them, as appropriate.

10. In every case, an office holder should make an initial assessment of whether there could be any matters that might lead to recoveries for the estate and what further investigations may be appropriate.

11. An office holder should determine the extent of the investigations in the circumstances of each case, taking account of the public interest, potential recoveries, the funds likely to be available to fund an investigation, and the costs involved.

(c) CDDA reporting obligations

There is also a positive duty on liquidators, administrators and administrative receivers to report on the conduct of directors under s7(3) of the Company Directors Disqualification Act 1986 ('CDDA 1986'). SIP 4 (which provides guidance on office-holder's statutory obligations under CDDA 1986 and The Insolvent Companies (Reports on Conduct of Directors) Rules 1996) requires an administrator to submit information as to the conduct of directors to the disqualification unit of the Secretary of State on the appropriate statutory forms ('D-Forms') within six months of the administration order. However, paragraph 10 of SIP 4 (entitled 'extent of work') states that: **6.184**

> The practitioner is expected to base his report, or decision that only a return is necessary, on information coming to light in the ordinary course of his work and is not required to carry out investigations specifically for the purpose of fulfilling his duties under the Act.

Nevertheless, corporate office-holders may also, as part of their proposals (in the case of administrators), confirm their proposed investigations and the steps they propose to take in that respect. In addition to the guidance in SIP 2 those proposals (which may be proposed and approved under paragraph 68 of Schedule B1 to the Act) will provide a potentially fertile ground on which to found an allegation of negligence if the office-holder fails to carry out the contemplated investigatory work. **6.185**

(d) Bankruptcy

A trustee in bankruptcy also has investigatory duties as a necessary adjunct to his positive duty to realise the bankrupt's property for the benefit of creditors. Those duties require an investigation into the bankrupt's available assets, and such investigation will ordinarily require an inquiry as to what assets may have been dissipated in the five years before the commencement of the insolvency process (having regard to the ability to upset transactions at undervalue within that time frame under IA 1986 s339) and potentially further back in time if IA 1986 s423 is under consideration. **6.186**

(e) Case examples – administrations

An example of such alleged failures of investigation arose in the context of the administration of *Re Our Price Entertainment Ltd*, already considered in paragraphs 6.174–6.175 above in the context of conflicts. As noted above, part of the complaint concerned an alleged failure to investigate adequately or properly the validity of floating charges and whether it was capable of being invalidated under IA 1986 s245. In short it was alleged that a reasonably competent, diligent and objective administrator would have investigated thoroughly whether the floating charge was valid or not. For the purposes of the causes of action in contemplation the key issue **6.187** related to the true financial position of the company – Entertainment – as at the date of the acquisition, having regard to all the information available to the administrators relating to events before and after that date. It was alleged the administrators needed to investigate thoroughly and objectively whether Entertainment was insolvent at the time the floating charges were granted, or became insolvent by reason of the acquisition pursuant to which the floating charges were granted. The question of insolvency and ascertaining the causes of insolvency is a core function of any office-holder, as reflected in the drafting of paragraph 1 of SIP 2 referred to above. The case settled before trial and so the underlying allegations were not tested, but they provide an example of a situation where investigatory failings were alleged and which provided for risk for the IP.

6.188 Another, and similar, example of an allegation of an investigatory failing was made in the unreported case of *Re Altala Group Ltd (in liquidation)*, in respect of which permission to bring misfeasance proceedings under paragraph 75(6) of Schedule B1 of the Insolvency Act 1986 against the former administrators was granted by Deputy Registrar Middleton in May 2017. In short, and as described by the applicants, the claim related to alleged negligence by the respondents whereby the companies in question lost the benefit of pursuing claims against insured directors of the companies with £15 million of directors and officers ('D&O') cover. The principal complaint against the former administrators was a failure to investigate properly claims against the former directors and in circumstances where they were on notice that any claims needed to be made within four months of the administration appointment if the benefit of insurance cover was to be preserved. The Deputy Registrar considered that the application had sufficient merit for permission to be granted to bring the claim against the former administrator.

5. Sales and transactions

(a) Introduction and receivers

6.189 A classic situation for a claim against an IP relates to sales and in particular transactions involving asset realisations where it is alleged the asset in question was sold at an undervalue. When disposing of assets an office-holder will have to achieve the best price obtainable. The duty is analogous to the duty owed by a mortgagee to the mortgagor to obtain the best price reasonably obtainable on a sale of the mortgaged property.[370] Before considering claims against administrators and liquidators it is worth briefly considering case law concerning receiverships as many of the principles have developed from those cases.

6.190 In the context of receivers, or administrative receivers, the duty is owed primarily to the appointor. A receiver, or an administrative receiver, is under a duty to realise assets in order to repay the money owed by the debtor company to the appointor.[371] There are circumstances when third parties may seek to make a claim against a receiver. The circumstances arise where it can shown that a receiver has caused loss and damage to their interests. The typical scenario is where it is alleged there is a sale at an undervalue.

---

370   *Cuckmere Brick Co Ltd v Mutual Finance Ltd* [1971] 2 WLR 1207.
371   *Silven Properties Ltd v Royal Bank of Scotland* [2003] EWCA Civ 1409, [2004] 1 BCLC 359 at [27].

When a mortgagee or his agent (a receiver) does exercise the power to sell, the equitable duty **6.191** to obtain a reasonable and fair price is triggered. A thorough exposition of the duty to obtain the best price reasonably obtainable is provided by Lightman J sitting in the Court of Appeal in *Silven Properties Ltd v Royal Bank of Scotland*.[372] In this case, which concerned the sale of mortgaged property, the duty to exercise reasonable care to obtain the best price was emphasised, but it was also emphasised this did not extend, so far as receivers were concerned, in taking steps to improve value, by for example seeking planning permission or grant leases. That was because of the primacy of the receiver's duty to the mortgagee and to the expeditious repayment of their debt. Many of the recent alleged sales at undervalue have focused on alleged failures by receivers in the context of portfolio sales. In those cases the receivers must ask themselves, and be satisfied, that a portfolio sale will achieve the best price, particularly where it might be said that one of the assets would have sold for more if sold individually.[373]

(b) Administrators and liquidators

One of the first reported cases in the field of professional negligence claims against IPs, namely **6.192** *Re Charnley Davies Ltd (No 2)*,[374] is an example of a transaction case, as is one of the most recent reported cases, namely in *Davey v Money; Dunbar Assets plc v Davey*.[375] Both of those cases were misfeasance claims against administrators where the essential complaint was that assets had been sold at an undervalue, and both claims failed on their facts, but similar claims may be made against liquidators: the liquidator has the power to realise assets of the debtor company by virtue of Schedule 4 paragraph 6,[376] and his or her duty is to realise the assets in the most efficient way in order to obtain the highest possible value for creditors.

It should be noted however that in *Davey v Money* Snowden J rejected the notion that an **6.193** administrator owes the more onerous duties of a trustee selling property as described above.[377] Instead their duty, when acting as agents to sell the assets of a company in administration, is simply to take reasonable care to obtain the best price which the circumstances of the case permit. The relevant standard of care is that of an ordinary skilled practitioner.

Observations of Snowden J in *Davey v Money* also contain some words of warning about **6.194** assuming that the dicta in the receivership cases apply without qualification to claims against administrators. In particular Snowden J confirmed he agreed with analysis of Professor Goode as follows:[378]

> Administrators operating in accordance with paragraph 3 of Schedule B1 are plainly intended by the legislature to have regard to wider considerations than receivers or administrative receivers, whose primary duty is to their appointor. In Goode, *Principles of Corporate Insolvency Law*, 4th ed. at 11-27, Professor Goode commented,

---

372 Ibid 368. See further the discussion in relation to receivers in Chapter 3 at paras 3.128 ff.
373 See *McDonagh v Bank of Scotland plc* [2018] EWHC 3262 (Ch) (Morgan J) and *Centenary Homes v Gershinson* (unreported, 15/12/2017).
374 [1990] BCLC 760.
375 [2018] EWHC 766 (Ch).
376 See Annexes I and II at pp 297, 302.
377 *Davey v Money* at [383]–[384].
378 *Davey v Money* at [391]–[392].

'In this respect, [an administrator] has less freedom than that possessed by the administrative receiver, because the latter, whilst under a duty to use reasonable endeavours to obtain the best price, was free to determine the timing of any realisations and could thus proceed to an early sale even if delay would have resulted in enhancement of the value of the security and would not have prejudiced his debenture holder. Now he has to avoid unnecessary harm to the general body of creditors. "Harm" is considered to be the equivalent of "prejudice". He is still entitled to subordinate the interests of the general body of creditors to those of secured and preferential creditors, since para.3(2) of Sch.B1 makes it clear that his duty to the general creditors is subject to the pursuit of the third objective. But he must avoid causing harm which is not necessary for the protection of the creditors for whom his realisations are intended. This imposes on him the duty to consider all aspects of the administration, including the timing of realisations. It is also a signal that the existence of security substantially in excess of the debt owed to the secured creditor or creditors does not entitle him to be lax in managing the business and realising the assets.'

6.195 Snowden J's judgment also provides helpful guidance on the circumstances in which the administrator may decide to adopt proposals which involve only repaying the secured creditor (the third 'objective' as defined in para 3(1) of Sch B1). An administrator may do so under paragraph 3(3) Schedule B1 if 'he thinks' that it is not reasonably practicable to achieve anything else, but even then he must not unnecessarily harm the interests of creditors as a whole.[379] However, the expression the administrator 'thinks' is an indication that Parliament intended a degree of latitude to be given to an administrator in deciding upon the objective to be pursued, and that he is not lightly to be second-guessed by the court with the benefit of hindsight. An administrator's decision not to pursue the first objective (rescue) will only be open to challenge if it was made in bad faith or was clearly perverse in the sense that no reasonable administrator could have thought that it was not reasonably practicable to rescue the company as a going concern.[380] This applies to the choice of objective but not to the methods adopted by the administrator to pursue his chosen course. Those methods are subject to a more objective standard of review.[381]

(c) Lack of funds & time

6.196 In determining whether an IP has fallen below the standard, it is very relevant to consider that in many insolvencies, an IP will not have ready funds at his disposal (e.g., for the purposes of availing himself of legal advice) and time will often be short. This lack of funds played a decisive part in the rejection (on the facts) of an alleged breach of duty (failure to obtain best price reasonably obtainable for sale of business by reason of alleged undue haste) in *Re Charnley Davies Ltd (No 2)*.[382] That said, as noted in paragraphs 6.205 and 6.183, this has to be

---

379 *Davey v Money* at [254]. Another case where there appears to be a challenge to the decision by the administrator not to seek to recuse the company, which has been reported in relation to interim disclosure matters, is the case of *Re One Blackfriars Ltd* (unreported, 18 December 2019, John Kimbell QC sitting as a Deputy High Court Judge, [2019] 12 WLUK 283). The case settled before trial.

380 Ibid at [255]. This case appears to have been the first case to consider the meaning of 'thinks' in para 3 of Sch B1. For previous commentary on how this might be interpreted see *Insolvency and the Enterprise Act 2002*, Guildhall Chambers Insolvency Team and edited by Stephen Davies QC (Jordans, 2003) at para 7.25, which suggested a similar test to that adopted by Snowden J.

381 [2018] EWHC 766 (Ch) at [256].

382 [1990] BCLC 760.

balanced against the need for the IP to gather in information before appointment, and to carry out certain irreducible investigations post-appointment (whether as an administrator or liquidator).

Whilst the cases failed on the facts in *Charnley Davies Ltd* and in *Davey v Money*, it is in practice not always easy to ensure that the duty has been discharged. The assets in question may be of uncertain or diminishing value. An administrator or liquidator may not have the time or resources to continue to trade the business or to engage in any extended period of marketing. Nevertheless, it is important to distinguish between errors which constitute negligence and what may be described as errors of commercial judgment, where a greater latitude is allowed for. The court has repeatedly recognised that office-holders have to make commercial judgments and that it should not interfere with these or be called upon to make such decisions itself.[383] **6.197**

(d)   Market exposure and pre-packs

Whenever possible effort should be made to expose the assets to the market and/or to create an environment in which competitive bidding occurs. It is acknowledged that this will not always be possible and that is particularly so in the case of pre-packaged sales. It is instructive that (despite all the controversy about pre-packs) there are still no reported cases of office-holders being successfully challenged for disposing of assets on this basis, although it may well be that the insurers for the office-holders have settled such claims below the reporting radar. **6.198**

It is nevertheless essential in every case that the office-holder takes steps to satisfy himself that the best price reasonably obtainable has been achieved. **6.199**

(e)   Check-list or 'warning flags'

A failure to consider the following matters, or follow the following steps, may be considered to be 'warning flags' and give rise to a potential for liability on the part of the IP. **6.200**

(i)   Nature and extent of assets

A failure to investigate fully the extent and nature of the assets to be sold is a risk area for the IP. It is instructive to note that the Code stipulates, as an aspect of professional competence, that an IP is required to obtain knowledge and understanding of the nature of the entity's business.[384] So, where an IP has failed properly to ascertain which assets are theirs to sell this may be said to constitute a breach.[385] Liability could also arise where the IP fails to consider whether assets may be worth more individually, rather than being sold as a portfolio.[386] **6.201**

(ii)   Enhanced value and special purchasers

As part of that investigation identifying any obvious potential to add value, for example where a complaint might be made that no account was taken of the fact that the property had **6.202**

---

383   See the cases and discussion in Section D, paras 6.125 to 6.128 above.
384   Code, 37(b).
385   Such an allegation was made in the receivership case of *Devon Commercial Property Ltd v Barnett* [2019] EWHC 700 (Ch).
386   See the portfolio sale cases referred to above at para 6.191.

planning permission for development.[387] Another risk area may be where there is a potential special purchaser identified.[388]

(iii) Independent valuation advice

6.203 A failure to take independent expert valuation advice is a key red flag.[389] Such advice helps safeguard the IP from risk, and is usually easily obtained in respect of real property and plant and machinery values. There may be more difficulties in respect of intellectual property or intangible assets; see further the case of *Brewer v Iqbal* discussed in paragraph 6.209 below, where arguably the wrong expert was instructed.

(iv) Basis of instruction

6.204 A further potential risk area may lie, even if the right type of expert is instructed, in whether or not the instruction has been provided on a correct basis. This can occur where there is a particular market or purchaser which the IP knows or ought to know of but which does not form part of the instructions to the expert valuer.[390]

(v) Unnecessary haste or delay

6.205 Either excessive haste or undue delay in taking realisation steps, resulting in a depressive effect on value, are potential risk factors. Those who are considering should also bear in mind that ordinarily IPs will be familiarising themselves with the entity and its affairs, and so the need to act quickly post-appointment will not necessarily be decisive.[391] For example, consideration should be given to assets that can be realised, such as debtors and work in progress, in reasonably short order, and whether they are time sensitive assets. The rights to the debtors can be sold to debt collection enterprises, but before selling the office-holder should consider exposing such an asset to the market.

(vi) Market exposure

6.206 Overlapping with the above, but worth considering as a category in its own right is the failure to properly market the property or expose it to the market place, and public advertisement is the norm (especially outside the pre-pack scenario). As stated in *Fisher & Lightwood* 'whatever *the mode of sale, it should be properly advertised'*.[392] However, on appropriate facts the court may absolve an IP from exposing property to the open market.[393]

---

387 See *Cuckmere Brick* at [1971] Ch 949. Cf. the dissent of Cross LJ at 962E–H, 978H–979B, D.

388 Again the Code of Ethics (at para 37(a)) encourages a focus on obtaining knowledge, pre-appointment, of the entity and its owners etc. See *Devon Commercial Property Ltd v Barnett* [2019] EWHC 700 (Ch), where the special purchaser was the occupier and also the appointor.

389 The need to use experts where necessary is trite, and emphasised in para 37(f) of the Code.

390 In *Devon Commercial Property* the complaint was made that marketing was not performed or targeted at drinks companies.

391 Indeed the Code emphasises, at para 37, that professional competence and relevant information gathering is to be considered prior to accepting an appointment.

392 *Fisher & Lightwood's Law of Mortgage* (15th edn, 2019) at 30–28, referring to *Michael v Miller* [2004] EWCA Civ 282, [2004] 2 EGLR 151. See also *Aodhcon LLP v Bridgeco Ltd* [2014] EWHC 535 (Ch), [2014] 2 BCLC 237 and for an example of a property not being properly exposed to the market, see *Bishop v Blake* [2006] EWHC 831 (Ch) at [107].

393 As occurred on the facts in *Davey v Money* at [455].

(vii) Consideration, deferral and security

Many deals may involve an element of deferred consideration and an IP may be under a duty to **6.207** secure the benefit of any deferred consideration. Where assets are sold on the basis that there will be a deferred consideration they should, as a matter of practice, ensure that the deferred consideration is secured in case of default.[394] If the purchaser is a newco or is otherwise unable to give adequate security personal or parent company guarantees should be considered.

(f) Intangibles

As noted above, particular difficulties may arise in relation to intangible items such as goodwill **6.208** and intellectual property rights. Whilst these assets may not be immediately apparent or may not feature on the balance sheet, they are nevertheless assets and the office-holder will have a duty to obtain the best price possible.[395]

A recent example of a case involving a negligent sale by an IP of intangible assets occurred in **6.209** *Brewer v Iqbal*.[396] Chief ICC Judge Briggs held that the administrator had placed too much reliance on the directors of the company to provide a value for certain Guides (known as 'EPGs'), approval for marketing on a website, and the timing of the sale of the EPGs. Therefore, while ascertaining the views of stakeholders will not necessarily go against the grain of the IP's duty,[397] if there is undue reliance on those views, then the IP will expose himself to liability. This principle may be more likely to apply where there is something unusual about the asset. The EPGs in *Brewer v Iqbal* were a specific category of intangible asset with a '*restrictive but competitive*' market. There were specialist EPG acquisition and sales agents, and it appears that knowledge of this fact should have been acted on by the IP for him to have discharged his duty to the company. This was the type of case where a competent administrator would probably have taken independent advice as to the marketing and selling from more than one agent, as the asset class was unusual and unfamiliar.[398] By not taking such advice, the IP ran the risk that the sale would be for an undervalue, and appears to have chosen the wrong valuer who did not have the right expertise.

(g) Bankruptcy

A trustee in bankruptcy is under a similar duty.[399] However when carrying out a sales function, **6.210** the IP must bear in mind that they may be expected to strain for a better result than an ordinary vendor (who, e.g., might be embarrassed to accept a gazumping offer – an office-holder may not be so embarrassed, in the exercise of their statutory functions). In the case of a trustee in bankruptcy the guiding principles for trustee vendors are: (i) to sell 'under every possible advantage' to the beneficiaries; (ii) to secure 'a proper competition' to obtain the best

---

394 Whilst not arising in the context of a sale by an IP, the royalty agreement in question in *Fraser Turner Ltd v PricewaterhouseCoopers LLP* [2018] EWHC 1743 (Ch) at [69] (upheld on appeal: [2019] EWCA Civ 1290), might be said to illustrate a case where security for future obligations ought to have been secured (though the fault in that case may have been laid at the door of the solicitors in question).

395 See the dicta of Jacob J in *Western Intelligence Ltd v KDO Label Printing Machines Ltd* [1998] BCC 472.

396 [2019] EWHC 182 (Ch).

397 See *Davey v Money* at [592].

398 *Brewer v Iqbal* at [88].

399 With similar powers set out in IA 1986 Sch 5 para 9. See Annexes I and II at pp 297, 302.

price; (iii) to investigate higher offers – even at a late stage; and (iv) not to advance the interests of one party at the expense of any other.[400]

6.211 Before moving away from liability for transacting office-holders and sales of assets it is worth briefly considering a case where liability was established. This arose in the personal insolvency context in *McAteer v Lismore*.[401] Mr Lismore was trustee in bankruptcy over the estate of the late Mr McAteer from 4 April 1995. In the discharge of his duties Mr Lismore obtained possession of and sold the former matrimonial home. Mrs McAteer contended that the sale had been at an undervalue and that Mr Lismore was in breach of the duty of care owed to the estate of her late husband. In the judgment of Deeny J, this complaint was well founded, principally on the basis that the property had not been marketed or advertised for nearly five years before 15 March 2005 when it was sold.

6. Conduct of litigation

(a) Introduction

6.212 In one sense it might be argued that IPs are almost always involved in the conduct of proceedings, because, for example, bankruptcies and liquidations are proceedings. However, the particular situation we consider here is the potential liability which may arise in relation to an office-holder's control and conduct of litigation. The first situation to consider is where an IP may be criticised for failing to commence litigation. We then turn to consider the circumstances where an IP may be at risk in the conduct of that litigation.

(b) Commencing litigation – limitation issues

6.213 So far as a failure to commence litigation, this may be said to be an instance of 'non-feasance' that is, a culpable failure or omission by the practitioner to act by bringing a claim in time. An example of such allegation is *A&J Fabrications Ltd v Grant Thornton*.[402] This was a strike-out case where the claim was brought by majority creditors against the firm of accountants (not the individuals). Perhaps somewhat benevolently, Jacob J took the view that a claim against the firm of accountants could be maintained – the conventional claim would be a misfeasance claim under IA 1986 s212 (or similar) against the office-holder personally. The complaint on the facts, which was not struck out, was that the liquidators failed to keep the plaintiffs informed of the state of their investigations, and did so for such a long time that any possibility of a claim became statute-barred.

(c) The use it or lose it rule – bankruptcy

6.214 A similar type of failing may be said to arise in the context of a trustee in bankruptcy where they miss a limitation period for bringing a claim against a third party. Unique to trustees in bankruptcy however is the obligation to realise the bankrupt's home before it ceases to form part of his estate by reason of the statutory provisions, and in particular the so-called 'use it or lose it' provision in IA 1986 s283A, whereby title to real property of the type specified in that

---

400 As summarised in *Killearn v Killearn* [2011] EWHC 3775 (Ch) at [16].
401 [2012] NICh 7, [2012] BPIR 812 (Deeny J).
402 [1998] 2 BCLC 227.

section (usually the bankrupt's former home) will re-vest in the bankrupt if the trustee omits to take steps to realise it within the statutory period.

(d) Use of court directions

When assessing legal competence and negligence, the ability to seek legal advice as well as directions[403] from the court should be noted. In *Re Home and Colonial Insurance Co*[404] the liquidator admitted a claim founded on a contract for the reinsurance of marine risks in circumstances where rejection would have left the company completely solvent. After dissolution, it became apparent that the reinsurance contract was unenforceable, and the company restored for the purpose of bringing proceedings against the liquidator. Maugham J noted the ability of the liquidator to obtain legal advice and the fact that a liquidator 'is entitled, in every case of serious doubt or difficulty in relation to the performance of his statutory duties, to submit the matter to the Court, and to obtain its guidance' which he described as being '*a most important consideration*'.[405] The liquidator had done neither. Rather he had chosen to 'navigate in these narrow seas, to him unaccustomed and unknown, without either chart or pilot; and for this temerarious conduct he must bear the responsibility'.[406] However, the ability of the office-holder to apply to court for directions (at least in the modern context) does not absolve them of the need to take difficult decisions that may arise out of and are inherent to their appointment. Where an office-holder is taking a commercial or administrative decision[407] or otherwise adjudicating upon a proof of debt for voting purposes[408] (save perhaps in circumstances where the validity of the proof is dependent upon a developing area of jurisprudence[409]) the court is unlikely to be receptive to such an application.[410] The corollary of that is that the theoretical ability of the office-holder to make such an application should not be overstated and consideration given as to the likelihood of the court entertaining an application for directions on a given set of facts before reliance is placed upon the proposition for which *Re Colonial Insurance* is commonly relied. **6.215**

(e) Use of lawyers

In relation to legal competence more generally, it has been observed by the Supreme Court of Southern Australia, in colourful terms, that '*a liquidator is not expected to be a bush lawyer*' and is to be judged primarily in relation to the accepted standards of his own discipline.[411] **6.216**

That said, obtaining legal advice from solicitors (or indeed guidance from the court) is not necessarily a bomb shelter, or safe harbour. IPs need to be astute to the fact that a determined claimant will look behind the legal advice, and enquire, for example, as to the quality and extent of the instructions which the IP gave to their lawyers, and also the extent of the **6.217**

---

403 Under IA 1986 ss112 (voluntary winding up); 168(3) (winding up by the court); and s303 (bankruptcy).
404 [1930] 1 Ch 102.
405 Ibid 125.
406 Ibid 126.
407 *Re T&D Industries plc* [2000] 1 WLR 646, 657.
408 *Parker v Nicholson* [2015] EWHC 3881 (Ch).
409 Ibid citing *Day v Haine* [2007] EWHC 269.
410 The appropriate procedure, which is dictated by the Insolvency Rules, is that the IP shall adjudicate on the proof, and the creditor has a right of appeal against that decision: see IR 2016 r15.35.
411 *Maelor Jones Investments (Noarlunga) Pty, Ltd v Heywood-Smith; Van Reesema v Heywood-Smith* [1989] SASC 1928 (Olsson J) at 36.

investigations which the IP had undertaken which informed those instructions. That is in effect what happened in *Top Brands Ltd v Sharma*.[412] This is not a case which concerns the conduct of litigation, but it is noteworthy that the IP's reliance on legal advice was insufficient to relieve her from liability. HHJ Simon Barker QC considered that the relevant insolvency practitioner (acting in an MVL) was unable to get off the hook on the basis of legal advice that she had received. In other words, the safe harbour principle is only available where practitioners have reasonably and properly obtained advice and have acted on that advice. As was explained by HHJ Simon Barker:[413]

> a liquidator will not have taken proper advice where the instructions to the adviser were flawed (partial or incorrect) by reason of a failure on the part of the liquidator to identify relevant considerations, or a failure to use all proper care and diligence in obtaining information relevant to the instructions given, or a failure to use all proper care and diligence in obtaining information relevant to the advice obtained.

7. Trading

(a) Introduction

6.218 A well-known trading claim is the decision in *Medforth v Blake*[414] where a claim was made by a company (against the appointed receivers) for failure to run its pig farming business efficiently so as to maximise returns. In particular, a properly informed IP would have realised they could have secured substantial discounts on the supply of foodstuffs for the purposes of carrying on the business. The judge held that there was a duty of care, over and above a duty of good faith, the standard to be expected being that of a reasonably competent receiver. However, such claims are not common. The circumstances in which an IP will trade a business (for example) in administration is less likely than it used to be. It is even rarer in the context of liquidations. Nevertheless, it is worth briefly considering this situation and the potential liabilities an IP may face if they trade the business in question.

(b) In liquidation

6.219 A liquidator is given power to carry on the business by Schedule 4, paragraph 5 to the Act, but he must have reasonable grounds for believing that carrying on the business is beneficial. In *Re Wreck Recovery & Salvage Co*[415] the Court of Appeal held (in the context of a compulsory winding up) that it must be both necessary and beneficial:

> Now the word 'necessary' means that it must not be merely beneficial, but something more, though the necessity must be determined by the court having regard to all the circumstances of the case. It does not, of course mean that no other course would be possible. Then it must [also] be for the 'beneficial winding up' of the business of the company, not with a view to its continuance.

---

412 [2014] EWHC 2753 (Ch), [2015] 1 BCLC 546.
413 Ibid at [33].
414 [1999] 3 WLR 922.
415 (1880) 15 ChD 353, 362.

A claim was made by a creditor against a liquidator pursuant to IA 1986 s212 in *Re Centralcrest* **6.220** *Engineering Ltd.*[416] The claim alleged misfeasance in allowing the company in liquidation to trade without the sanction of the court or the liquidation committee (as was required by IA 1986 s167) and misfeasance for the way the liquidator conducted the liquidation in allowing the company to trade when she should have realised its assets very quickly after her appointment. The liquidator had allowed the company to trade from October 1992 to January 1995 and during the period of trade had caused the company to make losses of £120,826.

(c) In administration

The recent decision in *Stevensdrake Ltd v Hunt*[417] is best known for, and was reported for, the **6.221** court ruling on the meaning and effect of a conditional fee agreement between the IP and their former lawyers. It considered in detail recovery only CFAs and the practice of solicitors agreeing to engage in such agreements with IPs. The underlying claim which was being pursued, however (and which the CFA related to), was a claim by the liquidator against the former administrators for (amongst other things) losses sustained by the business being wrongly traded by the administrators. That claim was ultimately conceded or settled by the former administrators, though difficulties in making a recovery led to the subsequent dispute between the lawyers and the accountants.

8. Payments

(a) The decision in Top Brands v Sharma

An office-holder has an obligation to ascertain the different categories or classes of creditors **6.222** and decide who should be paid and how much. This can give rise to claims for failings by the office-holder in the administration of such functions. An example of such a claim being successful is the decision in *Top Brands Ltd v Sharma*[418] which has already been referred to briefly in paragraph 6.217 above. The relevant facts are considered in more detail here. It is a rare instance of a case where liability and causation were made out against an IP for breach of fiduciary duty, and therefore justifies the following treatment.

In *Top Brands* the claimant companies were creditors of another company (Mama Milla Ltd or **6.223** MML for short). They issued proceedings, pursuant to IA 1986 s212 seeking an order that the first defendant former liquidator of MML pay compensation to MML for £548,074.56. The second defendant was MML's new liquidator, who gave evidence that, within two months of his appointment, he had discovered that MML had been used to defraud the Revenue and Customs Commissioners. The claimants contended that the sum was money belonging to MML and that, while acting as liquidator, the first defendant had negligently misapplied the sum when paying it out or in having authorised 18 transfers. The first defendant contended that, after receipt of an indemnity, she had acted on the reasonable belief, based on legal advice from an experienced insolvency lawyer, that the sum had been subject to a *Quistclose* trust in

---

416 [2000] BCC 727.
417 [2016] EWHC 342 (Ch), [2017] 1 BCLC 64 (upheld on appeal: [2017] EWCA Civ 1173, 167 NLJ 7759, [2017] 4 Costs LR 781, [2017] BPIR 1408).
418 [2014] EWHC 2753 (Ch), [2015] 1 BCLC 546.

favour of MML's customer and that the transferees had been the customer's nominees. IA 1986 s107, concerning distribution of company's property in voluntary liquidators, was also considered.

6.224   Section 107 provides that:

> Subject to the provisions of this Act as to preferential payments, the company's property in a voluntary winding up shall on the winding up be paid in satisfaction of the company's liabilities *pari passu* and, subject to that application, shall (unless the articles otherwise provide) be distributed among the members according to their rights and interests in the company.

The order of priorities as to distributions will be considered further in the next section, section 9 below.[419]

6.225   Ultimately however the judge found the claim was well founded, and that the first defendant had acted in breach of the duty implicit in IA 1987 s107, to pay unsecured creditors on a *pari passu* basis, and had acted negligently in paying out the sum to the wrong party. The judge found (amongst other things): (i) inadequate steps had been taken to ascertain MML's state of affairs at liquidation; (ii) inadequate, if any, consideration had been given to the material available as to MML's trading, assets and liabilities; (iii) important missing information was not obtained; (iv) inadequate instructions had been given by the first defendant to the lawyer (already referred to in paragraph 6.217 above), who had advised that repayment could be made; and (iv) overall inadequate enquiries had been made.

(b)   Payments of solicitor's costs

6.226   Another risk area for IPs is the payment of their own solicitors' costs. Where the costs of any person are payable as an expense of the insolvent estate, the amount payable must be decided by detailed assessment unless agreed between the office-holder and the person entitled to payment.[420] This means that an IP may in certain circumstances be under a positive obligation to require their own solicitor's costs to be sent for assessment. This can cause problems for IPs and solicitors who have not ironed out a formal agreement and the IP then makes payments in an informal manner following a successful realisation. It does not cause an immediate problem for them, but may do so if a successor IP or third party takes an interest in the level of fees paid out.

9.   Distributions

6.227   A liquidator is under a positive duty to apply the debtor company's property in satisfaction of its debts and liabilities before making a distribution to shareholders. This duty arises under IA 1986 s107.

6.228   Of course, this is to the 'free assets' of the company, and not to assets which are subject to a fixed or floating charge. This has been emphasised in decisions of the House of Lords (such as

---

419   See also para 4.088 above.
420   IR 2016 r12.42(1).

Re Leyland DAF Ltd[421]) and the Supreme Court (*In re Nortel GmbH*[422]). Lord Neuberger summarised the position in relation to liquidations and administrations as follows:[423]

> In a liquidation of a company and in an administration (where there is no question of trying to save the company or its business), the effect of insolvency legislation (currently the 1986 Act and the Insolvency Rules, and, in particular, sections 107, 115, 143, 175, 176ZA, and 189 of the 1986 Act (as amended), and paras 65 and 99 of Schedule B1 (as inserted by section 248 of and Schedule 16 to the Enterprise Act 2002), and rules 2.67, 2.88, 4.181 and 4.218 of the Insolvency Rules, as various amended), as interpreted and extended by the courts, is that the order of priority for payment out of the company's assets is, in summary terms, as follows: (1) Fixed charge creditors; (2) Expenses of the insolvency proceedings; (3) Preferential creditors; (4) Floating charge creditors; (5) Unsecured provable debts; (6) Statutory interest; (7) Non-provable liabilities; and (8) Shareholders.

In order to ascertain who should be paid out and in which order it has been said that: **6.229**

> It is the duty of a Liquidator to inquire into all claims, to see whether they are well founded or not, to pay the good claims, to reject the bad, to settle the doubtful, or if need be, to contest them. It is only in this way that a Liquidator can fulfil his duty [...] of seeing that the property of the company is applied in satisfaction of its liabilities *pari passu*.[424]

In undertaking this task, the office-holder is acting in a quasi-judicial capacity[425] and must reject all proofs that are not properly payable. The office-holder is both entitled to and even obliged (in appropriate circumstances) to look behind any judgment giving rise to the liability[426] and take account of all defences that may be available be they by way of limitation,[427] estoppel[428] or otherwise.

If the company or bankruptcy estate suffers loss as a consequence of the office-holder wrongly **6.230** admitting to proof a debt which is not properly owing, the office-holder may acquire personal liability.[429] Similarly, they may also be liable if they make payment to a contributory in circumstances where there are insufficient assets available in the liquidation to discharge the company's remaining liabilities.[430] As will be apparent, claims against IPs based on misfeasant payments and distributions are a real flash point.

There are particular difficulties however for IPs who make distributions contrary to the **6.231** statutory scheme, since there is some authority for the proposition that in this scenario the courts will approach the question on a strict liability basis, as happened in *AMF International*

---

421 [2004] 2 AC 298.
422 [2013] UKSC 52, [2014] AC 209.
423 Ibid at [39].
424 *Austin Securities Ltd v Northgate & English Stores Ltd* [1969] 1 WLR 529.
425 *Re Menastar Finance Ltd (in liquidation)* [2002] EWHC 2610 (Ch), [2003] 1 BCLC 338 at [44], citing *Tanning Research Laboratories Inc v O'Brien* [1990] LRC (Comm) 664 at 670.
426 *Re Van Laun, ex p Chatterton* [1907] 2 KB 23; *ex p Kibble, Re Onslow* (1875) LR 10 Ch App 373.
427 *Tanning Research Laboratories Inc v O'Brien* [1990] LRC (Comm) 664, 674.
428 *In re Exchange Securities & Commodities Ltd* [1988] Ch 46.
429 *Re Home and Colonial Insurance Co* [1930] 1 Ch 102; *Re Windsor Steam Coal Co* [1929] 1 Ch. 151; *Lord Advocate v Liquidators of Purvis Industries Ltd* 1958 SC 338.
430 *Re AMF International Ltd* (No 2) [1996] 1 WLR 77.

Ltd.[431] In that case a liquidator was appointed to conduct a members' voluntary liquidation. In a declaration of solvency made prior to the winding up the surplus assets of AMF available to contributories were said to amount to £5.9m. However, the declaration failed to take account of a lease either as an asset or a liability. Moreover, s sum of £4.5m said to be owed by 'trade creditors' was in fact due from the parent company. After the commencement of winding up the liquidator paid in full most of the creditors but made no payment to the landlords under the lease. He paid the accruing rent and sought to sublet the unoccupied parts of the premises, but the receipts from the subletting were not enough to cover the passing rent.

6.232   The liquidator paid a sum of £920,000 to the parent company as contributory and filed a notice of disclaimer on the landlord making the landlord a creditor to the extent of any loss or damage suffered. The loss and damage suffered was put at about £800,000 and the liquidator admitted it as a proof for about £600,000. Only £200,000 was paid in respect of the debt and a meeting was called under IA 1986 s95. A new liquidator was appointed. Registrar Buckley made an order that the first liquidator was guilty of breach of duty by failing to deal with the proof of the landlord in a diligent manner and breached his duty by paying the contributory ahead of creditors. The first liquidator was bound to pay for the loss and damage suffered by the landlord and was not entitled to challenge the original proof submitted of £759,511. In addition, the liquidator was liable to pay interest, costs and the second liquidator's remuneration.

6.233   *AMF* provides an example therefore of a successful allegation that the former liquidator should not have made a distribution. The allegation is sometimes put on the basis that a distribution should not have been made without a provision.[432] Returning to s107 and distribution of company's property in liquidation, it states as follows (with emphasis added):

> Subject to the provisions of this Act as to preferential payments, the company's property in a voluntary winding up shall on the winding up be applied in satisfaction of the company's liabilities pari passu and, *subject to that application*, shall (unless the articles otherwise provide) be distributed among the members according to their rights and interests in the company.

This statutory provision reflects what has been described as the '*cardinal principle*' that 'in a winding up, shareholders are not entitled to anything until all the debts have been paid'.[433]

6.234   As reflected in the *AMF* litigation, there is on one view no power to distribute to shareholders before creditors are '*satisfied*'. In the first reported judgment in *Re AMF International Ltd*, Ferris J found, when addressing arguments as to costs, that a liquidator in an MVL who made a distribution to a parent company (in that case in the US) in return for an indemnity did so '*at his peril*'.[434] He went on to find that the liquidator might find himself personally liable in relation to any deficiency of assets if the indemnifier did not honour its undertaking. In the second judgment it was recorded that the liquidator did not subsequently contest his liability[435] so in that sense it may be said the precise issue, as to whether or not personal liability

---

431   Reported initially at [1996] 1 WLR 77 (and subsequently at [1996] 2 BCLC 9 in a related sequel judgment).
432   Based on IA 1986 s107 and IR 2016 r14.39 and see IA 1986 s324(4) in the bankruptcy context.
433   *Re Armstrong Whitworth Securities Co Ltd* [1947] Ch 673 (Jenkins J) at 689 (cited in *AMF*).
434   [1996] 1 WLR 77 at 536.
435   [1996] 2 BCLC 9 at 11.

automatically (or strictly) follows in the event that there is a deficiency of assets to creditors where a distribution has been made to shareholders does not arise.

The judge in *Re AMF International Ltd* also referred back to the decision in *Pulsford v* **6.235** *Devenish*.[436] It should be noted that *Pulsford v Devenish* has subsequently been characterised as being a case of breach of statutory duty where 'the liquidator in a voluntary liquidation negligently omitted to inform the company's creditors of the liquidation, and distributed the company's assets to its contributories without regard to the creditors' claims'.[437]

Nevertheless it is at least arguable that the 'cardinal principle' referred to in *Re Armstrong* **6.236** *Whitworth Securities Co Ltd*,[438] and reflected in the drafting in s107, provides that there is to be no distribution to shareholders until all the debts have been paid or satisfied if the process for determining the company's liabilities (as laid down in the rules) has not been followed (or completed). In this sense it may be said the liquidator acted outside his powers (ultra vires) and strict liability results.[439]

The equivalent wording for distributions by administrators is also worth having in mind. **6.237** Paragraph 65 of Schedule B1 states as follows:

(1)   The administrator of a company may make a distribution to a creditor of the company.
(2)   Section 175 shall apply in relation to a distribution under this paragraph as it applies in relation to a winding up.
(3)   A payment may not be made by way of distribution under this paragraph to a creditor of the company who is neither secured nor preferential unless the court gives permission.

IA 1986 s175 provides that preferential creditors have priority to other creditors. IR 2016 **6.238** provide that unsecured creditors rank *inter se* on a *pari passu* basis.[440] Accordingly, an administrator may make a distribution to an unsecured creditor to the extent permitted by the court.[441] This may be said to provide an additional layer of potential protection to the administrator when faced with an allegation of negligence in relation to a distribution (at least for a strict liability claim).

Where the office-holder does not pay a dividend, the position is different to that described **6.239** above with any action lying against them being excluded by statute.[442] However the same provisions confer upon the court a discretion to order the office-holder to pay the dividend out of their own money along with interest.[443] The exclusion of any action whilst expressly providing for a judicial discretion to impose a personal liability is an unusual statutory technique which finds its origin in BA 1914 s68. It is suggested that it is best understood as

---

436   [1903] 2 Ch 625.
437   See, e.g., in the Court of Appeal in *Kyrris v Oldham* [2004] 1 BCLC 305.
438   [1947] Ch 673.
439   In a slightly different context see also the debate as to whether or not directors who pay out unlawful dividends should be strictly liable to repay those (in effect as quasi-defaulting trustees): see the analysis and cases referred to in the decision of Popplewell J in *Madoff Securities International Ltd* [2013] EWHC 3147 (Comm).
440   IR 2016 r14.126.
441   Subject to the qualification they may only make distributions to unsecured creditors on a *pari passu* basis.
442   IA 1986 s325(2) (bankruptcy) and IR 2016 r14.45(1) (liquidation).
443   IA 1986 s325(2) (bankruptcy) and IR 2016 r14.45(2) (liquidation).

(i) a statutory acknowledgment of the general principle that absent an assumption of responsibility, an office-holder owes no duty to an individual creditor; and (ii) an exception to that principle, created by operation of statute, with the appropriate mechanism for seeking the exercise of the discretion being an application in the insolvency.

10. Remuneration

6.240   The principles surrounding the office-holder's right to be remunerated for their work and the methods of approval of remuneration are discussed in Chapter 3.[444] IPs encounter a level of risk in relation to remuneration when they incur or pay fees which are considered to be excessive or are outside the statutory scheme. Similarly, office-holders may be criticised for the expenses which they incur in administering insolvent estates. This risk, and opportunity for criticism, arises because office-holders are 'not principals looking after their own assets, but fiduciaries charged with managing assets belonging to creditors, to whom they are ultimately answerable'.[445]

6.241   As an example, in the case of *Re Salters Hall School Ltd*[446] the creditors' choice of liquidator gave an undertaking that the costs and expenses of the prior members' liquidator would be paid out of the first realisations in the estate. There were insufficient funds in the estate to pay the fees of both liquidators in full, and the members' liquidator argued that his costs ranked in priority. The undertaking did not operate to alter the statutory scheme of priority of expenses found at r4.218 of the Insolvency Rules 1986 ('IR 1986').[447] Further IR 1986 r4.138[448] did not provide any greater priority to the members' liquidator. In this case his fees had not yet been fixed at the time the company's assets were handed over to the creditors' liquidator, but even if they had been so fixed and paid, he would not have been entitled to retain his remuneration if it subsequently emerged that there were expenses of the liquidation ranking no lower in priority than his remuneration. The rules are inflexible as to the order of priority and the office-holder's powers, and there is no general discretionary 'override' that can enable a different result,[449] save perhaps for rare instances where the rule in *ex parte James* is engaged so as to constrain IPs from taking steps they would otherwise be entitled to take.[450]

6.242   The introduction of IR 2016 brought into one rule the provisions in relation to remuneration and expenses challenges by a creditor or members in administrations, liquidations and

---

444   Paras 3.023–3.028.

445   *Re Super Aguri F1 Ltd* [2011] BCC 452 at [14], citing *Mirror Group Newspapers Plc v Maxwell* [1998] BCC 324 at 333–334 (Ferris J). There is also an illuminating discussion in the decision of the Court of Appeal in *Brook v Reed* [2012] 1 WLR 419.

446   [1998] 1 BCLC 401 where the company had entered a CVL *Centrebind* procedure.

447   IR 2016 r6.42 in relation to creditors' voluntary liquidations.

448   IR 1986 r4.138 stated at the time:

Where the liquidator ceases to be in office as such, in consequence of removal, resignation or cesser of qualification as an insolvency practitioner, he is under obligation forthwith to deliver up to the person succeeding him as liquidator the assets (after deduction of any expenses properly incurred, and distributions made, by him) … .

This has been replaced with IR 2016 r6.32 in relation to creditors' voluntary liquidations.

449   See also *Re London Bridge Entertainment Partners Ltd* [2019] EWHC 2932 (Ch) and *Re Stanford International Bank Ltd* [2019] UKPC 45.

450   See paras 4.041–4.045 above.

bankruptcies.[451] An application may be made by one or more creditors (or in a members' voluntary liquidation by one or more members)[452] on the grounds that:

(a) the remuneration charged by the office-holder is in all the circumstances excessive;
(b) the basis fixed for the office-holder's remuneration … is inappropriate; or
(c) the expenses incurred by the office-holder are in all the circumstances excessive.[453]

Such an application must be made within a defined timescale, being 'no later than eight weeks **6.243** after receipt by the applicant of the progress report under rule 18.3, or final report or account under rule 18.14 which first reports the charging of the remuneration or the incurring of the expenses in question'.[454] Note that the Rule refers to remuneration 'charged' and expenses 'incurred': no payment needs to have been made from the estate in order for the relevant remuneration or expenses to be challenged. The court must make an order if it considers the application to be well-founded. Amongst the options available to the court are: to reduce the amount or rate of remuneration; to change the basis on which remuneration is charged; to require that some or all of the remuneration or expenses are not to be treated as expenses of the insolvency procedure; and to require the office-holder to pay all or part of the excess to the company or for the benefit of the bankruptcy estate.[455] Therefore an IP could find themselves not only having to repay remuneration charged by themselves or their firm, but also paying third-party expenses from their own pocket.

The bankrupt has the right to challenge the trustee's remuneration and expenses where there is **6.244** or is likely to be a surplus available to the bankrupt (or would be but for the remuneration or expenses complained about). The application must be made no later than eight weeks after receipt by the bankrupt of the trustee's final report[456] and the same options are available to the court as for an application made by a member or creditor. In order to obtain permission, the bankrupt will first need to establish a commercial or pecuniary interest in the outcome by meeting one of the two requirements set out in IR 2016 r18.35(4) which necessitates a comparison between the assets remaining in the estate, and the liabilities and costs to be paid out of the estate, leaving out of account the remuneration and expenses which are challenged by the bankrupt. It is a hard edged or binary question which does not require the court to form a view as to the prospects of the bankrupt being successful in his proposed challenge.[457] If the bankrupt is able to meet this threshold requirement, the court will go on to exercise its discretion. That discretion is a broad one[458] and the likelihood of the bankrupt eventually establishing a surplus if permission is given may be (and in all probability will be) a very material

---

451 Although it should be noted that even though a creditor may not avail themselves of this challenge procedure, a subsequent office-holder may seek to invoke the summary misfeasance procedure under IA 1986 s212, which is widely worded. See further discussion in para 6.245 below.
452 IR 2016 r18.34(2) – the creditor(s) or member(s) making the application must represent 10% in value of the total voting rights, otherwise the permission of the court is required.
453 IR 2016 r18.34(1).
454 IR 2016 r18.34(3).
455 IR 2016 rr18.36 and 18.37.
456 Ibid r18.35.
457 *In re Singh (A Bankrupt)* [2018] EWHC 3277 (Ch), [2019] Bus LR 575 at [21].
458 Ibid at [33].

consideration.[459] Alternatively the bankrupt can make an application where they are seeking annulment of the bankruptcy on the basis of payment in full of the debts and expenses.[460]

6.245 An alternative route to challenge the remuneration and expenses of an IP may be via a misfeasance or breach of duty claim,[461] on the basis that the amounts paid out of the estate were not justified in the circumstances. On such an application the court will enquire as to whether a reasonably prudent man would lay out or hazard his own money in doing what the office-holders have done.[462] If an office-holder were to take remuneration in priority to those further up the order set out in the priority rules, such an act would also seem to constitute a breach.[463] However, where payment has been made out of sums provided by a third party for that specific purpose, it may be that the money provided (even when mixed with that of the company) is not the company's money. It follows that such payment would not constitute a breach of the rules and *a fortiori* would not give rise to misfeasance on the part of the office-holder.[464] Where however the money is provided in satisfaction for a prior debt, such sums cannot be used to discharge remuneration (or make payment of any other expense) other than in accordance with the order of priority because the effect would be to use company assets to prefer one creditor.[465] Creditors have standing to bring such claims (as does the bankrupt with the permission of the court) and there is no constraint of an eight-week timetable in which to bring a claim. A further potential claimant may be a subsequent office-holder, who may have the advantage of having access to additional evidence via the working files of their predecessor. Dissatisfied creditors may seek first to remove the incumbent IP and replace them with an alternative who in their view will administer the estate in a more effective manner and will consider challenging any inappropriate actions (or inactions) of the original IP.[466]

6.246 In *Overfinch*[467] an application was made under IA 1986 s112 to direct the liquidators to call a meeting to consider a resolution for their removal (or alternatively for the court to remove the liquidators), citing concern over the level of liquidators' fees amongst other matters. The liquidators had not called the requested meeting and sought an order directing them not to do so, on the basis that the proper route for challenge of liquidators' fees was IR 1986 r4.131.[468] The liquidators' arguments were rejected by HHJ Cooke and it was directed that the meeting be convened.

6.247 It is always open to any party who is unhappy with the conduct of an IP, including remuneration and expenses incurred in the estate, to bring a complaint.[469] Since the introduction of the Regulatory Objectives,[470] the RPBs have a responsibility to promote a

---

459 Ibid at [36].
460 IR 2016 r10.134.
461 IA 1986 s212 for claims against liquidators and administrative receivers, s304 for trustees, para 75 of Sch B1 for administrators.
462 *Re Borodzicz; Borodzicz v Horton* [2015] Lexis Citation 286, [2016] BPIR 24. See also *Brook v Reed* [2012] 1 WLR 419.
463 For example, *Katz v Oldham* [2018] EWHC 540 (Ch), [2019] BCC 48.
464 Ibid at [86].
465 Ibid at [87].
466 See Chapter 3 for a discussion on the procedure for removal of an IP.
467 *Autobrokers Ltd, Overfinch Finance Ltd and Sloane v Dymond and Hogg* [2015] EWHC 2691 (Admin).
468 IR 2016 r18.34.
469 See Chapter 2 for a discussion on complaints against IPs: paras 2.074 and 2.075.
470 Through the SBEEA 2015.

profession which provides *'high quality services at a cost to the recipient which is fair and reasonable'*[471] and may decide to take further action if an IP's costs are not considered to live up to this objective.

There is always likely to be a degree of subjectivity in determining what is 'excessive' in terms of   **6.248** remuneration and expenses. There are a number of principles which provide some guidance. When fixing the basis of the office-holder's remuneration, factors to be considered are: the complexity of the case, exceptional responsibility falling on the office-holder, the effectiveness of the office-holder, and the nature and value of the property in the estate.[472] A principle of SIP 9 is that payments to an office-holder and expenses incurred should be fair and reasonable reflections of the work necessarily and properly undertaken.[473] Similar principles are to be found in the Practice Direction on Insolvency Proceedings in respect of applications made in relation to the remuneration of office-holders, but they go a step further in stating that any element of doubt on the part of the court should be resolved against the office-holder.[474] The concept of fair and reasonable is arguably somewhat vague and only serves to increase uncertainty and unpredictability. It leaves office-holders starting any assessment procedure in an unenviable position and facing a regime which assumes they are in the wrong.[475]

G. CONTRIBUTION CLAIMS

The above situations have been considering the scenario where the IP is the defendant to a   **6.249** claim brought by the claimant. An IP may also face a claim brought by a co-defendant, as a contribution claim. Such an attempt was made by director defendants in *Re International Championship Management Ltd.*[476] The IPs were joined in relation to proceedings issued against the director for wrongful trading and misfeasance under IA 1986 ss212, 214, 238 and 239 on the ground that the IPs had been in breach of their duty to exercise skill and care when giving pre-insolvency advice. It was argued that the claims for contribution were misconceived because the statutory requirements for claiming contribution under the Civil Liability (Contribution) Act 1978 were not satisfied.

In order to succeed in a claim for contribution under the 1978 Act there has to be a common   **6.250** liability of one or more persons to another person who has suffered damage for which the claimant can claim compensation from those persons.[477] The claims brought by the liquidator under ss214, 238 and 239 of the Act could not be treated as claims brought by the companies who had been advised. They were claims brought by the liquidator which had been conferred on him by statute. It followed that the IP could not be under a common liability to the liquidator; as there was no common liability and thus the claim against the IP was struck out.

---

471   IA 1986 s391C(3)(b)(i).
472   IR 2016 r18.16(9).
473   SIP 9 (England and Wales), para 3 (effective from 1 December 2015).
474   Para 21.1 of the Practice Direction – Insolvency Proceedings.
475   For a discussion of the history of IP remuneration from the Cork Report onwards see the Guildhall Chambers seminar paper, Christopher Brockman and Paul French 'Office-holder Remuneration' (Seminar Paper, April 2008).
476   [2007] 2 BCLC 274.
477   *Royal Brompton NHS Trust v Hammond* [2002] 1 WLR 1397.

6.251 A different position may apply where there is a joint appointment of office-holders and where one of them takes on the main responsibility for certain tasks, for example, investigating the causes of failure, and they are alleged to have failed to carry out that task with reasonable diligence. In those circumstances the joint office-holder may incur joint liability (depending on how the terms of any appointment are framed). Ordinarily such joint appointments are made from one firm and both IPs will have the same insurer and so the issue will only be an academic one. However, the position may arise where the IPs are from different firms and/or have different insurers (such as, e.g., the situation where one has retired and has run-off cover from a different insurer). In those circumstances the 'innocent' IP may seek a contribution claim against the 'guilty' IP. It is considered that such a contribution claim would be likely to have reasonable prospects of success on conventional principles, and is different from the position of a director seeking a contribution claim from the IP.[478] This is considered further below in Chapter 7, at paragraphs 7.096–7.099 below.

H. OTHER LIABILITIES: REGULATORY AND CRIMINAL

1. Additional sources of liability

6.252 In addition to liabilities arising as a result of the operation of the civil law, office-holders are subject to obligations imposed upon them by their RPBs designated by the Insolvency Practitioners (Recognised Professional Bodies) Order 1986.[479] Additionally, office-holders can be liable under the criminal law both in respect of default under a number of provisions in IA 1986 and also by statutory extension of offences committed by the companies of which they have taken responsibility.

2. Regulatory liability

6.253 As already noted in Chapter 2 above, all IPs are required to be members of an RPB[480] with those bodies having power to impose sanctions upon their members. In order to ensure consistency, sanctions are imposed in accordance with the Common Sanctions Guidance produced by the RPBs. Additionally, the Secretary of State may apply to the court for a direct sanctions order to be made against an office-holder.[481] In practice, it is likely to be the RPBs who impose sanctions upon their membership rather than the court on the application of the Secretary of State with the power being a residual safeguard rather than the primary mechanism for imposing sanction on the delinquent office-holder.

6.254 The sanctions regime is addressed in greater detail in Chapter 2 with the reader being referred to the content set out at paragraphs 2.076ff in particular.

---

478   Assuming that the damage is the 'same debt or damage' for the purposes of ss1 and 3 Civil Liability (Contribution) Act 1978. Whether the professional indemnity insurer is entitled to be subrogated to the claim of the IP against the joint office-holder is perhaps a more complicated question.

479   SI 1986/1764. This is considered in more detail in Chapter 2 above.

480   IA 1986 ss390(2) and 390A.

481   Ibid s390P(1) as introduced by s141 SBEEA 2015.

3. Criminal liability

The insolvency legislation imposes a number of obligations on office-holders, default of which **6.255** may give rise to criminal liability. Examples include the absolute prohibition on an individual acting as an IP at a time when they are not qualified to do so[482] and the provision of a corrupt inducement with a view to the securing an appointment as a liquidator.[483] Schedule 10 to the IA 1986 sets out a comprehensive list of punishments for contraventions of the various provisions of IA 1986 which give rise to criminal sanction,[484] with similar provision being found at Schedule 3 to the IR 2016 in respect of similar contraventions of IR 2016.

In addition to possible criminal sanction arising as a result of contravention of the Insolvency **6.256** Legislation, an IP, on a corporate appointment, may find themselves exposed to criminal liability in circumstances where legislation (other than IA 1986) imposes criminal liability upon the company and by statutory extension, upon the party responsible for the management of the company. A standard example of such statutory extension is found in 37(1) of the Health and Safety at Work Act 1974 which provides as follows:

> Where an offence under any of the relevant statutory provisions committed by a body corporate is proved to have been committed with the consent or connivance of, or to have been attributable to any neglect on the part of, any director, manager, secretary or other similar officer of the body corporate or a person who was purporting to act in any such capacity, he as well as the body corporate shall be guilty of that offence and shall be liable to be proceeded against and punished accordingly.

Similar provision is found in a number of legislative instruments including (but not confined **6.257** to): the Environmental Protection Act 1990;[485] the Environmental Permitting (England and Wales) Regulations 2010;[486] the Private Security Industry Act 2001;[487] the Bribery Act 2010;[488] the Regulatory Reform (Fire Safety) Order 2005;[489] the Transfrontier Shipment of Waste Regulations 2007;[490] the Fluorinated Greenhouse Gases Regulations 2009;[491] the Social Security Administration Act 1992;[492] and the Trade Union and Labour Relations (Consolidation) Act 1992.[493]

In order for criminal liability to be imposed on an IP on a corporate appointment under those **6.258** provisions, three elements will need to established, namely:

---

482 Ibid s389.
483 Ibid s164.
484 Ibid s430.
485 Environmental Protection Act 1990 s157. See Redman, 'Environmental law for bankers and insolvency practitioners' (1993) 8(3) *JIBL* 85–94.
486 Environmental Permitting (England and Wales) Regulations 2010 reg 41.
487 Private Security Industry Act 2001 s23.
488 Bribery Act 2010 s14(2).
489 Regulatory Reform (Fire Safety) Order 2005 Art 32(8).
490 Transfrontier Shipment of Waste Regulations 2007 reg 55(11).
491 Fluorinated Greenhouse Gases Regulations 2009 reg 52(1).
492 Social Security Administration Act 1992 s115.
493 Trade Union and Labour Relations (Consolidation) Act 1992 s194(3).

(i)   That an offence under the Act in question has been committed.

(ii)   That the offence was committed with the 'consent or connivance' of the office-holder or otherwise that the offence in question was 'attributable' to their 'neglect'.

(iii) That the office-holder falls within those classes of persons upon which those provisions impose liability such persons being: directors; managers; secretaries; other similar officers; and persons purporting to act in the aforementioned capacities.

6.259 The first element is governed by the law applicable to and as set out in the Act in question. Where the company has a defence to any proceedings brought under that Act, it necessarily follows that any proceedings brought against an officer of the company (or similar) cannot succeed. As was held by Lord Hope in *R v Chargot Ltd* (a prosecution brought under the provisions of the Health and Safety at Work Act 1974):[494]

> So [the officer] can say in his defence that there was no breach of that provision by the body corporate or, if there was, that it was not reasonably practicable for the body corporate to avoid it. It is only when it is proved that an offence under one of those provisions has been committed that the question can arise as to whether the breach was something for which the officer too can be held criminally responsible.

6.260 Where the company is in a formal insolvency procedure, the prosecuting authority will need the leave of the court to commence (or continue) proceedings against the company.[495] Whilst this may not be forthcoming, there is no requirement that the company be convicted of the relevant offence as a prerequisite of liability being established as against the relevant individual.[496] It is sufficient to establish as a matter of fact that the company committed the offence which can be established, like all other necessary facts, by placing before the jury such credible evidence as would, when properly charged and directed, enable it to find that an offence has been committed.[497]

6.261 As to the second element *viz* that the offence was committed with the 'consent or connivance' of the IP or otherwise in a manner that is attributable to their 'neglect', it will need to be shown, at least in respect of the first formulation, that they had direct knowledge of the material facts.[498] The word 'neglect' requires proof of more than mere failure to see that the law is observed, an identification of a duty and either careless discharge of that duty or a failure to comply with that duty which was causative of the commission of the offence is required.[499] The state of mind contemplated by 'connivance' and 'neglect' may be established by inference.[500] Per Lord Hope in *R v Chargot Ltd (t/a Contract Services)*:[501]

> Where it is shown that the body corporate failed to achieve or prevent the result that those sections contemplate, it will be a relatively short step for the inference to be drawn that there was connivance or neglect on his part if the circumstances under which the risk arose were under the direction or control

494   *R v Chargot Ltd (t/a Contract Services)* [2008] UKHL 73, [2009] 2 All ER 645) at [32].
495   *Re Rhondda Waste Disposal Ltd* [2001] Ch 57 and see para 43(6) Sch B1.
496   *R v Dickson* [1991] BCC 719, 722.
497   *The People (at the suit of the DPP) v Hegarty* [2011] IESC 32 (Irish Supreme Court) at [44].
498   *Huckerby v Elliott* [1970] 1 All ER 189.
499   *R v Hewitt (Paul)* [2017] EWCA Crim 1726 at [18(4)] (citing: *Huckerby v Elliott* ibid, 195b–c).
500   Ibid at [18(7)].
501   *R v Chargot Ltd (t/a Contract Services)* [2008] UKHL 73, [2009] 2 All ER 645) [34].

of the officer. The more remote his area of responsibility is from those circumstances, the harder it will be to draw that inference.

Further, the words 'attributable to' require proof of a causal connection between the neglect and the commission of the offence by the company[502] albeit the fact that the relevant individual was unaware that their actions gave rise to an offence will provide them with no defence to the charge.[503] However, where the IP has acted conscientiously and honestly, it seems that there will be no question of criminal liability being imposed upon them. Further, there is no obligation on that IP to introduce funds into the company in order that it comply with its regulatory obligations. As was held by Neuberger J in *Re Mineral Resources Ltd, Environment Agency v Stout* (albeit *obiter*):[504]   **6.262**

> [criminal liability] need [not] concern a conscientious honest liquidator. If the company has run out of money, and is therefore incapable of complying with the conditions of a Waste Management Licence, I cannot see how it could be said that, unless the liquidator has in some way behaved imprudently or worse, he could be liable under s 157 of the EPA90 because he has not come up with his own money to enable the company to comply with its obligations. Nor do I see how the liquidator could be held liable, whether criminally or otherwise, for the company having failed to comply with its obligations due to lack of funds, simply because some of the funds of the company had been used to pay the liquidator his reasonable fees, whether in connection with the Licence or other reasonable matters in connection with the liquidation.

The third requirement is that the IP be shown to fall within those classes of persons upon whom the relevant provision imposes liability with such persons being: directors; managers; secretaries; other similar officers; and persons purporting to act in the aforementioned capacities. There appears to be no reported decision on whether an office-holder will fall within those classes of persons albeit that in *Re Mineral Resources Ltd; Environment Agency v Stout*[505] Neuberger J (as he then was) proceeded on the basis that a liquidator was in principle capable of being impressed with criminal liability as a result of s157 of the Environmental Protection Act 1990. The case concerned the liquidator's ability to disclaim a waste management licence with the point being made on behalf of the liquidator that were he not able to disclaim he would run the risk of, inter alia, exposing himself to criminal liability. Neuberger J's judgment does not indicate that he was invited to consider in detail the question of whether a liquidator would fall within the relevant class of person upon whom such liability may be imposed and the court proceeded on the basis that the liquidator would be exposed to such proceedings but that this should be of little concern in circumstances where they had acted honestly and conscientiously.   **6.263**

In the different context of proceedings brought for misfeasance against an administrative receiver, it has been held in *Re B Johnson & Co (Builders) Ltd* that such an appointee is neither an 'officer' nor a 'manager' and therefore could not be subject to proceedings brought under s333 CA 1948 (now IA 1986 s212).[506] The legal effect of this decision has been curtailed   **6.264**

---

502   *R v Hewitt (Paul)* at [18(3)] (citing *Wotherspoon v HM Lord Advocate* 1978 JC 74, 78).
503   *A-G's Reference (No 1 of 1995)* [1996] 4 All ER 21, 26.
504   *Re Mineral Resources Ltd, Environment Agency v Stout* [1999] 1 All ER 746, 763.
505   Ibid.
506   *Re B Johnson & Co (Builders) Ltd* [1955] Ch 634.

following the coming into force of EA 2002, and the reformulation of IA 1986 s212(1)(b) expressly to include an administrative receiver as being amongst those classes of person upon whom civil liability can be imposed under IA 1986 s212. Whilst this is in no way determinative of the point, it is perhaps an indication that a court in appropriate circumstances would take a less restrictive view to that adopted in *Re B Johnson & Co (Builders) Ltd.*

6.265 The issue of whether IPs can be properly regarded as an 'officer' of the Company has also been addressed in the context of the relieving provision found at s1157 CA 2006 with the better view being that they can be.[507] The question arises in a very different context to that under discussion but nevertheless indicates that an office-holder may fall within the class of individuals exposed to potential liability as a result of the nature of the relationship that they have with the company. The authors tentatively suggest that if IPs can be 'officers' for the purposes of CA 2006 s1157, then they are likely also to be 'officers' for the purpose of legislation such as the Environmental Protection Act 1990.

6.266 The above decisions arise in a very different context to that under discussion but nevertheless indicate that it is arguable that an office-holder will fall outside the classes of individual exposed to criminal liability under the various provisions outlined above. However it is suggested that the better view is that an office-holder will in principle be exposed to such liability albeit that as indicated by Neuberger J in *Re Mineral Resources Ltd; Environment Agency v Stout* (albeit *obiter*) that such liability will only be imposed in circumstances where they have failed to act honestly and conscientiously. Such an approach would accord with the apparent intention behind such provisions namely that they seek to impose liability upon 'the decision-makers within the company who have both the power and responsibility to decide corporate policy and strategy'.[508]

---

507 *Re Powertrain Ltd (In Liquidation)* [2015] EWHC 3998 (Ch), [2017] 1 BCLC 95 at [13]. See also the discussion at para 8.018.
508 *R v Boal* [1992] BCLC 872 at 876–7, [1992] QB 591 at 597–8, cited in *Woodhouse v Walsall Metropolitan Borough Council* [1994] 1 BCLC 435, 442.

7

REMEDIES FOR BREACH OF IP'S DUTY

A. INTRODUCTION TO REMEDIES

1. Introduction

As noted by Lord Briggs JSC in *Perry v Raleys Solicitors*:[1] 'The assessment of causation and loss **7.001** in cases of professional negligence has given rise to difficult conceptual and practical issues which have troubled the courts on many occasions.' Some of these difficulties may be avoided, or best overcome, in the context of IP liabilities, by starting with consideration of the nature of the duty which has been breached. We have seen that IPs owe duties to companies, creditors, debtors, bankrupts and third parties both as a result of the statutory imposition of such duties by the insolvency legislation and also as a consequence of the operation of the general law. The office-holder will in many instances be acting in a fiduciary capacity. However, it is wrong to assume that all duties owed by an office-holder will be fiduciary in nature. Whilst the office-holder will doubtless be acting as a fiduciary in circumstances where they are acting as a custodian of company property or property vested in them by operation of IA 1986 s306, there will also be many instances where the duties imposed upon them will be non-fiduciary in nature. Such circumstances may include the duty to exercise reasonable skill and care in performing their statutory functions, with such a duty arising both in equity and in tort, as well

---

1 [2019] UKSC 5 at [15].

as contractual obligations which will be imposed upon them in the event that they enter into contractual relations with third parties.

7.002 The nature of the duty owed is significant in the context of the relief afforded for its breach. First, the remedy to which the wronged party is entitled will be determined by the nature of the duty, with the remedy for breaches of fiduciary duty being primarily restorative,[2] whilst the remedy for the breach of tortious and contractual duties is primarily compensatory.[3] Additionally, the nature of the duty breached has a significant effect on the way that the court will approach issues such as remoteness of loss and foreseeability as well as the rules on mitigation. For this reason we have structured the following discussion of remedies for breach of an IP's duty, in subsections 2–4 below, by reference to the source of the duty breached, before touching upon the impact of the office-holder's release in sub-section 5,[4] and finally how the power to remove the office-holder from office might also be considered a remedy in sub-section 6.[5]

2. Remedies for breach of fiduciary duties

7.003 By way of refresher, the core duty of a fiduciary is one of 'single-minded loyalty'. This was described by Lord Justice Millet in *Bristol & West Building Society v Mothew* as having several facets which include; acting in good faith; not taking unauthorised profits; avoiding conflicts of interest; not acting for his own benefit or that of third parties; without the informed consent of the fiduciary's principle.[6] A fiduciary must also exercise their powers for a proper purpose, the test for which is subjective[7] and which extends to not exercising powers capriciously.[8] In addition, they will owe a fiduciary duty to take account of relevant matters when exercising a power as fiduciary under the rule in *Re Hastings-Bass*.[9] The precise scope of the relevant duty is moulded according to the nature of the parties' relationship,[10] and it will be for the court to determine the scope of the office-holder's obligations.[11] Mere incompetence will not suffice to establish a breach of fiduciary duty.[12] However, conscious impropriety is not required, it seems enough that there be a conscious disclaimer or disregard of the office-holder's responsibilities.[13]

---

2   *Bray v Ford* [1896] AC 44; *McGregor on Damages* (20th edn) at 15-005–15-007.
3   *McGregor on Damages* ibid at 1-002 and 1-011. On an inquiry as to damages on the enforcement of a cross-undertaking in damages in a freezing order, the assessment is made on the same basis, by analogy, as that on which damages for breach of contract is assessed, save that adjustments may have to be made because the court is not strictly awarding compensation for breach of contract: *Abbey Forwarding Ltd v Hone* [2014] EWCA Civ 711.
4   Considered in Chapter 6.
5   Considered in Chapter 3.
6   *Bristol & West Building Society v Mothew* [1998] Ch 1.
7   *Brewer and another (as joint liquidators of ARY Digital UK Ltd) v Iqbal* [2019] EWHC 182 (Ch), [2019] 1 BCLC 487 at [45]; *Hindle v John Cotton Ltd* (1919) 56 Sc LR 625, 630.
8   *Davey v Money* [2018] EWHC 766 (Ch), [2018] Bus LR 1903 at [623].
9   *Re Hastings-Bass (Deceased)* [1975] Ch 25 and see: *Pitt v Holt* [2013] UKSC 26, [2013] 2 AC 108; *Brewer v Iqbal* at [48]; *Re Edennote Ltd* [1996] BCC 718; and *Faryab v Smith* [2001] BPIR 246.
10   *New Zealand Netherlands Society 'Oranje' Inc v Kuys* [1973] 1 WLR 1126, 1130A.
11   *Medsted Associates Ltd v Canaccord Genuity Wealth (International) Ltd* [2019] EWCA Civ 83, [2019] 2 All ER 959 at [45].
12   *Extrasure Travel Insurances Ltd v Scattergood* [2002] EWHC 3093 (Ch), [2003] 1 BCLC 598.
13   *Top Brands Ltd v Sharma* [2014] EWHC 2753, [2015] 2 All ER 581 at [143]–[144], [175].

The significance to a claimant of a duty being fiduciary in nature stems, in part, from the relief **7.004** to which they will be entitled in the event of the duty's breach. Where the relief sought is the payment of money (equitable compensation), different (less stringent) rules as to mitigation and remoteness may apply as would apply in a damages claim and proprietary remedies may be available (including the possibility of tracing). Additionally, while the aim of the remedy is likely to be restitutionary or restorative rather than compensatory,[14] it will commonly include an account of the profits made by the errant fiduciary (which may be more lucrative than simple compensation). Further, losses arising out of a breach of fiduciary duty are usually assessed at the time of judgment with the benefit of hindsight.[15] Relief may also include an order restraining continuation of the breach, and allowing a company to avoid a transaction which is tainted by the breach of fiduciary duty.

The appropriate remedy is likely to be determined by the type of duty breached by an **7.005** office-holder. By way of illustration, the Supreme Court identified three types of duty that will be owed by trustees in *AIB Group (UK) plc v Mark Redler & Co Solicitors*:[16]

(1) a custodial stewardship duty, that is, a duty to preserve the assets of the trust except insofar as the terms of the trust permit the trustee to do otherwise;
(2) a management stewardship duty, that is, a duty to manage the trust property with proper care;
(3) a duty of undivided loyalty, which prohibits the trustee from taking any advantage from his position without the fully informed consent of the beneficiary or beneficiaries.[17]

The Supreme Court then provided a useful summary of the approach to relief that the court **7.006** will take in respect of breaches of each duty.

A breach of the first of these duties, the custodial stewardship duty, will require the party in **7.007** breach to reconstitute the trust fund *in specie* or make good the loss in monetary terms.[18] Historically, the remedy for breach of all of the above duties took the form of orders made on account with the court disallowing (or falsifying) the unauthorised disposal and either requiring the trust fund to be reconstituted *in specie* or ordering that the trustee makes good the loss in monetary terms. Whilst the relief may be described as equitable compensation, it is not compensation for loss; it is restitutionary (or restorative) and is sometimes described as 'substitutive compensation'.[19]

A breach of the second type of duty, the management stewardship duty, is different. Conscious **7.008** wrongdoing is not required (i.e., negligence will suffice) and the remedy is likely to require the party in breach to make good the loss resulting from the breach. This is sometimes called

---

14 *Bristol & West Building Society v Mothew* [1998] Ch 1, 18.
15 *Target Holdings Ltd v Redferns* [1996] AC 421; *Brewer v Iqbal* at [99].
16 *AIB Group (UK) plc v Mark Redler & Co Solicitors* [2014] UKSC 58, [2015] 1 All ER 747. For the avoidance of doubt, the Supreme Court did not directly consider the role of a trustee *in bankruptcy*.
17 *Boardman v Phipps* [1967] 2 AC 46 (HL).
18 *AIB v Redler.*
19 *Libertarian Investments Ltd v Hall* [2014] 1 HKC 368 at [168] (Court of Appeal of Hong Kong) cited with approval by the Court of Appeal in *Interactive Technology Corporation Ltd v Ferster* [2018] EWCA Civ 1594, [2018] 2 P & CR DG22 at [19].

'reparative compensation' albeit that, as Lord Toulson observed in *AIB v Redler* both types of remedy may be fairly described as reparative compensation in a practical sense.

7.009 The third type of breach, the breach of a fiduciary's core duty of undivided loyalty, may result in an order for the party in breach to account for the benefit with such relief being 'primarily restitutionary or restorative rather than compensatory'.[20] Alternatively, the court may order the party in default to compensate the beneficiary of the trust for their losses. It follows that equitable compensation extends to both gain-based or restitutionary relief (i.e., substitutive compensation) and relief which is compensatory in effect (i.e., reparative compensation).[21]

7.010 The appropriate measure of compensation is the difference between what the company or estate had in fact received and the amount which it would have received but for the office-holder's breach. This will normally be assessed at the date of trial, with the benefit of hindsight.[22] Foreseeability of loss is not generally material albeit that it must be shown that the loss was caused by the breach in the sense that it must flow directly from that breach.[23] Further, the claimant will not be required to mitigate their losses. However, losses resulting from clearly unreasonable behaviour on the part of the claimant will be adjudged to flow from that behaviour, and not from the breach.[24]

7.011 Where an office-holder (in breach of their fiduciary duties) obtains a benefit they will be liable to account to the company or the bankruptcy estate for that benefit irrespective of whether the company or the estate could have taken advantage of the same opportunity.[25] Any benefit which results from a breach of fiduciary duty to the principal is held on trust for that principal. The agent cannot rely on his own breach of duty in order to claim the benefit for himself. Rather, he will be assumed to have acted in accordance with his duty and to have acquired the benefit for his principal.[26] Relief is proprietary in nature with the party in breach holding the proceeds of the breach on constructive trust[27] for the benefit of the company or bankruptcy estate. The obligation of the office-holder to account in such circumstances will be strict[28] with the proprietary nature of the relief entitling the company or estate to rely upon equitable tracing (as opposed to the more restrictive common law rules).[29]

3. Remedies for breach of tortious and/or statutory duties

7.012 An office-holder will owe a duty to act with reasonable skill and care in the discharge of their duties both as a result of their statutory duties arising under the Act and in appropriate

---

20   *AIB Group v Redler* at [55]; *Bristol & West Building Society v Mothew* at 711.

21   *Interactive Technology Corporation Ltd v Ferster* [2018] EWCA Civ 1594, [2018] 2 P & CR D59 at [26].

22   *AIB Group v Redler* at [57] (citing *Libertarian Investments* at [168]).

23   Ibid at [136].

24   Ibid at [135]; *Canson Enterprises Ltd v Boughton & Co* [1991] 3 SCR 534 at 552–3.

25   Provided that the opportunity came to the office-holder by reason of his or her office. See e.g., *Boardman v Phipps* [1967] 2 AC 46, [1966] All ER 721; *FHR European Ventures LLP v Mankarious (No 2)* [2014] UKSC 45, [2014] 2 BCLC 145.

26   *First Subsea Ltd v Balltec Ltd* [2017] EWCA Civ 186, [2018] 1 BCLC 20 [36] (citing *FHR European Ventures LLP v Mankarious (No 2)* at [35]–[36]).

27   *FHR European Ventures LLP v Mankarious (No 2)* at [46].

28   Ibid at [8].

29   Ibid at [44].

circumstances where the facts give rise to their owing a duty of care to third parties. By analogy with the regime applicable to company directors, such a duty can arise in both tort and equity.[30] However, the effect of the remedy available under both heads is likely to be identical. As the House of Lords held in *Bristol & West Building Society v Mothew*:[31]

> Although the remedy which equity makes available for breach of the equitable duty of skill and care is equitable compensation rather than damages, this is merely the product of history and in this context is in my opinion a distinction without a difference. Equitable compensation for breach of the duty of skill and care resembles common law damages in that it is awarded by way of compensation to the plaintiff for his loss. There is no reason in principle why the common law rules of causation, remoteness of damage and measure of damages should not be applied by analogy in such a case.

In *AIB Group v Redler*, Lord Reed noted that in *Target Holdings*, Millett LJ was not considering the liability of a trustee and also that 'the application by analogy of "the common law rules" is complicated by the fact that there is no single set of common law rules'. Nevertheless, *Bristol & West Building Society v Mothew* remains good law and it is notable that in *Brewer v Iqbal* (which contains a lengthy exposition of the relevant principles in this area) the court was content to proceed on the basis that, on the facts of the case, there was no requirement to consider separately the cause of action arising in equity as distinct from that arising in tort.[32] **7.013**

The primary remedy for a breach of a defendant's duty of care is damages. The assessment of damages is essentially a 'jury question' in which a judge will sometimes find themselves needing to do the best they can.[33] In *Capita Alternative Fund Services v Drivers Jonas*, the Court of Appeal accepted counsel's submissions as to the approach which the court will take in the following terms:[34] **7.014**

> The exercise required is not about the Court reaching an immaculate or absolute value, but about reaching the most likely figure on the basis of the evidence it has heard. That evidence may well not be perfect, indeed it is unlikely ever to be so.

The court will not adopt a mechanistic approach to calculation and whilst it will not engage in guesswork to make good a failure on the part of a claimant to adduce available evidence, the fact that the loss cannot be quantified with certainty will not relieve a defendant from the need to pay damages.[35] As Norris J stated in *Breitenfeld UK Ltd v Harrison*:[36] **7.015**

> The fact that damages cannot be assessed with certainty does not relieve the wrongdoer of paying damages. The court's task is to make whatever findings it can on the evidence before it, recognising

---

30   *O'Keefe (In Their Capacity as Joint Liquidators of Level One Residential (Jersey) Ltd and Special Opportunity Holdings Ltd) v Caner* [2017] EWHC 1105 (Ch), [2017] WTLR 615 at [93]–[94].
31   *Bristol & West Building Society v Mothew* [1996] 4 All ER 698, 711.
32   *Brewer v Iqbal* at [56].
33   *Capita Alternative Fund Services (Guernsey) Ltd v Drivers Jonas (a firm)* [2012] EWCA Civ 1417, [2013] 1 EGLR 119 at [43(i)] (citing *Dennard v PricewaterhouseCoopers* LLP [2010] EWHC 812 (Ch)). See also *Breitenfeld UK Ltd v Harrison* [2015] EWHC 399 (Ch), [2015] 2 BCLC 275 at [120].
34   *Capita v Drivers Jonas (a firm)* at [43(i)].
35   Ibid at [123].
36   *Breitenfeld UK Ltd v Harrison* at [122].

that the evidence is unlikely ever to be perfect. But a claimant who obviously fails to obtain and present available, good quality, precise evidence runs a risk that the court may be unpersuaded by such evidence as is produced, because the court will not embark upon guesswork to make good a failure to adduce reliable evidence.

7.016 Where a claim is advanced in conversion or under the so-called economic torts, the focus remains on the loss suffered by the claimant rather than upon the defendant's gain,[37] thereby reflecting the compensatory nature of relief in tort.[38]

4. Remedies for breach of contract

7.017 Office-holders may enter into contractual relations with third parties in a wide variety of different circumstances, albeit that they are likely to take steps to minimise the extent to which they incur personal contractual obligations. They may however contract for the provision of services, causes of action may be contractually assigned and claims vested in the office-holder personally may be contractually compromised. In the event that the contractual counterparty proceeds against the office-holder to enforce the terms of the parties' bargain, the usual principles of the law of contract will apply.

7.018 The principal remedy for a breach of contract is an award of damages. In addition, and in appropriate circumstances, the party who institutes proceedings may also seek equitable remedies in the form of injunctive relief or specific performance. When assessing damages, the general rule is that damages are based on the claimant's loss[39] and, unlike breaches of fiduciary duty, do not focus on the defendant's gain.[40] In assessing those damages the court will look to place the victim in the same position as they would have been in had the contract in fact been performed.[41] The protection of the contracting party's expectation interest can be contrasted with the tortious measure of damages which seeks to put the tort victim in the same position that he would have been in had the tort not been committed. Unlike a party who is the victim of a breach of fiduciary duty, the claimant in a claim for breach of contract will be under a positive obligation to mitigate his loss. Further, the loss suffered must not be too remote to be recoverable[42] with that test being more restrictive in contract than in tort[43] or for breach of fiduciary duty.[44]

---

37 Ibid at [120].

38 Cf. *Morris-Garner v One Step (Support) Ltd* [2018] UKSC 20, [2018] 2 W.L.R. 135 at [95].

39 Exceptions to the general rule include circumstances where a party seeks *Wrotham Park* or 'negotiating' damages and those 'exceptional' cases where damages are not 'sufficient' to compensate the claimant (e.g., *Attorney-General v Blake* [2001] 1 AC 268).

40 *Tito v Waddell (No 2)* [1977] Ch 106, 332.

41 *Robinson v Harman* (1848) 1 Ex 850, 855.

42 *Hadley v Baxendale* (156) 9 E.R. 145, (1854) 9 Exch 341; *Victoria Laundry (Windsor) Ltd v Newman Industries Ltd* [1949] 2 KB 528; *Transfield Shipping Inc v Mercator Shipping Inc (The Achilleas)* [2009] 1 AC 61.

43 *Wellesley Partners LLP v Withers LLP* [2015] EWCA Civ 1146, [2016] 2 WLR 1351.

44 Cf. *AIB Group v Redler* at [136].

5. Impact of release

It must be noted that where an IP has obtained their release pursuant to the provisions of the **7.019** Insolvency Act 1986 they will be discharged from liability in respect of claims against them, with some exceptions: see Chapter 6, section C.2 above for a fuller discussion of this topic.

6. Removal of IP from office

The ability to seek the removal of an IP from office is a powerful tool in the arsenal of an **7.020** aggrieved party. As a general rule, the stakeholder(s) entitled to appoint an office-holder also have the power to remove him or her from office. Where the matter is not capable of democratic resolution (i.e., by a decision-making process that can appoint an alternative office-holder), removal can also be effected by order of the court. The circumstances in which removal will be contemplated are discussed in detail in Chapter 3 above. Removal is not a remedy per se, because while there must be a 'good ground' for removing the sitting office-holder, it is not necessary to show any personal unfitness or misconduct on their part (what is a good ground depends on the purpose of the office and the facts of the case).[45] However, such applications do commonly arise in the context of or as a precursor to a wider liability claim against that office-holder, particularly in respect of conflicts of interest.[46]

B. CAUSATION

In order to recover damages in proceedings against an IP, a claimant will need to establish that **7.021** the wrongful act or omission of the IP caused (both as a matter of fact and as a matter of legal attribution) the relevant loss with the burden of establishing causation being upon the claimant.[47] In doing so, it will need to be established that the damage claimed is attributable to the breach of duty relied upon[48] as a claimant cannot recover in respect of a loss which falls outside the scope of the duty owed.[49] Where the breach relied upon is an omission, the claimant will need to prove that compliance with the defendant's duty would have prevented

---

45   In the context of administrators, see *Sisu Capital Fund Ltd v Tucker* [2005] EWHC 2170 (Ch), [2006] BCC 463; *Clydesdale Financial Services Ltd v Smailes* [2009] EWHC 1745 (Ch); *Finnerty v Clark* [2011] EWCA Civ 858, [2012] 1 BCLC 286. In the context of liquidations, see *Re Keypak Homecare Ltd* (1987) 3 BCC 558. *Re Keypak* emphasises that the burden lies on the applicant to show cause (which, Millett J observed, is different to the court thinking it fit to remove the liquidator), and the court will act and remove a liquidator if it is to the advantage of those interested in the assets of the company. Such applications are most common in the bankruptcy context, and examples include *Re Birdi (Miles v Price)* [2019] EWHC 291 (Ch), [2019] BPIR 498 (removal is to be measured by reference to the real substantial, honest interests of the process, and to the purpose for which the office-holder was appointed).

46   For example, in *Sisu v Tucker, Beattie v Smailes; Re VE Interactive* [2018] EWHC 186 (Ch), albeit one answer to a potential conflict might be to appoint a conflict liquidator: *Re York Gas Ltd* [2010] EWHC 2275 (Ch), [2011] BCC 447; *Davey v Money* [2018] EWHC 766 (Ch).

47   *Lexi Holdings (in administration) v Luqman* [2008] EWHC 1639 (Ch), [2008] 2 BCLC 725 at [69] (overturned on the facts).

48   *Lexi Holdings v Luqman* [2009] EWCA Civ 117, [2009] 2 BCLC 1 at [36].

49   *South Australia Asset Management Corp v York Montague Ltd* [1997] AC 191 (HL), 218; *Hughes-Holland v BPE Solicitors* [2017] UKSC 21.

the damage.[50] Such an approach has been described as requiring the construction of 'a necessarily hypothetical edifice so as to ascertain what would probably have happened if the relevant duties had been performed, so as to ascertain whether in that event the losses actually suffered ... would, probably, not have been suffered.'[51]

7.022 The fact that recovery is sought by way of an application within the insolvency proceedings[52] as opposed to fresh proceedings does not alter the need to establish causative loss and it will be for the applicant to properly plead their case on causation.[53] As Jonathan Gaunt QC[54] described it in *French & Mummery v Cipollettar:*[55]

> In my judgment, it is quite clear from the authorities [...] that proof of loss to the Company is a necessary ingredient of a cause of action for breach of fiduciary duty or negligence under section 212. I do not accept that the section justifies a laxer approach to pleading than would be called for in a writ action. In my judgment the Defendant director is entitled to know what case is being made against him and it is necessary that the Claimant should (a) allege loss to the Company and (b) at least make clear the types of loss that are alleged to have been caused by the breaches of duty or negligence in question.

7.023 A distinction needs to be drawn between breaches of non-fiduciary and fiduciary duty. In respect of the former, the claimant will need to establish foreseeability of loss (also known as remoteness) and mitigation to the common law standard. In respect of the latter, different rules apply and it will be sufficient for a claimant to establish causation on the 'but for' test.[56]

7.024 A distinction also needs to be drawn between breaches of tortious duty and breaches of contract since the test for whether damage is too remote differs slightly between them. In contract law the question is whether the damage can be said to be in the reasonable contemplation of the parties at the time of contracting, either in the ordinary course of things or in the special circumstances known by them.[57] It has been recently clarified that the enquiry is really about identifying the common expectation as to the scope of each party's assumption of responsibility and therefore liability under the contract.[58] In tort law, the question is whether the kind of damage suffered was reasonably foreseeable by the defendant at the time of the breach of duty.[59] The defendant will be liable for any type of damage which is reasonably

---

50 *Bishopsgate Investment Management Ltd (in liquidation) v Maxwell (No 2)* [1993] BCLC 1282; *Cohen v Selby* [2001] 1 BCLC 176 at [30] (see also *Dickinson v NAL Realisations (Staffordshire) Ltd* [2017] EWHC 28 (Ch), [2018] 1 BCLC 623 at [160]).

51 *Lexi Holdings (in administration) v Luqman* [2008] EWHC 1639 (Ch), [2008] 2 BCLC 725 at [28]. Cf. *Lexi Holdings plc v Luqman* [2009] EWCA Civ 117, [2009] 2 BCLC 1 at [48] and see *Weavering Capital (UK) Ltd v Dabhia* [2013] EWCA Civ 71.

52 For example, by way of IA 1986 s212.

53 *Cohen v Selby* [2001] 1 BCLC 176 [20]; *Raithatha (as liquidator of Halal Monitoring Committee Ltd) v Baig* [2017] EWHC 2059, [2018] BPIR 743 (Ch) at [25]; *Re E D Games Ltd, French v Cipolletta* [2009] EWHC 223 (Ch).

54 Sitting as a Deputy High Court Judge.

55 *Re E D Games Ltd, French v Cipolletta* [2009] EWHC 223 (Ch) at [16].

56 *Target Holdings Ltd v Redferns* [1996] AC 421; *AIB Group v Redler.*

57 *Hadley v Baxendale* (156) 9 E.R. 145, (1854) 9 Exch 341.

58 *Transfield Shipping Inc v Mercator Shipping Inc* [2008] UKHL 48 *(The Achilleas).*

59 *Overseas Tankship (UK) Ltd v Morts Dock and Engineering Co Ltd (The Wagon Mound No 1)* [1961] AC 388.

foreseeable as liable to happen even in the most unusual case, unless the risk is so small that a reasonable man would in the whole circumstances feel justified in neglecting it.[60]

The court's approach to establishing causation in the context of claims against office-holders is demonstrated by the decision in *Top Brands Ltd v Sharma*.[61] In that case, the applicants were two creditors of the company who brought proceedings under IA 1986 s212 against the company's liquidator seeking an account of monies which had been misapplied by the liquidator. The relevant payments had been authorised by the liquidator in circumstances where she believed that the payees were nominees of one of the company's former customers but where it subsequently transpired that the instruction was fraudulent. **7.025**

The liquidator sought to argue that the starting point was that the loss was caused by the sophisticated fraud which had resulted in the payments being made. HHJ Simon Barker QC (sitting as a Judge of the High Court) rejected the submission and held that the loss was caused by the liquidator's negligence in that had she acted in accordance with the relevant standard: (i) she would have been aware that the true nature and purpose of the company had been to engage in VAT fraud; (ii) the solicitor instructed by the liquidator would have been differently instructed and would have been unlikely to have given that advice which he did; and (iii) any attempt to 'set up' the liquidator to make the payment would have failed. **7.026**

Whilst obtaining legal advice may in many circumstances insulate an office-holder from liability insofar as they follow and act in accordance with that advice,[62] where obtaining that advice (as in *Top Brands*) does not provide a defence to breach, it seems (at least where the advisers were competent and their instruction not negligent) that the provision of that advice will not break the chain of causation. **7.027**

C. MEASURE OF LOSS

1. The contractual and tortious measures

The classic contractual measure of loss is that which places the claimant in the position they should have been in had the contract been properly performed. This is sometimes described as the 'expectation' measure. The central tenet is the fact that the parties had a particular bargain, and the defaulting party must see that come to fruition either by performance or by damages to mimic the effect of performance so far as possible.[63] **7.028**

By contrast, the tortious measure of loss is often stated to be that which is required to put the claimant in the position they would have been in had the tort not occurred.[64] This involves consideration of the relevant hypothetical counterfactual: what would have occurred *but for* the defendant's breach? If the claimant can establish they would have avoided suffering a loss or **7.029**

---

60 *Heron II* [1969] 1 AC 350.
61 *Top Brands Ltd v Sharma* [2014] EWHC 2753, [2015] 2 All ER 581.
62 *Brewer v Iqbal; Pro4Sport Ltd (in liquidation) v Adams* [2015] EWHC 2540 (Ch), [2016] 1 BCLC 257.
63 See generally *McGregor on Damages* (20th edn) at 4–002 ff.
64 Subject to the *SAAMCO* cap, discussed below in subsection 3.

gained a benefit, they can claim damages to reflect their loss. Most cases involving IPs acting as office-holders are likely to be measured on the tortious approach.

7.030 Take the example of an IP who has, in breach of duty, sold an asset at an undervalue because they did not properly expose it to the market. The relevant enquiry will be the price which could have been achieved if a competent sale process had been followed. Thus in *McAteer v Lismore*,[65] where a trustee in bankruptcy had been negligent in selling the bankrupt's former matrimonial home without having actively marketed or advertised it for nearly a 5-year period before the sale (such that the property was not properly exposed to the market), the undervalue calculation was made on the balance of probabilities based on expert evidence adduced as to what the asset would have achieved at the time of sale if the marketing had been carried out properly. We have referred carefully to 'what the asset would have achieved if properly marketed' and not the 'market value'.[66] These will often be the same, but not invariably. For instance, where a 'special interest purchaser' had made an offer to pay over reasonable market value to secure a property they wanted because of the marriage value with their adjacent land. In that case, if the IP negligently failed to pursue such an offer, and the offer was genuine and proceedable, arguably the loss to the estate would be the difference between the price which would have been achieved on that particular sale, although in excess of the ordinary market value, and the actual price achieved.[67]

7.031 Where the claimant is relying only upon their own actions to establish their loss, this must be established upon the balance of probabilities – it must be more likely than not that the claimant would have acted in such a way as to have avoided the loss or achieved the benefit for which damages are sought, in which case the full amount of the loss will be recoverable as damages.

2. Loss of a chance

7.032 Where the hypothetical counterfactual involves the actions of a third party, the court can award a figure representing the 'lost chance' of the relevant outcome materialising.[68] This principle has been recently succinctly stated by the Court of Appeal thus:[69]

> where the claimant's loss depends, not on what he would have done, but on the hypothetical acts of a third party, the claimant first needs to prove (to the usual civil standard) that there was a real or substantial, rather than a speculative, chance that the third party would have acted so as to confer the benefit in question, thereby establishing causation; but that the evaluation of the lost chance, if causation is proved, is a matter of quantification of damages in percentage terms.

---

65 [2012] NICh 7, [2012] BPIR 812.

66 Defined by the Royal Institute of Chartered Surveyors ('RICS') as:

> [t]he estimated amount for which an asset or liability should exchange on the valuation date between a willing buyer and a willing seller in an arm's length transaction after proper marketing where the parties had each acted knowledgeably, prudently and without compulsion.

67 For some consideration of a case involving an alleged special purchaser and special purchase value in a receivership context, see *Devon Commercial Property Ltd v Barnett* [2019] EWHC 700 (Ch).

68 As recognised in the seminal case of *Allied Maples Group Ltd v Simmons & Simmons* [1995] 1 WLR 1602.

69 *McGill v The Sports and Entertainment Media Group* [2016] EWCA Civ 1063 at [60].

It would seem that a loss of chance measure is justified where due to the passage of time, or because obtaining disclosure or witness evidence has become impossible, or because the court may consider it absurd for a claimant to recover in full if their prospects are assessed at 51 per cent but nothing if their prospects are assessed at 49 per cent.[70]

The measure of damages in such a case is the sum which the claimant would have recovered in **7.033** the underlying transaction multiplied by the percentage chance of the claimant making that recovery, giving rise to the moniker: a 'loss of a chance' claim. Such a claim might be made, for instance, where an IP fails to issue a claim belonging to the estate before it is extinguished by limitation – losing the chance of success in that claim. To recover, it would not be necessary to show prospects were greater than 50 per cent. Instead, a claim can be made for the lost chance, multiplying the likely value of the claim by its percentage chance of success.[71] The decision will be one for the trial judge, and unlikely to be amenable to appeal. For example, in *Assetco Plc v Grant Thornton*, Bryan J reached an assessment of greater than 90 per cent for each contingency in the counterfactual, and had therefore been entitled to treat it as being a 'racing certainty'; it was a conclusion of certainty, as understood within the confines of judicial decision-making.[72]

The chance must be more than speculative or the claim will be dismissed, as nothing of real **7.034** value will have been lost. Thus in *Prosser v Castle Sanderson*,[73] a professional negligence claim was brought by the debtor against the IP who had become the supervisor of his IVA, where the allegations of negligence concerned the lack of advice given to the debtor during the course of a break taken after the relevant creditors' meeting to consider the IVA proposals had begun. The court was not satisfied that there was a realistic chance of a better outcome even if the debtor had been properly advised to seek an adjournment (no doubt informed by the judge's 'dim view' of the claimant and his activities). The judge thought the chances of proper and full information being provided to creditors and for them to change their mind as to whether or not to accept the proposals were 'very speculative indeed'.[74] However, in professional negligence cases lost chances of as low as 20 per cent have been found to be sufficient to attract compensation.[75]

---

70 *Perry v Raleys Solicitors* [2019] UKSC 5 at [17]–[18] (Lord Briggs JSC), citing *Hanif v Middleweeks* [2000] Lloyd's Rep PN 920 at [17] (Mance LJ).

71 In this lost litigation scenario it is important to understand that the relevant enquiry is not, or not ordinarily, a trial within a trial: it is the prospects in the lost litigation and not the hypothetical decision in the lost trial which has to be investigated; see *Sharif v Garrett & Co (a firm)* [2001] EWCA Civ 1269; *Dixon v Clement Jones Solicitors (a firm)* [2004] EWCA Civ 1005. That said, in *Kitchen v RAF Association* [1958] 1 WLR 563 the court rejected the notion that a claim which was bad in law might still justify a nuisance payment and, by an extension to this principle, in *Perry v Raleys*, the Supreme Court has held that there may also be a trial of whether the claimant would have made the original (lost) claim honestly. These provide some inroads into the principle that there is to be no 'trial within a trial' in lost claims cases. The focus is on whether it is said to be fair to require a claimant to prove something on the balance of probabilities and where this is a point of law, or something which involved acts to be taken by them, then there is no inherent lack of fairness in requiring them to do so. Query however, how this can be reconciled with cases where a point of law arose but the case is most likely to have settled in the earlier proceedings. It ought to be open for the claimant in those circumstances to seek the sum of money likely to have been achieved on a hypothetical assessment, at least outside cases which are simply nuisance claims (obviously bad in law) and dishonest claims.

72 [2020] EWCA Civ 1511 at [206]–[209].

73 [2002] EWCA Civ 1140, [2002] BPIR 1163. See comment at Co. L.N. 2003, 11, 6.

74 At [89].

75 See *Ball v Druces & Attlee* (No 2) [2004] EWHC 1402 (QB).

3. Scope of duty: the *SAAMCO* cap

7.035 In recent times the courts have begun to favour an approach which, instead of simply looking at what would have happened but for the breach and seeking so far as possible to place the claimant in that position, instead limits a defendant's liability to those consequences of their negligent acts which are acts attributable to that which made the act wrongful. This is sometimes referred to as 'the *SAAMCO* cap', after the first case where it was articulated.[76] A good example of the application of *SAAMCO* in the context of IP liabilities is the case of *DeMarco v Perkins*.[77] The appellant, Mr DeMarco, was adjudged bankrupt in March 1997. The respondent IPs were retained to act on his behalf with regard to obtaining an IVA and a subsequent annulment of his bankruptcy order. Negligently, they failed to advise him that it was necessary to seek the annulment prior to discharge from bankruptcy, with the result that Mr DeMarco got his automatic discharge in March 2000 and lost the opportunity to seek an annulment via an IVA. The relevant hypothetical was that, if the IP had not been negligent, Mr DeMarco would have been an annulled bankrupt, rather than a discharged bankrupt.

7.036 Mr DeMarco argued that the only way for the IP properly to compensate him was to pay off all his pre-bankruptcy debts, thereby allowing him to obtain an annulment by a different means. His debts were such that he claimed in the region of £170,000. The trial judge, and the Court of Appeal disagreed. The IP's 'wrongful act' was the failure to warn Mr DeMarco that he could exit the bankruptcy through an IVA, rather than by discharge, only if he put an acceptable proposal to his creditors before discharge. The IP should, therefore, be liable only for the foreseeable consequences of not putting an acceptable proposal to the creditors within the proper time, which were that he was discharged after three years and his post-bankruptcy debts were eradicated, but he was left with the stigma of being a discharged bankrupt. This is the consequence of acts *'attributable to that which made the act wrongful'*. The Court of Appeal therefore awarded damages of £6,000 for stigma/loss of reputation.

4. Mitigation and collateral benefits

7.037 A further constraint on the measure of loss is the principle that a defendant cannot be held liable for losses that the claimant could reasonably have been expected to avoid.[78] The essence of the principle is that if the claimant unreasonably fails to act to mitigate its loss, or unreasonably acts so as to increase its loss, the law treats those actions as having broken the chain of causation in respect of that proportion of the damages and measures them as if the claimant had instead acted reasonably.[79] As a result the claimant is said to have a 'duty to mitigate'. It should however be noted that this is not an enforceable legal duty, but a shorthand recognition that if the claimant fails to act reasonably their recoverable loss will be affected by

---

76 *South Australia Asset Management Corporation v York Montague Ltd* [1997] AC 191 (HL). It has more recently been described by the Supreme Court as being a tool for determining the loss flowing from negligently wrong information as opposed to the loss flowing from entering into the transaction at all: *Hughes-Holland v BPE Solicitors* [2017] UKSC 21 at [45] (Lord Sumption).

77 [2006] EWCA Civ 188.

78 Alternatively the constraint may be analysed as an aspect of the law on causation, which operated as a filter serving to limit the matters for which a wrongdoer is legally responsible. See e.g., *Hughes-Holland v BPE Solicitors* at [20].

79 In other words, the law assumes the claimant will act reasonably, even if he does not.

that failure. This includes both a passive element[80] and an active element.[81] If the claimant is found to have acted reasonably, then they can recover their actual losses, including the cost of mitigation even if it has not been successful.[82] Conversely, where steps taken in mitigation lead to a financial benefit to the claimant, then that may be taken into account too and credit given to the defendant for that benefit in the calculation of loss.[83] A separate, but closely related concept which may impact on the measure of loss is the concept of collateral benefits obtained in the course of subsequent steps being taken by the claimant. If the court considers they are truly collateral then they are not taken into account. There is no universal test which is applied by the courts in this respect, though causative proximity will often be relevant.[84]

D. INTEREST

1. Sources of the obligation to pay interest

Lord Goff once lamented that 'one would expect to find, in any developed system of law, a **7.038** comprehensive and reasonably simple set of principles by virtue of which the courts have power to award interest … Sadly, however, that is not the position in English law'.[85] Instead, the main bases for an award of interest by the court (prior to a judgment having been granted[86]) are:

(i)   pursuant to a right granted by contract;
(ii)   under the court's equitable jurisdiction;
(iii)   as a discrete head of damages, at common law; or
(iv)   under any statute which makes express provision for the payment of interest.

(a) Contract

Many commercial contracts provide for interest to be charged when payment of the contract **7.039** price (or other sum payable under the contract) is late. This express right to contractual interest arises without a court judgment (or tribunal award) but may be the subject of a claim to court if unpaid when due. An express interest clause will usually specify whether the interest is to be simple or compound and the period for which it is chargeable.

---

80   That is, deliberately not to make matters worse.
81   That is, a duty on claimants to take steps to improve their position. See Restatement (Second) of Contracts §350 (American Law Institute).
82   *Lagden v O'Connor* [2004] 1 AC 1067 at [78] (Lord Scott).
83   See e.g., *British Westinghouse Electric & Manufacturing Co Ltd v Underground Electric Railways Co of London Ltd (No 2)* [1912] AC 673 (where faulty turbines were replaced after three years and the replacement increased the claimant's profitability), and *Spar Shipping AS v Grand China Logistics Holding (Group) Co. Ltd* [2015] EWHC 718 (Comm).
84   For a recent discussion of the principles see *Globalia Business Travel SAU (formerly TravelPlan S.A.U) of Spain v Fulton Shipping Inc of Panama* [2017] UKSC 43.
85   *Westdeutsche Landesbank Girozentrale v Islington LBC* [1996] AC 669, 684 (Lord Goff).
86   Once judgment is granted, interest is payable under statute. High Court judgments carry interest under the Judgments Act 1838 s17(1). The rate of interest on High Court judgment debts in sterling has been 8% since April 1993: see the Judgment Debts (Rate of Interest) Order 1993 SI 1993/564. Further, most County Court judgments over £5,000 also carry interest pursuant to the County Courts Act 1984 s74, subject to some exceptions (which are outside the scope of this text).

7.040 To be effective after judgment, such a clause must expressly state that it applies after judgment, as well as before. If not, the right to contractual interest will end at judgment, as a result of the 'merger' principle[87] such that the creditor is no longer entitled to contractual interest, but may be entitled to statutory interest on the judgment debt. An express interest clause will displace the wide discretionary powers of the courts to decide the principal, period and rate of interest up to judgment (dealt with in section (d) below).

(b) Equity

7.041 Under the court's general equitable jurisdiction, simple interest can be awarded as an adjunct to equitable remedies such as specific performance, rescission and taking of an account. Further, simple or compound interest can be awarded against a fiduciary accountable for profits made from their position, to ensure they do not make a profit from their own wrongdoing.[88]

7.042 The court's equitable jurisdiction to award compound interest against a non-fiduciary was considered in *FM Capital Partners Ltd v Marino*.[89] The claim was for an account as equitable compensation for dishonest assistance (as distinct from a claim for common law damages). Cockerill J held that, although compound interest was most clearly applicable to cases where money had been obtained and retained by fraud or misapplied by a fiduciary, the balance of case law favoured the view that compound interest can also be awarded against a dishonest assistant who is not a fiduciary, making the assistant's liability co-extensive with that of the fiduciary/trustee whom he has assisted.

(c) Common law

7.043 The question of when interest was available at common law was helpfully addressed and clarified by the House of Lords in *Sempra Metals Ltd v IRC*.[90] While an unparticularised claim for interest as general damages is impermissible, the Lords indicated unanimously that simple or compound interest should, in principle, be recoverable as an independent head of loss, subject to the usual rules of proof of loss and remoteness. The actual interest loss, which may be the cost to the claimant of borrowing money, or the loss of an opportunity to invest promised money, must be proved. The proof required will depend on the nature of the loss and the circumstances of the case, and there are no special rules for the proof of facts in this area.[91] While *Sempra Metals* involved a cause of action in contract and restitution, the Court of Appeal confirmed the principle also applies to tortious claims in *Parabola Investments ltd v Brownwallia Cal Ltd*.[92] Further clarification must also be given in light of the Supreme Court's decision in *Prudential Assurance Co Ltd v Revenue and Customs Commissioners*,[93] which in

---

87   See *Director General of Fair Trading v First National Bank plc* [2001] UKHL 52; *Parr v Tiuta International Ltd* [2016] EWHC 2 (QB).

88   *Westdeutsche Landesbank Girozentrale v Islington LBC* [1996] AC 669 (HL), 701.

89   [2019] EWHC 725 (Comm).

90   [2007] UKHL 34, [2008] 1 AC 561.

91   At [95]–[96] (Lord Nicholls).

92   [2010] EWCA Civ 486. Examples of cases where claims for interest as damages were rejected for lack of evidence include: *Cassa di Risparmio della Repubblica di San Marino SpA v Barclays Bank* Ltd [2011] EWHC 484 (Comm); *JSC BTA Bank v Ablyazov* [2013] EWHC 867 (Comm) and *Mortgage Express v Countrywide Surveyors Ltd* [2016] EWHC 1830 (Ch).

93   [2018] UKSC 39.

practice has significantly curtailed the availability of awards of compound interest in the context of unjust enrichment claims.

(d) Statute

Simple interest is recoverable, at the discretion of the court, under various statutes the most important of which in respect of claims against IPs are s35A of the Senior Courts Act 1981 for claims in the High Court and its County Court equivalent, s69 of the County Courts Act 1984. The statutory discretion to award simple interest is an additional power which does not displace the common law remedy, but it will not be awarded where interest already runs under a contract. Although at the discretion of the court, in practice interest awards are made as a matter of course to the successful party. **7.044**

2. Exercise of the court's discretion

Statutory interest payable under s35A of the Senior Courts Act 1981 and s69 of the County Courts Act 1984 is sometimes referred to as discretionary interest because of the breadth of the court's discretion in awarding it. The rate of interest is at such rate as the court thinks fit or as rules of court provide, and may be calculated at different rates for different periods. The period of interest runs for all or any part of the period between the date that the cause of action arose and the date of payment or the date of judgment. What is clear is that the purpose of interest is to compensate the claimant in respect of money they should have had, not punish the defendant.[94] Some guidance can be gleaned from the usual treatment of claims to interest in the authorities. **7.045**

(a) Period

While there is no invariable rule, interest will generally run from the date of accrual of the cause of action in respect of money then due or loss which then accrues; and in respect of loss which accrues at a date between accrual of the cause of action and judgment, from such date.[95] **7.046**

Factors which may persuade the court to depart from this general rule include the position of the defendant (who may not know and have no way of knowing about the claimant's cause of action, in which case it might be appropriate for interest to run from the date of the claim itself) and the conduct of the claimant (who may have delayed unreasonably in prosecuting the claim, or otherwise lulled the defendant into a false sense of security).[96] **7.047**

---

94 See e.g., *Kuwait Airways Corp v Kuwait Insurance SAK* [2000] EWHC 191 (Comm); *Tate & Lyle Industries Ltd v Greater London Council* [1982] 1 WLR 149 (QB); *Banque Keyser Ullmann SA v Skandia (UK) Insurance Co Ltd* Lloyd's Rep at [1896] 1 Lloyd's Rep 336.

95 For a brief discussion as to when this might arise in an insolvency context, albeit not involving a claim against an IP, see *Re DCL Hire Ltd (UK)* [2019] EWHC 2086 (Ch).

96 See e.g., *Birkett v Hayes* [1982] 1 WLR 816, (CA):

Far too often there is unjustifiable delay in bringing an action to trial. It is, in my view, wrong that interest should run during a time which can properly be called unjustifiable delay after the date of the writ. During that time the plaintiff will have been kept out of the sum awarded to him by his own fault. The fact that the defendants have had the use of the sum during that time is no good reason for excusing that fault and allowing interest to run during that time.

See also *Derby Resources AG v Blue Corinth Marine Co Ltd (No 2) (The 'Athenian Harmony')* [1998] 2 Lloyd's Rep 425, 427.

7.048   In *Claymore Services Ltd v Nautilus Properties Ltd* [97] Jackson J derived three propositions from a review of authorities. First, where a claimant has delayed unreasonably in commencing or prosecuting proceedings, the court may exercise its discretion either to disallow interest for a period or to reduce the rate of interest. Second, in exercising that discretion the court must take a realistic view of delay. In the case of business disputes, litigation is for all parties an unwelcome distraction from their proper business, and it is not reasonable to expect any party to take every litigious step at the first possible moment, or to concentrate on litigation to the exclusion of all else. Thus delay should only be characterised as unreasonable when, after making due allowances for the circumstances, it can be seen that the claimant has neglected or declined to pursue his claim for a significant period. Third, when determining what disallowance or reduction of interest should be made to mark a period of unreasonable delay, the court should bear in mind that the defendant has had the use of the money during that period of delay. Having regard to those three propositions, Jackson J held that the defendant should pay interest but at 2 per cent above base rate being the minimum rate that the claimant would have to have paid to borrow the same amount as the debt.

7.049   There are no strict rules as to the manner in which delay on the part of a claimant might affect an interest award. One common approach is to disallow the delay period from the total possible period of interest from the accrual of the cause of action to judgment.[98] Another approach is to allow interest only from the accrual of the cause of action to the date the matter ought to have come to trial, if it had been pursued with reasonable diligence, or to delay the start of the running of interest to reflect the fact that the claimant delayed starting proceedings.

(b)   Rate

7.050   A broad-brush approach is taken to determine what rate of interest is just and appropriate. In commercial cases, the rate of interest awarded is usually (although not invariably) based upon the estimated rate at which the claimant[99] could have borrowed the sum of which they had been deprived, not what they could have expected as a return had they had it to invest.[100] Historically there was a tendency, if not a presumption, for the commercial court to award interest at base rate + 1 per cent, which could be displaced by evidence that this would be unfair or otherwise inappropriate[101] (and claimants who are individuals could sometimes persuade the

---

97   [2007] EWHC 805 (TCC), [2007] BLR 452.

98   See e.g., *Oyesanya v Mid-Yorkshire Hospital NHS Trust* [2015] EWCA Civ 1049.

99   Although note that the courts do not have regard to the specific rate at which a particular claimant might have borrowed funds, instead considering their general characteristics in order to decide whether to assess interest at a rate that is higher or lower than conventional. See *Tate & Lyle v Greater London Council* [1982] 1 WLR 149, 154; *Jaura v Ahmed* [2002] EWCA Civ 210 at [25]; *Fiona Trust & Holding Corporation v Privalov* [2011] EWHC 664 (Comm) at [16]; *Attrill v Dresdner Kleinwort Ltd* [2012] EWHC 1468 (QB) at [2]; *Persimmon Homes (South Coast) Ltd v Hall* [2012] EWHC 2429 at [10]–[17] and *West v Ian Finlay and Associates (A Firm)* [2013] EWHC 868 (TCC) at [75].

100   *Tate and Lyle Food; Shearson Lehman Hutton Inc v Maclaine Watson and Co Ltd (No 2)* [1990] 3 All ER 723. However, this could be departed from in the right case, see e.g., *Bataillon v Shone* [2015] EWHC 3177 (QB), where interest was awarded to the claimants at c 20 per cent, being 'the sort of money that they would have earned if that capital had been placed in investments elsewhere' at [22] (HHJ).

101   As confirmed in *Kitcatt v MMS UK Holdings Ltd* [2017] EWHC 786 (Comm).

Court to go up to 3 per cent[102] or even 5 per cent[103] above base). However, this presumption may no longer be particularly useful given that current interest rates are the lowest in modern history.[104]

3. Pleading a claim for interest

7.051 A claim for interest must be pleaded. CPR rr16.4(1)(b) and (2) require the claimant to state in the particulars of claim (or counterclaim) that they are seeking interest and to state whether they are claiming it under a contract, an enactment and if so which or some other basis and if so which. Further, if the claim is for a specified amount of money, the claimant must state:

(i)   the percentage rate at which interest is claimed;
(ii) the date from which it is claimed;
(iii) the date to which it is calculated, not later than the date of issue of the claim form;
(iv) total amount of interest claimed to the date of calculation; and
(v)   the daily rate of interest at which interest accrues after the date of calculation.

7.052 A failure to plead the matters above will need to be corrected by an application to amend the statement of case, which will engage the usual considerations for such an application. In *Zagora Management v Zurich*[105] the defendant argued that they would be prejudiced by a late application to amend the particulars of claim to include a claim for discretionary interest because they did not have an opportunity to respond to such a pleading, engage in disclosure or adduce lay or expert evidence on the proper rate and period for the interest to run. The court concluded it was not unfair to the defendant to allow the late amendment given the well-established approach by which interest claims are disposed of by the courts and the fact the court was not concerned with the personal circumstances of the claimants. It concluded that further evidence and exploration suggested by the defendant to be necessary to do justice to them was irrelevant and thus unnecessary.[106]

E. INSURANCE AND PROFESSIONAL INDEMNITY REQUIREMENTS

1. Introduction

7.053 For reasons already discussed in Chapter 2 above, an IP will be a member of a recognised professional body ('RPB'), as defined by IA 1986 s391. The RPBs set out requirements in relation to professional indemnity insurance ('PII'). Whilst these requirements pre-date s391B, the requirements for PII are consistent with the duties of the RPBs, and the regulatory

---

102   For example, *Challinor v Juliet Bellis & Co* [2013] EWHC 620 (Ch); *Harris v Charalambous* [2013] EWHC 2557 (QB).
103   For example, *Attrill v Dresdener Kleinwort* [2012] EWHC 1468 (QB).
104   Recognised in *Hamad M Aldrees & Partners v Rotex Europe Ltd* [2019] EWHC 526 (TCC).
105   [2019] EWHC 205 (TCC).
106   See [20]–[23] for a useful summary of the authorities on the court's approach to the factual matters relevant to its discretion.

objectives or principles under s391B, that regulatory activities should be 'transparent, account-able, proportionate, consistent and targeted only at cases in which action is needed'.[107]

7.054 Typically, of course, PII will not respond to acts of dishonesty by the office-holder. In the case of insolvency practitioners there are specific regulatory requirements which require security to be provided in the form of a bond. Those regulatory requirements were first introduced by the Insolvency Practitioners Regulations 1986 alongside the IA 1986, and are now set out in the Insolvency Practitioners Regulations 2005. These are discussed in further detail at section A.4 in Chapter 2 above.

7.055 In the next section the focus is on PII requirements, and not on bond requirements, although we return to consider both later on in this chapter when moving on to consider some of the practical consequences of the regulatory regime. What follows is a summary of the require-ments general to all RPBs and then consideration of some of the provisions applicable to particular RPBs.

2. General professional indemnity requirements

7.056 All of the RPBs require that those to whom appointment taking insolvency licences are issued hold adequate PII. The RPBs each have their own requirements surrounding the terms of cover, in particular the limit of indemnity, and these requirements are updated periodically. What follows is a description of the limits applicable at the time of writing. The reader should consult the links indicated below for any updates or amendments.

7.057 PII is provided on a 'claims made' basis, which means that cover is given for claims first made or circumstances arising and notified to the insurers during the term of the policy, regardless of when the work was carried out. Therefore, insurance must continue to be maintained if cover is to be available for work carried out in the past. Insurance may include retroactive cover for liabilities arising from work carried out prior to the start date of the policy, except for claims known about at the time the insurance was first taken out. Insurers will frequently put a retroactive date on the policy, meaning that a claim will not be accepted if the original work was done before the retroactive period started.

7.058 Typically, the required minimum limit of indemnity is £1.5 million for each claim. However, the limit may be less than this where the fee income of the IP's firm is less than £600,000 per annum. RPBs may also take into account the size of the largest fee raised by the firm in the previous accounting year when determining the minimum limit.

7.059 Minimum terms may be published by RPBs, with which insurance policies must comply. Some RPBs produce a list of participating insurers. These insurers use approved wording and the RPB may require that those whom they regulate obtain cover with one of the insurers on the list.

---

107   IA 1986 s391C(4)(a). See also s391C(3) which defines 'Regulatory objectives' as 'the objectives of (a) having a system of regulating persons acting as insolvency practitioners that (i) secures fair treatment for persons affected by their acts and omissions'.

The RPB may also require appointment takers who are part of a firm which employs full- or **7.060** part-time staff to hold fidelity guarantee insurance ('FGI'). This provides cover against any acts of fraud or dishonesty by any partner, director or employee.

Where an IP retires or ceases to act as an IP, he or she may be required to satisfy the RPB that **7.061** adequate run-off cover is in place for a period of time after ceasing to act, at an indemnity level not less than that applying immediately prior to retirement or cessation. The recommended minimum period is six years, although two years is the required minimum for some RPBs.

The position can be more complicated when an IP leaves one firm and joins another. The **7.062** retroactive part of the cover will need to be maintained in order for prior work carried out to be covered under an insurance policy. This may be achieved via retroactive cover in the new firm, as a former principal in the old firm or through a special policy section.

If an IP cannot obtain suitable PII, depending upon the RPB, it may be possible to obtain **7.063** cover via the RPB's assigned risks pool for a period of time. The assigned risks pool can provide cover in an emergency and for up to two years, although the premium is likely to be higher than that of a standard policy.

Having set out some of the general requirements we shall turn to consider summaries of the **7.064** requirements particular to the RPBs, or groups of them, focusing in particular on the minimum requirements or limits, which is likely to be of most interest to those considering claims against IPs. For the detailed requirements, the reader should refer to the up-to-date regulations of each RPB, available on the websites referenced.

3. The PII requirements of ICAEW/ICAS/CAI

In this section we consider the current PII requirements of the following RPBs: the Institute of **7.065** Chartered Accountants in England and Wales ('ICAEW'), the Institute of Chartered Accountants of Scotland ('ICAS') and Chartered Accountants Ireland ('CAI'). They are considered together as their requirements are very similar.[108]

These RPBs currently require a minimum limit of indemnity £1.5m for any one claim or a **7.066** number of claims, with a participating insurer which uses approved minimum wording, and 'if the gross fee income of a firm is less than £600,000, the minimum limit of indemnity for any one claim and in total must be equal to two and a half times its gross fee income, with a minimum of £100,000'.[109] There are additional requirements if activities of the firm come under the ambit of the Financial Conduct Authority and/or the firm is accredited to carry out probate work. All firms are required to consider whether the minimum limit of indemnity is sufficient.

---

108 See https://www.icaew.com/technical/practice-resources/regulations-standards-guidance-and-ethics/professional-indemnity-insurance; https://www.icas.com/regulation/professional-indemnity-insurance; https://www.chartered accountants.ie/Professional-Standards/Authorisations/Professional-indemnity-insurance (accessed 8 May 2020).

109 Reg 3.3 ICAEW Professional Indemnity Insurance Regulations. The ICAS and CAI wording is similar.

7.067   A member who ceases to be engaged in public practice is expected to use their best endeavours to ensure that they are covered by arrangements which satisfy the regulations for at least two years from the date they ceased in public practice. The ICAEW recommends that run-off cover is maintained for at least six years.

7.068   If a member cannot obtain cover which satisfies the PII regulations they may be able to enter the assigned risks pool for a period of time until cover is obtained in the market. The assigned risks pool is effectively an insurer of last resort and was set up to ensure that members are almost always able to comply with the regulations whatever their circumstances. Every participating insurer has agreed to subscribe to the assigned risks pool. This can provide cover in an emergency and for up to two years.

4.   The PII requirements of ACCA

7.069   This subsection addresses the current PII requirements of the Association of Chartered Certified Accountants ('ACCA').[110]

7.070   ACCA's Global Practising Regulations 2003 require that:

> PII shall provide cover in respect of all civil liability incurred in connection with the conduct of the firm's business by the partners, directors, members and designated members of limited liability partnerships or employees and FGI shall include cover against any acts of fraud or dishonesty by any partner, director or employee in respect of money or goods held in trust by the firm.[111]

7.071   They further require that 'the limit of indemnity on PII in respect of each and every claim shall be:

(i)   in the case of a person whose firm's total income for the accounting year immediately preceding the year in question (the 'relevant total income' and 'relevant accounting year') is less than or equal to £200,000, at least the greatest of:
(aa) two and one half times that firm's relevant total income; and
(bb) 25 times the largest fee raised by the firm during the relevant accounting year; and
(cc) £50,000;

(ii)   in the case of a person whose firm's relevant total income exceeds £200,000 but is less than or equal to £700,000, at least the greater of:
(aa) the aggregate of £300,000 and the firm's relevant total income; and
(bb) 25 times the largest fee raised by the firm during the relevant accounting year;

(iii)   in the case of a person whose firm's relevant total income exceeds £700,000, at least the greater of:
(aa) £1 million; and
(bb) 25 times the largest fee raised by the firm during the relevant accounting year'.[112]

---

110   See the ACCA Rulebook at https://www.accaglobal.com/gb/en/about-us/regulation/rulebook.html which incorporates the Global Practising Regulations 2003 (accessed on 8 May 2020).

111   Reg 9(2) The Chartered Certified Accountants' Global Practising Regulations 2003 (amended 1 January 2019).

112   Ibid reg 9(3).

Where a practitioner's firm employs full- and/or part-time staff, the firm must also hold a **7.072** policy of FGI in respect of all partners, directors, members and designated members of limited liability partnerships and employees.[113]

Practitioners subject to ACCA's regulations must ensure that they have in place arrangements **7.073** for the continued existence of PII and, as the case may be, FGI for a period of six years after they cease to engage in public practice.[114]

5. The PII requirements of the IPA

This subsection considers the current PII requirements of the Insolvency Practitioners **7.074** Association ('IPA').[115]

For the IPA, under the Professional Indemnity Insurance Regulations, 'each Individual **7.075** Member is required to have a minimum PII cover for any one claim of whichever is the greater of £250,000; or 2.5 times his or her Gross Fee Income',[116] subject to the required minimum referred to below. However:

> Where an Individual Member is in partnership or association with other Insolvency Practitioners and they are covered by a single PII policy, the minimum PII cover required shall be calculated by aggregating each Individual Member's Gross Fee Income.[117]

Perhaps in recognition of the fact that the above requirements could lead to a very high level of **7.076** cover, 'the required minimum cover under the policy need not exceed £1,500,000'.[118]

In relation to policy terms: **7.077**

> PII policies must comply with any IPA approved minimum terms for PII policies, as may be published from time to time, and shall include fidelity insurance covering the dishonest acts or omissions of principals and employees of the Individual Member to the same level of cover as applies to the PII itself.[119]

Members who retire or cease to act as IPs are 'required to satisfy the Association that adequate **7.078** run-off cover is in place for a minimum of six years after ceasing to act at an indemnity level not less than that applying immediately prior to retirement or cessation'.[120]

---

113 Ibid reg 9(1)(a).
114 Ibid reg 9(5).
115 See https://www.insolvency-practitioners.org.uk/regulation-and-guidance/ipa-regulations-guidance (accessed on 8 May 2020).
116 IPA Professional Indemnity Insurance Regulations reg 3(1).
117 Ibid reg 3(2).
118 Ibid reg 3(3).
119 Ibid reg 3(4).
120 Ibid reg 5.

6. Practical implications of PII and bond cover

7.079 The fact of having two types of cover, PII and bond cover, can provide for complications for the person who is framing or defending the claim in question. There are two areas where potential complications may arise which are worth considering here. The first is the nature of the claim advanced and whether it is a professional negligence claim or a dishonesty claim, or both. The second is the impact of a release.

(a) The nature of the claim being advanced

7.080 The complications this can create can be considered in the context of *Re Varden Nuttall Ltd (in administration)*.[121]

7.081 *Varden Nuttall* involved both the administration of a company providing or facilitating the provision of services of IPs as nominees and supervisors of IVAs and a claim by the current supervisors of the individual IVAs. The claim was brought against Mr Nuttall and Mr Varden jointly, as directors of the company, and against Mr Nuttall as former supervisor. The claim arose from a deficiency in excess of £1.3m being discovered on the company's trust accounts, where funds belonging to various different estates had been pooled. Further investigations led to the discovery of what appeared to be frauds on the estates managed by the licensed IPs employed by the company resulting from allegedly fraudulent arrangements (or 'commissions') made by or with the approval of Mr Nuttall and Mr Varden with third-party service providers. It was claimed this (and certain other claims) amounted to a dishonest breach of Mr Nuttall's duties in his capacity as a licensed IP and a breach of director's duties by him and Mr Varden in their capacity as directors. Mr Varden did not appear or defend the claims and so the trial only proceeded against Mr Nuttall.

7.082 The claim was advanced on the basis that the company and current supervisors' claim against Mr Nuttall was being advanced solely to enable a recovery to be made against insurers.[122] Somewhat unusually in order to establish a claim against Mr Nuttall the claimants looked to two sources: Mr Nuttall's insurers for his acts as a director under a D&O policy and, secondly, losses suffered by the IVA estates from the underwriters of Mr Nuttall's bonds. This resulted in the claims being framed purely as negligence claims so far as the breaches of director's duties were concerned but claims incorporating allegations of dishonesty for the purposes of the claims against Mr Nuttall *qua* supervisor. Of course, where an allegation of dishonesty is raised, the standard of proof remains the balance of probabilities test, but the more serious the allegation the more cogent must be the evidence if that standard of proof is to be discharged.[123]

7.083 So far as the breaches of director's duties were concerned, the judge found Mr Nuttall liable. He placed particular reliance on the fact that from at least April 2014 government guidance on the monitoring of IVA providers warned RPBs of the need to ensure that all IPs had 'full oversight and control over estate accounts with adequate safeguard arrangements in place which should include appropriate financial controls'.[124] Mr Nuttall failed to do this. This

---

121 [2018] EWHC 3868 (Ch) (HHJ Pelling QC).
122 *Varden Nuttall* at [7].
123 *Re H (Minor: Sexual abuse: Standard of proof)* [1996] AC 563 (HL) at [10] (Lord Nicholls).
124 *Varden Nuttall* at [35].

coincided with the well-known responsibility of a director to acquaint themselves with the financial affairs of the company.[125] While Mr Nuttall was entitled to delegate management of the account, he failed to take any steps to ensure that Mr Slater (the delegated individual) had taken any adequate steps to safeguard the monies. Mr Nuttall also failed to resume control once he knew or ought to have known that Mr Slater was not performing the tasks delegated to him. It was the failure to carry out any reconciliation that caused the shortfall.

Not all of the claims against Mr Nuttall for breach of supervisor duty were successful. The claims relating to secret commissions are of most relevance to this text. In this respect the debate focused on the obligations of the IP under Statement of Insolvency Practice ('SIP') 9. As noted by the judge, the manner in which fees, disbursements and expenses are dealt with is primarily governed by the terms of the IVAs, typically in standard form.[126] However, the way in which a supervisor should conduct themselves is also governed by SIP 9, in this case the version applicable to all appointments after 1 November 2011. In particular, so far as payments to associates were concerned, paragraphs 24 and 25 of SIP 9 provided as follows: **7.084**

> 24. Where services are provided from within the practice or by a party with whom the practice, or an individual within the practice, has a business or personal relationship, an office holder should take particular care to ensure that the best value and service is being provided …
>
> 25. Payments that could reasonably be perceived as presenting a threat to the office holder's objectivity by virtue of a professional or personal relationship should not be made unless approved in the same manner as an office holder's remuneration or category 2 disbursements … .

So far as the fee arrangements were concerned, the judge was satisfied that sham documentation had been created in order to hide the true position from the relevant RPB. Accordingly, the finding was that secret commissions had indeed been paid. He also found that Mr Nuttall was aware of and involved in the arrangements. The judge found that the payments could only have been properly made if administered and disclosed in accordance with SIP 9 paragraph 25. He found that the secret commission was, in truth, a mechanism by which a sum in excess of the agreed supervisor's fee could be obtained from each estate. SIP 9 paragraph 6 required disclosure of payments or remuneration or expenses by an IP to himself or herself or associates. That meant fully-informed disclosure and consent. In those circumstances the judge found that a dishonest breach was made out: right thinking people would have concluded that these were dishonest acts. **7.085**

In the circumstances the claimants were successful in their claims against Mr Nuttall both for negligent breaches of his duties as a director and for dishonest breaches of his duties as a supervisor. However, it does not necessarily follow that the D&O insurers would or would be required to pay out under the policy. Even though the claimants restricted the claims in relation to acts as directors to complaints of negligence, bearing in mind the findings made in relation to the claims relating to supervisory duties, there must be a risk that cover might be rejected. In short, selective advancement of claims may enable the claimant to advance claims against two different insurers where it can be said they involve different duties, but that must be a rare case, and it will not be determinative as to coverage issues. **7.086**

---

125 *Re Barings plc (No 5)* [2000] 1 BCLC 523.
126 *Varden Nuttall* at [9].

7.087 Moving away from the decision in *Varden Nuttall*, the typical case involving an IP will not also include them acting as a director. In those circumstances, it is likely that the claimant will have to evaluate the likelihood of cover being rejected on the basis of facts known to the claimant and depending on that decide whether to advance claims of dishonesty, with a view to claiming under the bond, or restrict the claims to those of negligence (or similar, falling short of dishonesty, such as, for example, acting for an improper collateral purpose) with the hope that this will not trigger coverage issues for the PII cover.

7.088 There is, however, a secondary consideration when considering the interaction between PII and bond claims, and that is the impact of release.

(b) Impact of release

7.089 There are two practical issues which arise in relation to the question of release. The first concerns restrictions on the ability to make the claim. The second concerns restrictions on ability to recover in relation to insurance.

7.090 So far as the first consideration is concerned, the impact of release is considered elsewhere in this book in relation to the different types of estates.[127] In brief terms, in the context of claims against former liquidators or administrators, for example, IA 1986 s212 and Schedule B1 pararaph 75, misfeasance claims may still be brought under these provisions after an office-holder has obtained their release, with permission of the court. The permission gateway is to provide a level of protection to the former office-holder to prevent them from being subject to vexatious claims, and will require the court to be satisfied of benefit to the estate from bringing the claim, but generally speaking the courts will grant permission if those hurdles are crossed, and the claim is supported and advanced by a successor office-holder who is supported by experienced lawyers.

7.091 It is the second consideration which is of more interest for the purpose of the discussion in this section of this chapter, namely what impact release may have on the ability to *recover*. As noted above, PII cover is ordinarily framed on the basis of a claims made basis, such that the cover will ordinarily respond in relation to a claim being made during the period of the cover. By contrast, bond cover may differ.

7.092 In particular, bond cover typically operates on the basis that it may only provide for cover in relation to claims made up to a certain period after release has been obtained. This can, for example, be as short as two years. This means that there may be considerable advantages of PII cover over bond cover. Moreover, if bond cover is the principal target, and the successor IP considers that PII cover may not be effective, then they would be well advised to take steps to object to any application for release or discharge, or seek to have that set aside if they are able to do so (though the grounds upon which it may be possible to set aside or vary may be limited if no objection was raised at the time). Certainly, it is advisable to take steps to protect those measures pending visibility as to the terms of any bond cover.

---

127   See paras 6.066–6.086 above.

(c)   Operation of bond cover

Finally, it is worth noting that bond cover tends to operate in a different way to PII cover in that, typically, the cover will be by deed and not just be operational between the IP and the underwriter, but will also involve the RPB. The reason for this seems to be on the basis that the rights under the bond may be assigned by the RPB to the successor IP, who may then seek to enforce the rights against the underwriter (as surety for the IP as principal) directly without needing to involve or obtain the consent of the dishonest IP.   **7.093**

F. JOINT AND SEVERAL LIABILITIES; CONTRIBUTION CLAIMS

1.   Contribution claims

The focus of this section of this chapter is remedies between office-holders and in particular contribution claims. Brief mention is also made at the end of this section, in F.5. below, on potential contribution claims against third parties (not IPs).   **7.094**

Claims for contribution may be made under an application or claim advanced under the IA 1986 (e.g., under IA 1986 s212 or Sch B1 para 75), but the court is likely to decide the question of the level of any contribution by reference to general principles of law, and in particular under the Civil Liability (Contribution) Act 1978 ('CLCA 1978'). There is no need to bring a contribution claim until liability has been established against an IP,[128] although it may be thought to be more cost-effective and preferable to make a contribution claim as soon as a claim is brought if it is considered it has reasonable prospects of success.[129] What follows involves a brief introduction to the general principles provided by the Act as interpreted in leading case law and then a brief consideration of how this might be applied in the context of IPs.   **7.095**

2.   The Civil Liability (Contribution) Act 1978

Section 1(1) of the CLCA 1978 provides as follows: 'any person liable in respect of any damage suffered by another person may recover contribution from any other person liable in respect of the same damage (whether jointly with him or otherwise)'.   **7.096**

The key issue which has arisen in the case law concerns the concept of 'same damage' and the leading case in this respect remains *Royal Brompton Hospital NHS Trust v Hammond (No 3)*.[130] Lord Bingham (with whom the rest of the House agreed), observed that the issue 'same damage' was to be approached as follows:[131]   **7.097**

---

128   A claim for contribution must be brought within two years of a judgment, arbitration award, or the date of any settlement: see Limitation Act 1980 ('LA 1980') s10.

129   Not least because of the potential for limitation issues to arise. For a useful general discussion of the application of the Act to contribution claims involving professionals see Chapter 4 of *Jackson & Powell on Professional Liability* (8th edn).

130   [2002] UKHL 15, [2002] 1 WLR 1397. See also *Hampton v Minns* [2002] 1 WLR 1.

131   At [6].

When any claim for contribution falls to be decided the following questions in my opinion arise. (1) What damage has A suffered? (2) Is B liable to A in respect of that damage? (3) Is C also liable to A in respect of that damage or some of it? ... I do not think it matters greatly whether, in phrasing these questions, one speaks (as the 1978 Act does) of 'damage', or of 'loss' or 'harm', provided it is borne in mind that 'damage' does not mean 'damages' (as pointed out by Roch LJ in Birse Construction Ltd v Haiste Ltd [1996] 1 WLR 675, 682) and that B's right to contribution by C depends on the damage, loss or harm for which B is liable to A corresponding (even if in part only) with the damage, loss or harm for which C is liable to A.

7.098 The House of Lords also approved[132] as a practical (though not threshold) test for assessing whether a contribution claim might lie for the 'same damage' the following passage in *Howkins & Harrison v Tyler*:[133]

Suppose that A and B are the two parties who are said each to be liable to C in respect of 'the same damage' that has been suffered by C. So C must have a right of action of some sort against A and a right of action of some sort against B. There are two questions that should then be asked. If A pays C a sum of money in satisfaction, or on account, of A's liability to C, will that sum operate to reduce or extinguish, depending upon the amount, B's liability to C? Secondly, if B pays C a sum of money in satisfaction or on account of B's liability to C, would that operate to reduce or extinguish A's liability to C? It seems to me that unless both of those questions can be given an affirmative answer, the case is not one to which the 1978 Act can be applied. If the payment by A or B to C does not pro tanto relieve the other of his obligations to C, there cannot, it seems to me, possibly be a case for contending that the non-paying party, whose liability to C remains un-reduced, will also have an obligation under section 1(1) to contribute to the payment made by the paying party.

7.099 CLCA 1978 s2(1) also provides, so far as assessment and apportionment is concerned, that 'the amount of the contribution recoverable from any person shall be such as may be found by the court to be just and equitable having regard to the extent of that person's responsibility for the damage in question'. As the words might suggest, this provides the court with considerable latitude to make adjustments for relative blame as well as causative impact and influence. It also enables the defendant to such a claim to raise any defences which might have been available against the original claimant, such as contributory negligence.

3. Joint and successive appointments

7.100 Where an IP is appointed to act on their own and there has been no previous office-holder then the question of contribution claims is unlikely to arise.

7.101 It is conceptually possible they might arise in relation to successive appointments, possibly by a defendant in order to encourage the court to reduce any claim on the basis of default by a successor office-holder.

7.102 The other area where liability for a contribution can arise is where there is a joint appointment and therefore joint liability. Joint appointments will frequently be made from the same firm who will have the same insurer, but different firms may be involved. This can arise where an

---

132 At [28].
133 [2001] Lloyd's Rep. P.N. 1, (CA) (Scott VC).

appointment is made due to particular concerns raised by a creditor and the court may appoint a second set of administrators to act concurrently.[134] A joint appointment involving different firms may also arise where they agree to share an appointment as a compromise (e.g., where they both have support of different creditors) or because one firm alone does not have the resources or expertise necessary to cover the whole appointment. Where such appointments are made, however, the delineation of roles or tasks are such that it is unusual for an issue in relation to joint liability across two firms and insurers to arise.

The most likely area where the issue will arise is where the appointment originally involves two IPs from the same firm, but then they move their separate ways, such that by the time the claim has been made there are two different insurers involved. This issue has arisen in the context of joint appointment of administrators and this is discussed in the next section.   **7.103**

4. Joint and concurrent administrators

The requirements in relation to joint and concurrent administrators are set out in Sch B1 paragraphs 100–103. Where more than one person is appointed paragraph 100(2) requires it to be stated: **7.104**

(a) which functions (if any) are to be exercised by the persons acting jointly, and
(b) which functions (if any) are to be exercised by any or all of the persons appointed.

Where the appointment provides that each office-holder may act jointly and severally then it may become relevant to enquire as to who in fact discharged the activities in question which are sought to be impugned. If the acts were undertaken by one office-holder alone the court may conclude that the other office-holder should not be liable for their joint office-holder's acts. This was the view reached by Sarah Worthington QC in *Re MK Airlines Ltd (in liquidation)*.[135] However, this passage in the judgment was *obiter dicta*, and not necessary for the Deputy Judge to reach the conclusion she did on the case overall. In these circumstances the point remains an open one.   **7.105**

It should also be noted here that if the court were to conclude that the joint holder is liable then as well as considering apportionment or contribution claims under the CLCA 1978, the court may consider whether it would be appropriate to grant relief from liability. There is not much direct authority on the point in the context of Schedule B1 paragraph 75, but the analogous gateway under IA 1986 s212 has generated a number of cases. The courts appear to have taken the view that the legislation provides them with a discretion (at least partly) to relieve a former officer from liability exercising its discretion to do so and independently of the ability to do so under s1157 of the Companies Act 2006 ('CA 2006'). See for example *Re Loquitur Ltd*,[136] which suggests a power to reduce liability (though arguably not to exonerate entirely).[137] See paragraphs 8.064–8.067 below for further detail.   **7.106**

---

134   For example, *Re BHS Ltd* [2016] EWHC 1965 (Ch), [2016] BCC 609. See paras 3.029–3.033 above.
135   Sitting as a Deputy High Court Judge. *Oldham v Katz (acting as joint liquidator of MK Airlines)* [2018] EWHC 540 (Ch) at [143]–[159].
136   [2003] EWHC 999 (Ch).
137   See also *Holland v Revenue & Customs, Re Paycheck Services 3 Ltd* [2010] UKSC 51.

7.107 Finally, the office-holder might seek to obtain relief from liability under CA 2006 s1157. There is some doubt as to whether an administrator may do so, following the decision in *Rawnsley v Weatherall Green & Smith North Ltd*,[138] although in *Re Powertrain Ltd*,[139] where the matter was more fully argued, Newey J concluded that a liquidator was an 'officer' and accordingly entitled to relief.

5. Contribution claims against third parties

7.108 Given that the nature of a contribution claim involves seeking to obtain a contribution from another party who is also liable to the claimant for the same damage it may be thought that it will be a relatively rare case where an IP might be able to make a contribution claim against a third party. One situation where this might arise however may be said to be where the IP is acting for a company and the company has also instructed solicitors who are acting for that company, not just for the IP. In those circumstances the solicitors may be said to be liable, if negligent, for the same damage to the same entity. It may be however that the solicitors are not retained by the company or the estate but instead by the IP and in those circumstances it may be said that they are not liable to the same claimant. If such a contention is made, however, the IP might still have the ability to bring in that third-party adviser, whether solicitor, surveyor or other professional or third party, for causing or contributing to the IP to be exposed to losses to the claimant.

---

138 [2009] EWHC 2842 (Ch).
139 [2015] EWHC 3998 (Ch).

8

DEFENCES

A. INTRODUCTION

As with claims brought against other professionals, once a claim is made out against an IP for **8.001** breach of duties causative of some loss this will usually result in liability. There are however potential additional lines of defence which may be raised. It is the main purpose of this chapter to consider those. The exact nature of the liability must be accurately identified, as sometimes this can carry important ramifications for the availability of some defences.

As discussed further in Chapter 7 above, for claims brought at common law for negligence, or **8.002** for breach of contract, the default remedy is an order for damages. The extent of any such liability may therefore be reduced if the claimant has failed to comply with the so-called 'duty to mitigate', and is subject to the common law rules on remoteness and *Hadley v Baxendale*.[1] Although these operate practically in much the same way as defences, in that the defendant will be ordered to pay a smaller sum than he otherwise would, the 'duty to mitigate' is really an aspect of causation; the law assumes claimants will act reasonably in reducing their losses, even if they do not. The principle that claimants cannot claim for losses which are too remote is, at root, guided by policy. But again, it is an aspect of the claim itself, rather than a standalone defence.

Claims brought against IPs acting under a contract, or in theoretically possible circumstances **8.003** where the IP voluntarily assumes responsibility to another party, will therefore be considered by the courts in the same way as any other professional.

---

1 [1854] EWHC Exch J70.

8.004   The picture is more complicated when a claim is made against an IP in their capacity as an office-holder. It is settled law that, at least insofar as claims are brought against directors, the statutory avenues for claiming against a liquidator or administrator for misfeasance are procedural only; they do not create any new causes of action.[2] It is suggested that the same principle applies to any claim brought against a trustee in bankruptcy under IA 1986 s304 as well, although breaches will of course be made out under negligence or breach of fiduciary duty rather than under a breach of any provisions of the Companies Act 2006 ('CA 2006').[3] It is doubtful whether a claim can be brought at common law in addition, although a trustee may possibly be liable outside a claim brought under s304.[4]

8.005   However, although the character of the cause of action itself is not changed, there is a peculiarity in the drafting of section 212(3) in that:

> The court may, on the application of the official receiver or the liquidator, or of any creditor or contributory, examine into the conduct of the person falling within subsection (1) and compel him (a) to repay, restore or account for the money or property or any part of it, with interest at such rate as the court thinks just, or (b) to contribute such sum to the company's assets by way of compensation in respect of the misfeasance or breach of fiduciary or other duty as the court thinks just.[5]

8.006   The first point to note about the nature of this language is the use of the word 'may' which suggests discretion on the part of the court. In an ordinary common law professional negligence claim the court does not have a discretion to grant a remedy beyond the usual common law rules. The drafting of s212(3) suggests the court has a discretion in relation to insolvency claims under this section which goes wider than the common law principles. The precise scope of this discretion is a matter of debate, but it might include, for example, limiting an award of damages by reference to a shortfall in the insolvency estate. This is considered further below.

8.007   The language of subsection (3)(a) is directed towards misapplications of company property. That this is the primary intention of the drafter is also seen by the reference in s212(1) to officers, liquidators, or other persons involved in the promotion, formation or management of the company who have 'misapplied or retained, or become accountable for, any money or other property of the company, or been guilty of any misfeasance or breach of any fiduciary or other duty in relation to the company'.

---

2   There is a potential distinction between IPs and directors, which may particularly arise in the bankruptcy context (and where there is no prior nexus between a company and its officer). There is possibly scope for damages arising as a result of breach of statutory duty, notwithstanding the limitations placed on such claims by *X v Bedfordshire CC* [1995] 2 AC 633 (HL). However, the claimant's position is unlikely to be improved over and above any claim for negligence at common law: see *Stovin v Wise* [1996] AC 923, 952E–953D.

3   On one view, CA 2006 ss171–177 did nothing more than codify the pre-existing law in any event.

4   *Oraki v Bramston* [2015] EWHC 2046 (Ch). In *Oraki v Bramston* [2017] EWCA Civ 4405, David Richards LJ disagreed with Proudman J's view of liability exclusively arising under s304, although did not elaborate on the point.

5   There is no material distinction between Sch B1 para 75(4) and this part of IA 1986 s212, save of course that the former only applies to administrators and purported administrators: para 75(1). IA 1986 s304 is materially identical insofar as it applies to trustees in bankruptcy.

That a trustee may be accountable for money or other property of the company that has been **8.008** misapplied or retained is uncontroversial; a breach of fiduciary duty will usually result in an order for equitable compensation, or for an account to be given of those same sums.[6]

For claims that are brought in respect of 'other' breaches of duty, such as claims in negligence, **8.009** given the nature of the drafting of s212(3), the position may be said to be a little less clear. It might be said it is not clear whether the nature of any relief that will be granted under s212(3) actually takes on the character of a liability to contribute a sum, although it is considered this is tolerably clear from the wording in s212(3)(b). This wording is the counterpart for the words referring to breaches of 'other' duties at the end of s212(1). While the relevance of this argument is unlikely often to be crucial, it may be so when questions of a failure to mitigate arise, which are applicable to claims sounding in damages, but not to debts or orders to account. The likely answer would seem to be that the court will take into account issues such as a failure to mitigate at the stage of deciding what the amount of compensation should be under s212(3)(b), which will then be reflected in the amount of the final order.

Also excluded from the verbs 'repay, restore, account, and contribute' appears to be the **8.010** possibility of seeking an injunction against a liquidator. This is to be contrasted with the position at common law, and in particular in relation to directors, where the court may grant a prohibitive injunction on a *quia timet* basis, to prevent a proposed or intended breach of duty. It would seem unlikely that the court's inherent jurisdiction to grant injunctions is limited by the mere omission of reference to such a power in s212(3). It is suggested that the intention of Parliament cannot have been to restrict the court's inherent jurisdiction to grant such injunctions, particularly in respect of an IP who is an officer of the court, and therefore subject to the court's control. That said, it may be said to be doubtful whether such an injunction is necessary. That is because the complainant could readily invoke other procedural routes, such as a directions application or an application alleging that a contemplated act would constitute unfair harm. These matters are discussed in Chapter 5 and in particular paragraphs 5.089–5.119 above. The question of a directions application is also considered further below, at paragraphs 8.045–8.050, in the context of its use as shield.

In summary therefore, a distinction must be drawn between cases where a defendant or **8.011** respondent succeeds in an action because an element of the cause of action is or is not made out, and cases where the cause of action may or may not be made out, but the defendant is not rendered liable.

Reference should be made to the foregoing chapters, in particular Chapters 6 and 7, for **8.012** instances of the first category of 'non-liability'. So where, for example, a liquidator is negligent in the conduct of his office, but that negligence causes no loss to the company in liquidation, the claim will fail for want of causation.[7] The defendant in litigation succeeds because an essential element of the claim is lacking. The same applies if it transpires that the claimant does

---

6 *Barnes v Addy* (1874) LR 9 Ch App 244.
7 See paras 7.021–7.027 above.

not in fact have standing to bring the claim, for example because the claim is reflective of a company's loss,[8] or because the claimant does not have a sufficient interest in the claim.[9]

8.013 The second category of defence is an element of the defendant's case that exists aside from the elements of the cause of action. These are true or standalone defences. Continuing with the example of a claim in negligence against a liquidator, for example, if that claim is brought more than six years after the cause of action accrued, the defendant will be entitled to raise a complete procedural defence under the Limitation Act 1980 ('LA 1980'). It is this second category of defences with which this chapter is primarily concerned and to which we now turn.

B. LIMITATION

8.014 As intimated above, the most obvious and in one sense the most powerful defence a defendant or respondent can raise is a limitation defence. As also mentioned above, the fact that a claim is brought via IA 1986 s212, Schedule B1 paragraph 75, or IA 1986 s304 does not change or alter the juridical nature of the claim.

8.015 There are two main questions that must be asked with regard to any issue of limitation:

(1)   what is the limitation period?
(2)   when did the limitation period start to run?

1.   Limitation periods

8.016 The duration in respect of which time runs depends on the nature of the substantive claim. The same act or omission may therefore give rise to a number of causes of action, with distinct limitation periods. The same acts or omissions may give rise to multiple causes of action. If so, the claimant has the option to plead alternative and concurrent causes of action, even if a shorter limitation period has expired.[10]

(a)   Breaches of contract and negligence

8.017 Claims against an IP for breach of contract,[11] for a sum of money,[12] or for negligence,[13] will be subject to a limitation period of six years from the date the cause of action accrued. If there is a difference between the date of breach and the date the loss is suffered, time will run in contract from the date of the breach, and in negligence from the date the final element of the cause of action exists. This will usually be the loss element.

8.018 There are two exceptions to the six-year period, which apply generally, and there is no basis for considering that they should not apply to IPs. First, in a claim for negligence (only), a possible

---

8   *Johnson v Gore Wood & Co (No 1)* [2002] 2 AC 1 (HL); *Rawnsley v Weatherall Green & Smith North Ltd* [2009] EWHC 2482 (Ch).

9   *Doffman v Wood* [2011] EWHC 4008 (Ch); *Deloitte & Touche v Johnson* [1999] 1 WLR 1056 (PC).

10   *Henderson v Merrett Syndicates Ltd (No 1)* [1995] 2 AC 145 (HL).

11   LA 1980 s5.

12   Ibid s9.

13   Ibid s2.

exception is created by s14A of the Limitation Act 1980, which may extend the prima facie applicable period up to 15 years from the date the cause of action accrued.[14] If the conditions are met, it provides that s2 does not apply and, instead, time for the bringing of the action expires at the later of six years from the date when the cause of action accrues and three years from the 'starting date'. That date is defined in s14A(5) as 'the earliest date on which the claimant or any person in whom the cause of action was vested before him first had both the knowledge required for bringing an action for damages in respect of the relevant damage and a right to bring such an action'. Reference should be made to specialist texts on the interpretation of the following subsections.[15] For present purposes, the key subsection is 14A(10), which provides that a person's knowledge includes 'knowledge' which he might reasonably have been expected to acquire from facts observable or ascertainable by him, or from facts ascertainable by him with the help of appropriate expert advice which it is reasonable for him to seek.

This subsection may be of particular use to creditors, who are often not privy to the day-to-day **8.019** progress of a liquidation, and who may only discover years after the event that there was a valid claim. In such circumstances, and assuming it cannot be said that the creditors could not with reasonable diligence have discovered the breach, it is suggested that the court should be prepared to grant leave to bring a claim against a liquidator who has had his release.[16]

The second exception lies in LA 1980 s32, and provides that no limitation period will apply in **8.020** cases of fraud, concealment, or mistake. However, by reason of the IP's position as a trustee-like fiduciary, LA 1980 s21 is likely to apply, and claimants may be able to take advantage of that section without the need to demonstrate fraud for the purposes of s32.[17]

(b)   Breaches of fiduciary duty

Section 21 of the LA 1980 provides that: **8.021**

> (1) No period of limitation prescribed by this Act shall apply to an action by a beneficiary under a trust, being an action—
>
> (a)   in respect of any fraud or fraudulent breach of trust to which the trustee was a party or privy; or
> (b)   to recover from the trustee trust property or the proceeds of trust property in the possession of the trustee, or previously received by the trustee and converted to his use.

Notwithstanding that this section appears to have been drafted to be of direct relevance to **8.022** claims brought by a beneficiary against a trustee, it has been consistently interpreted by the courts as applying to directors, who owe a 'trustee-like' fiduciary duty to their company. The word 'beneficiary' has correspondingly been given a wide interpretation to encompass the company within its ambit. There would seem to be no good reason why the same principle should not apply to IPs.[18]

---

14   That is, the statutory longstop: LA 1980 s14B.
15   See, generally, McGee, *Limitation Periods* (8th edn).
16   Under IA 1986 s212(4).
17   Although that option may still be available, where appropriate: *Williams v Central Bank of Nigeria* [2014] UKSC 10 (Lord Neuberger PSC) at [119].
18   See *Taylor v Davies* [1920] AC 636 (PC).

8.023   There are different types of trustee, and not every imposition of a constructive trust will enable a claimant to take advantage of s21. As explained by Millett LJ in *Paragon Finance v Thakerar*,[19] trustees who have undertaken to be a custodian of trust property fall into the first category, and are trustees, properly understood.[20]

8.024   This is to be distinguished from those who, although holding property that becomes subject to a constructive trust, are not trustees in the fullest sense. An example is where a third party receives property and a constructive trust is imposed, thereby requiring the property to be transferred to the beneficiary. Constructive trusts of that kind do not give rise to a 'true' trustee-beneficiary relationship; the imposition of the constructive trust only arises because it is unconscionable for the recipient to retain the property, and the response of the court's equitable jurisdiction is a constructive trust. Such individuals never assume or intend to assume the status of a trustee, but are exposed to the equitable remedy by virtue of their participation in the unlawful misapplication of trust assets.[21]

8.025   Given the responsibility of a liquidator to get in, realise, and distribute the assets of the company, it is difficult to see how, where a claim is brought against that office-holder, they were not already responsible for those assets.[22] They are therefore likely to be a 'class 1' trustee within the categories defined by Millett LJ in *Paragon Finance*. Correspondingly, it means that IPs are likely to fall within LA 1980 s21(1)(a) in appropriate cases.[23]

8.026   The lack of protection afforded to IPs in this situation is plainly justified. Like directors or trustees, they have lawfully assumed fiduciary obligations in relation to trust property, with a formal appointment. They are also remunerated for their work. They generally have the option to seek advice or directions when difficulties arise. The costs of taking that step can also generally be paid from the estate.

8.027   Section 21(1)(b) may potentially apply, but only where an IP improperly retains property of the company or bankrupt or converts it to their own use. Such cases will by their very nature be rare, and inherently much rarer than in cases involving directors, where the general flow of assets is likely to be much greater.

8.028   The Supreme Court considered the application of s21(1)(b) in the case *Burnden Holdings (UK) Ltd v Fielding*[24] on an application made by the defendant directors in that case for summary judgment on limitation grounds.[25] The assumed facts were that the defendant directors had breached their fiduciary duties owed to the company by causing the company to make a distribution of an asset (a shareholding in a subsidiary). The distribution took place six years

---

19   [1999] 1 All ER 400 at 413. It is 'the distinction between an institutional trust and a remedial formula–between a trust and a catch-phrase'. See also *Selangor United Rubber Estates Ltd v Cradock (No 3)* [1968] 1 WLR 1555.
20   Although LA 1980 s38(1), which refers to the definition in the Trustee Act 1925 s68(17), describes this including 'implied and constructive trusts … and to the duties incident to the office of a personal representative, and "trustee" where the context admits, includes a personal representative …'.
21   See *Williams v Central Bank of Nigeria* at [56].
22   Affirmed by *Re Mama Milla* [2014] EWHC 2753 (Ch), [2016] BCC 1 at [40].
23   *Williams v Central Bank of Nigeria.*
24   [2018] UKSC 14, [2018] AC 857.
25   After the limitation defence failed, the main proceedings were heard by Zacaroli J: *Burnden Holdings (UK) Ltd (in liquidation) v Fielding* [2019] EWHC 1566 (Ch).

and three days before the claim was issued. Unless s21(1)(b) applied, it was common ground that the directors had a good limitation defence pursuant to s21(3). The defendants argued that s21(1)(b) could not apply to them because the relevant shareholding had always been legally owned by a corporate entity, and not by them and had never been received by them and converted to their use. The Supreme Court rejected that contention. It held that the defendant directors were, in view of their office, the fiduciary stewards of the company's property, so that the shareholding had been previously received by them, and it had been converted to their use as a result of the economic benefit that they stood to gain (they were the majority shareholders of the entity to which the shareholding was distributed). As a result, s21(1)(b) applied, and the directors were not able to deploy a limitation defence.

2. Time runs notwithstanding absence of potential claimant

The accrual of the cause of action is independent from the notion that a claimant exists or is prepared to bring the claim. In claims brought *by* liquidators against directors, the logic of this proposition gives rise to an oddity, in that there will be a period of limitation which will run, notwithstanding that the claimant will not yet have been appointed (i.e., in the period between breach and appointment).[26] In the context of a claim brought by an IP against a former IP, this would appear to give rise to a similar oddity, in that as long as the misfeasant IP remains in office, the company will not be able to bring a claim against the IP as the IP will remain in control of the insolvency process while time continues to run. **8.029**

The possibility of a creditor bringing a claim against the IP under the relevant sections mitigates this position somewhat. However, even if a creditor's claim is successful, it will result only in an augmentation of the assets in the estate available for distribution generally. It may therefore increase the dividend an unsecured creditor may receive, but it will not be often that a creditor will seek to run the risk of bringing such a claim, particularly because of the identifiable risk of 'throwing good money after bad'. Instances where a creditor will take such a commercial risk perhaps include situations where there is a creditor with a large percentage of the debts in the insolvency, or perhaps where a creditor committee is formed. **8.030**

Where, however, an actionable wrong has taken place under the watch of an IP and there is a delay in their replacement then it is quite likely that the claim may be brought either on the basis that no limitation period applies, where there has been a misapplication of trust property or dishonest breach, or on the basis that time should be extended on the grounds that relevant knowledge was not acquired in time, or, in extreme cases, where deliberate concealment takes place. That may include instances of an IP committing a deliberate breach of an actionable duty in circumstances where they are aware it may not be discovered for some time.[27] **8.031**

There may also be the prospect of relying on later breaches by an IP where an earlier breach has become statute-barred. Simply because it may be said there is recoverable damage arising from **8.032**

---

26 *Re Eurocruit Europe Ltd* [2007] EWHC 1433 (Ch), [2007] 2 BCLC 598; *Hill v Spread Trustee Co Ltd* [2006] EWCA Civ 542.

27 In *Cave v Robinson Jarvis & Rolf (a firm)* [2002] UKHL 18, [2003] 1 AC 384 (a solicitor's negligence case) it was held that deliberate concealment for the purposes of s32(1)(b) and (2) of the LA 1980 included a deliberate breach of duty either concealed or undisclosed and committed in circumstances such that it was unlikely to be discovered for some time and also the taking of active steps to conceal a breach of duty after becoming aware of it; but that it did not include failure to disclose a negligent breach of duty that the person in question was not aware of committing.

an earlier statute-barred tort does not mean a fresh cause of action is barred if that gives rise to (further or future) recoverable loss. An example of this may be where it can be alleged that the IP had a duty to report their own earlier breaches or misconduct. A failure by them to do so may therefore itself be said to be a separate breach and the level of loss equivalent to the value of the claim which might otherwise be statute-barred. A similar argument has gained traction in several cases in which it was held that directors might have a duty to disclose their own misconduct to the company, if a director acting in good faith would have concluded the disclosure was in the best interests of the company.[28] Since the disclosure obligation was not an independent duty but arose as a facet of the director's fiduciary obligations, there appears to be no reason why the same reasoning could not apply to IPs (where they owe similar fiduciary duties) by analogy.

8.033 In a similar vein, an IP might commit a fresh breach of duty which has the effect of concealing a prior breach of duty – in such a case, the loss of the right to sue in respect of the prior breach from the passage of time might conceivably be claimed as damage caused by the later breach.[29] Similarly, where an IP fails to bring a claim for the benefit of the estate, or otherwise fails to protect the interests of the estate, and the window of time for doing so has expired, a subsequent office-holder may be able to claim a breach of duty against the original IP for damages in respect of the lost chance that that (now expired) claim would have resulted in a successful recovery.[30]

C. SET-OFF

8.034 Claims brought against directors for breaches of fiduciary duty are often met with the response that a director in fact contributed a greater sum to the company, and so the director should be entitled to extinguish or reduce the value of the claim. This argument is an attempt to engage insolvency set-off, which is provided for by the Insolvency Rules 2016 ('IR 2016') r14.25 in respect of mutual debts or dealings.[31]

8.035 The advantage of a successful allegation of set-off is that the funds introduced will be set off pound for pound against the order made against the director as a result of the misfeasance. The alternative is that the misfeasant director will be required to contribute the whole sum, and

---

28   *Fassihi v Item Software (UK) Ltd* [2004] EWCA Civ 1244. Further, in *Haysport Properties Ltd v Ackerman* [2016] EWHC 393 (Ch), a director had breached his duty to avoid a conflict of interest by approving the grant of security by the relevant company to support a facility advanced to a separate business in which the director was interested. The claim relating to the original breach of duty would have been time barred but the director was held to be subject to an additional, continuing duty to disclose the original breach of fiduciary duty for so long as he remained a director.

29   *Gold v Mincoff Science & Gold (a firm)* [2000] All ER (D) 2412 at [99] (Neuberger J):

>   if the subsequent instruction was also negligently implemented by the solicitor, and, this later negligence concealed the earlier negligence then, subject to normal questions such as causation and remoteness, if the earlier negligence only comes to light outside the limitation period, the loss of the right to sue in respect of it can properly be the subject of a claim based on the later negligence.

30   See paras 7.032–7.034 above.

31   There is no possibility of legal set-off in these circumstances. Insolvency set-off in this context is probably equitable in origin, although is now governed by the IR 2016. It is suggested that any attempt to circumvent the scheme in IR 2016, by reference to equity, would be unlikely to succeed as the rules effectively set down a complete code, at least insofar as set-off is concerned: see *Re Stanford International Bank Ltd* [2019] UKPC 45.

then receive only a *pari passu* dividend in respect of any debts owed.[32] However, such attempts to 'set off' a misfeasance against contributions will usually fail for want of mutuality.[33]

The position of the office-holder is different because, as explained above at paras 5.192–5.203, **8.036** the IP will be entitled to claim priority of his expenses, which includes remuneration. The question arises as to whether the IP can therefore waive the expenses already claimed, or otherwise set them off by virtue of r14.25,[34] so as to reduce any liability for breach of trust.

It is suggested that, if the remuneration already claimed was properly incurred, then there will **8.037** usually be no particular advantage in alleging a set-off under r14.25. This is because the IP is already entitled to be paid, pound for pound, ahead of the unsecured creditors. In other words, the IP will already have an advantage that is tantamount to a set-off being available to him.

This does, however, assume that there will be sufficient assets in the estate to remunerate the **8.038** IP accordingly. If an estate is particularly depleted of assets, then the IP, or their insurer, may still prefer to set-off the remuneration received against the claim made against the IP. This argument is unlikely to work for two reasons. First, r14.25 is said only to apply to relationships as between creditors and the company.[35] Even if the IP were said to be a 'creditor' (in the sense that the company owes a sum of money to the IP), it runs into the same problem created by *Manson v Smith*, in that there can be no mutuality between a breach and the remuneration incurred.

Further, if an order is made against an IP in respect of a breach of duty, it is suggested that the **8.039** court may simultaneously order that the IP is not entitled to remuneration in respect of a part of the work carried out by the IP. It is clear from IR 2016 rr7.108(4)(a)(ii) and 7.108(4)(r) that expenses may only rank as an expense of the liquidation if they are 'properly chargeable'.

Consequently, it is suggested that only proper remuneration should be chargeable to the estate. **8.040** Far from giving a basis for set-off, therefore it appears that a successful claim may also be a basis for or a springboard for a reduction in available remuneration. For the same reasons, namely that the creditors should not be made indirectly to bear the costs of the IP improperly incurred (or which are incurred purely for the purposes of protecting the IP's position), it will also usually be directed in such a case that the IP must bear the costs of any such application personally.[36]

---

32 The director will receive nothing if the funds were introduced *qua* shareholder rather than *qua* creditor unless, exceptionally, there is a surplus in the estate.
33 *Manson v Smith (liquidator of Thomas Christy Ltd)* [1997] 2 BCLC 161; *Re CJ & RA Eade LLP (in liquidation)* [2019] EWHC 1673 (Ch).
34 IA 1986 s323 applies in bankruptcy.
35 IR 2016 r14.25(1).
36 See *Re VE Interactive* [2018] EWHC 186 (Ch) (an application to remove the administrators) at [41]:

> It is also right in principle that the [administrators] should not be able to recover costs and expenses, including their remuneration, insofar as they now prove to be unnecessary or wasted. Similarly, they should be responsible for costs and expenses to be incurred as a result of their resignation which would not otherwise have been incurred.

D. STATUTORY AND PRIVATE APPOINTMENTS

8.041   As set out above, there are likely to be substantial differences, depending on whether a claim is brought against an IP on the basis of a duty owed to a particular individual (such as under a contract), or where the claim is brought against the IP while acting as an office-holder. In this context, the distinction can be described as 'in-court' and 'out-of-court', although this is not to be confused with the statutory methods of appointing an IP.[37]

8.042   Where the claim is brought directly under contract or tort, there would appear to be no principled basis to depart from the general position that such liability might be limited by an exclusion clause and/or notice. Such attempts to exempt or otherwise limit liability will, correspondingly, be subject to the usual statutory controls.[38] It would appear to be a very unlikely state of affairs that would give rise to the type of trader-consumer relationship that would engage the Consumer Rights Act 2015.

8.043   That still leaves the potential application of the Unfair Contract Terms Act 1977, assuming that the requirements of the Act are met.[39] In such a case attempts to render a contractual performance substantially different from that which was reasonably expected of him, or to render no performance at all, will be subject to the test of reasonableness.[40]

8.044   Once an IP takes office, the IP becomes subject to the supervision of the court and the statutory requirements of his role. It is not possible for the IP to limit the scope of his duties or otherwise to limit his liability in the context of carrying out his role as office-holder, since to do so would otherwise have the potential to conflict with the IP's duties under the statutory scheme. In doing so, it would oust the jurisdiction of the court.[41] However, the IP is not prevented from limiting or excluding liability under contracts entered into as office-holder, provided that such terms do not interfere with the statutory scheme. It will not be possible for the office-holder to exclude or limit liability below the minimum statutory standard. Indeed, if it were possible so to contract, it would undo much of the work of the Cork Report in ensuring that IPs are held to certain and identifiable standards.

E. APPLICATION TO COURT FOR DIRECTIONS

8.045   IPs are often required to make complex and important decisions, which occasionally require input from solicitors and/or counsel, and to which there may be no clear answer, but rather a

---

37   For example, where an administrator is appointed by a QFC holder 'out of court', or a resolution is passed for a liquidator to be appointed in a CVL.

38   See, e.g., *Chitty on Contracts* (33rd edn) generally at Chapter 15.

39   Of these, the requirement that one deals on the other's written standard terms of business may pose a particular challenge: Unfair Contract Terms Act 1977 s3(1).

40   Unfair Contract Terms Act 1977 s3(2)(b).

41   It is for this same reason that a claim cannot be brought under contract against an IP, separately or in addition to the statutory avenues for doing so: *Reynard v Fox* [2018] EWHC 433 (Ch) at [36]; *Oraki v Bramston* [2017] EWCA Civ 403.

range of reasonable responses. It is, of course, also central to the IP's role that they must make a wide range of commercial decisions. Such decisions are also often made under significant time pressure.

The threats of criticism, challenge and possible litigation are always at the back of office-holders' minds and, particularly in cases involving large estates that are more commercially viable to litigate over, are increasingly at the forefront. It is suggested that there is a growing trend towards such claims being intimated or brought. However, it remains within the power of the IP to make an application to court for directions, which may act as a bar to later criticisms.[42] The scope of such applications can vary widely, but the most common will involve seeking clarification on the ranking or priority of debts and expenses, which might prevent an unintended distribution of assets to the wrong party.[43] Such applications can even go to the core of the IP's position, as has been demonstrated by the flurry of applications to verify the appointment of administrators outside the usual court opening times.[44] **8.046**

As explained by Snowden J at first instance in *Nortel*, a direction from the court will 'prevent subsequent challenge'.[45] In general, a direction from the court sanctions the actions of the office-holders before they are taken. They are not, therefore, defences that can be raised after the event, but are instead a pre-emptive move that an IP can make *before* committing the act in question.[46] **8.047**

1. Limitations to applications for directions

Such applications can therefore offer some comfort to IPs. There are, however, certain downsides to making an application. The first is the obvious cost involved in making an application. There is no small irony, for example, in applications being made to court by administrators to verify that their *out of court* appointments were valid,[47] meaning that the supposed time and cost efficiencies of such out-of-court appointments were lost. **8.048**

The second limitation is that the courts are not generally prepared to intervene in what are essentially commercial decisions. As it was put by Neuberger J (as he then was) in *Re T & D Industries* 'commercial and administrative decisions are for [administrators], and the court is not there to act as a sort of bomb shelter'.[48] This is part and parcel of the division between courts and office-holders appointed under the court's supervision, in that the court will be the **8.049**

---

42 IA 1986 ss7 (in a CVA), 112 (in a voluntary liquidation), 168 (in a court winding up), 263 (in an IVA), 303 (in a bankruptcy), para 63 Sch B1 (in an administration).

43 In *Re London Bridge Entertainment Partners LLP* [2019] EWHC 2932 (Ch), e.g., an application for directions was used to determine whether a landlord's claim was to rank as expense or a provable debt.

44 *Re Skeggs Beef* [2019] EWHC 2607 (Ch); *Re HMV Ecommerce Ltd* [2019] EWHC 903 (Ch); *Re SJ Henderson and Co Ltd* [2019] EWHC 2742 (Ch); *Re Keyworker Homes (North West) Ltd* [2019] EWHC 3499 (Ch). See further at paras 3.076–3.077 above.

45 [2016] EWHC 2769 (Ch).

46 See paras 5.089–5.119 above.

47 Of course, if the finding were to go against the administrator, then it would transpire that they were not entitled to make the application in the first place. It is suggested that this raises the possibility of the administrators being personally liable for those costs, rather than them being treated as part of the expenses of the process.

48 *Re T & D plc (in administration); Re T & D Automotive Ltd (in administration)* [2000] 1 WLR 646, 657.

ultimate arbiter of legal matters[49] and in 'commercial matters, administrators are generally expected to exercise their own judgment rather than to rely on the approval or endorsement of the court to their proposed course of action'.[50] Notwithstanding those judicial statements, which would seem to caution against such applications,[51] in practice once the court is faced with such an application for directions, the legal aspect of the intended course of action will usually be decided (i.e., that the IP has the power to do X), rather than to sanction the entire course of action (i.e., there being no decision that the IP can exercise his powers properly to do X, or that X is the best course). In this respect, it would seem that an application for directions would in fact offer little prospective protection to the IP's acts, but it is suggested that in practice the prior investigation and blessing of the court is likely to discourage a would-be claimant from launching a challenge to the IP's conduct.

8.050 The third limitation is the speed with which the court can act. Although the overriding objective requires the courts to ensure that cases are dealt with expeditiously and fairly,[52] this must be balanced against the needs of other court users.[53] However, timescales can often be short in insolvency matters, particularly in challenges to CVAs and IVAs on grounds of unfair prejudice or material irregularity.[54] The courts and judges will often do their best to accommodate those timescales, particularly if the case is of a high value. Recent examples include the urgent request for directions in a CVA in *Re MF Global UK Ltd*,[55] *Carluccio's*,[56] *Debenhams*,[57] and the memorable 'disclaimer' provided by Warren J in *SISU Capital Fund Ltd v Tucker*.[58]

---

49 For example, in relation to questions of whether so-called 'currency conversion claims' exist, and could enable creditors to seek more from the insolvent estate that had already been proved for, in circumstances where foreign exchange markets had shifted since the insolvency cut-off date to the creditors' advantage: *Re Lehman Brothers International (Europe) (in administration)* [2017] UKSC 38 (they cannot).

50 *Re MF Global UK Ltd (in special administration) (No 5)* [2014] EWHC 2222 (Ch) at [41]. The application centred on the issue of whether certain Chapters 7 and 7A of the Client Assets Sourcebook ('CASS'), which formed part of the Financial Services Authority Handbook, impinged on the power to compromise claims found in section 15 of the Trustee Act 1925. The 'clear power' for administrators to compromise such claims lay in para 60 of Sch B1.

51 These statements also chime with CPR r1.1(2)(e), which states that dealing with a case justly and at proportionate cost includes allotting to each case 'an appropriate share of the court's resources, while taking into account the need to allot resources to other cases'.

52 CPR r1.1(2)(d).

53 CPR r1.1(2)(e).

54 The deadline for such applications is just 28 days from the date of filing: IA 1986 ss6(3), 262(3).

55 The Court of Appeal's judgment was handed down just 24 hours before the CVA lapse date.

56 *Re Carluccio's Ltd* [2020] EWHC 886 (Ch), on the availability of the Coronavirus Jobs Retention Scheme in administration.

57 *Re Debenhams Retail Ltd* [2020] EWHC 921 (Ch) [2020] EWCA Civ 600.

58 [2005] EWHC 2170 (Ch); [2005] EWHC 2321 (Ch):

   This application has come on in the Long Vacation as a matter of urgency. I have needed to digest a mass of written material … of over 1,000 pages. It is impossible for me, in the time available to write this judgment, to review the evidence in the detail which I would ordinarily wish to do in arriving at, and expressing, my conclusions. The fact that I do not do so does not mean that I have ignored it—although it would be a pretence at perfection to say that I had not overlooked anything.

2. Costs of applications for directions

Applications for directions can range from those that are made for the benefit of the insolvency **8.051** where there is, for example, an unopposed application to determine a point of law arising from the interpretation of the Insolvency Act so that the estate can be properly administered. At the other end of the spectrum lie applications for directions that have more of the character of adversarial litigation about them. This has a bearing on the costs orders that may be made in such applications. The general starting point of costs 'following the event' in litigation is well-known. But there is equally no doubt that, by analogy with developed practice in the context of litigation to resolve contested issues in a deceased's or insolvent's estate, where the proceedings have in effect been sponsored by the estate administrator, and the parties' involvement has in effect been as contributors to a necessary judicial inquiry, the court will usually depart from the general 'costs follow the event' principle and allow costs as an expense in the relevant insolvency process.[59] The question is ultimately one of discretion, and the resolution of the same issue (such as the interpretation of a contract) may be relevant to the resolution of stakeholders who have adopted neutral or aggressive stances. However, it is cautiously suggested that the starting point for such applications is that the costs will generally be in the estate, as long as there is some identifiable benefit to the creditors as a whole for the issues to have been determined.

F. CONSULTATION WITH CREDITORS

Aside from applications to court, a similar prophylactic can possibly be obtained from the body **8.052** of creditors, for whose benefit the insolvency process ultimately exists.[60]

1. Sanction from creditors

Before the reforms brought about by the SBEEA 2015, it was necessary for IPs to seek **8.053** sanction from creditors or the Secretary of State before embarking on some types of claim.[61] In light of the amendments of the SBEEA 2015,[62] there is now no general requirement on IPs to seek sanction from creditors. However, that does not restrict the power of the IP to seek the consent from creditors. It is suggested that informed consent should act as a shield against a challenge from creditors in the future.

The downside of seeking such consent is the same that beleaguers creditor involvement more **8.054** generally, in that the majority of creditors choose not to play any active role in the conduct of

---

59 See *Re Lehman Brothers International (Europe) (in administration)* [2018] EWHC 924 (Ch) (Hildyard J) at [6]–[7].

60 There is perhaps a parallel here with the principle in *Re Duomatic*, which provides that as long as the company's shareholders unanimously agree to a particular course (and the company is not insolvent or of dubious solvency), then the act of the company will be *intra vires*. The principle is similar in that, assuming the creditors have given their informed consent to a particular action, it would seem to be contrary to that consent for them later to complain of that very same act.

61 Claims brought by the IP under IA 1986 ss213, 214, 238, 239, 339, 340 and 423, and claims brought or defended in the name of the company in a court winding up and relating to property comprised in the bankruptcy estate. The categorical distinction is still visible in the divisions of the parts to IA 1986 Schs 4 and 5.

62 SBEEA 2015 s120.

the insolvency.[63] The introduction of the deemed consent procedure introduced by the SBEEA 2015 would seem to offer a solution to that particular issue,[64] although silence from the creditors generally will be unlikely to be interpreted by the IP as a ringing endorsement of their proposed claim.

8.055 The advantage of seeking the sanction of creditors is that it can be made before or after the act has been carried out. Therefore, unlike an application to court which may result in an immediate decision being taken by the court contrary to the IP's wishes, there is more room for flexibility between the creditors and the IP, and there is perhaps scope for finding a satisfactory middle ground if the parties start from opposing positions.

8.056 Notwithstanding the availability of this method of 'shielding', it does not appear to be commonly in use, perhaps due to lack of creditor engagement. Progress reports will usually simply refer to the IP's decision to bring or not bring a claim, rather than opening up the decision to the creditors as a whole. While the IP is within his rights to do so, modern technology would seem to offer many possibilities for creditor engagement in insolvency processes than has previously been the case. There would appear to be scope for innovation in this respect which could provide better protection to IPs.

8.057 One difficulty in seeking a decision from creditors arises where the IP is proposing a claim against the company's directors (as is frequently the case), who themselves may well be listed as creditors of the company. Such directors cannot be expected to endorse the IP's proposed claim, but may be the only creditors who engage in the decision procedure. This issue could lead to a reluctance from IPs to seek decisions from the body of creditors in such circumstances. There are further issues in terms of disclosing sensitive information which may prejudice the claim which the IP wishes to bring.

2. Indemnity in respect of costs orders

8.058 A more common aspect of communication with creditors arises in respect of costs. If the estate appears to have a good claim against a potential respondent, but there are no liquid assets available to fund the claim, the IP may often look to the creditors to take on the risk of fulfilling any costs order that will be made against the company in due course. This may be necessary even if the IP is acting under a CFA.[65] The logic of this is that the creditors will stand to gain from an increase in the assets available for distribution, and so they may decide to take on the risk of paying the other side and/or their own costs. Whether or not they do so will turn on the risk appetite of the particular creditor(s) and their ability to meet any future costs order.

---

63   Baister, 'Class consciousness and the creditor' (2018) 31(4) *Insolv Int* 107 at 109.

64   As claims no longer require sanction under the IA 1986: IA 1986 s246ZF(1)(a).

65   The alternative may be for every professional party acting for an insolvent company to act under a CFA. In such circumstances, an application for security for costs may be made by the defendant. But it also may amount to an attempt to stifle a genuine claim, and so be dismissed: *Absolute Living Developments v DS7 Ltd* [2018] EWHC 1432 (Ch) at [34].

G. CONTRIBUTORY NEGLIGENCE

In claims for negligence brought against an IP, there would seem to be no reason why the Law **8.059** Reform (Contributory Negligence) Act 1945 should not apply. There is, however, no reported authority where the partial defence has been raised, and the Act clearly cannot be extended to apply to breaches of fiduciary duty. The effect of the Act is that any award of damages 'shall be reduced to such extent as the court thinks just and equitable'. This appears not to add anything to the wording of IA 1986 s212(3) or CA 2006 s1157, and it would seem that the court would take into account those same considerations, regardless of the exact statutory basis for doing so. While it may be available in principle, it is difficult to think of an example of a factual scenario where contributory negligence is ever likely to feature as a defence to claims brought against the IP, and it does not tend to fare that well as a defence in claims brought by lay people against professionals generally in cases involving specialist work where they might reasonably be expected to leave the matter entirely to the professional.[66]

H. RELIEF FROM LIABILITY

CA 2006 s1157 provides for total or partial relief, even in circumstances where the respondent **8.060** has been found to have been liable. Subsection (1) provides as follows:[67]

(1) If in proceedings for negligence, default, breach of duty or breach of trust against

    (a) an officer of a company, or

    (b) a person employed by a company as auditor (whether he is or is not an officer of the company), it appears to the court hearing the case that the officer or person is or may be liable but that he acted honestly and reasonably, and that having regard to all the circumstances of the case (including those connected with his appointment) he ought fairly to be excused, the court may relieve him, either wholly or in part, from his liability on such terms as it thinks fit.

This section has long been a feature of English company law,[68] and is materially identical to **8.061** the provision applicable to trustees.[69] The term 'officer' is defined in CA 2006 as including directors, managers and secretaries.[70] There is, however, no explicit reference in the act to office-holders. It is suggested that, in the process of codification that took place in the drafting of the Companies Act 2006, the section could usefully have been revised so as expressly to refer to office-holders as well as directors.

---

66 *Bollom (JW) & Co Ltd v Byas Mosley & Co Ltd* [2000] Lloyd's Rep IR 136 at [152]:

    When a person engages a professional man to provide specialist services the law will not ordinarily impose a duty on that person to take steps to protect himself against negligence on the part of someone who has himself undertaken to act with reasonable skill and care. Negligence involves a failure to guard against a risk that is reasonably foreseeable and there cannot therefore be contributory negligence in a case of this kind unless the plaintiff ought reasonably to have foreseen that his adviser might fail to carry out his responsibilities.

67 Subsection (2) provides for an anticipatory application for relief.

68 It repeats s727 of the Companies Act 1985.

69 Trustee Act 1925 s61.

70 CA 2006 s1173.

8.062 The answer as to whether or not an office-holder even falls within this category is consequently subject to conflicting authority. *Rawnsley v Weatherall Green & Smith North Ltd* stated that it was 'seriously arguable that a liquidator is not within the ambit of s. 1157'.[71] Conversely, in the later case of *Re Powertrain Ltd*,[72] Newey J departed from the view in *Rawnsley*. This could be said to conflict with the definition contained in s1173, although that definition is intended to be inclusive, rather than exclusive. Further, it would also appear to be arguable that, in light of the terms of s212(3) and its parallels in other insolvency processes, which will almost always grant a judgmental discretion in terms of the amount of relief to order, the additional stage in the analysis incorporated by CA 2006 s1157 probably adds little of substance, save perhaps for an additional focus on whether the IP acted honestly and reasonably in all the circumstances.[73]

8.063 However, it makes little sense to give a jurisdictional basis of relief to directors and secretaries, but not to IPs. If there is surplusage in the drafting of IA 1986 s212(3) and CA 2006 s1157, then that is a criticism that would appear to be equally strong in the case of claims against directors, in respect of whom there is no doubt that the jurisdiction also applies. It seems likely therefore that the position in *Re Powertrain*, that an IP can seek relief from liability in appropriate circumstances, will be followed.

1. Relationship with IA 1986 s212(3)

8.064 Reference has already been made above to IA 1986 s212(3). The subsection confers on the court a judgmental discretion as to the quantum of compensation.[74] This appears to suggest that, even if the court is unable to grant relief under s1157 because the respondent is unable to demonstrate that he acted honestly and reasonably, it might still be able to exercise its *further* discretion under s212(3) by limiting the amount that should prima facie be paid by a respondent.[75] It may be asked why this is so, and whether it makes sense as a matter of statutory interpretation to ask, in effect, three questions: (i) should the respondent IP prima facie be liable under IA s212(3)? (ii) if the IP is liable, is there a possibility for partial or total relief under CA 2006 s1157? (iii) if the IP is still liable, and the relief cannot be granted under s1157, is there still a basis in any event for lowering the amount of compensation required to be paid under s 212(3)?

8.065 The issues of total or partial relief under CA 2006 s1157 and IA 1986 s212(3) may be said to pose the same or substantially the same judicial question, 'what should this respondent be ordered to pay?'. In any event, if that broader discretionary exercise has already been undertaken as the first step in the chain of logic, then it makes little sense to then turn to s1157, which is an inherently narrower test.

8.066 This logic would also appear to be supported by the fact that an 'officer' of a company would only seem to be apt to extend to IPs who act as liquidators, administrators, and possibly

---

71 [2009] EWHC 2482 (Ch) (HHJ Behrens) at [66].

72 [2015] EWHC 3998 (Ch).

73 See, e.g., *Re Mama Milla* [2014] EWHC 2753 (Ch), [2016] BCC 1 at [47], where HHJ Simon Barker QC (sitting as a High Court Judge) appeared to subsume the issues of honesty and reasonableness into the issue of discretion under IA 1986 s212(3).

74 *Liquidator of Glasgow and Weir Blacksmiths Ltd v Glasgow* 2016 SLT (Sh Ct) 171.

75 *Re Loquitur* [2003] EWHC 999 (Ch) at [245] and [247].

supervisors. Trustees in bankruptcy, and arguably also voluntary liquidators,[76] who cannot be said to be 'officers' in the same sense, would not appear to be able to take advantage of CA 2006 s1157. That therefore creates a possible inconsistency between two IPs, both of whom honestly and reasonably (but mistakenly) distribute assets, where one acts as a liquidator of a company and the second is a trustee in bankruptcy. It would seem to be inconsistent that only the first should be able to take advantage of the possibility of discretionary relief for acting honestly and reasonably, but the second should not (albeit a trustee in bankruptcy might arguably benefit from similar provisions in relation to trustees[77]). These points may be said to support the argument that it must be inherent in the provisions of the IA 1986 that the court is permitted – as a matter of discretion – to adjust the quantum of the relief beyond what conventional principles of causation and equitable accounting would require.

The disparity between office-holders in the corporate and personal contexts could also give rise to an argument that CA 2006 s1157 should simply not apply to any type of IP. However, for the reasons stated above in relation to *Re Powertrain*, that would seem only to create a different disparity, that is, between directors, secretaries, and IPs. The better view, consequently, is that CA 2006 s1157 does apply to IPs, but that its impact as a discrete provision in addition to the discretionary powers granted to the court under the IA 1986 provisions is probably minimal.   **8.067**

2. Application of section 1157 to IPs

CA 2006 s1157 has rarely been relied on successfully. The burden rests on the party seeking relief under s1157 to demonstrate that he acted honestly and reasonably in the circumstances and, consequently, that he should be entitled to relief under s1157.[78] There are limited instances of IPs relying on it, and no reported case where it has been used successfully as a defence by an IP.[79] There are, however, many instances of directors applying for relief under CA 2006 s1157, and it is part of the arsenal of defences that will be deployed by directors in response to a claim for breach of his or her duties.   **8.068**

It is, however, suggested that the authorities on CA 2006 s1157 cannot simply be transplanted from the context of director duty claims to claims brought against IPs. The question of who has the real economic interest in a particular transaction, and consequently who will lose out as a result of that transaction, was identified by Hoffmann LJ in *Re D'Jan of London* as a basis for granting partial relief under the forerunner of CA 2006 s1157.[80] This consideration obviously cannot arise in the context of an insolvency, where the IP acts only in the interest of creditors,   **8.069**

---

76 For the reason that liquidators in a voluntary liquidation are not officers of the court: *Re TH Knitwear (Wholesale) Ltd* [1988] Ch 275. The counter-argument is that, whether or not they are officers of the court, they remain 'officers' of the company.

77 Trustee Act 1925 s61.

78 Although in practice, it will often not be productive to take a strict or prescriptive approach to the burden of proof, and such an approach is not required by IA 1986 s212: see *Mama Milla* at [49].

79 *Re Powertrain* was an instance of prospective relief, on an application for directions brought by the liquidators.

80 [1993] BCC 646 at 649:

> although Mr D'Jan's 99 per cent holding of shares is not sufficient to sustain a Multinational defence, it is relevant to the exercise of the discretion under sec. 727. It may be reasonable to take a risk in relation to your own money which would be unreasonable in relation to someone else's. And although for the purposes of the law of negligence the company is a separate entity to which Mr D'Jan owes a duty of care which cannot vary according to the number of

and would undoubtedly be conflicted from so acting if he were a creditor. However, there is perhaps scope for argument that, even if the views of creditors do not give a sufficient basis for ratification of a particular act,[81] it may still be relevant for the purposes of exercising discretion under s1157.[82]

8.070 The reason for the differences in approach as between directors and IPs is at least partly due to the different appetite for risk that a director can be expected to take on, as compared with an IP. For example, a director may honestly and reasonably choose to ensure a particular trader is paid, notwithstanding that he harbours some doubts about whether the trader will provide certain goods. The IP's position will habitually be more formulaic, and will be guided by the provisions of the IA 1986; distributions must be made according to the proofs submitted.[83] That said, there are often instances when IPs have to act quickly and in time-sensitive scenarios. One example might be where a decision must be made whether or not to continue trading. In such circumstances, it would be anticipated that the court would give a greater degree of leeway to the IP, who acts in a more quasi-directorial manner in such instances. In any event, the question of whether he should obtain relief is plainly fact sensitive and should be determined at a trial. It is, consequently, highly unlikely that such issues will be suitable for summary determination.[84]

8.071 It has also recently been held that CA 2006 s1157 can in principle be extended to proprietary claims.[85] However, the comments of Newey LJ in *Dickinson* were strictly *obiter*, because of the factual findings in that case, which the Court of Appeal felt unable to interfere with.

8.072 Reasonable reliance on advice may also engage s1157.[86] In this respect, the section can perhaps be seen as a mid-point where reliance on advice is not deemed to be sufficient to give rise to total relief under the principle in *Pitt v Holt*, but where the effect of the statutory provision can otherwise mitigate the binary decision between relief and no relief.[87] The IP's proceedings on an assumption unless and until advice is received may also limit a particular period of liability, and should be subject to a grace period for the advice to be digested and a decision made as to how it will be acted upon.[88] However, just as a failure properly to instruct will prevent reliance on advice received from being reasonable for the purposes of a *Pitt v Holt*-type defence, logic would seem to dictate that a failure properly to instruct advisers should also preclude relief under s1157.[89]

---

shares he owns, I think that the economic realities of the case can be taken into account in exercising the discretion under sec. 727.

81 See paras 8.052–8.057 above.

82 See, e.g., *Re Barry and Staines Linoleum Ltd* [1934] Ch 227.

83 There is no scope for the IP to distribute the assets of the estate otherwise, no matter how 'equitable' the IP considers such a distribution to be: *Re Stanford International Bank Ltd* [2019] UKPC 45 at [40]: 'The applicable insolvency scheme may be good, bad or indifferent, but the liquidator takes it as he finds it, and his statutory duty is to apply it'.

84 *Rawnsley v Weatherall Green & Smith North Ltd* [2009] EWHC 2482 (Ch).

85 *Dickinson v NAL Realisations (Staffordshire) Ltd* [2019] EWCA Civ 2146.

86 *Re Claridge's Patent Asphalte Co Ltd* [1921] 1 Ch 543.

87 In this respect, s1157 can perhaps be seen as a parallel to the introduction of the Law Reform (Contributory Negligence) Act 1945, which released the courts from the strictures of determining total or zero liability in cases of tortious breach.

88 *Revenue and Customs Commissioners v Holland* [2009] BCLC 309 (CA).

89 *Mama Milla* [2014] EWHC 2753 (Ch), [2016] BCC 1 at [31]–[33] (ChD).

3. Section 1157 generally

There is a general lack of clarity on the exact ambit of s1157, even before one considers how it **8.073** might be applied to IPs. As was noted by Hoffmann LJ in *Re D'Jan*, which remains a rare instance of relief being granted under the section, there is tension in a court proceeding logically through the body of the claim, finding that a claim is made out, which may include a failure to act with reasonable skill and care, and then granting relief anyway on the basis that he acted '*honestly and reasonably*'. Notwithstanding this tension, it is settled law that the words of the section make this plain.[90]

The modern trend outside claims against IPs appears to be an increasingly narrow application **8.074** of s1157. The tension between prima facie liability and relief being granted is still yet to be fully articulated in any appellate authority.[91] The better analogy may be with director disqualification terms, which look to the liability/disqualification as an expression of opprobrium rather than being premised on a restitutionary basis.[92]

There is a particular difficulty in the case of IPs, which has never been addressed in any **8.075** reported authority, in that a balance must be struck between relieving the IP from liability, and the interests of creditors who in effect must pay for that relief.[93] From the perspective of commercial realism, it is suggested that the usual insurance policy that IPs will have in place will mean they are better placed to absorb the loss than are the creditors. That may make it more appealing to some judges to decide that the balance should weigh in favour of imposing liability in full, rather than requiring (in effect) the creditors to pay for the IP's breach. If that is so, then that will mean that relief will be even more difficult for IPs to obtain under s1157 than for directors. Nevertheless, s1157 remains good law and it is tolerably clear that the jurisdictional basis for its application exists. The question remains open however as to when, if ever, the court will accede to an IP's application for it to apply.

I. ILLEGALITY

In principle, there also seems to be no reason why the general bar on *ex turpi causa non oritur* **8.076** *actio* should not apply in instances involving IPs. The modern approach to the defence of illegality should now be guided by *Patel v Mirza*.[94]

The general principle is that expressed by the general policy that the law should not be used to **8.077** give effect to illegal transactions, or otherwise protect those who have engaged in criminal activity. A clear example is that an agreement to pay for a so-called 'contract killing' cannot be enforceable. The effect of the principle is that the loss (if it can be described as such) will lie as it falls. At the other end of the spectrum are cases where the illegality is an irrelevant part of the background.

---

90   *Re MDA Investment Management Ltd* [2004] 1 BCLC 217; *PNC Telecom plc v Thomas (No 2)* [2008] 2 BCLC 95.
91   Hoffmann LJ sat as an additional judge of the High Court in *Re D'Jan*.
92   Which is also explicable on the basis that director disqualification terms are really a form of sentence passed in response to breach.
93   In cases such as *Powertrain*, e.g., there was no risk of this indirect financial burden being placed on creditors.
94   [2016] UKSC 42.

8.078 *Re Mama Milla* raised this issue, although it was unable to provide any defence to the IP in that claim.[95] By way of background, the 'real business' of the company was VAT fraud.[96] The starting point raised by the respondent was that the property of the company was in fact criminal property, within the meaning of s340(3) of the Proceeds of Crime Act 2002. Reference was also made to *Stone & Rolls v Moore Stephens*.[97] At first instance, it was held that the nature of the 'inquiry' into the liquidator's conduct, required by s212, meant that a further fraud on the liquidator (as appears to have happened) was unable to provide a defence to the more historic frauds that had led to the company holding the assets in the first place. The finding was that the prior illegality was a 'peripheral' matter.[98]

8.079 The Court of Appeal observed that the law on the illegality defence was, at that time, unstable.[99] As a result, there was no thorough exposition of the case law, or consideration of how it might apply to office-holders. It was, however, said to be clear that there was no basis for the defence to apply. There was no inextricable link between the VAT fraud and the claim; the act had been collateral and was not causally connected with the fraud.[100] Indeed, there is a clear policy objective in ensuring that the office-holder's duty properly to get in, realise, and distribute the assets of the estate is upheld, which would come into conflict with an *ex turpi causa* defence. In this respect, *Mama Milla* appears to be consistent with the test that was later expounded in *Patel v Mirza*.

8.080 Further, the sums were not criminal property, because the sums were transferred pursuant to contracts, and there was no agreement between the company and the other alleged conspirators.[101] Even if it had been criminal property, that in itself has no bearing on the common law principle of *ex turpi causa*.[102]

8.081 The facts may be different if, for example, the office-holder had exercised all reasonable care and skill to protect the assets, in which case the tension between the policies to be upheld by the *ex turpi causa* doctrine on the one hand, and the requirement that office-holders carry out their duties properly, would not exist. Another example might be where the suspense or liquidation account is the target of a malicious computer hack. In those circumstances, it would seem to be unjust to hold the office-holder responsible, although the response of the court

---

95 In *Griffin v UHY Hacker Young & Partners* [2010] EWHC 146 (Ch) [2010] PNLR 20, Vos J rejected an application for strike out or summary judgment brought by a defendant insolvency practitioner on the grounds of illegality.

96 [2014] EWHC 2753 (Ch) at [7].

97 [2009] UKHL 39. That case also concerned a 'one-man' company, although the claim was brought by the director, who was said to be unable to benefit indirectly from his own fraud. The case has however been subject to criticism on numerous occasions, and it is not to be followed in the future: see most recently discussion of it in *Singularis Holdings Ltd (in liquidation) v Daiwa Capital Markets Europe Ltd* [2019] UKSC 50.

98 [2014] EWHC 2753 (Ch) at [204].

99 Due to the decisions in *Tinsley v Milligan* [1994] 1 AC 340 and *Allen v Hounga* [2014] UKSC 47. *Tinsley* is probably no longer good law in light of *Patel v Mirza*. See [2016] UKSC 42 at [110].

100 [2015] EWCA Civ 1140 at [47] and [54].

101 Ibid at [44]–[47].

102 Ibid at [48]. The concept of *'realisable property'* in any event appears to run alongside and, in some instances, contradict notions of title and ownership as understood in insolvency law (specifically) and common law and equity (more generally). See, e.g., POCA 2002 ss84(2)(d), 150(2)(d), 232(2)(d); *R v Shahid* [2009] EWCA Crim 831; *R v Waya* [2012] UKSC 51. But see also s418(3), which repeats the 'first come, first served' principle insofar as there is a conflict between the timing of a restraint order and a bankruptcy order.

might well be to exercise its discretion under IA 1986 s212(3) (or the applicable equivalent) or CA 2006 s1157 so as to relieve the office-holder from liability. The reliance on a full *ex turpi causa* defence in such circumstances would appear to be unnecessary.

J. INDEMNITY

If a claim is successfully brought against an IP, the professional and financial ramifications are likely to be significant. Although it is of course not a defence to a claim, every IP is required to be covered by a policy of professional indemnity ('PII'). The advantage of such policies is that the IP will not suffer the 'crushing liability' that may arise from a claim, and the prospect of a claim not being financially viable for a claimant to bring is also lowered.[103] Reference should also be made to paragraphs 7.053–7.078 above, which discuss the relevant regulatory framework. **8.082**

Although the principles that apply to the construction of a contract of insurance are not generally different from any other contract, such PIIs are generally considered to be comprehensive, and will typically extend to those in the firm of the IP as well as the IP herself (notwithstanding that IP appointments are personal). **8.083**

IPs should also take care to notify their insurer in line with the terms of the policy. A failure to notify the insurer in time may render the policy useless. Returning to *Mama Milla*, it also appears that, in that case, the insurer was not notified in time. The respondent therefore had no insurance in place in respect of the claim. That consideration carried no weight for the purposes of the proceedings, but clearly spelled *'financial ruin'* for the IP herself.[104] **8.084**

1. Limits to the policy and bond cover

As with any policy of insurance, there will be limits to its application, and it is unlikely to provide cover in cases of actual fraud or criminal activity. In that instance however the IP's bond may provide some possibility of recompense. This is discussed further in Chapter 2 at paragraphs 2.047–2.059. **8.085**

K. CONCLUDING OBSERVATIONS

It is apparent from the above discussion that the IP is unlikely to be able to have successful recourse to standalone defences once the usual elements of a claim are established against them. The statutory discretion to limit or reduce claims, under IA 1986 s212(3), may carry some weight, for example, by reference to limiting the amount of losses. Relief from liability under CA 2006 s1157 is also theoretically available, although in practice it is rarely likely to succeed for an IP who has been found to be negligent. Limitation defences, as procedural **8.086**

---

103 From the perspective of the IP, this may actually be an undesirable consequence, as it causes the IP (who is appointed personally) to appear a more attractive, 'deep-pocketed' target.
104 [2014] EWHC 2753 (Ch) at [21].

defences, are one area where the IP may establish a complete defence, although again in relation to such lines of defence there are many exceptions or 'work-arounds' for the well-advised claimant. The main battle ground in relation to claims is therefore most likely to occur at the stages of breach, causation and losses.

ANNEX I

Table A1.1   Comparison of Schedules 1, 4 and 5 to the Insolvency Act 1986 (numerical order)

Schedule 1	Schedule 4	Schedule 5
1 Power to take possession of, collect and get in the property of the company and, for that purpose, to take such proceedings as may seem to him expedient.	1 Power to pay any class of creditors in full.	1 Power to carry on any business of the bankrupt so far as may be necessary for winding it up beneficially and so far as the trustee is able to do so without contravening any requirement imposed by or under any enactment.
2 Power to sell or otherwise dispose of the property of the company by public auction or private contract …	2 Power to make any compromise or arrangement with creditors or persons claiming to be creditors, or having or alleging themselves to have any claim (present or future, certain or contingent, ascertained or sounding only in damages) against the company, or whereby the company may be rendered liable.	2 Power to bring, institute or defend any action or legal proceedings relating to the property comprised in the bankrupt's estate.
3 Power to raise or borrow money and grant security therefor over the property of the company.	3 Power to compromise on such terms as may be agreed (a) all calls and liabilities to calls, all debts and liabilities capable of resulting in debts, and all claims … subsisting or supposed to subsist between the company and a contributory … or other debtor or person apprehending liability to the company, and (b) all questions in any way relating to or affecting the assets or the winding up of the company, and take any security for the discharge of any such call, debt liability or claim and give a complete discharge in respect of it.	2A Power to bring legal proceedings under section 339, 340 or 423.

Table A1.1 (continued)

Schedule 1	Schedule 4	Schedule 5
4 Power to appoint a solicitor or accountant or other professionally qualified person to assist him in the performance of his functions.	3A Power to bring legal proceedings under section 213, 214, 238, 239, 242, 243, or 423.[1]	3 Power to accept as the consideration for the sale of any property comprised in the bankrupt's estate a sum of money payable at a future time subject to such stipulations as to security or otherwise as the creditors' committee or the court thinks fit.
5 Power to bring or defend any action or other legal proceedings in the name and on behalf of the company.	4 Power to bring or defend any action or other legal proceedings in the name and on behalf of the company.	4 Power to mortgage or pledge any part of the property comprised in the bankrupt's estate for the purpose of raising money for the payment of his debts.
6 Power to refer to arbitration any question affecting the company.	5 Power to carry on the business of the company so far as may be necessary for its beneficial winding up.	5 Power, where any right, option or other power forms part of the bankrupt's estate, to make payments or incur liabilities with a view to obtaining, for the benefit of the creditors, any property which is the subject of the right, option or power.
7 Power to effect and maintain insurances in respect of the business and property of the company.	6 Power to sell any of the company's property by public auction or private contract, with power to transfer the whole of it to any person or to sell the same in parcels.	7 Power to make such compromise or other arrangements as may be thought expedient with creditors, or persons claiming to be creditors, in respect of bankruptcy debts.
8 Power to use the company's seal.	7 Power to do all acts and execute, in the name and on behalf of the company, all deeds, receipts and other documents for that purpose to use, when necessary, the company's seal.	8 Power to make such compromise or other arrangement as may be thought expedient with respect to any claim arising out of or incidental to the bankrupt's estate made or capable of being made on the trustee by any person.

---

1   IA 1986 s212 is curiously missing from this paragraph.

Schedule 1	Schedule 4	Schedule 5
9 Power to do all acts and to execute in the name and on behalf of the company any deed, receipt or other document.	8 Power to prove, rank and claim in the bankruptcy, insolvency or sequestration of any contributory for any balance against his estate, and to receive dividends in the bankruptcy, insolvency or sequestration in respect of that balance, as a separate debt due from the bankrupt or insolvent, and rateably with the other separate creditors.	9 Power to sell any part of the property for the time being comprised in the bankrupt's estate, including the goodwill and book debts of any business.
10 Power to draw, accept, make and endorse any bill of exchange or promissory note in the name and on behalf of the company.	9 Power to draw, accept, make and indorse any bill of exchange or promissory note in the name and on behalf of the company, with the same effect with respect to the company's liability as if the bill or note had been drawn, accepted, made or indorsed by or on behalf of the company in the course of its business.	9A Power to refer to arbitration, compromise on such terms as may be agreed, any debts, claim or liabilities subsisting or supposed to subsist between the bankrupt and any person who may have incurred any liability to the bankrupt.
11 Power to appoint any agent to do any business which he is unable to do himself or which can more conveniently be done by an agent and power to employ and dismiss employees.	10 Power to raise on the security of the assets of the company any money requisite.	9B Power to make such compromise or other arrangement as may be thought expedient with respect to any claim arising out of or incidental to the bankrupt's estate made or capable of being made by the trustee on any person.
12 Power to do all such things (including the carrying out of works) as may be necessary for the realisation of the property of the company.	11 Power to take out in his official name letters of administration to any deceased contributory, and to do in his official name any other act necessary for obtaining payment of any money due from a contributory or his estate which cannot conveniently be done in the name of the company. In all such cases the money due is deemed, for the purpose of enabling the liquidator to take out the letters of administration or recover the money, to be due to the liquidator himself.	10 Power to give receipts for any money received by him, being receipts which effectually discharge the person paying the money from all responsibility in respect of its application.

Table A1.1 (continued)

Schedule 1	Schedule 4	Schedule 5
13 Power to make any payment which is necessary or incidental to the performance of his functions.	12 Power to appoint an agent to do any business which the liquidator is unable to do himself.	11 Power to prove, rank, claim and draw a dividend in respect of such debts due to the bankrupt as are comprised in his estate.
14 Power to carry on the business of the company.	13 Power to do all such other things as may be necessary for winding up the company's affairs and distributing its assets.	12 Power to exercise in relation to any property comprised in the bankrupt's estate any powers the capacity to exercise which is vested in him under Parts VIII to XI of [the IA 1986].
15 Power to establish subsidiaries of the company.		13 Power to deal with any property comprised in the estate to which the bankrupt is beneficially entitled as tenant in tail in the same manner as the bankrupt might have dealt with it.
16 Power to transfer to subsidiaries of the company the whole or any part of the business and property of the company.		14 For the purposes of, or in connection with, the exercise of any of his powers under Parts VIII to XI of [the IA 1986], the trustee may, by his official name: (a) hold property of every description; (b) make contracts; (c) sue and be sued; (d) enter into engagements binding on himself and, in respect of the bankrupt's estate, on his successors in office; (e) employ an agent; (f) execute any power of attorney, deed or other instrument; and he may do any other act which is necessary or expedient for the purposes of or in connection with the exercise of those powers.
17 Power to grant or accept a surrender of a lease or tenancy of any of the property of the company, and to make a lease or tenancy of any property required or convenient for the business of the company.		
18 Power to make any arrangement or compromise on behalf of the company.		

Schedule 1	Schedule 4	Schedule 5

19 Power to call up any uncalled capital of the company.

20 Power to rank and claim in the bankruptcy, insolvency, sequestration or liquidation of any person indebted to the company and to receive dividends, and to accede to trust deeds for the creditors of any such person.

21 Power to present or defend a petition for the winding up of the company.

22 Power to change the situation of the company's registered office.

ANNEX II

Table AII.1   Comparing and contrasting Schedules 1, 4 and 5 to the Insolvency Act 1986

Schedule 1	Schedule 4	Schedule 5
1 Power to take possession of, collect and get in the property of the company and, for that purpose, to take such proceedings as may seem to him expedient.		
2 Power to sell or otherwise dispose of the property of the company by public auction or private contract ...	6 Power to sell any of the company's property by public auction or private contract, with power to transfer the whole of it to any person or to sell the same in parcels.	3 Power to accept as the consideration for the sale of any property comprised in the bankrupt's estate a sum of money payable at a future time subject to such stipulations as to security or otherwise as the creditors' committee or the court thinks fit. 9 Power to sell any part of the property for the time being comprised in the bankrupt's estate, including the goodwill and book debts of any business.
3 Power to raise or borrow money and grant security therefor over the property of the company.	10 Power to raise on the security of the assets of the company any money requisite.	4 Power to mortgage or pledge any part of the property comprised in the bankrupt's estate for the purpose of raising money for the payment of his debts.
5 Power to bring or defend any action or other legal proceedings in the name and on behalf of the company.	3A Power to bring legal proceedings under section 213, 214, 238, 239, 242, 243, or 423.[1] 4 Power to bring or defend any action or other legal proceedings in the name and on behalf of the company.	2A Power to bring legal proceedings under section 339, 340 or 423. 2 Power to bring, institute or defend any action or legal proceedings relating to the property comprised in the bankrupt's estate.

---

1   IA 1986 s212 is curiously missing from this paragraph.

Schedule 1	Schedule 4	Schedule 5
6 Power to refer to arbitration any question affecting the company.		9A Power to refer to arbitration, compromise on such terms as may be agreed, any debts, claim or liabilities subsisting or supposed to subsist between the bankrupt and any person who may have incurred any liability to the bankrupt.
8 Power to use the company's seal.	7 Power to do all acts and execute, in the name and on behalf of the company, all deeds, receipts and other documents for that purpose to use, when necessary, the company's seal.	
9 Power to do all acts and to execute in the name and on behalf of the company any deed, receipt or other document.	7 Power to do all acts and execute, in the name and on behalf of the company, all deeds, receipts and other documents for that purpose to use, when necessary, the company's seal.	10 Power to give receipts for any money received by him, being receipts which effectually discharge the person paying the money from all responsibility in respect of its application.
10 Power to draw, accept, make and endorse any bill of exchange or promissory note in the name and on behalf of the company.	9 Power to draw, accept, make and indorse any bill of exchange or promissory note in the name and on behalf of the company, with the same effect with respect to the company's liability as if the bill or note had been drawn, accepted, made or indorsed by or on behalf of the company in the course of its business.	
4 Power to appoint a solicitor or accountant or other professionally qualified person to assist him in the performance of his functions.	12 Power to appoint an agent to do any business which the liquidator is unable to do himself.	See para 14(e) below.

303

Table AII.1 (continued)

Schedule 1	Schedule 4	Schedule 5
7 Power to effect and maintain insurances in respect of the business and property of the company. 12 Power to do all such things (including the carrying out of works) as may be necessary for the realisation of the property of the company.	13 Power to do all such other things as may be necessary for winding up the company's affairs and distributing its assets.	12 Power to exercise in relation to any property comprised in the bankrupt's estate any powers the capacity to exercise which is vested in him under Parts VIII to XI of [the IA 1986]. 13 Power to deal with any property comprised in the estate to which the bankrupt is beneficially entitled as tenant in tail in the same manner as the bankrupt might have dealt with it. 14 For the purposes of, or in connection with, the exercise of any of his powers under Parts VIII to XI of [the IA 1986], the trustee may, by his official name: (a) hold property of every description; (b) make contracts; (c) sue and be sued; (d) enter into engagements binding on himself and, in respect of the bankrupt's estate, on his successors in office; (e) employ an agent; (f) execute any power of attorney, deed or other instrument; and he may do any other act which is necessary or expedient for the purposes of or in connection with the exercise of those powers.
13 Power to make any payment which is necessary or incidental to the performance of his functions.	1 Power to pay any class of creditors in full.	
14 Power to carry on the business of the company.	5 Power to carry on the business of the company so far as may be necessary for its beneficial winding up.	1 Power to carry on any business of the bankrupt so far as may be necessary for winding it up beneficially and so far as the trustee is able to do so without contravening any requirement imposed by or under any enactment.

Schedule 1	Schedule 4	Schedule 5
15 Power to establish subsidiaries of the company.		
16 Power to transfer to subsidiaries of the company the whole or any part of the business and property of the company.		
17 Power to grant or accept a surrender of a lease or tenancy of any of the property of the company, and to make a lease or tenancy of any property required or convenient for the business of the company.		
18 Power to make any arrangement or compromise on behalf of the company.	2 Power to make any compromise or arrangement with creditors or persons claiming to be creditors, or having or alleging themselves to have any claim (present or future, certain or contingent, ascertained or sounding only in damages) against the company, or whereby the company may be rendered liable.	7 Power to make such compromise or other arrangements as may be thought expedient with creditors, or persons claiming to be creditors, in respect of bankruptcy debts. 8 Power to make such compromise or other arrangement as may be thought expedient with respect to any claim arising out of or incidental to the bankrupt's estate made or capable of being made on the trustee by any person. 9B Power to make such compromise or other arrangement as may be thought expedient with respect to any claim arising out of or incidental to the bankrupt's estate made or capable of being made by the trustee on any person.

Table AII.1 (continued)

Schedule 1	Schedule 4	Schedule 5
19 Power to call up any uncalled capital of the company.	3 Power to compromise on such terms as may be agreed (a) all calls and liabilities to calls, all debts and liabilities capable of resulting in debts, and all claims… subsisting or supposed to subsist between the company and a contributory … or other debtor or person apprehending liability to the company, and (b) all questions in any way relating to or affecting the assets or the winding up of the company, and take any security for the discharge of any such call, debt liability or claim and give a complete discharge in respect of it. 11 Power to take out in his official name letters of administration to any deceased contributory, and to do in his official name any other act necessary for obtaining payment of any money due from a contributory or his estate which cannot conveniently be done in the name of the company. In all such cases the money due is deemed, for the purpose of enabling the liquidator to take out the letters of administration or recover the money, to be due to the liquidator himself.	
20 Power to rank and claim in the bankruptcy, insolvency, sequestration or liquidation of any person indebted to the company and to receive dividends, and to accede to trust deeds for the creditors of any such person.	8 Power to prove, rank and claim in the bankruptcy, insolvency or sequestration of any contributory for any balance against his estate, and to receive dividends in the bankruptcy, insolvency or sequestration in respect of that balance, as a separate debt due from the bankrupt or insolvent, and rateably with the other separate creditors.	11 Power to prove, rank, claim and draw a dividend in respect of such debts due to the bankrupt as are comprised in his estate.

Schedule 1	Schedule 4	Schedule 5
21 Power to present or defend a petition for the winding up of the company. 22 Power to change the situation of the company's registered office.		

INDEX

Printed and bound by CPI Group (UK) Ltd, Croydon, CR0 4YY

25/06/2023

03229922-0001